D1126320

Managing Information Quality

Martin J. Eppler

Managing Information Quality

Increasing the Value of Information
in Knowledge-intensive Products
and Processes

Second Edition

With 39 Figures and 34 Tables

 Springer

Professor Dr. Martin J. Eppler
University of Lugano (USI)
Chair of Information
and Communication Management
School of Communication Sciences
Via Buffi 13
6900 Lugano
Switzerland
martin.eppler@lu.unisi.ch

ISBN-10   3-540-31408-3 Springer Berlin Heidelberg New York
ISBN-13   978-3-540-31408-0 Springer Berlin Heidelberg New York
ISBN   3-540-23571-X 3. edition Springer Berlin Heidelberg New York

Cataloging-in-Publication Data
Library of Congress Control Number: 2006927427

Springer is a part of Springer Science+Business Media

springeronline.com

© Springer Berlin · Heidelberg 2003, 2006
Printed in Germany

Hardcover-Design: Erich Kirchner, Heidelberg

SPIN 11617303   42/3153-5 4 3 2 1 0 – Printed on acid-free paper

Preface to the Second Edition

It still holds true: information is not always the answer. Information is often part of the problem. While the main goal of information in the business place is to enable adequate decisions and actions, it can also lead to numerous negative effects: it can confuse, block creativity, or it can lead to hectic activism, stress and fatigue. Information can distract and divert attention, and it may even delay important decisions – the paralysis by analysis. Strategies to avoid these dysfunctional effects of information can be divided into sender-based strategies and receiver-based strategies. In my previous research, I have looked at receiver-based strategies that outline effective ways of dealing with information overload. This book, by contrast, analyzes *sender-based strategies* that aim at making content actionable by increasing its information quality. By offering relevant and sound information in a convenient and reliable manner, managers and information providers ranging from analysts to CEOs can not only optimize communication, they can also improve their reputation, employee satisfaction and customer loyalty. In a time where information has become a commodity or even a nuisance, this is a valuable strategy. The main premise of this book is consequently that information quality has already become a (if not *the*) decisive factor of the information economy. Many companies, however, are not managing this factor systematically.

I personally became aware of the relevance of information quality when working on an interactive supplement to a weekly economic newspaper in the early nineties. The central question in developing the supplement was how the value of the provided information changed by offering it in an interactive format. To answer this question, I had to look at the factors that make information useful to the reader. I had to examine issues such as *timeliness*, *convenience*, or *clarity*. Since then, I have spent a great amount of time finding out what these and other information attributes really mean to information consumers. The results are documented in this book. It contains the key insights gained during a four year research project on information quality at the Institute for Media and Communications Management of the University of St. Gallen. It is the synthesis of a research report (a habilitation) that also included survey and focus groups results, as well as an extensive theoretical discussion. The book is aimed at scientists, students and practitioners who are interested in understanding and managing the attributes of information that make it valuable to diverse information consumers.

Since this book was first published in 2003 my work on the topic has continued and evolved. The current second edition reflects this evolution and incorporates new research conducted at the University of Lugano (USI), namely an additional extensive case study, further considerations regarding principles and tools of information quality management, as well as insights and a short case study on information quality in e-government. This new edition also discusses ways of moving beyond data and information quality by considering communication and knowledge quality (illustrated through a short corporate case study).

Lugano, March 2006   Martin J. Eppler

Table of Contents

List of Figures

List of Tables

1. Introducing the Notion of Information Quality

The first chapter introduces the notion of information quality by discussing three real-life business cases where the quality of information is of crucial importance. Specifically, the notion of information quality will be discussed in the context of strategy consulting, product development, and web design. The chapter also provides an overview of the main goals, target groups, and chapters of the book.

Chapter Overview

Everything that can be said, can be said clearly.

LUDWIG WITTGENSTEIN

What makes information useful? This broad and general question is the central concern of this book. Information quality – the fitness for use of information[1] – is a term that is vague and general, yet promising and pertinent: Amidst the increasing *quantity* of available information, the *quality* of information becomes a crucial factor for the effectiveness of organizations and individuals. Information quality is not only, as we will see, an issue that involves graphic designers, information systems architects, communication trainers, or technical authors. It is also (and perhaps primarily) a management challenge, as knowledge work[2] – which requires information both as input and output factors – becomes increasingly collaborative and distributed and thus requires continuous and systematic coordination and management. This text will therefore examine the concept of information quality from a *general management perspective*.[3] Specifically, it will look at *criteria* that enable

Information Quality: A General Management Topic

A Focus on Criteria

---

[1] We shall use this definition as a preliminary proxy. Extensive definitions will be provided below.

[2] Knowledge work involves analyzing and applying specialized expertise to solve problems, to generate ideas, or to create new products and services (Zidel 1998). Schultze defines knowledge work as the production and reproduction of informational objects (Schultze 2000).

[3] Unlike many prior studies on information quality that focus on specific applications such as data warehouses, management in-

Knowledge-intensive Processes as the Context of the Book

management to better define information quality goals, analyze information quality problems, and improve the way that individuals and teams create and manage information in knowledge-intensive processes which rely heavily on the individual's expertise and personal contribution in the form of information. Examples of *knowledge-intensive*[4] *processes* are such complex endeavors as product development, market research, strategy development, business consulting, or on-line publishing. There are, however, many other less prominent tasks which can also be considered as knowledge-intensive processes such as reading or writing a report, presenting a concept or teaching a course. All of them, it will be argued, can benefit from an analysis of the quality of information.

Business Scenarios as Starting Points

Below, we present three brief real-life scenarios that illustrate why the notion of information quality is a highly relevant management and research topic. They show typical problems in managing the quality of information in knowledge-intensive processes. The following scenarios (or mini case studies) are based on the experience of the author and represent authentic business situations. Each scenario includes a series of key questions that will be addressed in this book.

Scenario 1: Strategy Consulting

A strategy consulting company receives feedback from its clients that the delivered report and the accompanying presentations are inadequate and too difficult to use by the managers who have commissioned the analysis. The managers find the reasoning of the consultants hard to interpret and difficult to put into practice. They have problems communicating the results to their peers in the company. They also claim to have problems in locating crucial evidence in the large document quickly. In addition, they indicate that they require more detailed information on the market situation, and less analysis of their internal status-quo. Specifically, they ask for more current market information to be included in the report. Nevertheless, they do not want the report to become any longer than it already is (namely, over eighty pages).

---

formation systems, multimedia, library services and so forth, the present study is addressed to researchers and practitioners with an interest in general management topics beyond individual disciplines or functional sectors.

4   The term 'knowledge-intensive' was used in a similar way by Starbuck, 1992. He states that "labeling a firm as knowledge-intensive implies that knowledge has more importance than other inputs" (Starbuck, 1992, p. 715, see also Nurmi, 1998). The same reasoning can be applied to processes. The term will be described in more detail in section 3.1.2. For a definition of a knowledge-intensive process see Eppler et al., 1999, or section 3.1.2.

In consequence, the consulting company has to re-work a major part of the project and rewrite many sections of the original report. This results in higher costs and lower margins for the consulting company and in delays for the client. As a result of this negative experience, the consulting company realizes that it has to pay greater attention to the expectations and information needs of its clients. The problem in doing so, however, consists of articulating these implicit expectations (which may also change over time). Very often, the management of a client company can only articulate its main problem or question and not in what way the answer should be presented. The real challenge therefore consists in finding a way that the information parameters of a consulting engagement can be negotiated between the consulting company and the client. The key questions inherent in this problem are the following ones:

How can the consulting company make the customer's expectations for such a complex information product as a strategic analysis explicit? How can it develop a vocabulary to describe the (desired) characteristics of such a report? What are the parameters that have to be specified in order to get it right the first time? Which quality management activities should be implemented to assure that the final product meets or exceeds customer expectations? Who should be involved in this task?

The consulting company found a first tentative solution to this problem and some answers to the above questions. In regular, brief meetings with the client, the consultants ask a set of diagnostic questions to determine the crucial vectors of the client's information needs. This may regard the timeliness of the analysis (at what point in time it should be completed), the scope of the analysis (what should be in- or excluded), and the factors that make the analysis useful or applicable (i.e., the format of the recommendations). For the last issue, applicability, the consulting team closely examines the client community that will use the final results of the analysis. The consultants pay special attention to the community's working style and habits, to its terminology and constraints. The consulting company's infrastructure (its intranet) is partially opened to the client, so that he can monitor the progress on a day-to-day basis, give instant feedback, and access more detailed information.

The main insight from this scenario is the following one: In order to improve the quality of information, the consulting company should not only modify the final information product (the report and the presentations that go with it). It has to improve the content production process and its infrastructure. It has to invest considerably more time in understanding the target community and make sure that it keeps close contact with it in order to understand the information needs and (changing) expectations of that community. Unlike the quality of a physical product, information quality thus requires a periodic re-negotiation and adaptation of such information characteristics as scope, timeliness, or applicability. This requires a list of information quality criteria that are explicit and systematic and hence allow for a productive discussion between the client and the consulting firm. Such a list should also reveal potential tradeoffs between various criteria[5] in order to avoid potential conflicts early on.

Scenario 2: Product Development

A product development team, consisting of marketing, medical, and technical specialists from the US and Germany is working on a new portable device to monitor the glucose level of diabetes patients. Early on in its development efforts, the (distributed) team realizes that it requires more information from other development teams and other (marketing as well as technical) specialists to prevent making the same mistakes again and to be aware of developments that are going on else-where in the company (such as an initiative to standardize specific elements of all devices currently under development). When the team researches the available documents in the various corporate databases, it discovers that they are only of limited value. Often, the team cannot understand the context of the retrieved documents and whether they are applicable to their current situation or not. Many times the documents are incomplete or it is unclear how they originated or who wrote them (and where that person is working now). Many of the retrieved documents take too much time to read, only to discover that they do not contain any relevant information. Consequently, the stored documents of other development teams are either inaccessible, incomplete and thus difficult to understand, or outdated and irrelevant.

Another major problem that the team faces is its own internal communication. Since a part of the development team is working in the United States and the rest of the team is located in Germany, face-to-face communication is more the exception than the rule. Most of the communication happens via e-mail, stored documents, or phone conversations. Due to the time

---

[5]   Typical tradeoffs (or goal conflicts) exist between scope and conciseness or between scope and timeliness: The more elaborated a report has to be, the more space it will require and the more time it will take to produce it. These and other tradeoffs will be systematically discussed in chapter three.

difference, language problems, and the technical and cultural differences among the two sub-teams, knowledge transfer is not always easy or efficient.

Because of these problems, the team is looking for help and asks the following questions:

How can we learn from other teams about what works and what doesn't? How do we incorporate expertise from other parts of the company? How do we know which information is still valid and relevant for us? How can we activate our own experiences from prior projects to improve the current development project? How can we contribute to the knowledge base of the company with our experiences so that others get value out of our insights for future projects? How can we improve our own internal knowledge sharing and reduce the amount of misunderstandings?

In this situation, two answers to these questions were found: The first one consisted of installing electronic meetings rooms to facilitate and accelerate the exchange of information among the team members. To increase the interactivity and usability of the virtual team rooms, a human factors specialist was hired to analyze to which degree the platform was supporting the working processes. This analysis was then used as a basis for a complete redesign. In addition, a taxonomy for documents was created based on a synthesis of various file- and document-naming policies used by the project team members. After the launch of the modified system with a common taxonomy, the project team members stopped complaining about having difficulties finding team information or making contributions. Thus, the accessibility, interactivity, convenience, consistency, and timeliness of the stored information was immediately improved for the team (as far as its internal communication was concerned). The second answer to the questions above regarded the use of prior or related experiences and the documentation of experiences for future development projects. Instead of searching for documents of past projects, it was decided to organize systematic knowledge sharing and review workshops with key experts and the team in order to make past experiences "come alive" and judge their relevance and validity as a team. These one-day workshops brought the team members and experts physically together in one location. Through meta-plan sessions[6] prior experiences and insights were elicited,

---

[6]   A metaplan session is an interactive workshop in which the participants contribute their thoughts on colored cards that are then combined on a pin-board and clustered into groups. Thus, individual insights can be combined and discussed. The workshop can then be documented visually as a series of process charts.

discussed, and combined visually. In this way, the context of prior experiences was reconstructed and explained and the consequences of the experience for the current project became clear through collective deliberation and discussion. Since every such workshop ended with a to-do list that converted the gathered insights into an action plan with deadlines and responsibilities, the applicability or impact of the discussed experiences was assured.

The visualized experiences of the team members (which were placed on cards along the standard product development steps that were drawn horizontally) were documented electronically and thus made available in a concise and clear format. Besides the metaplan charts, which were used to increase the clarity of the discussed information, the team relied heavily on real-time visual protocols that showed at every instant of a workshop what was being discussed (through a beamer that projected the agenda as a visual discussion trail)[7]. This timely access to team information increased the understanding among the various specialists. It made the final workshop protocols more concise and more convenient, since central insights could be grasped at one glance (instead of having to read many pages of a text-based protocol). As a final measure, one team member wrote a short case study on the experiences of the team, to make the insights available in a more authentic and lively format for other development teams.

The insights that can be derived from this mini-case are the following ones: In order to increase the quality of information for a knowledge-intensive process, information has to be made relevant and actionable by embedding it in a context that all team members can relate to. In this case, this mutual context was given by electronic team rooms structured according to an agreed upon taxonomy, and by the standard product development steps (which were used to structure the collected project insights during the workshops). Another way of increasing the applicability of information is by discussing it in a group of peers and transforming it into specific action items. This enables the collective evaluation of the information and its application for a new context. This would never be possible by individually searching and reading old project documentations.

Improving information quality is therefore also a question of choosing the right medium for the right kind of information and acknowledging the limits of computer-based communication for the transfer of (implicit) knowledge or experience.

---

[7]   An example of such an instant visual protocol is given in section 3.3.2.

The final business scenario shows the relevance of the information quality concept for the domain of website development. A project team of an Internet agency is hired to develop an Internet website for an industrial client. The team consists of graphic designers and animators, project consultants and managers, database- and HTML- specialists, as well as copy editors and advertising professionals. As the team advances in the project, more and more conflicts arise. It seems that the graphic designers and the consultants have different notions of what constitutes a high-quality website. Whereas the graphic designers stress creative and original artwork, the consultants insist on the timely delivery of the website and its easy maintainability. Never-ending discussions among the various team members lead the project head to take actions. He is looking for help to answer the following questions.

Scenario 3: Website Design

Is there a set of common quality criteria on which we can all agree in developing a website? How do we bridge the gap between our rational, efficient consultants and the more intuitive, aesthetic graphic designers? How can we match the criteria that we agree on in the team (once we have come that far) with the customer's expectations and needs?

As with all complex problems, there is no single activity or answer that resolves all of the above conflicts or questions. However, with the notion of information quality as a systematic set of criteria which are related to one another in either a positive or negative way, the team can reach a consensus and compare that consensus to the client's view. Specifically, the project head can ask the team members (for examples during a kick-off meeting) to list all the adjectives that they associate with a high-quality website. The team members are asked to distinguish between attributes that are subjective and those which can be evaluated objectively (such as criteria related to the content management process or the infrastructure of the website). After these individual quality criteria have been written down by each team member, they are combined and clustered. Once they have been consolidated and grouped, they can be 'democratically' rated through a voting mechanism. From this, a list of ten to twenty quality criteria is established. These criteria can then be analyzed in terms of their mutual relation-

---

[8] For this task, standard Total Quality Management (TQM) tools such as the House of Quality or Quality Function Deployment (QFD) can be adapted to the Internet context and used to match information quality criteria with functionalities of a website. For examples of such e-QFDs (quality function deployment charts) for the Multimedia context see Merx, 1999, pp. 58-62.

ships. In the remainder of the meeting (which should have been held at the very beginning of the project), the team only needs to discuss criteria which are conflicting, such as creative value versus timely delivery. In discussing the forces between these two criteria, the team can reach an agreement of what constitutes a fair compromise. The team can then use this weighted list of quality attributes and ask the client which characteristics he or she considers to be of crucial importance and how they can be achieved in the implementation of the website.[8]

The central insight from this scenario lies in the crucial role of information quality criteria to establish a common (explicit) goal and common values in a team that collaborates to create an information product. In addition, the scenario shows that information quality criteria can be used to identify customer expectations.

Conclusion from the Scenarios

These typical business situations show that the quality of information is a crucial and pervasive management problem. Unlike a tangible product, information as the outcome of an intellectual process cannot easily be specified or monitored. Criteria such as efficient, error-free, or pretty are not as easily defined and implemented for information products as, let us say, in the case of a car, a shampoo, or a fast-food meal. Nevertheless, there are effective ways of describing and improving the quality of know-how intensive information products, such as a strategic analysis report, a concept for a new product, or an e-commerce website. In this book, we will look at such ways and examine the problems and possible solutions involved in achieving high-quality information. We will examine a great number of business situations where high-quality information is crucial for the success of a knowledge-intensive process, such as research, consulting, planning, on-line communication, or even selling. In doing so, we will argue that a small number of systematically organized quality criteria can be used to achieve superior results. Before outlining our own approach, we briefly discuss other perspectives on information quality. This will help us to understand the background of the concept. It can also highlight the fact that various disciplines choose similar criteria to define high quality information. The final paragraphs of this introductory chapter hence summarize some older and sometimes more exotic notions of information quality.

This book is of course not the first one to address the issue of information quality.[9] It is also not the first one to start with the premise that information quality management is not just a sub-topic of traditional quality management, but does indeed require a different approach, since physical goods have inherently different characteristics than information used in intellectual processes (see for example Agosta, 2000, for this view).[10] There are numerous disciplines, ranging from pedagogy, legal studies[11] to rhetoric or epistemology, that have discussed the notion of information quality (section 2.3 describes some of the more recent examples in more detail). The definition of information quality in these disciplines – whether explicitly stated or not – depends on the *use of information*. HUANG, LEE, and WANG point out this aspect in their study on information quality from an information systems perspective: "Clearly, the notion of information quality depends on the actual use of information" (Huang, Lee, Wang, 1999, p.17). As a consequence, one has to analyze the use of information[12] in order to determine which notion of information quality is adequate.[13]

Other Notions of Information Quality

---

[9]   For an "early" study on information quality and its effects on decision processes, see Grotz-Martin, 1976. This study has not taken new media into account, but it includes an extensive discussion of information quality criteria. For reasons why information quality has long been a neglected issue in electronic information delivery see Arnold (1995).

[10] There are also studies which argue the exact opposite, namely that information quality management can be sufficiently described with the vocabulary and instrumentation of traditional total quality management, see for example English, 1999, who applies Deming's fourteen quality factors (see Deming, 1986) to information quality in the data warehousing context or Waterman, 1996, who applies TQM to knowledge work (but also sees the limits of this approach). This line of argumentation seems plausible for automatic data processing, but not for the context of knowledge-intensive processes. A study that backs my line of argumentation is Prahalad and Krishnan's view on software quality (see Prahalad and Krishnan, 1999, p. 114). Another possible reason against traditional TQM-approaches lies in their often limited impact (and administrative overhead), see Zbaracki, 1998.

[11] For insightful studies that examine information quality from a legal point of view see Gasser, 2000, or Zulauf, 2000.

[12] The meaning of the term "information" at this point is the one articulated by Driver and Streufert in the *Administrative Science Quarterly*: "Information can be defined as all inputs that people process to gain understanding (see Driver and S. Streufert, 1969). The term is further defined in section 2.1.

An analysis of the use of information can begin with a delineation of the territory in which information is discussed. Such a territory may be the academic discipline in which information is discussed. The quality of information is a topic that is not only discussed in management, but also in fields such as medicine, cartography, linguistics, rhetorics, or history to name but a few of the areas where the topic is crucial. Below we look at a few of the quality criteria that are cited in these disciplines.

Information Quality Criteria from other Domains

Information quality has been a long standing concern for accountants and auditors (a fact that is highlighted by recent scandals in this domain). PAUL M. CLIKEMAN, professor of *accounting* at the University of Richmond, states that "internal auditors must ensure that their managers receive *relevant*, accurate, and timely information at an affordable cost" (Clikeman, 1999). Outside the domain of management, there is extensive literature on information quality in the *medical* profession. Criteria of information quality for this domain can be found in the guidelines of leading medical journals.[14] These guidelines stress the validity or empirical evidence for the provided information. Besides validity, many of the criteria that are discussed in accounting resurface in this fundamentally different context. Information quality is also discussed in the legal professions. *Legal* scholars stress the fact that information pertaining to a particular situation should be comprehensive. Examples of other information quality criteria from a legal perspective can be found in Gasser, 2000 or Zulauf, 2000. Besides completeness or comprehensiveness, these studies cite timeliness, clarity, correctness, security, interpretability, and conclusiveness as critical information quality criteria. A final example of a discipline that is concerned with information quality is cartography. The fact that *maps* should be accurate enough for the intended use (that accuracy is thus a context-dependent criteria) is highlighted in BRIAN and JEFF AMBROZIAK's monumental book on two thousand years of three-dimensional

---

[13]   Arnold (1995) asks a similar question and finds similar answers in his review of electronic information quality practices: "Can electronic information be measured like an automobile fender? When does a database have quality? The answer depends on *who asks the question*, the *expertise* of the person evaluating the database and its records, and the *use* to which the electronic information will be put (Arnold, 1995, p. 29).

[14]   They are taken from Goodman et al., 1994, Oxman et al. 1983, and Lionel and Herxheimer, 1970. For a further discussion of quality criteria for medical information in the context of medical publications see: Baker and Fraser, 1995.

mapmaking (Ambroziak and Ambroziak, 1999, p. 20), in GÜNTHER and VOISARD's analysis of geographic information quality (Günther and Voisard, 1997), and in RICHARD SAUL WURMAN's magnificent map collection (Wurman 1996). As other information products, maps must meet certain content and format requirements in order to provide value to their users.

Time, Format, and Content Aspects

What these approaches have in common is their primary concern, namely to provide the right information, in the right format and quantity, at the right time, to the right person, at reasonable costs. Although individual information quality criteria may vary (often cited criteria are accurate, timely, reliable, relevant, current, objective) there is a set of common dimensions that relate to *time, format*, and *content* aspects of information.

Synonyms and Closely Related Terms

This idea can be expressed through a number of terms or concepts. All of them are related to the notion of information quality. Since this book focuses on information quality *in the business context*, the terms that seem most closely related are the ones from the domains of information systems, marketing, multimedia management, information and knowledge management, as well as accounting. In these areas, one can find various terms that represent a set of characteristics that make information valuable and useful.[15] Examples of such terms and their background are given in the table below.

---

[15] Other terms sometimes used in connection with the topic of information quality are communication quality, media quality, information system quality, software quality, knowledge quality, or data quality. The differences among these terms will be explained in chapter two.

Synonyms and Related Terms	Source and Application Domain
Information(al) added-value	Taylor, 1986, Library Studies
Information liquidity	Teflian 1999, Marketing
Information effectiveness	Strassmann, 2000, Information Management
Information impact	English 1999, Saracevic 1999, Data Warehouse, Information Science
Information utility	Agosta, 2000, Data Quality Management
Knowledge content quality	Harris & Fleming 1998, Knowledge Management
Information Payoff	Strassmann, 1985, Information Management
Return on Information	Huesing, 2000, Knowledge Management
Information salience	Davenport 1997, Information Management, Media Studies
Cybervalue	Donath 1998, On-line Marketing
Information service excellence	Kinnel 1997, Information and Library Studies
Information systems service quality	Van Dyke et al., 1997, Management Information Systems

Table 1: Terms related to information quality and their background

Information Quality – the Business Challenge

If we look at these (theoretical) issues from the point of view of management and employees who struggle with information on a day to day basis, the topic of information quality becomes not only an interesting research topic, but also a pressing business challenge.

Quality management in knowledge-intensive firms has so far been limited to standard products, administrative services, and routine processes. Within knowledge-intensive processes, quality management has not been a pre-dominant topic. It is often considered difficult to operationalize and of limited practical value due to the creative nature of knowledge-intensive tasks. MARGARET KINNELL writes in her empirical investigation on quality management in the information service sector: "There was a general view that quality systems were not appropriate [for information staff]" (Kinnel, 1997, p. 5). She cites the fear of administrative costs and rigid procedures as prime

---

16   The overall topic of the survey was information overload and how well the employees cope with the high information load in their daily work. The final question of the questionnaire was an open one which asked the respondents what could help them in their

reasons for this view. HUMBERT and ELISABETH LESCA, two information management consultants and professors, conclude similarly that it is very rare that a company analyzes the costs resulting from non-quality information (Lesca & Lesca, 1995, p. 116). Finally, Strong, Lee, and Wang write that 'until recently there has been little awareness of the pervasiveness of IQ problems and their severe financial and operational costs to organizations (see Strong et al., 1997, p.46) Surveys conducted by our institute among professional management consultants (see Brocks, 2000) and among CIOs and webmasters (see Muenzenmayer, 1999) confirm this lack of quality management for know-how-intensive, non-routine tasks. The interviews we conducted revealed that information quality management was a topic that most practitioners had never heard of (unlike the problems associated with the term) or that they only used intuitively. At the Swiss bank CREDIT SUISSE (in its private banking section), for example, high information quality was explicitly stated as the first of ten corporate quality goals. There was, however, no single definition or explanation of the term available or known to the employees, when we conducted interviews on-site (Muenzenmayer, 1999, p. 45).

It seems that using any kind of rigid quality management system in a context as unpredictable as knowledge work is a dangerous undertaking. Knowledge workers may not like the idea that their intellectual energy and creativity should meet certain predefined standards or criteria. Nevertheless, many managers in knowledge-intensive firms have come to realize that information quality is a decisive competitive factor and that non-quality information can be a crucial cost driver. The typical statements listed below illustrate this practice gap between a clear need for information quality management and the discontent (or mismatch) with traditional quality methods for the context of knowledge-intensive processes. The quotes are taken directly from an on-line survey (and twenty-three follow-up interviews) that we conducted in a large multi-national insurance company in the first quarter of 2001 with over 650 responding employees of the company.[16] When asked whether they often received information in a form which is difficult to use for them (unstructured, unclear purpose), over fifty percent of all questioned managers and executives indicated that this was frequently the case.

Limits of Traditional Approaches

---

productivity in regard to information processing. The table lists original answers from that question. I have added the affected information quality characteristics beside each quote.

Survey Quotes from Managers and Staff	Affected Information Quality Characteristics
It would help me if the senders of e-mails would indicate more clearly *what they expect of me* and by when.	Applicable
People should not only be trained how to search for information. They should also be taught *how to pass it on.*	Convenient, targeted, relevant
Access to information should be better *structured.* Training to use existing tools and systems should be improved.	Accessible, easy-to-use information infrastructure
We need the following: to have the major sources of information *in one central area.*	Comprehensive, integrated sources
We should determine a *rating scale* on what is essential reading to what might be optional reading.	Relevant, evaluated
We need more *summaries* upfront; shorter, more *concise* texts, and generally information that gets to the main point right away.	Concise, focused
At the first contact with information I need *overview* not details, but that is not the case.	Concise, systematic
What I would need is *clear, structured information* on a *stable platform* with an executive summary at the beginning of each file.	Clear, stable platform, concise
I need information in clearer structure, and a *higher quality* of information *sources.*	Clear, high-quality source
I need more *targeted, short* and *concise* information. Electronic information has to be presented differently than print because one skims through it and looks for keywords.	Targeted, concise, adjusted to the medium
I would like more *focused* information provision – knowledge, not just information.	Focused, value added, concise
Clearer, more precise information would allow increase in time to comprehend important information.	Clear, precise, comprehensible
It would help a lot if I received the same information in the *same look and feel.*	Consistent
I have to make sure I don't waste time on information and e-mails that don't directly *impact* my work activities.	Applicable, relevant
Clearly defined subject headings with *action* indicators and deadlines would help, as well as information on the *background* of the information. Summaries upfront are key.	Traceable, concise
There are *too many formats and sources* for the information I need; one figure will be quoted by different sources and be different; how do you know which one is *reliable*?	Reliable, consistent

Table 2: The practice gap as illustrated by management complaints about internal information

This empirical evidence seems to indicate that there is a practice gap, in the sense of a discrepancy between problem awareness and solution deployment.[17] It illustrates the fact that further research in this domain is necessary (and that the transfer of the research results into practice are of crucial importance). The benefit of this research should thus be to resolve some of the problems articulated in the table above. This can be achieved by clarifying the vocabulary, structuring and examining the problem space, and offering systematic and exemplary solutions. As stated before, a major element of this endeavor will be the development of a conceptual framework.

Benefits of this Books

The resulting information quality framework should answer crucial business questions such as the ones listed below:

Questions Answered by the IQ-Framework

- How do you rate the quality of an information product, such as a white paper, a product concept, a knowledge portal, a business book, a project report, or a market research report?
- How do you make the expectations of a customer explicit in terms of the information he or she anticipates?
- Which are typical problems that occur in knowledge-intensive processes that can be traced back to poor information quality?
- Which are the limitations, tradeoffs or natural constraints when information has to be managed for high-quality in a real-life setting (e.g., for speed and convenience rather than for accuracy and security)?

---

[17] Specialized analysts of major research companies confirm this view. Daniel W. Rasmus, for example, of Giga Information Group concludes the following in his analysis of knowledge management technology from August 9th, 2001: "Organizations require formal transfer processes that *ensure the quality and consistency of the knowledge* being transferred." See Rasmus, 2001. Similar findings are reported by Connie Moore and Susan Wiener, also of Giga. They conclude that quality assurance and *quality of content* is one of the crucial pitfalls of web content management today. See Morre & Wiener, 2001. The Gartner Group also stresses the strategic role of information quality and acknowledges its current practice gap. In a report from October 1999, it concludes that *information quality architecture* is one of the key success factors for the future of business intelligence. See Anderson & Smith, 1999, p. 54.

- What is the required management infrastructure in terms of systems, processes, tools, roles, etc. to assure high-quality information in knowledge-intensive business processes?

Target Audiences   Besides the target groups in the scientific community, this book primarily addresses practitioners and students in the field of information and knowledge management. It should provide them with a systematic overview of the field of information quality and familiarize them with this perspective. Hopefully, it will also provide them with ideas and ways of improving information quality in their own context.

Structure of the Book   In terms of the book's structure, it will proceed deductively, starting with a conceptual framework that is then illustrated with the help of case studies. Having given a first overview of the topic in chapter one, *chapter two* will provide a survey on the main problems resulting from low-quality information. It will provide various perspectives from which information quality problems can be analyzed. Chapter two also provides a survey of current information quality management frameworks. Based on the findings of chapter two, *chapter three* will show how an information quality framework can be used to specify and improve the value of information products. Chapter three represents the main part of this book. It contains the four information quality principles that can be used to manage information quality. These principles are then applied in in various contexts in the case studies in *chapter four*. *Chapter five* provides a synthesis of the main findings and highlights the implications for various management levels.

Conclusion   The notion of information quality is both a promising concept and a vague and ambiguous term that seems to depend on the use of information. Consequently, numerous theoretical notions exist depending upon perspective and disciplinary background. In practice, these notions are often only implicit and not very systematic. This can lead to misunderstandings, conflicts, or customer complaints. Nevertheless, it has become clear that the notion of information quality relates to certain content, format, cost, and time characteristics of information which give it value to specific users. There is evidence that traditional quality management approaches may not work well for these intangible characteristics.

2. Information Quality Problems and Current Approaches

This chapter consists of four parts. In a first step, the information quality perspective will be introduced as a problem lens. Then, a survey of information quality problems from relevant literature and field research will be presented. This will result in a problem typology. In a third step, existing information quality frameworks will be presented and evaluated. In the last step of this chapter, research deficits and consequences of further framework development will be discussed.

Chapter Overview

2.1 Background and Key Terms

I do not say that definitions may not have a role to play in connection with certain problems, but I do say it is for most problems quite irrelevant whether a term can be defined or cannot be defined, or how it is defined. All that is necessary is that we make ourselves understood.[18]

SIR KARL R. POPPER

In this introductory section, key terms and concepts that will resurface in the problem description and in the analysis of information quality frameworks will be described and defined. Specifically, the relevant background and vocabulary of quality management and knowledge management (and their relationship) will be briefly discussed.

Goal of the Section

---

[18] Popper, 1994, p. 18. While I do not fully agree with this opinion and view definitions as one means of clarification, I do agree with Popper that explaining things by examples can lead to a better understanding than simply providing definitions (Popper, 1994, p.19).

*Quality
Management
& Knowledge*

If one examines the quality of information in knowledge-intensive processes, one inevitably has to rely on the concepts and terms of two 'disciplines', namely quality management and knowledge management. Although these two fields share many common goals, such as the documentation of procedural knowledge and the continuous improvement through systematic learning, exchange between the two disciplines seems to be neither frequent nor intensive, nor particularly fruitful.[19] Nevertheless, codification of experiences or insights (an issue that regards both disciplines) can only be productive and useful if the stored content is of high quality and can be turned into actionable knowledge. Hence, quality management may profit from a closer examination of the characteristics of knowledge and knowledge management, in return, may benefit from an analysis of the experiences of quality management and its conceptions of quality. In consequence, we will look at the background, differences, and key terms of both disciplines. This should give us a better understanding of the problems inherent in managing information quality in knowledge-intensive processes.

*Different
Backgrounds
and Origins*

Having stated that quality and knowledge management may be two fields with great complementarities and mutual benefits, one has to acknowledge the different backgrounds from which these disciplines originated. This regards both the academic background and the first practical applications of the two concepts. Whereas the quality management movement began with a focus on quantitative analysis and monitoring in a manufacturing context (see Evans & Lindsay, 1999), knowledge management evolved (much later than quality management) out of the organizational learning and organizational memory literature and was first applied systematically in research or consulting contexts (see Lehner, 2000). Although both areas have come to stress the importance of learning and communication, they do so from two distinct perspectives. One could argue that quality management focuses on processes and their reliability and how they lead to customer satisfaction. Knowledge management, in contrast, focuses on innovation (e.g., knowledge creation see von Krogh et al., 2000), and intellectual asset reuse (see Davenport & Prusak, 1998).

Two Mind-sets

This uncommon ground may not always be visible in the respective literature, but it does have consequences for the methodologies and tools that are used by these disciplines.

---

[19]   See for example Lim et al. 1999.

Particularly the epistemological paradigms employed by the two disciplines seem far apart. Whereas knowledge management literature often stresses a constructivist or autopoetic view of knowledge (emphasizing the collective, context-dependent sense-making of individuals and groups, see von Krogh et al., 1994), quality management tends to be rooted in a positivistic, Cartesian mind-set, that aims at the objective measurement of clearly given situations or problems.[20] These two different mind-sets may lead to, at times, incommensurable views on issues such as measurement, improvement, or learning. This is also the reason why information quality management for the context of knowledge-intensive processes is not just a replica or slight adaptation of concepts such as Total Quality Management or Quality Assurance. In other words: information quality management cannot be just an adaptation of traditional quality management concepts to the immaterial world. It has to be rooted in a knowledge-based view of the firm that differs in terms of the basic assumptions with many ideas inherent in quality management.

Nevertheless, many insightful ideas from quality management can be used in the knowledge work domain in spite of the great differences between the two disciplines. These ideas relate, for instance, to the mobilization of the workforce for quality issues, the forms of aggregation of data about quality, and the identification of non-quality costs.

To turn these ideas into concepts and to use them in a new (often immaterial) context, we must first clarify some of the key terms of knowledge and quality management. These terms are *quality, (total) quality management, data, information, knowledge, knowledge work(er),* and *knowledge-intensive process.* While there is a plethora of definitions available for these terms, the next few paragraphs will focus on definitions that represent a terminology which is both representative (of the academic field) and useful for the current context.

Required Definitions

In their review of quality management literature, Evans and Lindsay conclude the following about the term 'quality' and its definition:

Quality as a Concept

---

[20]   This distinction seems true for many typical "representatives" of the two disciplines. It does, of course, not apply to all scholars or practitioners active in the two fields. There are many knowledge management 'activitists' with positivistic mind-sets, and there are quality management advocates who stress the socially constructed nature of managerial challenges.

Quality can be a confusing concept, partly because people view quality in relation to differing criteria based on their individual roles in the production-marketing chain. (Evans & Lindsay, 1999, p. 10).

Standard Definitions of Quality

In spite of this confusion, one can actually find a limited number of recurring definitions that adequately describe the term. Two of the most frequently encountered definitions are the following ones: "Quality is the totality of features and characteristics of a product or service that bears on its ability to satisfy given needs." "Quality is meeting or exceeding customer expectations" (Evans & Lindsay, 1999, pp. 15). Variations of these definitions often include the terms 'high value', 'error-free', 'specifications' (which are met), or 'fitness for use'. Further definitions adapted to the information quality context will be provided in section 2.3.[21]

Twofold Nature of Quality
⇒ *Subjective and Objective Indicators*

What we can learn from these definitions is that quality has a *subjective* (e.g., meeting expectations) and an *objective* component (e.g., meeting requirements), or in other words an *absolute* ('error free', 'meeting specifications') and a *relative* dimension ('fitness for use', 'satisfy needs'). Any approach to quality, including information quality, has to take this twofold nature of quality into account. The duality of quality can have important consequences for the way that quality is measured. It cannot only be calculated with the help of automatically generated key indicators, but must also be evaluated according to the (subjective) judgments and opinions of the customers.

Quality Management

⇒ *Focus on the Present and the Future*

This view of quality as both an objective and a subjective phenomenon influences the definition of quality management. Managing quality becomes a task of not only assuring that the processes and their outcomes are under control and within specified limits, but also an activity that strives for customer 'delight' and loyalty. It becomes a systematic activity that is not only focused on the present, but also on future improvements. This understanding becomes clear in the following text book definition of total quality management:

Total Quality Management is a management concept (and associated tools) that involves the entire workforce in focusing on *customer satisfaction* and continuous *improvement*.[22]

---

[21]   For alternative definitions and their implications see also: Reeves, C.A., and Bednar, D.A. (1994) Defining Quality: Alternatives and Implications, in: *Academy of Management Review*, 19, no. 3, pp. 319-445.

[22]   See Evans & Lindsay, 1999, glossary.

Most quality management concepts that strive to reach these two goals, do so by employing a *management cycle*. A quality management cycle that has become well-known is the Deming-cycle[23], which consists of the phases *plan* (the quality activities and goals), *do* (what is necessary to improve quality), *check* (whether this has worked), and *act* (to correct still existing deficiencies). The management cycle is an essential element of any quality management concept, since it offers a sequence of steps and associated tools through which quality can be assured and improved.

Quality Management Cycle

Closely related to this understanding of managing quality is the cycle of total data quality management (TDQM), a field that is of course much younger than TQM, but obviously more closely related to the topic of this book. Huang et al. Define this cycle as follows :

Total Data Quality Management

The definition component of the TDQM cycle identifies Information Quality (IQ) dimensions. The measurement component produces IQ metrics. The analysis component identifies root causes for IQ problems and calculates the impacts of poor quality information. Finally, the improvement component provides techniques for improving IQ. They are applied along IQ dimensions according to requirements specified by the consumer (Huang et al., 1999, p. 16).

This cycle (which Huang et al. describe with the steps *define, measure, analyze*, and *improve*) highlights other important aspects of quality management, namely those of analyzing root causes of problems, and calculating the costs of non-quality information. Although Huang et al. refer to information quality dimensions, their cycle is clearly labeled as a data quality management cycle. Hence, they not dot distinguish information from data. The next section will show (by way of examples) that data and information quality problems are clearly distinct. Here, we will show that they are different by looking at the definitions of data, information, and knowledge. This will also highlight one of the goals of information quality management, namely to turn information into actionable knowledge.

Analyzing Causes, Calculating Costs

Whereas data designates 'raw,' unconnected, quantitative or qualitative items, the term information relates to answers to questions, statements about situations or facts. Information in this sense is a difference that makes a difference (Bateson,

Data ≠ Information Knowledge

---

[23]   See for example Deming 1986.

1972).[24] A piece of data is just a distinction or a registered item without context. Data in this sense becomes information when it is related to other data. In other words, when we link various sets of data to form one coherent statement, the resulting entity can be called a piece of *information:* a coherent set of statements that forms a message. In the context of this book we look at information as potential knowledge that has to be internalized by the receiver. We see information as a *production factor* and as the *input* and *output* of certain knowledge-intensive business processes. This information becomes knowledge when it is correctly interpreted and connected with prior knowledge.[25] Knowledge, in the traditional epistemological analysis of the term, only qualifies as such if it is a justified (e.g., it can be argued convincingly), true (i.e., corresponds to facts) belief (i.e., is held by an individual).[26] This 'platonic' notion of knowledge, however, has been extensively criticized.

One of the most prominent critics of this 'purist' approach to knowledge is MICHAEL POLANYI. He associates knowledge closely with an individual's *personal* commitment and passion to hold a certain belief. He stresses the activity of knowing over the reification of knowledge and views it as 'an active comprehension of the things known, an action that requires skill'. (see Polanyi, 1974, p., vii-viii, p. 17, p. 143, p. 252-257). Whereas critical rationalist thinkers like POPPER have argued for the superiority of objective knowledge (Popper's world three, see Popper, 1994), Polanyi stresses the value of subjective knowledge and the personal co-efficient that enters every act of knowing. In doing so, he emphasizes the fact that major discoveries – new knowledge – do not always ensue from deductive reasoning, but are often the result of an initially unjustified personal belief (a process that PEIRCE has

---

[24]   Davenport and Prusak (1998) provide a similar definition: Information is contextualized, categorized, calculated, corrected and condensed data that makes a difference. This definition already contains some of the information quality principles that will be presented in chapter 3, namely contextualizing, condensing (integrating), and correcting (validating).

[25]   Knowledge management's prime objective in this context is the same as the mission of information quality management: to **make information actionable** or ensure that stored experiences can be used again.

[26]   See Dance & Sosa, 1993, p. 234.

[27]   In chapter three of this book, the first issue has been incorporated in the validation principle, the second issue in the activation principle.

labeled as abduction, see Dancy and Sosa, 1993, p. 8, p. 332).

The consequences of these two views of knowledge for the current thesis are the following ones: Information can only be of high-quality if is validated, and if it is made actionable and stimulates the prior knowledge of the individual.[27]

Two brief examples can illustrate this important hierarchy of concepts and the differences between data, information, and knowledge: *Examples*

Data: When the digits 1 and 9 and 2 are *aggregated* with the help of the dot sign (.) the resulting data is a number: 1.92.

Information: When the data 1.92 is *combined* with other data to produce a coherent message, the resulting information could be the following: 1 US$ = 1.92 Swiss Francs. This piece of information states the fact that one US-Dollar is right now equivalent to one Swiss franc and 92 cents. Hence, information can be the answer to a question, e.g., what is the value of one US-dollar in terms of Swiss Francs.

Knowledge: When I *interpret* this equation and link it to my *prior knowledge*, I may realize that the Dollar is quite expensive right now in relation to the Swiss Franc. If I *apply* this fact to my current situation (my plans to travel to the United States) I may decide not to spend my vacation in the States because of the expensive exchange rate. Having *understood* this relationship, we can speak of knowledge (or, more precisely, in this case factual knowledge, know-what).

High-quality information makes it easier to transform information into knowledge, by helping to interpret and evaluate the information, by assisting the connection to prior knowledge, and by facilitating the application of the information to new contexts. Thus, increasing the quality of information means increasing the probability that information is again turned into knowledge.

Agosta, 2000, cites the following examples to illustrate the distinction between information and data:

An example of data is a knock at the door. The information presented is that my colleague has arrived for a visit. Likewise, that it is 55 degrees Fahrenheit today is data. That it is warm for this time of year is information.

He concludes that as soon as data is evaluated as to its *quality*, the data becomes information. Thus, we see another link between quality and information.

Based on the aforementioned distinctions (and the discussion of knowledge as a balance between objective insights and subjective opinions) we can now define how knowledge is used. The application of knowledge can be described from the point of view of the knower, i.e., who is applying it (e.g., the knowledge worker) or how it is applied (e.g., in a knowledge-   *Knowledge Work Definitions* intensive process). Thus, we are first going to define what a knowledge worker is (and what constitutes as knowledge work) and then outline our understanding of knowledge-intensive processes.

Professionals that are typically considered as knowledge workers are consultants, lawyers, professors, engineers, or managers (see Schultze, 2000). But what is it that makes these professionals 'knowledge workers' (a term that was coined by Peter F. Drucker)? Despress and Hiltrop offer the following definition of knowledge workers:

Knowledge workers manipulate and orchestrate symbols and concepts, identify more strongly with their peers and professions than their organizations, have more rapid skill obsolesce and are more critical to the long-term success of the organization (Despress & Hiltrop, 1995).

A synonym of knowledge workers is therefore symbolic analyst, i.e., somebody who analyses and manipulates (changes) symbols. The simplest definition of a knowledge worker is of course 'somebody who performs knowledge work'. While this is certainly true, it does not help in our understanding of the concept. Hence, we have to look at definitions that describe knowledge work itself. Following are six such definitions that show the scope of meanings that are associated with the term knowledge work:

Knowledge work is human mental work performed to generate useful information. (Davis & Naumann, 1997.)

Knowledge work is the production and transmission of knowledge. (Sther 1994)

Knowledge Work is any creative systematic activity undertaken in order to increase the stock of knowledge of man, culture and society, and the use of this knowledge to devise new applications. It includes fundamental research, applied research, and experimental development work leading to new devices, products and processes (Unesco Definition cited in: Despress & Hiltrop, 1995, p.14).

Knowledge work is the skillful collection, analysis, synthesis, and application of information. (Eppler 1998)

Knowledge work involves analyzing and applying specialized expertise to solve problems, to generate ideas, or to create new products and services (Zidel 1998).

Knowledge work can be classified as white collar work which uses and produces information, but unlike service work is not scripted, but creative and often non-routine. It relies on idiosyncratic knowledge and requires formal education (abstract, technical, theoretical knowledge). Knowledge workers need to constantly balance objective and subjective knowledge (Schultze, 2000).

What all of these definitions have in common is the fact that knowledge work focuses on information that has to be made useful; hence, the connection between knowledge work and information quality. The constant balance between objective and subjective knowledge mentioned by Schultze was already discussed in the definition of knowledge. The fact that knowledge work is not scripted, however, has not been addressed yet. Although knowledge work is often non-routine and creative, as Schultze writes, it can nevertheless be sequenced and broken down into specific steps. We refer to this standardization of knowledge work as knowledge-intensive processes. They are defined in the next paragraph.

We define a knowledge-intensive process as a productive series of activities that involves information transformation and requires specialized professional knowledge. Knowledge-intensive processes can be characterized by their often non-routine nature (unclear problem space, many decision options), the high requirements in terms of continuous learning and innovation, and the crucial importance of interpersonal communication on the one side and the documentation of (high quality) information on the other. Knowledge work can thus be organized into knowledge-intensive processes. This organization includes the management of knowledge. Knowledge-intensive processes require three types of knowledge: Knowledge about the process (which steps to follow), knowledge within the process (which information has to be gathered or used), and knowledge derived from the process, e.g., experiences and insights from the completed steps (see Eppler et al., 1999).

Knowledge-intensive Process

The following table provides a summary of the discussion so far and compares central parameters of quality management, information quality, and knowledge management. It highlights the fact that information quality in knowledge-intensive processes should combine insights from both existing domains.

Table Overview

Descriptors	Quality Management	Information Quality Management	Knowledge Management
		⟹	⟸
Goal	Reduce errors (before they occur) and meet specifications in the manufacturing process. Increase (internal and external) customer satisfaction.	Assure that information is of high value to knowledge workers who use it in knowledge-intensive processes. The goal is to improve the usefulness and validity of information.	Turn information into actionable knowledge, foster innovation, enable learning from mistakes and best practices and promote effective knowledge sharing. Value and exploit intellectual capital.
Object	Products (and processes) in the manufacturing context, at times also (scripted) services	Knowledge content (information that answers how and why questions)	Implicit and explicit knowledge (know-how, know-what, know-why, know-who) in all forms
Dominating mind-set	Positivistic, rational, Cartesian, quantitative	Systemic, qualitative and quantitative	Constructivist, systemic, qualitative
Implicit assumption	Quality affects the entire organization and every employee: it must be specified, measured, and continually improved through training, team work, and process adaptations.	To describe the quality of information, one can rely on a finite number of criteria which can be grouped into several meaningful dimensions.	Knowledge is often tacit (difficult to articulate) and thus depends on the individual. KM must connect knowledge workers, elicit their knowledge, map their skills, and use their experience.
Time of initial development	Early 1950s	Late 1990s	Early 1990s
Tools and methods	Ishikawa diagram, Pareto chart, House of Quality, Quality Function Deployment (QFD), Six Sigma and statistical analysis tools, Failure Mode and Effects Analysis (FMEA), Quality circles, audits, process manuals	Information quality frameworks, surveys, policies and guidelines, training seminars, portals, abstracts, review work-flows, monitoring software, indicators and standards, rating and ranking schemes	Knowledge maps, expert directories, groupware applications, document manage-ment systems, retrieval and mining software, debriefing workshops, intellectual capital reports, collaboration forms such as communities of practice
Management cycle	Plan – do – check – act (Deming)	Define – measure – analyze – improve (Wang)	Set goals – identify – store – develop – share – use – measure knowledge (Probst)
Advocates/ thought leaders	Deming, Ishikawa, Juran, Crosby, Imai, Feigenbaum	Wang, English, Redman, Lesca, Königer, Reithmeyer	Nonaka, Davenport, von Krogh, Probst, Sveiby

Table 3: A comparative view of Quality Management, Information Quality and Knowledge Management

If one studies the quality of information in knowledge-intensive processes, the context of one managerial discipline may not be enough. While both, knowledge management and quality management have developed powerful concepts in their respective fields, only a combination of both approaches can lead to superior results. A combination must take into account the differing mind-sets and definitions and accommodate them to the new context of knowledge work.

Conclusion

2.2 A Survey of Information Quality Problems in Knowledge-intensive Processes

The principal summary point to make is that the major problems in future information systems will revolve around the processes of reducing the amount of and raising the quality of information brought to the attention of the user.[28]

ROBERT S. TAYLOR

In the previous chapter, I have outlined how information quality management can be seen as a combination (or mediation) between quality management and knowledge management. I have argued that traditional quality management can only be directly applied in the information management domain if one focuses on data quality issues. As soon as one moves to the next level – meaningful and context-dependent information – quality management techniques alone no longer suffice. Insights from the domain of knowledge management now need to be incorporated. In order to further clarify this distinction between data quality and information quality, the following table lists typical problems from the two domains. This should illustrate the difference between the two concepts as discussed in the previous chapter (but this time from a problem-perspective).

Data vs.
Information
Quality Problems

---

[28]   Taylor, 1986, p. 58.

Data Quality Problems	Information Quality Problems
Duplicates, multiple data sources	Conflicting recommendations in a study or analysis
Missing data relationships	Unclear causal effects in a diagnosis
Garbling (meaningless entries)	Wordy reports that have no logical flow
Spelling Errors	Untidy language that contains grammatical errors
Obsolete or outdated entries	An analysis is not updated according to recent discoveries or changes in the organizational context
Inconsistent data formats or naming conventions	Inconsistent layout or navigation structures
Misplaced data that is saved in the wrong database	Lost or 'buried' documents
Complicated query procedures	Difficult information navigation and retrieval
Wrong data coding or tagging (adding wrong meta-data)	Inadequate or insufficient categorization (in-sufficient meta-information or contextual attributes)
Incorrect data entries because of lack of source validation	Unsubstantiated conclusions with inadequate evidence
Manipulation of stored data (deletion, modification)	Manipulation of decision processes (overloading, confusing, diverting)

Table 4: Data quality versus information quality problems

Key Differences

Data quality is often managed with traditional total quality management approaches and the first experiences show that these may indeed offer feasible solutions for many database or data warehouse applications (see English, 1999, Redman, 1996, Huang et al, 1999).

Having clearly differentiated data from information, we can easily see that information quality problems are distinct from data quality problems. This is particularly evident when one looks at the solutions to these problems.

Data Quality vs. Information Quality Solutions

Whereas data quality problems can be resolved through data cleansing algorithms, data profiling programs, stabilization algorithms (e.g., phonetic manipulation and error correction), statistical process control, or dictionary matching routines (see Strong et al., 1997, or Agosta, 2000), information quality problems can often not be solved through automated processes. They require (as do some data quality problems) fundamental analysis of business issues, a change in work practices and process redesigns, an analysis of the involved information community and its expectations and skills, an evaluation of the relevant knowledge domains and their attributes, as well as a rating of the content management process and infrastructure. Typical remedies for information quality problems may include design guidelines, publishing policies, authoring training, source validation rules, the purchase of additional information services and infrastructures, a re-design of the review and feed-back process, etc.

In the next three sections we will look at typical *information* quality problems, as they are described in the relevant literature, or as we have encountered them in our research. This will not only ground the subsequent work in the problems that need to be resolved, but it will also help to structure and categorize the encountered challenges.

Section Goals

2.2.1 Information Quality Problems in Overview

In this section we look at information quality problems as they have been described and compiled in the relevant academic literature. For that purpose several books and articles that treat the topic of information quality (and knowledge work) problems are reviewed and summarized. The three main criteria for inclusion of a text in this literature survey are the perspective (a general approach rather than a very focused one), the explicit connection to the topic of information quality and knowledge work, and the application within a corporate context. The analysis of these texts, particularly how they categorize information quality problems, will contribute to the problem taxonomy that is developed in section 2.2.2.

Section Goal

In his analysis of information quality problems, GARVIN distinguishes three types of major information problems (Garvin, 1993, pp. 50-58): First, *biased* information, that is to say information that is inaccurate or distorted due to the interests or motives of the source or information transmitter. Second, *outdated* information that is no longer current due to its tardy delivery or a failure to update it. While the first problem related to content and the second to time, the third relates to (inadequate) format. Garvin refers to this problem as '*massaged*' information. According to Garvin, 'massaging is the putting together of data in a manner that applies to a particular problem at hand.' The problem that lies in this massaging is that the very same information - when massaged (or represented) differently - may lead to different (and sometimes inadequate) interpretations. While Garvin's problem survey is very simple and narrow in scope, it does highlight the fact that information quality problems can be split into content, time and format problems. Garvin does not however, stress another important problem

Garvin's Three Information Quality Problems

⇒ Content, Time, and Format Problems

Lesca and Lesca's Information Maladies

dimension: that of *cost*. The same is true for the next information quality approach by Lesca and Lesca (1995). As we will see below, Lesca and Lesca have analyzed a variety of information quality problems.

A more complete (yet still general) analysis of information quality problems was conducted by Lesca and Lesca in 1995. It revealed eight clusters of information 'maladies', as the authors have labeled them. Below, we summarize the symptoms and causes of these eight information quality problems, as they are described by Lesca and Lesca, two French professors of information management (see Lesca & Lesca, 1995, pp. 75-165).

1. *Limited usefulness* of information due to an *overload*[29] of information caused by a lack of cleansing or maintenance activities or by neglecting analysis and synthesis. As counter-measures the authors suggest filtering according to relevance criteria, prioritization and hierarchical structuring of information.

2. *Ambiguity* of the provided information leading to differing or wrong interpretations due to lacking precision or accuracy, the use of abbreviations or jargon, or simply different points of view. Counter-measures suggested by the authors include the use of a glossary, establishing feedback loops, and using richer communication media.

3. *Incompleteness* of information that can lead to inadequate decisions. The main causes for this problem are the fragmentation of work and the resulting specialization that leads to fragmentation of information. Main causes for this fragmentation are infrequent communication and exchange of information between specialists, incompatible IT-systems, and an information management strategy that is not aligned with the business strategy. Counter-measures focus on these three areas.

4. *Inconsistency* of information that leads to confusion. Causes for inconsistencies or contradictory statements are a lacking co-ordination between information authors and distributors, unclear responsibilities, or the use of multiple, inconsistent, information sources. Counter-measures focus especially on clear responsibilities and co-ordination mechanisms.

---

[29]   The connection between information overload and lacking information quality is also pointed out by Simpson and Prusak, 1995.

5. An *inadequate presentation format* that leads to expensive conversion tasks. The main problem lies in the fact that information is not presented in an order, format or style that allows for a direct use, hence conversion is necessary. Causes for this problem are insufficient dialogue between information producers and consumers, constant time pressure, and a lacking adaptation of information to usage needs or styles (which would be the most effective countermeasure).

6. The information is *not reliable* or *trustworthy*, i.e., there is a great risk of errors, and the information's background cannot be checked. Causes for this problem are mistakes in the information production and distribution process, as well as unidentified sources.

7. The information is *not accessible*. It is lost over time because of unclear responsibilities or technological changes. This can demotivate staff and lead them to wrong decisions.

8. Finally, a big problem that Lesca and Lesca see, is the *distortion of information*, e.g., when the original message is no longer the same when it is received. Causes for this problem are too many intermediaries, too much specialization and jargon, or even voluntary distortion (e.g., misinformation) such as modifying, delaying or blocking the information to harm the receiver.

Lesca and Lesca structure these eight problems into two sections. The first one views information as a *product* with problems such as overload, ambiguity, incompleteness, inconsistency, or inadequate format. The second one views information as a *process* and contains the last three problems from the list, namely lacking reliability, lost access, or distortion. Every problem that is described in this way is also related to an information quality criterion, the criterion being the opposite of the problem, e.g., overload versus relevance, ambiguity versus clarity.

⇒ *Information Product and Process Problems*

⇒ *Problems as Opposites of IQ-Criteria*

What this approach has shown is that information problems must not only address the final information product, but also the process that leads to this product. This is of course an insight that traditional quality management has considered for quite a long time. In addition, the approach shows that information quality problems can be seen as the opposites of information quality criteria (an approach that other authors have also followed, see below).

Information
Quality 'Potholes'

The eight problems described above already provide helpful hints where and how non-quality information may cause problems. The above list is nevertheless neither complete, nor very systematic. A more systematic approach has been developed by Strong et al. (1997) and was later modified in Huang, Lee, and Wang (1999). As Garvin and Lesca and Lesca, the authors of this approach base their findings on incidents at real-life companies to illustrate the identified problems. In these approaches ten information quality problems were identified that relate to information producers, information custodians, and information consumers. The authors thus structure information quality problems along the *life cycle* of information: from origination (information producer/sources), storage and maintenance (information custodian/systems), to information use (information consumer/task environment). Since the authors examine information quality from a database and data warehouse point of view, not all identified problems are relevant to this study. Consequently, purely database-related problems[30] are left out at this point. The other problems, as well as their consequences and possible counter-measures, are summarized in the table below.

⇒ *Production,*
Storage and
Usage Problems
(Life Cycle)

---

[30]   They relate to non-numeric information and its indexing and to automated content analysis.

Problem Name	Description	Consequences	Solution
1. Multiple sources	Multiple sources of the same information produce different values and lead to confusion, less credibility and acceptance.	Use of information declines. Users distrust information. Maintenance is more difficult and costly.	Develop common definitions and consistent procedures.
2. Subjective roduction	Information is produced using subjective judgements, leading to bias.	The objectivity of the information decreases and information is difficult to evaluate.	More training, better rules, expert systems.
3. Production errors	Systemic errors in information production lead to lost information.	Information searching and correcting increases.	Process improvements, incentives, controls.
4. Too much information	Large volumes of stored information make it difficult to access information in a reasonable time.	Excess time is required to extract and summarize information.	Analyze information needs, develop regular, frequently extracted subsets of relevant information.
5. Distributed systems	Distributed, heterogeneous systems lead to inconsistent definitions, formats, and values.	Information can no longer be easily aggregated or combined, due to the format differences and incompatibilities.	Integrate systems in one platform (e.g., data warehouse) or reduce the amount of systems to one.
6. Changing task needs	As information consumer's tasks and the organizational environment change, the information that is relevant and useful changes.	Mismatches develop between available information and what is needed for tasks.	Anticipate changes in tasks and revise processes and systems before the mismatch becomes a crisis.
7. Security and privacy requirements	Easy access to information may conflict wit requirements for security, privacy, and confidentiality.	Mechanisms for security block or delay access, so the information provides less value.	Develop consistent policies and procedures for secure information.
8. Lack of computing resources	The IT infrastructure is insufficient and limits access to information.	Knowledge workers are demotivated and cannot work productively.	Develop technology upgrade policies so consumers know when to expect more resources.

Table 5: Information quality problems (compiled and adapted from: Strong et al., 1997)

⇒ *Relating Problems to Several Criteria*

Besides using the information life cycle to structure information quality problems, this approach also relates the problems to specific information quality criteria. Unlike Lesca and Lesca, however, who viewed an IQ-problem as the exact opposite of an individual criterion, this approach relates every IQ-problem to several criteria. Problem number three, for example, is related to the criteria of correctness, completeness, and relevancy. Problem number one is related to both consistency and believability.

⇒ *Systemizing IQ Problems into Patterns*

In addition to identifying a number of significant information quality problems (and relating them to IQ-criteria), Huang et al. (1999) based on Strong et al. (1997), have grouped these problems systematically in what they call 'IQ patterns.' These patterns relate various IQ-problems to one another and combine them with counter measures. An IQ-pattern thus consists of the symptoms, causes, and solutions of IQ-problems. Such a systematic arrangement can help to better understand the interdependencies between information quality problems. A pattern in this sense is a systematic problem perspective that helps users identify the problem type that they are facing and relate it to possible generic solutions. For our own information quality problem typology, we retain the idea of systematically relating information quality problems to one another and to solution elements.

Knowledge Worker Problems

Besides the information quality problems that are discussed in terms of quality criteria, there is a great body of literature on *knowledge workers* and their problems in dealing with information. The descriptions of knowledge work problems can highlight other issues associated with low information quality, since knowledge work is characterized by the fact that its input and output is information (see Drucker, 1991)[31].

⇒ *Input & Output, Process, and Infrastructure Problems*

If one scans the vast available academic literature and empirical surveys on knowledge workers (see for example Collins, 1997, Schultze, 2000, or Reuters, 1998), several problem areas become evident. They relate to the adequate *amount* of information (as an input factor), its *structure* and format, the working *habits* or *processes* and *workplace* parameters, the *communication media* or *IT-infrastructure*, and the *output characteristics* of knowledge workers. Especially the two first problem areas (amount and structure) are closely related to the informa-

---

[31] Drucker writes that 'knowledge work by definition does not yield a product. It yields a contribution of knowledge to somebody else. The output of the knowledge worker is always somebody else's input (Drucker, 1991, p. 173).

tion quality domain. They outline what happens when information is neither provided in the right amount nor in the right format. But the other three domains are also relevant to the IQ-domain, since they show in what ways information has to be integrated into the working habits and workplace of a knowledge worker. They also show how the infrastructure can cause knowledge worker productivity problems. The last problem area, output characteristics, can illustrate the potential of information quality to better specify the products of knowledge work efforts.

The following diagram illustrates the main clusters of knowledge worker problems that are discussed below.

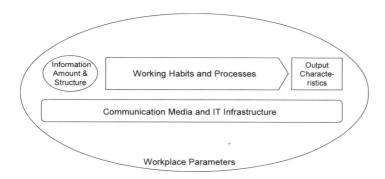

Figure 1: Knowledge work problem categories

That the sheer amount of information which has to be screened is a major knowledge worker problem has been documented in numerous studies (for an overview on such studies see Probst et al., 2000). There are literally dozens of investigations that have found information overload to be a key challenge of today's knowledge workers. The term information overload describes situations in which the individual is no longer able to integrate new information for decision-making, due to the great amount of information he or she is exposed to. He or she can no longer productively use the quantity of information in the available time scale. In consequence, decision quality, efficiency, and even well-being may be reduced. The reasons for this phenomenon are that the provided information does not come in the right *amount* or in the right *format* (e.g., lacking structure or focus). It is repetitious, unclear, irrelevant, or simply poorly organized. As a result of this, knowledge workers can no longer distinguish between what is important and what is not, how various pieces of information relate to one another, or which

Information Amount & Structure (Input)

⇒ Information Overload

information is trustworthy and which isn't. This problem area illustrates that quantity can directly have a negative influence on information quality and that the right amount of information, or its scope, are critical quality criteria. It also highlights the fact that comprehensiveness or completeness are relative terms.

Working Habits and Processes

Whereas the previous problem cluster related to information as an input factor, the problems described in this paragraph focus on information as it is used in the daily routines of knowledge workers. Here, a particular problem of knowledge workers is that they often do not act upon information. That is to say, they know what ought to be done and have all the right information, but don't act on it. Pfeffer and Sutton refer to this problem as the knowing-doing gap (Pfeffer & Sutton, 2000 and Pfeffer & Sutton, 1999). As MINTZBERG (1975) has pointed out, managers need to find a balance between information collection and action taking. If the working habits of knowledge workers consist of merely absorbing information, then they will suffer of what is called 'paralysis by analysis', a tendency to remain in the diagnostic mode and not switching to an action mode.[32] Although this problem relates mostly to the knowledge worker, the role of information quality should not be underestimated. Information that is already organized for action and stimulates a reader or user to remember and apply it, can help in overcoming this knowing-doing gap.

⇒ *Knowing-Doing Gap*

Workplace Parameters

The cluster labeled as workplace parameters contains such typical problems as constant distraction through co-workers (and their calls, e-mails, questions etc.), administrative overhead that needs to be managed, or generally a high workload without time for concentration and quiet work. Knowledge worker problems that relate to the workplace may also include other factors, such as an ergononomic chair and desk, the general working climate (e.g., no incidences of mobbing etc.), or the larger organizational context (e.g., reorganizations that bind resources, etc.). As far as information quality is concerned, the workplace has to make sure that information is not only provided, but can also be processed adequately (without distractions, interruptions, or other worries). This will have a direct influence on the quality of information as an output of knowledge work. How this output should be characterized is another problem, one which we look at in the next paragraph.

⇒ *Concentration Increases Output Quality*

---

[32] This danger is also described in one of the case studies, specifically in the description of major problems by Giga's head of research.

This problem cluster refers to the difficulties that exist in specifying the output of knowledge workers or measuring their productivity. Schultze (2000) in her in-depth analysis of knowledge work refers to this problem as the subjectivity-objectivity problem. It is based on the insight that many knowledge workers rely on idiosyncratic knowledge that they need to make understandable to their peers and superiors[33] (who may have difficulties evaluating their productivity). However, this is not an easy task. It requires a 'negotiation' of meanings, ideas, and opinions. In addition, it requires that the often intangible results of knowledge work are measured through indicators or criteria that allow for comparisons between employees and analyses over time.

Output Characteristics

⇒ Specification Enables Measurement and Comparisons

Especially in the context of interdisciplinary knowledge work teams, the lack of specification of knowledge work output can lead to major problems, such as performance gaps, lags, or simple misunderstandings. Specifying the characteristics that make up information quality for a given context can help reduce this problem cluster and it can provide management with metrics to measure knowledge worker productivity, one of the biggest challenges of management today according to PETER F. DRUCKER.[34]

The last problem cluster relates to the communication and information infrastructure that is available to knowledge workers. Here, problems range from complicated interfaces and low user-friendliness of these systems to incomplete deployment, slow performance, or insufficient control (e.g., the systems are not interactive enough). Employees find that knowledge work systems (see Laudon & Laudon, 2000), which should support them in their tasks, are not adjusted to their information needs or inconvenient to use. Standard IT-tools or communication media are purchased and not sufficiently adapted to the context of knowledge workers. The knowledge workers, in return, do

Communication Media and IT Infrastructure

⇒ User-centric Design and Training

---

[33] This topic is also discussed at length in Polanyi (1974) as stated in the previous chapter.

[34] Drucker (1994) views the two issues of quality and productivity as closely related. He writes: "Wee need systematic work on the *quality of knowledge* and the *productivity of knowledge* – neither even defined so far" (see also Drucker, 1991). In related research, Cornell and Brenner write that "many have tried to measure knowledge worker performance, but with little success." One of the reasons they give for this is that the output is often intangible and abstract. "You can't hold, weigh or put a caliper to the output of a knowledge worker" (Cornell & Brenner, 1993).

not receive enough training to master the offered IT-tools and use their functionalities. In consequence, the communication and information infrastructure contributes to information overload instead of reducing it through filtering mechanisms. The potential of these tools to improve information quality (e.g., making information more accessible, current, and easy-to-use) is hence often not fully exploited. As stated above, this is mainly due to design problems and insufficient training.

If we compare this analysis of knowledge work problems with that of other authors, we see that the presented framework does in fact cover the dominant knowledge work problems. Especially the problem cluster around 'output characteristics' dominates the current discussion of knowledge work.

Other Approaches   Pfiffner and Stadelmann (1995) emphasize the following two knowledge workers problems:

First, Pfiffner and Stadelmann see the difficult *control* of the working progress by the superior as a major problem (because of mostly *abstract* results). We have discussed this issue in the 'output' section above, where we stated that information quality criteria can provide indicators of whether a knowledge worker provides high or low quality work as far as his or her information is concerned (e.g., whether it is accurate, useful, timely etc.). Second, *lags* in the articulation and distribution of new knowledge cause many productivity problems (mainly because the assimilation of knowledge – learning – is always time consuming). The problem of lags was also addressed in the output section. One reason for process lags are time-consuming adjustments because of lacking initial information specifications. Lags of this type can be avoided through information quality specifications. Additionally, the use of high-quality learning content can accelerate the learning process and reduce lags in the application of new knowledge.

Another analysis of knowledge work problems can be found in Davenport et al. (1996). The authors describe the following seven problems associated with knowledge work:

Knowledge workers struggle with the multitude and *insecurity* of information *inputs* and *outputs*. Again, this problem can be directly linked to our discussion of input and output parameters.

Managers struggle with the *unstructured* and highly individual working rules and *routines* of knowledge workers. In our framework in the figure above, we have indicated that individual working habits and processes may cause problems. A way to reduce these individual (and at times conflicting) rules consists of specifying common criteria which everybody should adhere to.

It is difficult to separate work process, result, and original input due to the unstructured nature of knowledge work. For this problem, we have proposed to describe knowledge work in terms of knowledge-intensive processes that offer a greater degree of structure.

There are no clear indicators by which one could measure knowledge worker performance. This problem relates again to output characteristics and to finding reliable indicators.

Every knowledge worker demands a high degree of autonomy. This can lead to lacking coordination. This problem refers to our "habits and process" section.

There are great differences in terms of performance over time and between knowledge workers. As mentioned above, this is a problem of measuring the output of knowledge work.

Knowledge workers often struggle with lacking IT-support. This issue has been explicitly discussed in our last problem cluster. The reasons given were inadequate training and design

From these discussions of knowledge work problems we see that measurement and control problems are consistently affected, two activities that are at the heart of management. For both of these issues, information quality criteria that help to specify the outcome of knowledge work may offer feasible solutions.

⇒ Measurement and Control Problems

Conclusion

Literature on information quality problems categorizes these challenges according to their dimension (content, format, time), their view (information as product or process), or their phase in the information life cycle (production, storage, use). Some approaches directly relate the problems to information quality criteria.

The literature on knowledge work problems revealed that major problems are information overload (resulting from inputs that are too frequent and in an inadequate format), a knowing-doing gap due to the working habits of employees, frequent interruptions, an inadequate IT infrastructure, and missing measurement or control mechanisms (output specifications or indicators).

2.2.2 Information Quality Problem Patterns

You do not understand anything until you understand it in more than one way.

MARVIN MINSKY

Goal of this Section

Having provided an overview on the range of possible information quality problems, we can now summarize the insights from the previous sections in a systematic problem classification. The resulting problem typology – which will reduce the great number of encountered problems to smaller groups – will provide helpful categories or patterns for the framework that will be developed in the next chapter.

Review:

Categorizations of Information Quality Problems

When one analyzes the problems discussed in the previous sections, one can detect various ways of framing or categorizing various information quality problems. There is the abstract problem description that relates information quality problems to either information *content, timing,* or *format.* Then, on a more specific level, there are the problems themselves which are often described in terms of (deficient) information *attributes*, e.g., whether information is correct or flawed, to the point or rather wordy, delivered in a timely and convenient manner, consistent or not etc. These specific IQ-problems can be related to either information as a *product* (stressing stable 'entity' aspects of information) or information as a *process* (stressing the dynamic communication aspects).

Another such abstract way of categorizing information quality problems consisted of relating them to the *life cycle* of information from production (or input) problems to consumption (or output) and deletion problems. Yet another way of categorizing the problems consisted of relating them to certain '*master problems*' that represented a whole series of related issues. Problems that were mentioned in this context were information overload (or the 'volume problem'), the knowing-doing gap, and design and measurement problems. Another (crude) distinction that was made in categorizing information quality problems was the one between *real* information quality and *perceived* quality of information. Then, there was the categorization of problems based on the various information *stakeholders*. Problems affecting information producers (such as difficult publication procedures) were distinguished from those that information administrators face (such as maintaining an information repository), or the problems that information consumers face (e.g., judging the credibility of information). Finally the two categories of *content quality* and *media quality* were introduced to distinguish the different origins of information quality problems.

The section on surveys and focus groups did not yield any additional categorizations, but rather indicated which information attributes represent the greatest problem areas. Based on these crucial areas and the discussed categorizations, we will now group the multitude of problems to sets that allow systematic counter-actions.

In order to structure the problems encountered previously, we can look at them from three insightful perspectives. We can categorize the problems according to their *origin* (i.e., what causes the problems), according to their *consequences* for the information consumer, or according to the *responsibilities* for solving the problems. Below, we structure the encountered problems in those three ways. They seem especially apt because they represent a logical sequence from cause to consequence to remedy.

Three Bases of Categorization:

Origin, Consequence, Responsibility

As far as the origins of the various information quality problems are concerned, one can distinguish four possible causes. The first cause for information quality problems can be that the provided information is *not targeted* at the community that is supposed to use it. In other words, the problems exist because information is addressed to the wrong audience. This can result in irrelevant, incomplete, or simply not useful information for the information consumers. A second cause of information quality problems may simply be that the information producers create 'bad' information that is often incorrect, inconsistent, or outdated. The origin is not a wrong allocation of the information as in the first cause, but already a *wrong production* to begin with. A third possible cause may be that the information is provided in the *wrong manner*. The information may be correct and targeted to the needs of the information consumer, but it may not be provided in the right way or through the right process. A final, fourth possible origin or cause for a great number of information quality problems may be the *infrastructure* on which information is provided. If the hard- and software on which any information system is built (whether electronic or print-based) is not reliable, the information may not be accessible or secure.

Problem Origins

Let me summarize these causes as the following four generic information quality problem categories:

1. **Irrelevant Information**: selection, filter, and profiling problems.
2. **Unsound information**: source or authoring problems.
3. **Sub-optimal content management process**: workflow and management problems.
4. **Unreliable infrastructure**: hardware and software problems.

We can relate many information quality problems to these four causes. We can also articulate strategies against these four types of problems. These counter measures are to align information better to the needs of the user community (problem area one), to improve the training for the information producers and enforce certain minimal quality standards (for problem area two), to improve the co-ordination and the workflows in the content management processes, and to improve the hard- and software in order to make it more reliable and efficient. The following diagram summarizes this view.

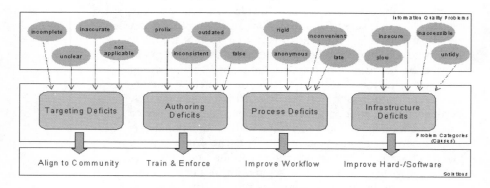

Figure 2: IQ Problems categorized in terms of heir origins

Problem Consequences

Whereas the above figure illustrates the means to overcome problems based on specific root causes, the next categorization helps to resolve information quality problems by analysing their *consequences*. Here, one can also distinguish four main issues. The following four consequences are a direct result of lacking information quality. They are all formulated from an information consumer's perspective:

1. **Information Overload**: I cannot identify the right information.
2. **Misjudgment**: I cannot judge or evaluate the information.

3. **Misinterpretation**: I cannot understand or interpret the information.
4. **Misuse**: I cannot use or apply the information.

Here is the logic behind these four categories: If an information consumer cannot *identify* (find and access) information, then this may be because it is difficult to get an overview on the available information because it is too dispersed, too vast, or because it is incomplete, inconvenient or impossible to access. Once the information has been found, it has to be evaluated by the user. If an information consumer cannot *evaluate*, judge, or trust a piece of information this may be due to inaccurate or inconsistent statements, or due to an insecure platform on which the information was found. If an information consumer can evaluate the credibility of an information source, but he or she cannot *interpret* a piece of information itself, this could be the result of lacking clarity, or simply because the information is not correct or does not refer to its sources. It may also be because the information is not kept current and not maintained and hence the user no longer knows what is still relevant and what has become obsolete. Finally, if the information consumer is not sure how to *apply* the information he or she has been provided with, then the resulting misuse could be the consequence of a wrong information format, a wrong timing or a wrong application context. Once again, a diagram can be used to illustrate this logic.

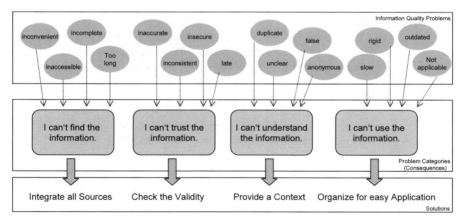

Figure 3: IQ Problems categorized in terms of their consequences for the user

Countermeasures

As the diagram shows, every one of the four problem categories has a specific counter-measure that can help to overcome it. In order to resolve the identification problem, sources need to be integrated or aggregated (e.g., through portals, maps, directories, summaries, etc.). To increase the trustworthiness of information its validity and background must be checked. To foster a better understanding of the information, a context must be provided that allows for an adequate interpretation of a piece of possibly isolated information. Finally, to avoid a misuse of the information or its non-use, it must be re-organized for easy application, that is to say it must be provided in a (interactive) format that can be directly used by the information consumer. An example of this would be a bank statement with account information that can be directly used for income tax forms.

Responsibilities

We have now grouped information quality problems according to their main causes and their main consequences. A third and final possible categorization criterion is the responsibility for the problems – that is to say who should do something about them. Here, we can distinguish between three professional communities: the information producers or *authors*, their superiors or *managers*, and their support staff or *IT-managers*. If the information quality problems result from providing the wrong kind of information (see the problem origins) then the managers must get authors to produce a different kind of information. If the information is relevant, but often false, outdated, or inconsistent, then the authors need to improve their content either on their own or with the help of their management. In contrast, if the way that information is provided is sub-optimal (slow, complicated, untraceable), then the information technology managers need to become active. The same holds true for deficits of the infrastructure, whether it is insecure or simple difficult to maintain. Thus, we can categorize information quality problems as either *content problems* that must be resolved by the information producers and their management, or as *media problems* that need to be resolved with the help of the information technology department that should improve the content management processes and infrastructures. The figure below illustrates this dual responsibility for information quality in a corporate setting.

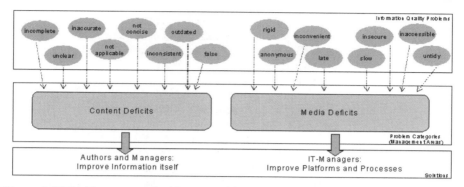

Figure 4: IQ Problems categorized in terms of their responsibility

Based on the three ways of categorizing IQ problems, we can now formulate the following definition of information quality problems:

Resulting Definition

We define an *information quality problem* as a situation in which the content or medium of information does not meet the requirements of its producers, administrators, or users. It can be expressed in terms of information attributes that are clustered according to their origin, consequence or responsibility.

Definition: Information Quality Problem

Information quality problems are the result of either providing the wrong kind of information (i.e., *irrelevant* or incomplete information), providing simply wrong information (i.e., *unsound* information that is inconsistent or incorrect), providing the information in the wrong way (i.e., in a non-convenient and rigid *process*), or providing the information on the wrong kind of *infrastructure* (e.g., not reliable or secure).

Information quality problems ultimately result in higher costs and a lower value of information use; in other words: the greater the information quality problems, the less informative the medium and its content.

This definition can help to better frame, delineate and analyze information quality challenges. It can further help to devise effective solution strategies by identifying the origins, consequences, and responsibilities of such problems.

Use of the Definition

We have now thoroughly analyzed the problem side of the information quality issue. In the next section, we are looking at the solution side in terms of already existing frameworks. We will examine how well they structure the possible information quality characteristics and their inherent challenges.

Transition to the Next Section

Conclusion   By categorizing the observed information quality problems according to their origin, their consequences for the information consumer, and their remedies or responsibilities, we have classified the main problem drivers and possible countermeasures. As far as *origins* are concerned, we distinguished information quality problems due to the lacking value of information for a specific community, problems due to intrinsic information deficiencies, problems caused by an inadequate content management process, and problems due to infrastructure deficits. As far as the *consequences* are concerned we distinguished information quality problems that made the efficient identification of information difficult, problems that lead to a wrong evaluation, problems that lead to a wrong interpretation or allocation of information, and problems that made the information difficult to use. The *responsibilities* for these problems can be split between information producers, line-managers, and information (system) administrators.

2.3 Information Quality Frameworks in Review

2.3.1 Recent Models from Various Domains

In the information quality field, researchers from such distinct domains as media studies, data warehouses, corporate communications, on-line publishing or knowledge management have pondered the question of what can be qualified as "good information". Regardless of the great differences of their research contexts, goals and methods, these scholars have built what seems at times an astonishing consensus in regard to the criteria that can be used to describe the value of information products such as newspapers, databases, websites, Intranets, or technical manuals.

Conceptual frameworks of information quality abound in management, communication, and information technology literature. In our review of information quality literature from the last ten years, we have found twenty information quality frameworks that define and categorize quality criteria for information (i.e., adjectives that describe information characteristics which make information useful for its users) in various application contexts (see Table 1). In this evaluation of information quality frameworks, we have found it useful to focus on approaches from the last ten years, since they take the new information infrastructure landscape (e.g. the Internet) into account. However, throughout this study, frameworks will be presented or referenced which may date back to the 1960s or 1970s, if they provide insights which recent frameworks have not incorporated.

Author & Year of Publication	Application Context
Horn 1989	Hypertext Instruction Manuals
Augustin & Reminger 1990	Management Information Systems
Russ-Mohl 1994 / 2000	Newspapers
Lesca & Lesca 1995	Corporate Communications
Morris et al. 1996	Management
Redmann 1996	Data Bases
Miller 1996	Information Systems
Wang & Strong 1996	Data Bases
Davenport 1997	Information Management
Eppler 1997	Corporate Communications
Ballou, Wang, Pazer & Tayi 1998	Data Warehouses
Kahn & Strong 1998	Information Systems
Harris & Flemming 1998	Knowledge Management
Königer & Reithmeyer 1998	Information Science
Moody & Shanks 1998	Data Models
Teflian 1999	Marketing
Rittberger 1999	Information Service Providers
English 1999	Data Warehouse and Business Information
Alexander & Tate 1999	Web Pages
Eppler 1999	Multimedia

Table 6: Information quality frameworks from 1989 to 2000

Besides these twenty frameworks, we have found a large number of simple information quality criteria lists from such domains as *scientific peer reviewing, medical data management* or *medical publication standards, accounting* and *auditing* information quality, *Internet publication* quality etc. These lists, however, were just that: simple listings of criteria without conceptual insights. They are not considered as frameworks in

Other Domains for Information Quality

the sense that they provide systematic orientation or problem solving potential like the twenty frameworks taken from academic sources in Table 1.

Goals of an Information Quality Framework

An information quality framework, in our view, should achieve four goals. First, it should provide a systematic and concise set of criteria according to which information can be *evaluated*. Second, it should provide a scheme to analyze and solve information quality *problems*. Third, it should provide the basis for information quality *measurement and benchmarking* (systematic comparisons). Fourth, it should provide the research community with a conceptual map that can be used to structure a variety of approaches, theories, and information quality related phenomena.

This understanding of a framework as a theory-building and practice-oriented tool is directly derived from Porter's conception of theory development as a choice for either limited models or comprehensive frameworks. Porter views frameworks as a legitimate form of research that can be validated through multiple case studies. He describes their aim as follows:

> Frameworks identify the relevant variables and the questions which the user must answer in order to develop conclusions tailored to a particular industry and company [...]. Frameworks seek to help the analyst to better think through the problem by understanding the firm and its environment and defining and selecting among strategic alternatives available. (Porter 1991, p.955)

In order to better understand whether the above information quality publications can achieve this facilitating function of a framework, we use six criteria to evaluate selected frameworks from the above list. By doing this, we hope to learn more about the design of such frameworks for the information quality context and whether one domain can provide insights for another application domain. If this is the case, then the information quality research area can truly be qualified as an interdisciplinary effort, where insights from one domain are accepted and incorporated into another discipline that uses both a different vocabulary and a different research methodology.

The Evaluation of IQ-Frameworks

From the twenty information quality frameworks above, we have evaluated seven more closely in order to learn more about the characteristics of information quality frameworks and their potential to improve the understanding of information quality and resolve information quality problems (such as outdated entries in a database, biased reporting in a newspaper, obsolete links on an Internet page, or inaccurate numbers in an annual report).

The seven frameworks that are evaluated in this chapter were chosen because they represent elaborated concepts and reflect the diverse field of information quality research in terms of *geographic origin* and *application context*. The authors of these frameworks come from France, Germany, USA, and England. Their research contexts range from database application to newspapers (see Table 2). The geographic context of a framework may be relevant, since it can influence the disciplinary background the information quality framework. Research domains such as information science or 'Publizistik' (an approach towards media studies) are for example typical for the German speaking world.

Author & Year of Publication	Country of Origin
Lesca & Lesca 1995	France
Redman 1996	USA
Wang & Strong 1996	USA
Russ-Mohl 1998	Germany
Königer & Reithmeyer 1998	Germany
English 1999	USA
Alexander & Tate 1999	USA

Table 7: Evaluated information quality frameworks

Evaluation Criteria

The frameworks are evaluated according to *analytic* (or scientific) criteria and *pragmatic* (or operational) criteria. The analytic criteria are based on academic standards and require clear *definitions* of the terms used in a framework, a *positioning* of the framework within existing literature, and a *consistent* and systematic structure. The pragmatic dimension consists of criteria which make the framework applicable, namely *conciseness* (i.e., if the framework is memorable), whether *examples* are provided to illustrate the framework, and the inclusion of *tools* that are based on the framework. As Huang, Lee, and Wang note in their analysis of information quality frameworks, the choice of evaluation criteria can either be based on intuitive understanding, industrial experience, literature review, or consumer interviews. They also conclude that there is no general agreement on information quality dimensions (Huang, Lee, Wang, 1999, p. 17). For meta-criteria such as the ones used in this chapter, the same holds true. They have been chosen based on existing literature (e.g., articles on scholarly writing and academic journal review policies), common sense and interviews with practitioners. The following table outlines the key questions behind every meta-criterion (i.e., the criteria used to evaluate criteria-sets of information quality frameworks).

Meta-Criteria	Evaluation Questions
Definitions	Are all individual information quality criteria clearly defined and explained? Are all the dimensions to which the individual criteria are grouped (if existing) defined and explained?
Positioning	Is the context of the framework's application (and its limits) clear? Is the framework positioned within existing literature?
Consistency	Are the individual criteria mutually exclusive and collectively exhaustive? Is the framework overall divided into systematic dimensions that are also mutually exclusive and collectively exhaustive? Is it clear why a group of criteria belongs to the same dimension?
Conciseness	Is the framework concise in the sense that it can be easily remembered? Are there (as a minimal rule of thumb) less than seven dimensions and less than seven criteria per dimension?
Examples	Are specific and illustrative examples given to explain the various criteria (e.g., case studies)?
Tools	Is the framework accompanied by a tool that can be used to put it into practice, such as a questionnaire, a software application, or a step-by-step implementation guide or methodology?

Table 8: Meta-criteria for the evaluation of information quality frameworks

Having outlined the goal and methodology of this article, we can now turn to the actual evaluation of the seven frameworks with the six meta-criteria in the two (analytic and practical) dimensions

2.3.2 Evaluation of Seven Information Quality Frameworks

Before we briefly discuss the seven information quality frameworks and their characteristics according to the six meta-criteria presented in part one of this article, we start by discussing the most common definitions of information quality that can be found in information quality frameworks. We do this, since the type of definition that a framework uses typically affects the criteria which are included in such a framework.

In the review of existing literature on information quality, we have found seven different definitions of information quality.

Information Quality Definitions

1. Information quality can be defined as information that is *fit for use* by information consumers (Huang, Lee, Wang, 1999, p. 43).
2. Information quality is the characteristic of information to meet or exceed customer *expectations* (Kahn & Strong, 1998).
3. Quality information is information that meets *specifications* or *requirements* (Kahn & Strong, 1998).
4. Information quality is the characteristic of information to be of *high value* to its users (Lesca & Lesca, 1995, my translation).
5. "The degree to which information has *content, form, and time characteristics* which give it *value* to specific end users" (Brien, 1991, p. G-7).
6. "Quality of information can be defined as a *difference* between the required information determined by a goal and the obtained information. In an ideal situation there will be no difference between the required and obtained information. A qualitative measure for information quality is expressed by the following tendency: the smaller this difference, the greater the quality of information" (Gerkes, 1997).
7. Information quality is the characteristic of information to meet the *functional, technical, cognitive,* and *aesthetic* requirements of information *producers, administrators, consumers,* and *experts* (Eppler, 1999).

The most commonly used definitions are those ranked one through four. The seven frameworks evaluated in this chapter typically use combinations of these four definitions.

With the exception of the framework by Lesca and Lesca, all seven frameworks include a *time dimension* in their criteria set. Some frameworks refer to it as timeliness, stressing the rapid delivery process, while others stress the quality aspect of the information of being current or up-to-date (for which the timely delivery is a necessary but not sufficient prerequisite).

Common Elements of the Frameworks

Five out of the seven frameworks rate *accessibility* or obtainability as an information quality criterion. Neither Russ-

Mohl in the newspaper context, nor Alexander and Tate in the Web context give this important criterion any weight, which seems surprising, since both, newspapers and websites, depend on a rapid and stable distribution channel in order to be of value to users. Four out of the seven frameworks use *objectivity* as an information quality criterion. While most frameworks refer to it as an unbiased representation of reality, this criteria seems to be one of the most difficult ones in terms of a clear definition. Five out of the seven frameworks use the vague term *relevancy* as an information quality criterion. Definitions range from 'contextual impact' to synonyms such as pertinence to the end-user. *Accuracy* is only seen as a central information quality criterion in three out of the seven frameworks. This is surprising since a great part of information quality literature with a background in information technology views this criteria as a central notion in the concept of information quality (see Wang, Strong, 1996). However, four of the seven frameworks use the closely related terms *precision* or preciseness as information quality criteria. *Consistency* is only stated as an explicit information quality criterion in three of the frameworks. It refers to the systematic, non-contradicting, format and content of information. *Completeness* is seen as a crucial information quality factor in four of the seven frameworks. It is viewed as a characteristic of a set of information to represent reality with all required descriptive elements.

General Features of the Seven Frameworks

Besides the individual criteria used in the frameworks, one can also compare the general features of information quality frameworks. In doing so, we have found six distinct patterns in the evaluation of the seven frameworks. Below, we discuss these insights into the nature of information quality frameworks.

As the overall evaluation of the seven frameworks in the appendix shows, only three out of the seven frameworks are generic, while four contain criteria that are *specific* to a certain application context. This seems representative of the whole of information quality frameworks, where we have found the majority of frameworks to be context-specific rather than generic and widely applicable.

The seven frameworks are also typical information quality frameworks in the sense that they do not explicitly deal with *tradeoffs*[35] between individual information quality criteria (as, for example, in Ballou and Pazer, 1987). Typical tradeoffs that probably exist between information quality criteria are:

- The tradeoff between security and accessibility (for this issue, see also Huang, Lee, Wang, 1999, pp. 50-52): the more secure an information system is, the less convenient is its access.
- The tradeoff between currency and accuracy: the more current a piece of information has to be, the less time is available to check on its accuracy.
- The same tradeoff holds for the criteria of correctness or reliability and timeliness: the faster information has to be delivered to the end-user, the less time is available to check its reliability or correctness.
- The tradeoff between right amount of information (or scope) and comprehensibility: more detailed information can prevent a fast comprehension, because it becomes difficult "to see the big picture."
- The tradeoff between conciseness and right amount (scope) of information: the more detail that is provided, the less concise a piece of information or document is going to be.

With the exception of the framework by Wang and Strong (see also Strong et al., 1997b, for this point), the seven frameworks often fall short in including problem categories and specific indicators (i.e., means of measurement) into the actual framework. Most frameworks only provide limited assistance to resolve information quality problems with the help of a frame of analysis, which a framework could and should provide. This is closely related to the fourth point revealed by our analysis, namely the lack of adequate tools.

Most of the frameworks evaluated in this chapter lack supporting tools that put the framework into practice, except for English (1999) and again Wang and Strong (1996) which provide elaborate tools to go with their framework, but do not include them in their framework. As far as tools

---

[35] The term tradeoff in this context refers to possible goal conflicts between IQ-criteria. The improvement in one quality criteria may lead to a decreasing value in another. To explore and acknowledge tradeoffs is a research strategy, according to Weick (1979), that can lead to fruitful insights into a domain.

are concerned, most frameworks only convert the criteria into questionnaires that specify various aspects of the criteria. An exception is the model by Taylor (1986, p. 50) which is not included in this review since it is older than ten years. Taylor's framework combines information quality criteria with specific solutions. It is however, not adapted to the open standards of the Internet. The framework by Taylor can also be found in the appendix.

The evaluation matrix in appendix one also illustrates that only the Wang and Strong (1996) framework offers both a solid foundation in existing literature and practical applications. It is the only framework in the series of seven that strikes a balance between theoretical consistency and practical applicability.[36] It does not, however, address the important cost or maintainability issues.

As a final point, not one single framework has addressed the *cost dimension* involved in information quality. This seems surprising, in spite of the fact that most IQ-frameworks have not been authored by economists (except the one by Lesca and Lesca). The cost dimension is a vital one for organizational contexts that should not be neglected, since quality is also a relation between cost and benefit. With the help of these findings we can identify future research needs in the area of information quality frameworks. They are outlined in the next section.

2.3.3 Five Development Imperatives

The review of selected examples of information quality frameworks showed that they are often strong in their analytic dimension with thorough definitions and an extensive recapitulation of prior literature (and a systematic structure), or alternatively in their pragmatic dimension – offering concise criteria sets, many examples, and facilitating tools– but rarely strong on both dimensions at the same time. The evaluation also revealed that the IQ frameworks are often domain-specific (i.e., for a specific application such as data warehouses or corporate communications), and that they rarely analyze interdependencies between the information

---

[36]   A study on information systems quality framework from Adelakun and Enholm (1998) finds the same to be true, namely that "they are either too theoretical or too technical" (Adelakun and Enholm, 1998, p. 116).

quality criteria. From these insights, we have derived five future directions for information quality frameworks: first, the quest for more *generic models*; second, the development of information quality frameworks that show *interdependencies* between different quality criteria; third, the inclusion of problem areas and *indicators* into these frameworks; fourth, the development of *tools* or solutions which are based on an information quality framework; fifth, the development of frameworks that are at the same time *theoretical and practical* (e.g., a framework that acknowledges the importance of cost and implementation issues*)*.

2.4 Conclusion: The Need for a New Framework

Problems with low-quality information abound today in many knowledge-intensive processes, whether it is the lack of clarity in a project report, the confusing design of a website, or the lengthy and wordy style of a research book. These problems can lead to unproductive knowledge work, to overloaded information consumers, and ultimately to wrong or late decisions and low quality products and services.

Information QualityProblem abound

We have seen in the previous chapters that these problems have been recognized by academics and practitioners alike. We have seen that various frameworks exist that treat these problems mostly from a static database perspective. They sometimes lack the process dimension and their view of information as isolated entities does not emphasize crucial interpretation or sense-making processes. A new, versatile and teachable framework is needed that takes the specificities of information in knowledge-intensive processes into account; specificities such as *ambiguity*, the crucial role of *context*, or the *cognitive* and *behavioral* dimension of information: information has to be interpreted and it should be acted upon to be of value. Another specificity that has been underemphasized in current approaches is the cost dimension of information quality. Conceived as a management issue (and not only as an information technology topic), information quality must be related to the investments that are needed to achieve that quality.

A Lack of Knowledge-focused Approaches

In summary, one can say that the current academic discussion can benefit from a fresh perspective on the topic. The approach is 'fresh' in the sense that it uses a new perspective (a knowledge-based view) and an interdisciplinary background to analyze a topic that has so far been mostly dis-

Consequences

cussed by information system scholars, library science researchers, and data warehouse specialists.

Chapter
Conclusion

This chapter has given an overview on the domain of information quality in the context of knowledge-intensive processes. It has discussed a wide range of problems (from various sources) that are associated with this concept. These problems were then categorized in order to further improve their understanding. The chapter also discussed the existing frameworks that try to resolve these problems. Information quality frameworks from various domains were compared and evaluated and five development imperatives were articulated. The gathered insights prepared the ground to develop a new information quality framework that overcomes the current deficits and helps to resolve some of the problems associated with knowledge-intensive processes. This model will be presented in the next chapter.

3. A Framework for Information Quality Management

This chapter contains the framework for information quality management and describes its elements in detail. The chapter is divided into three sub-chapters, which outline the aim of the framework as well as its application context, its main elements, and its application in various settings. The chapter closes with a summary of the key findings. The largest part of this chapter is dedicated to the second sub-chapter, where the elements of the framework are described, such as the information quality criteria and the principles to assure them. The main principles discussed are the integration, validation, contextualization, and activation principles which improve the value of information products.

Chapter Overview

3.1 Aim and Context of the Information Quality Framework

3.1.1 Aim: Analysis, Evaluation, Management, and Education

Organizational scientists should be viewed not as engineers offering technical advice to managers but as providers of conceptual and symbolic language for use in organizational discourse.

W. ASTLEY and R. ZAMMUTO

The goal of the present framework is neither prognosis nor precise description or explanation. It should help (as PORTER points out in his discussion on the use of conceptual frameworks, see Porter, 1991) to better *think through a problem* and *select* among strategic alternatives. It should serve – as ULRICH (1984) has called it – as a frame of reference where useful thoughts can be placed and organized systematically. This in return can foster a more rapid problem solving process.

General Purpose of Frameworks:

Orientation & Guidance

Frameworks in this understanding identify the relevant variables and the questions which an analyst must answer in order to develop conclusions tailored to a particular company (see Porter, 1991, p. 955). Frameworks provide a *conceptual language* which practitioners can use to facilitate their mutual problem understanding and coordinate their collaborative actions (for this point, as already noted, see Astley & Zammuto, 1992, p. 443). In the information quality context, a framework should thus provide a systematic and concise set of terms which practitioners and researchers can use to analyze and resolve information quality issues.

Specific Goals of the IQ-Framework

As a framework in this understanding of the term, the information quality framework is a frame of reference that should allow management practitioners and researchers to do five things. First, it should help them to *identify* information quality problems more systematically and more comprehensively. Second, it should enable them to *analyze* these problems in more detail and rigor and find their root causes. Third, the framework should be useful to *evaluate* (or *monitor*) solutions to information quality problems based on this problem analysis. Fourth, it should provide means to *design* and *manage* sustainable solutions based on the prior evaluation of feasible improvement measures. Finally, the framework should also be instrumental in *teaching* the aforementioned four processes to students or novices in the field. It should offer a systematic mnemonic map that illustrates the core issues in identifying, analyzing, evaluating, and managing information quality in knowledge-intensive processes.

Resulting Requirements of the Framework:

Elements and their Connections

Because of these five purposes the framework itself has to meet certain criteria. In order to be useful in the identification and analysis of problems, as well as in the evaluation of solutions, it has to provide a *diagnostic heuristic* through which management problems can be viewed. It has to provide *diagnostic steps and views* that can be used in 'dissecting' a domain. It has to isolate and 'compartmentalize' aspects of reality so that they become less complex. Nevertheless, the framework must not neglect interdependencies between these compartments or aspects of reality.

Implementation Steps

As far as the design and management of solutions is concerned, the framework must prove to be easily applicable. It must offer a sequence of generic steps that can be followed to improve the current situation. It must not only outline the *activities* included in each step, but it should also refer to specific ('prototypical') ways in which these steps can be implemented.

Finally, in order to assure that the framework is teachable, the framework must adhere to certain *pedagogic standards*. It must have a plausible logic, a modular design (that can be taught in several steps), and a parsimonious design (in order not to overload students with details).

Pedagogic Value

The following framework strives to fulfill most of these requirements. In doing so, however, one should not neglect the fact that its application for diagnostic or management purposes is primarily focused on business processes which are knowledge-intensive. One characteristic of these processes is that they rely heavily on information products, both as input and output factors of their tasks. These processes will be more specifically described in the next section.

Limitations: Process Context

3.1.2 Context: Knowledge-intensive Processes

In section 2.1 we defined some of the central terms of this book and stated that the prime difference between the concept of knowledge work and knowledge-intensive processes is the degree of structure or formalization. Below we outline this view in more detail and show why it is a fruitful one for the information quality discussion.

Overview

MICHAEL HAMMER defines a process as a group of familiar tasks, which eventually lead to a value for the customer (Hammer, 1996). He stresses the value added for the customer as a final outcome of a business process. THOMAS DAVENPORT sees the definition of process rather from the perspective of structured task splitting. He defines a process as „a specific *ordering* of work activities across time and place, with a beginning, an end, clearly identified inputs and outputs: a *structure for action*.“ (Davenport 1993, my italics). In the context of knowledge-intensive processes this structure mostly serves to organize what can be labeled as informative action (Eppler 1998), namely to inform oneself or others in order to convey or create knowledge.

Process Definitions

Listed below are various examples of activities which meet these criteria and which are described as knowledge-intensive processes (or closely related terms) in the referenced literature.

Examples

Knowledge-intensive Process	Sources
Product Design	Carslisle & Dean, 1999, Windrum & Tomlinson, 1999
Product Development	Starbuck, 1992
Market Research	Windrum & Tomlinson, 1999, McDermott, 1995
Consulting	Windrum & Tomlinson, 1999, Waterman, 1996
Auditing	Nurmi, 1998
Planning	Eppler et al., 1999, Nurmi, 1998
Training	Windrum & Tomlinson, 1999, Nurmi, 1998
Patent Filing	Waterman, 1996
Legal processes	Burkert & Eppler, 1999
Professional Training	Götz & Hilt, 1999
Managerial Decision-making	Joshi, 2001
On-line communication	Ware & Degoey, 1998
Medical Diagnosis	Starbuck, 1992
Software Development	Laudon & Starbuck, 1996, Starbuck 1992

Table 9: Examples of knowledge-intensive processes

Common Elements of the Examples

What is it exactly hat makes these activities knowledge-intensive processes? We have already said that their structure and their productive outcome are the characteristics that qualify them as a process. But which factors determine their knowledge-intensity? Knowledge-intensity is a debatable concept that has been used to describe companies (Starbuck 1992), professions (Waterman, 1996), and even entire industries (Prusak & Davenport 1998).

'Knowledge-intensive'

MATS ALVESSON (Alvesson, 2000, p. 1103) of the University of Lund finds that „the concept of knowledge-intensiveness is vague." Nevertheless, he argues, it is a concept that makes sense and can be a meaningful category that highlights crucial domains, although it cannot be defined in exact terms. In the context of knowledge-intensive companies, Alvesson writes:

Nevertheless, it encourages an interest that goes beyond the single case without aspiring to talk about organizations in general, loosely pointing at an organizational category about which one may say something interesting.

The same, I believe, holds true for the application of the concept of 'knowledge-intensiveness' to processes. Here the notion of a knowledge-intensive process can sharpen the focus on a domain that is often difficult to describe or define. It is the diversity of activities that can be summarized with this term that allows for fruitful comparisons and contrasts within the same focus area. The attributes that are generally associated with the concept of knowledge-intensity are a focus on information interpretation, analysis and application, as well as a high degree of expertise or specialized knowledge. Other aspects associated with knowledge-intensity are high learning requirements, a need for creative, non-routine problem solving and the need for frequent mediated and direct communication (see Schultze, 2000).

Based on these considerations, we propose the following definition of knowledge-intensive processes. This definition should make the crucial role of information quality explicit.

> We define a knowledge-intensive process as a productive series of activities that involve information transformation and require specialized professional knowledge.
>
> Knowledge-intensive processes can be characterized by their often non-routine nature (unclear problem space, many decision options), the high requirements in terms of continuous learning and innovation, and the crucial importance of interpersonal communication on the one side and of documentation (or codification) of information on the other.

Definition: Knowledge-intensive Process

Knowledge-intensive processes thus rely heavily on the experiences and know-how of the relevant people. From this evident conclusion, we can derive two main questions as far as the management of these processes is concerned:

Knowledge in the Process

1. *Which* knowledge is crucial for the success of such a process (its quality and timing) and should therefore be observed more closely?
2. *How* can that crucial knowledge be managed and systematically exploited? In other words, how can we assure that the knowledge is documented as high-quality information that is likely to be transformed into knowledge again by individuals who rely on it.

The first question can be answered as follows: critical process knowledge consists of three types of intellectual assets, they are: the know-how regarding the management of business processes or knowledge *about* the process, knowledge regarding the contents of a process or knowledge that is generated *during* or *within* a business process (know-what), and insights gained from a completed process or knowledge derived *from* a process (know-why). These three types of knowledge need to be analyzed more closely. In doing so, we will answer the second fundamental question raised above, since each of the three types of knowledge has to be represented differently in an enterprise knowledge medium (see Eppler et al, 1999). The figure below represents this basic distinction graphically.

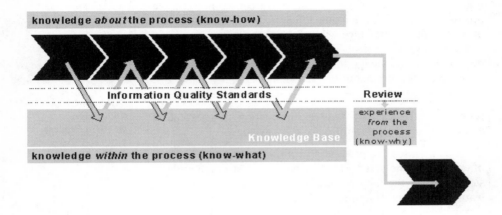

Figure 5: Relevant knowledge dimensions for knowledge-intensive processes

Three Relevant Types of Process Knowledge

This simple model summarizes the three crucial knowledge types that need to be managed carefully in knowledge-intensive processes. Each one of them is further discussed below and illustrated with examples. The figure also shows the central role of information quality standards in knowledge-intensive processes. These standards (as explicit quality criteria) assure that the acquired knowledge is adequately documented for later use. Specifically, the consistent quality of a knowledge-intensive process depends on the accuracy, timeliness, maintainability, and currency of the codified know-what, on the applicability, conciseness and clarity of the codified know-how or procedural knowledge, and - among other things – on the traceability and correctness of the know-why or gathered insights and experience. Why these three knowledge types form the basic context for knowledge-intensive processes is described below, where each one of them is outlined in more detail.

Knowledge about the Process

The first type of process knowledge can be found in *explicit* forms in such documents as quality manuals, process design handbooks or in workflow applications. These formats typically visualize all important process steps and their sequence and inherent logic. In *implicit* form, this type of knowledge lies in the heads of process owners or other people that are involved in the process. It relates to the experience they have in managing a business process, that is to say in coordinating activities, people and time during a process. These people typically know where critical process steps lie, where to contact which person, and how to detect process deviations. This type of knowledge can be made explicit by integrating it into the process chart, i.e., by adding key people to the visualized process steps, or mark time-critical process steps in different colors. Another way of eliciting this type of process knowledge consists in adding time indications regarding the expected duration of a process steps to its documentation

In summary, this type of process knowledge – knowledge about the process – should answer the following questions:

- How is the process organized? What are the main steps, problems, responsibilities and deliverables?
- Which are the main and which are the sub-tasks and how are they coordinated?
- Which resources (time, expertise, staffing, money) are necessary for the process? How are they allocated?
- How is the quality of the process assured?

This type of knowledge is mostly heuristic or procedural knowledge. It assures the effective coordination of people over time. Because of its dynamic character, it is, however, difficult to grasp (summarize or condense) and comprehend or keep current. Visualization offers a valuable aid in developing procedural notions.

Knowledge within the Process

The know-what, factual knowledge, or mostly explicit domain knowledge that is generated during a knowledge-intensive business process represents the second type of crucial knowledge which has to be documented as high-quality information. Examples of this type of knowledge are test results, written analyses, recorded events, meeting outcomes, or reached agreements.

The following types of questions are answered by this type of knowledge:

- What has to be documented during the process?
- Who has done what at what time? What has happened at what point in time?
- What data has been gathered during a process step? What are the outcomes?
- What is going on right now in the process? What are deviations and critical situations at the present state?

One of the greatest management challenges regarding this type of knowledge is the sheer volume in which it is generated. Another difficult aspects results from the dispersed locations in which it is stored. In terms of information quality criteria, the main challenges consist of making the information easily accessible in a timely manner and in a concise format. One way to assure this is through information quality standards. Another way consists of providing various personalization, notification- filter- or source integration functionalities (such as portals or personal profiles).

Knowledge Derived from the Process

At the end of every completed process, knowledge has been created through the experience that was gathered over the course of its completion. By introducing feedback loops into the process, continuous improvements can be achieved. This form of experience is often only available in implicit form and thus difficult to share or store. The main challenge in documenting this type of knowledge as high-quality information consists in allocating time to make it explicit, to combine individual experiences and insights and put them into a common format that can be found, understood and re-used by others.

By documenting lessons learned, insights from the process can not only benefit the people who were directly involved, but also successors in the process that can anticipate common mistakes or critical phases. An enterprise knowledge medium or knowledge base can systematically gather these lessons learned in the form of process descriptions ('best practices') or key success factors that have been validated and contextualized. The main questions answered by this type of knowledge are:

- If we were to do the process all over, what would we tackle differently?
- Are there successful (or best) practices to be deduced from the project, that is to say can we transfer the methodology to other domains?
- Are there critical success factors to be isolated?
- How can we further improve the process?
- Who was able to gain what kind of experience?

The crucial question in all of these issues is how the management can assure the quality of the lessons learned that are documented for later use. One possibility lies in establishing a review board that checks the documented lessons learned for their consistency and their value for other processes. The review board can be a central mechanism to assure the information quality of such a documentation. But in order to evaluate the quality of information, a review board has to rely upon generally accepted criteria of what constitutes information quality. In the upcoming sections, we will look at these criteria systematically.

The main contexts for the present study of information quality are knowledge-intensive processes. The information that is needed to manage these non-routine, sequential tasks of information transformation is consequently the central object of our quality related inquiries. This information is threefold: it relates to the knowledge *about* the process, the knowledge generated *during* the process, and the knowledge derived *from* the process. For the part of this know-how, know-what, and know-why that can be made explicit and documented, the quality of information is a crucial prerequisite for the effective knowledge transfer among knowledge workers and thus ultimately for the functioning of the knowledge-intensive process itself.

Conclusion

3.2 Elements of the Framework

3.2.1 Overview of the Framework and its Elements

In section 2.3, we have analyzed information quality frameworks from the last decade and found that they required further development in five areas in order to be useful for practitioners and researchers (i.e., the general applicability, the visualization of tradeoffs, a categorization of problems and possible solution elements, tool, practical and theoretical relevance). With the following information quality framework, we try to overcome these shortcomings. We strive for a generic framework (in the sense of wide applicability) that can be used for any kind of knowledge-intensive process, as described in the previous section. Generic also means that the framework can be used for various purposes, such as evaluation and assessment, improvement, management or monitoring. The framework will explicitly show tradeoffs between specific criteria (drawn as arrows that connect two criteria). It can be used to position information quality problems, and it consists of four principles which help to find solutions to IQ-problems (the integration, validation, contextualization, and activation principle). It will be shown that the framework is rooted in an existing theory (the media reference model) and nevertheless provides practical tools that are based upon it (such as the information quality radar which uses the frame-

Framework Deficits as a Starting Point

work as a means of visualizing IQ-deficits). Additional requirements for the framework have been generated in the previous section, for example the pedagogic design of the framework that makes it more easily understandable for students in the field.

Elements of the Framework: Levels, Criteria, Phases, Principles

The information quality framework I propose consists of four major elements: The first element is the framework's vertical structure. It consists of *four levels* or views on information quality that categorize crucial information quality *criteria* according to their relation to the target community, the information product, the information process, and to its infrastructure. The next element of the framework is the horizontal structure, which is divided into *four phases*. The four phases represent the life cycle of information from a user's point of view: it is searched and found, evaluated, adapted to a new context (allocated in our terminology), and applied. The information quality *criteria* – the third component of the framework – are placed along these phases according to their importance for the different phases. How these criteria can be improved is answered by the last element of the framework, the management principles. The *principles* help to improve the quality of information in every phase. In the following sections we describe these elements in detail.

3.2.2 Levels of Information Quality

Four Views on Information Quality

The overall structure of the present framework is derived from an implicit convention which most recent information quality frameworks seem to follow, whereby they are divided into two sections: a category section, and a criteria (or dimensional) section. Thus, in most IQ-frameworks, the individual quality criteria are grouped into a few information quality categories. These categories typically do not include qualifiers, but often have standard names (which are not self-explanatory) such as *intrinsic IQ* (Wang & Strong, 1994) or *quality of structuring* (Königer & Reithmayer, 1998). In the current framework this twofold structure is also used, but with qualifying category names, which already include a quality criterion on a higher level. The four IQ-categories or views are:

1. **Relevant information**: This category relates to whether information is comprehensive, accurate, and clear enough for the intended use, and whether it is easily applicable to the problem at hand. This category is also called the *community view,* since the relevance of a piece of information depends on the expectations and needs of a certain (writer, administrator, or user) community.

2. **Sound information**: This second category contains criteria which describe the intrinsic or *product characteristics* of information, such as whether it is concise or not, consistent or not, correct or not, and current or not. Whereas the criteria in the first category (relevance) are subjective (indicated through the term „enough") the criteria in this category should be relatively independent of the targeted community (indicated through the term „or not").

3. **Optimized Process**: The third category contains criteria which relate to the content management process by which the information is created and distributed and whether that process (or information service) is convenient (for writers, administrators, and users), and whether it provides the information in a timely, traceable (attributable), and interactive manner.

4. **Reliable Infrastructure**: The fourth and final level contains criteria which relate to the infrastructure on which the content management process runs and through which the information is actually provided. Reliability in this context refers to a system's easy and continuous accessibility, its security, its maintainability over time and at reasonable costs, and its high speed or performance.

The logic of these four levels or IQ-views is based on the knowledge media theory of BEAT SCHMID (see Schmid and Stanoevska-Slabeva, 1999). It states that any design of knowledge media (in the sense of a platform that enables the transfer of knowledge) must begin with the analysis of the community of people who need to share knowledge, and must analyze their needs, activities, and work practices. Then, the services and information objects which must be provided to and by this community need to be analyzed and a process has to be designed in order to deliver these information services or information objects. Only at this point can the infrastructure requirements and parameters be determined.

Media Theory Background & Framework Diagram

Thus, the following framework can be used in a top-down approach.

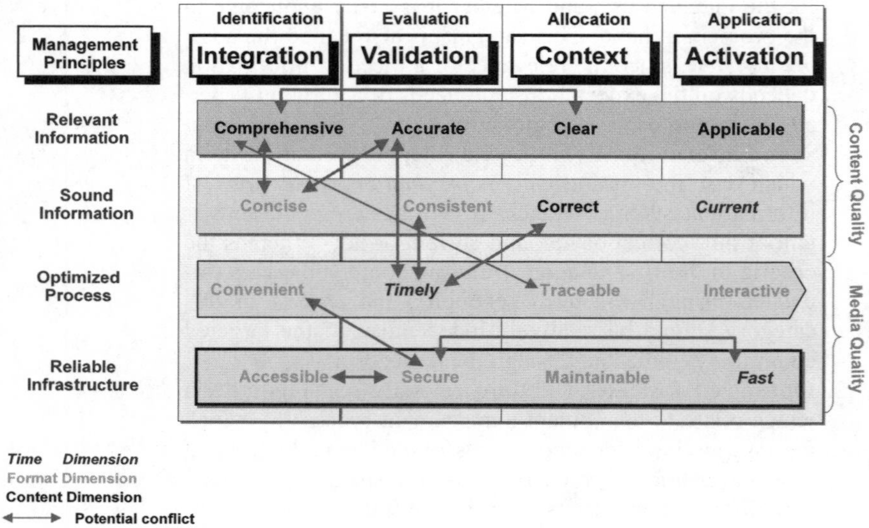

Management Principles	Identification	Evaluation	Allocation	Application	
	Integration	**Validation**	**Context**	**Activation**	
Relevant Information	Comprehensive	Accurate	Clear	Applicable	Content Quality
Sound Information	Concise	Consistent	Correct	Current	
Optimized Process	Convenient	Timely	Traceable	Interactive	Media Quality
Reliable Infrastructure	Accessible	Secure	Maintainable	Fast	

Time   *Dimension*
Format Dimension
Content Dimension
◄──────► **Potential conflict**

Figure 6: The information quality framework

Content and Media Quality

As the figure shows, the upper two levels of the framework are labeled *content quality*, while the lower two are referred to as *media quality*. The first two categories, relevance and soundness, relate to the actual information itself, hence the term content quality. The second two categories, process and infrastructure, relate to the management of that information, and whether the delivery process and – infrastructure are of adequate quality, hence the term media quality, which stresses the channel by which information is transported. For the end-user, both segments, media and content quality, may be perceived as one final product – the information and its various characteristics. For the information producers and administrators however, this difference is crucial, since the authors usually cannot influence the media quality, and the administrators only have limited possibilities of influencing the content quality. The framework separates these areas because they fall into separate areas of responsibility. In order to be of practical value, the framework has to distinguish between these responsibilities and indicate which areas are the responsibility of management or the information producers (the area labeled as content quality), and which domain is the responsibility of the support or IT-staff (the two levels labeled media quality).

Having described the levels of the framework, we can now turn to the specific information quality criteria that are included in the framework and their relationships.

3.2.3 Information Quality Criteria

In this section we will reduce the great amount of possible information quality attributes to a manageable quantity of criteria. In order to achieve this, we will first give an overview on the possible criteria and then select the ones that have the least redundancy (i.e., that are mutually exclusive), and cover the main aspects of information quality (i.e., are collectively exhaustive).[37]

Steps in this Section

3.2.3.1 Overview of Possible Criteria

Huang et al. (1999, p. 33) state that information quality has been conventionally described as how accurate information is. In the last couple of years, however, it has become clear that information quality encompasses multiple dimensions beyond accuracy. These dimensions can be gathered in various ways. Huang et al. (1999) distinguish between three different approaches: the intuitive, systematic, and empirical one. The *intuitive* approach is one where IQ-criteria are based on the intuitive understanding or experience of one or several individuals. The main disadvantage of this approach is that it does not yield representative results. The *systematic* approach, according to Huang et al., focuses on how information may become deficient during the information production process. Few research strategies have followed this deductive-analytic or ontological approach (where real-life states are compared to the represented data states). One reason may be the fact that it is difficult to convey the results to information consumers. The third approach is an *empirical* one. Here, the criteria are gathered by asking large sets of information consumers about their understanding of information quality in specific contexts (as we have done with the online focus groups described earlier). The disadvantage of this approach,

Three Ways of Gathering Information Quality Criteria

---

[37]   For this meta-criteria of any conceptual framework see Minto (1995) or Roehl (2000).

according to Huang et al. (1999, p. 34) is that the correctness or completeness of the results cannot be proven based on fundamental principles (as in the deductive systematic approach). There is also a risk, in my view, that the empirical results will not always be consistent or free of redundancies. It is also unclear, whether information consumers are always capable of articulating the information quality attributes which are important to them.[38] Besides distinguishing the ways in which the criteria can be gathered, one can also distinguish the types of criteria that exist.

Quality Criteria Types

In their general discussion on quality criteria, Evans & Lindsay (1999) distinguish four types of criteria, namely: *judgmental criteria* (such as well-designed/aesthetic), *product-based criteria* (such as free-of-errors), user-based criteria (such as relevance), and *manufacturing-based criteria* (such as timeliness).[39] Another, similar classification is from Naumann and Rolker (2000). They distinguish between *subject-oriented criteria* (such as relevance and understandability), *object-oriented criteria* (such as price and reliability), and *process-oriented criteria* (such as response time and availability).

Overview of Common Criteria

These distinctions are perhaps not the most elegant or insightful ways to categorize information quality criteria. They can, however, ensure that we think of all possible criteria. In the list below, we have compiled criteria that have been gathered intuitively, systematically, and empirically and we have included criteria which are based on judgment (of the subject), on the information product (or object) and on the (manufacturing) process.

70 IQ-Criteria

The following table lists seventy of the most widely used information quality criteria to be explicitly discussed and defined in the information quality literature. They provide the basis for the criteria that are organized in the framework.The numbering does not imply a ranking of the criteria. Such a ranking or screening is possible (and has been done, see Taylor, 1986), but it does not yield a systematic result. It would

---

[38] This is also one of the reasons why it may not be easy to construct a house of quality (HoQ) for information products, as some have advocated (see for example Merx, 1998). Many information consumers may not be able to articulate their criteria consistently, let alone see which functionalities improve which criteria.

[39] Evans & Lindsay, 1999, pp. 10-12. For examples of empirical criteria selections, see Barry & Schamber 1998.

merely show that the most commonly cited criteria include notions of accuracy, timeliness, correctness, clarity and related terms.

1. Comprehensiveness	27. Verifiability	48. Response time
2. Accuracy	28. Testability	49. Believability
3. Clarity	29. Provability	50. Availability
4. Applicability	30. Performance	51. Consistent Representation
5. Conciseness	31. Ethics/ ethical	52. Ability to represent null
6. Consistency	32. Privacy	values
7. Correctness	33. Helpfulness	53. Semantic Consistency
8. Currency	34. Neutrality	54. Concise Representation
9. Convenience	35. Ease of Manipulation	55. Obtainability
10. Timeliness	36. Validity	56. Stimulating
11. Traceability	37. Relevance	57. Attribute granularity
12. Interactivity	38. Coherence	58. Flexibility
13. Accessibility	39. Interpretability	59. Reflexivity
14. Security	40. Completeness	60. Robustness
15. Maintainability	41. Learnability	61. Equivalence of redundant
16. Speed	42. Exclusivity	or distributed data
17. Objectivity	43. Right Amount	62. Concurrency of redundant
18. Attributability	44. Existence of meta infor-	or distributed data
19. Value-added	mation	63. Nonduplication
20. Reputation (source)	45. Appropriateness of meta	64. Essentialness
21. Ease-of-use	information	65. Rightness
22. Precision	46. Target group orientation	66. Usability
23. Comprehensibility	47. Reduction of complexity	67. Cost
24. Trustworthiness (source)		68. Ordering
25. Reliability		69. Browsing
26. Price		70. Error rate

Table 10: Seventy typical information quality criteria

This extensive list of information quality attributes can be (and should be) significantly shortened because it contains various inconsistencies and redundancies and is not a practical directory for use in real-life contexts. We can systematically reduce the above list by eliminating criteria that are expendable. There can be seven reasons why a criterion is expendable. We briefly discuss each of these in the following paragraphs.

Seven Reasons to Eliminate IQ-Criteria

First, there are criteria in this list that are already a *result of other criteria;* these include believability, authority or reputation which are the result of correct or consistent information. We will not include these derived or secondary IQ-criteria in the framework. Second, some criteria are *synonyms* or closely related terms such as ease-of-use, convenience and

---

[40]   Polysemy refers to a term's multiple meanings.

usability or verifiability, testability and provability or and what correctness and rightness. Similar criteria are combined using one term only. Third, there are criteria that are *too context-specific* (like reflexivity or exclusivity from the newspaper quality context) or too technical for the management context (such as the ability to represent null values from the database context) . Such criteria are excluded from the final list. Fourth, some of the criteria that are not really quality attributes of the content or the media, but rather sophisticated information services or *functionalities*. Such services have not been included. Examples are ordering, browsing, or linking. Fifth, there are criteria that do not meet the same level of *abstraction* as most of the criteria in the list above. Response time, for example, is already an indicator for speed or timeliness. Such very specific terms have not been included either. Sixth, there many criteria from the list are not really qualifications or characteristics, but rather relevant terms in the context of information quality. Such general terms *without direction* are price, cost or value. These terms are not self-explanatory and they do not contain a qualifier. They are consequently excluded.

Finally, some criteria should be excluded because they are *difficult to operationalize* due to their polysemic nature[40]. Grand concepts like relevance, objectivity or ethical value pose various management problems. They are not irrelevant, but they should be broken down into more tangible criteria (such as target-group orientation, traceability or correctness) in order to be less confusing or ambiguous.

Relevance and Objectivity as Problematic Criteria

Let us look more closely at two of these problematic criteria that can be excluded because of the last reason, that of difficult specification or ambiguity. We take the attributes of *relevance* and *objectivity* as examples to show that it is not always fruitful to take the most common or intuitive criteria. The problem with relevance is that it contains various types of pertinence which should be distinguished and cannot be reduced to one term only. The problem with objectivity is that it is a concept that is highly normative and not always seen in association with the value or quality of information (especially in the area of knowledge content, where highly subjective expertise is documented). These two complex concepts are briefly reviewed in the next two paragraphs.

Relevance Types

That relevance is a complex issue has been shown effectively by information scientist Saraceciv (1999). He writes the following in a review on recent information science research regarding relevance:

An (uneasy) consensus has emerged in information science that we can distinguish between several differing relations that account for different manifestations or types of relevance.

Subsequently, he distinguishes between no less than five different notions of relevance. In the following quote, he outlines their differences:

1. System or algorithmic relevance: relation between a query and information objects (texts) in the file of a system as retrieved, or as failed to be retrieved, by a given procedure or algorithm. Comparative effectiveness in inferring relevance is the criterion for system relevance.

2. Topical or subject relevance: relation between the subject or topic expressed in a query and topic or subject covered by retrieved texts, or, more broadly, by texts in the system file, or even in existence. Aboutness is the criterion by which topicality is inferred.

3. Cognitive relevance or pertinence: relation between the state of knowledge and cognitive information need of a user and texts retrieved, or in the file of a system, or even in existence. Cognitive correspondence, informativeness, novelty, information quality, and the like are criteria by which cognitive relevance is inferred.

4. Situational relevance or utility: relation between the situation, task or problem at hand and texts retrieved by a system, or in the file of a system, or even in existence. Usefulness in decision-making, appropriateness of information in resolution of a problem, reduction of uncertainty, and the like are criteria by which situational relevance is inferred.

5. Motivational or affective relevance: relation between the intents, goals, and motivations of a user and texts retrieved by a system, or in the file of a system, or even in existence. Satisfaction, success, accomplishment, and the like are the criteria for inferring motivational relevance.

In concluding, Saracevic states that the only type of relevance that information retrieval systems can provide is systems relevance. In terms of information quality, we nevertheless are interested in all aspects of relevance, hence we include them in various other criteria instead of in the one that is highly ambiguous and clearly too complex to be used in every day management practices. Saracevic follows this line of argumentation in the following quote (Saracevic, 1999, p. 1052, my italics):

Practically, IR [information retrieval] systems assess systems relevance only – that is, they respond to queries – hoping that the objects retrieved may also be of cognitive relevance, and even more so of utility. However, a user may judge an object by any or all types of reevance – for a user they may interact dynamically.

Other information scientists have come to similar conclusions that highlight the problematic nature of relevance. Schamber et al. (1990) conclude their in-depth study of relevance with the confirmation that „information scientists have not reached a consensus in defining the central concept of relevance" (Schamber et al, 1990, p. 755). In addition, Schamber et al. argue that relevance is a concept that is extremely difficult to operationalize or measure (p. 757). Because of these reasons, relevance is not included as a single criterion in the framework but rather as a view that is composed of various other criteria.

Reasons against the Inclusion of Objectivity

The concept of objectivity is as complex as the criterion of relevance. In my view, it does not constitute a useful criterion because the subjective nature of knowledge can contribute to its added value when documented as information. As POLANYI (1974, p. viii) has shown in his analysis of personal knowledge and its role in scientific progress, the subjectivity of information may not always equal a lack of quality:

I have shown that into every act of knowing there enters a passionate contribution of the person knowing what is being known, and that this coefficient is no mere imperfection but a vital component of his knowledge.

Similarly, an ethnographic study on knowledge work has found that the idiosyncratic and subjective nature of knowledge is of great value. SCHULTZE (2000) writes in her empirical examination on knowledge work:

Even though the role of tacit knowledge and subjective insight in science has been recognized (e.g., Polanyi 1966), the scientific agenda has been to minimize their effect on knowledge production (Deetz 1996). This agenda is rooted in the subject-object dualism, which posits that reality is made up of objects that stand in fundamental opposition to subjects, i.e., individuals with minds and feelings. This scientific agenda has been successfully challenged, however, by social constructionism (Berger and Luckman 1966) and work on the sociology of science and knowledge (e.g., Kuhn 1970). Social constructionism posits that neither a position of absolute subjectivity nor of absolute objectivity is possible. Instead, both become relative positions in the intersubjective social consciousness. Thus the scientistic subject-object dualism is replaced by a subject-object duality, i.e., a view of subjects and objects as inextricably intertwined and mutually constitutive.

Due to this intertwined and mutually constitutive nature of knowledge we exclude the notion of objectivity from an information quality framework that is used in knowledge-intensive business processes.

Having given an overview on the existing information quality criteria and their types, and having argued why not to include many of them (and having given two examples of difficult or controversial information quality attributes) we can now turn to the criteria that we are going to include in the framework and the reasons for doing so.

There is a wide range of possible information quality criteria that are generated intuitively, systematically or empirically. Some of them relate to the information consumer and his or her judgment of information. Others relate to the information object itself, while still others focus on the process of information provision. This multitude of possible criteria can be reduced to a smaller number of attributes by eliminating synonyms and closely related terms, by excluding criteria that are either too context-specific or too vague, and by splitting-up or leaving out controversial and debatable criteria, such as relevance or objectivity.

Conclusion

3.2.3.2 Selection of Feasible Criteria

In the previous section we have given an overview on the range of existing information quality criteria and we have given reasons why we exclude a certain number of attributes. This seems reasonable since any type of conceptual management framework that consists of seventy items can no longer be used effectively. For practical as well as instructive reasons a framework should not consist of considerably more than a dozen criteria and not of more than seven elements per level. The frameworks we have reviewed earlier consisted of 6 (Lesca and Lesca, 1995) to 27 criteria (Redman, 1996). Four of the seven frameworks consisted of 12 to 18 criteria. This, then, seems to provide an adequate scope of criteria. For reasons of simplicity and symmetry we have included 16 criteria in the framework, four on each individual level. Each one of them is defined in the glossary in the appendix. The criteria and their opposites are listed in the table below. The list does not contain any synonyms, context-specific, vague or multifaceted attributes anymore. It is also cleansed of attributes that are on another level of abstraction (such as browsing) or that are the result of information quality principles (such as reputation or credibility).

Information Quality Level	Information Quality Criteria	Opposite
Community Level (Relevance)	Comprehensiveness	Incompleteness
	Accuracy	Inaccuracy
	Clarity	Obscurity
	Applicability	Uselessness
Product Level (Soundness)	Conciseness	Prolixity
	Consistency	Inconsistency
	Correctness	Falsity
	Currency	Obsolescence
Process Level	Convenience	Inconvenience
	Timeliness	Lateness
	Traceability	Indeterminacy
	Interactivity	Rigidity
Infrastructure Level	Accessibility	Inaccessibility
	Security	Exposure
	Maintainability	Neglect
	Speed	Slowness

Table 11: The sixteen selected information quality criteria and their opposites

As a result of this juxtaposition, one can define the opposite of quality information as follows:

Definition: Low Quality Information

Low quality information is incomplete, inaccurate, obscure, useless, prolix (or wordy), inconsistent, false, obsolete, delivered in an inconvenient, late, undeterminable and rigid way, via an infrastructure that is inaccessible, exposed to manipulation and other security risks, cumbersome or costly to maintain, and slow.

Discussion of Selected Criteria

Most of these criteria are self-explanatory or they become clear when contrasted with their opposites. Some of them, however, merit further discussion in the context of knowledge-intensive processes, mainly because they are either interpreted in different ways or because they are not always included in standard information quality frameworks (and hence need to be explicitly discussed). Below, we will discuss six such criteria in more detail, namely accuracy, traceability, interactivity, convenience, applicability, and maintainability.

The most widely used information quality criteria is accuracy (see Huang et al., 1999, p. 33). The term may seem self-explanatory at first sight, but – as with many other IQ-criteria – one can find various interpretations of the concept in the relevant IQ-literature. Accuracy can be used to designate notions of precision, level of detail, or even correctness, as Huang et al. find: *Accuracy*

> Although the term „accuracy" has an intuitive appeal, there is no commonly accepted definition of what it means exactly. For example, Kriebel characterizes accuracy as „the correctness of the output information." Ballou and Pazer describe accuracy as when „the recorded value is in conformity with the actual value." (Huang et al., 1999, p. 17)

Here, we define the term accuracy as how closely information matches a real-life state. It is in this sense a synonym of precision. Technically speaking, it is the degree of conformity of a measure to a standard or a true value. This may include the level of detail, in terms of precision, but not in terms of scope.

Unlike accuracy, traceability (or attributability) is not a standard information quality criterion. The crucial role of traceability to assure information quality is highlighted by a team of information quality researchers and professionals which implemented a knowledge management system at IBM Global Services Consulting Group (Hu et al., 1997, p. 358): *Traceability*

> In addition to the data quality, every step of the information extraction and information fusing need [sic] to be accounted for with reasons so that a human can trace back the whole process if needed. Since the information or knowledge generated by the customer knowledge management process will be highly summarized, credibility will not be established without such tracing facility.

Traceability is thus a prerequisite for the credibility of information. It also enables a more comprehensive evaluation of the information because its sources and its methodology can be reviewed. But traceability can also mean that the hidden interests of an author are traced, for example tracing the stocks that an equity research analyst holds when reporting on companies (see the Economist, September 8th, 2001, p. 86 for this aspect of traceability).

Interactivity

Interactivity, as in the capacity of an information system to react to the inputs of an information consumer and to generate instant, tailored responses to a user's actions or inquiries is an information quality that is especially relevant in (but not limited to) the realm of new media. More and more information is not just delivered to the information consumer but explored by him or her. Consequently, the flexibility of the information manufacturing and provision process becomes a key success factor. The domain that aims at improving this criterion is sometimes referred to as interactivity design. In the quote below design guru CLEMENT MOK explains what this discipline is all about (Mok, 1996, p. 127):

Interactivity design borrows many concepts and models from the study of ergonomics, semiotics, artificial intelligence, cognitive science, and theater. The computer medium is quickly absorbing the principles behind those disciplines and art forms, which is making it possible for visual, sensory experiences to materialize on screen. The interactivity arts can transform those experiences into meaningful, humane communication.

Interactivity as an information quality criterion thus describes the flexibility of a content management process and its underlying system to provide an optimal interface to the information consumer. In the context of new media, interactivity is the responsibility of designers and engineers. In the context of regular face-to-face communication the attribute of interactivity reflects a speaker's or writer's empathy with his or her audience or target community and the willingness to react quickly and spontaneously to their preferences or reactions.

Convenience

The criterion of interactivity is closely related (but not identical) to convenience. Convenience designates the ease-of-use or seamlessness by which information is produced, administered and (most importantly) acquired. Too much interactivity can in fact reduce convenience, for instance if an information consumer has to determine too many parameters of his or her information environment. A high-quality information system will achieve convenience by making some of the choices for the information consumer. The terms that are used normally to refer to this concept are ease-of-use, usability, or ergonomic design. The term convenience, however, stresses the fact that information can and should be viewed as a *service* that has to be delivered in a convenient way.

Applicability

That information is not only conveniently accessible, but also of practical use is one of the prime concerns of information consumers in the management context. This is especially true in times of information overload and data smog where there is an abundance of easily accessible information. Applicability is consequently of cardinal importance. It can be defined as the characteristic of information to be directly useful in a given context. Applicable information is already organized for action and doesn't have to be converted, transformed, or repackaged to be of use in a particular situation. Applicability is the quality of a piece of information to directly contribute to the solution of a problem. It is a subjective criterion because only the information consumer can judge whether a piece of information is helpful for him or not. Closely related terms are usefulness, closeness to problem, stimulation, or value-added.

While applicability is a user-centered criterion, maintainability is primarily a relevant attribute for information administrators or information custodians (such as webmasters, knowledge managers, database managers, IT-support staff, etc.). It designates the characteristic of an information environment to be manageable at reasonable costs in terms of content volume, frequency, quality, and infrastructure. This cost factor is frequently overlooked by quality frameworks that do not take a management perspective on the topic. Quality per se, however, cannot be a management goal. The question in the context of management is: what quality (in terms of scope, currency, convenience etc.) can we afford, or: quality at what price? The criterion of maintainability takes this reasoning into account and defines the quality of information and its underlying system also in light of its sustainability. Hence, maintainability can be defined as the characteristic of an information system and the information included in it to be manageable over time at reasonable costs. As we will see below in the analysis of criteria-tradeoffs, this attribute is in direct conflict with the comprehensiveness of information, since more information is bound to be more difficult to maintain.

Maintainability

As important as the individual criteria discussed above is their overall logic and structure. The rationale for their (vertical) arrangement is described in the next few paragraphs.

From Individual Criteria to the Set

In this section, the logic of the individual criteria and their relation to the category names are explained. The potential conflicts between the individual criteria are also discussed in this segment.

The Criteria and their Logic

The logic for the criteria contained in the first level is the following: *Relevant information* is information that is adequate for the community that requires it. Adequate in this context signifies that the scope (or breadth) of the information is right (comprehensive enough), that the precision and level of detail is sufficient (accurate enough), that the clarity of argumentation is sufficient (comprehensible, interpretable, or clear enough) and that the information is easily applicable for the target community.

The criteria of the second level follow this rationale: *Sound information* is information that has certain intrinsic (product) characteristics which make it of high quality independently of the community that deals with the information. The information can said to be sound if it does not contain superfluous or non-related elements (conciseness), if it is internally consistent (does not contradict itself and uses the same format conventions) , if it does not contain errors or false elements (correctness), and if its it not outdated by more recent information (currency).

The criteria of the third level all relate to information as a process: We refer to the information delivery process as an *optimized information process* if the following conditions are met: the information creation, administration, and delivery is as convenient as possible for the three information stakeholders (author, administrator, user), e.g., there are no superfluous or tedious steps; the access to the information is secure in the sense that both the information and the user are protected against unauthorized manipulation; the information is continuously maintained (cleansed, updated); and the manner in which the information is accessed or retrieved can be adapted to one's personal preferences through interactive elements.

The criteria of the fourth level all deal with infrastructure requirements: For the information *infrastructure* to be *reliable*, it is important that it is always accessible (no downtimes, otherwise the information itself is not accessible), that it is secure (protected against unauthorized access or information manipulation), that it is maintainable (that is to say that the information can also be accessed easily in the future), and that it enables fast interaction between the stored information and the users (or the authors or administrators). Infrastructure in this framework not only relates to the hardware and operating system software of information systems. The information infrastructure can be any kind of channel that allows for information to be documented and shared, such as a paper archive, a library, a documentation center, an intranet, a war room-like control center, a television studio etc.

Information Quality Criteria Dimensions:

As indicated in Figure 6, the criteria selected for the framework all relate to at least one dimension of *time, content, format* or *cost*. This convention will be briefly described below.

The first level of information quality, the relevance criteria, contains subjective notions of information quality that mainly relate to the *content* of the information (although one could argue that applicability is also a question of format and timing). The second level, the soundness criteria, contain criteria of three dimensions, since information has to be sound in terms of format, content, and time aspects. Again, one could argue that criteria such as consistency are not only related to a consistent format of the information, but also to consistent content (that it is free of self-contradictions). While this is certainly true, it is often easier to detect inconsistencies in the format than in the content. For the other criteria in this group, the dimensions seem obvious. The last two levels of the framework do not contain any content criteria, as they relate to media quality and not the content quality of the information. The process and the infrastructure can directly influence the format (the presentation) of the information and its timely delivery[41], as well as the costs involved in assuring high-quality information (captured in the maintainability criterion).

The four information quality dimensions (as a third perspective on the criteria besides the levels and phases) described above can be summarized in the following statement: In order to be of value to information producers, administrators, and consumers, information must be provided at the right time, with relevant and sound content, in the right format, and at reasonable costs.

As far as possible *tradeoffs* between individual criteria are concerned, one can argue that the most critical criteria here are *comprehensiveness, security, timeliness,* and *accuracy* since they provide the greatest number of potential conflicts with other criteria (see Figure 6).

A tradeoff in this context refers to possible goal conflicts, that is to say when the increase in quality in one criterion leads to a decreasing quality in another. One tradeoff that has been discussed in the information quality literature is the accuracy-timeliness tradeoff (see Ballou & Pazer, 1987), which consists of a choice between accurate or timely information, since the very fact of a timely delivery often impedes the careful consideration of accuracy issues. A similar tradeoff exists between timeliness and correctness: the faster the

Time

Content

Format

Cost

⇒ *Summary of the Criteria*

Making Tradeoffs Visible

Critical Criteria: Comprehensive, Secure, Timely, Accurate

---

[41] The process can only indirectly affect the content quality of information, for example through rating and validation workflows that double-check the information before it is published or distributed.

information has to be delivered, the less time is available to fully check its correctness (or completeness) for the given context. The same may be said for consistency and timeliness: the faster the information must be delivered, the less time can be spent on improving its format and content consistency. Another tradeoff that may exist is between accuracy (in the sense of precision or level of detail) and conciseness: the more accurate information is, the less concise is its presentation. This tradeoff is similar to the one between conciseness and comprehensiveness: the greater the scope of the information, the more difficult is its presentation in a concise format. The quest for comprehensive information may also lead to less clarity, since the increased scope reduces clear distinctions between central and peripheral information and thus makes the information more difficult to comprehend. There is another important tradeoff associated with the comprehensiveness (or completeness) of information, namely between it and maintainability or costs in general. More information usually means more costs, both in terms of acquisition and in terms of maintenance (more information has to be indexed, reviewed, cleansed, updated etc. which leads to higher maintenance costs).[42]

The tradeoffs related to the security criteria are threefold: First, there is a potential conflict between convenience and security, since many security measures lead to inconvenient authorization for information producers, administrators, or consumers. Second, there is a clear conflict between providing quick access to an information infrastructure and keeping the infrastructure secure. A typical example of this tradeoff in the computer context is the number of times one has to enter passwords to access a certain information system. Third, there may be a tradeoff between the speed of an information infrastructure and its security, since security measures require additional resources which in turn may slow down the functioning of an information infrastructure.

Making these tradeoffs visible can help the designer of an information system or information product in his or her interaction with information consumers and authors, since it highlights the constraints under which one has to operate. In the context of consulting and market research, we have used the tradeoffs in the framework to show clients that is not possible to request a report that is delivered within two weeks (timeliness), contains no errors whatsoever (correctness and consis-

---

[42] The tradeoff between completeness and (maintainability) costs has been highlighted in Arnold, 1995, p. 21.

tency), has a high level of accuracy and is very comprehensive and at the same time not more than fifteen pages (conciseness). Finally, the tradeoffs can also underline differences between various user groups of information: while one group may require information in a very comprehensive format, another information consumer group may require the same information in an extremely concise format (due to time constraints).

We have now discussed the information quality criteria contained in the framework, their opposites, the logic behind them, as well as their mutual relationships. The table below summarizes the sixteen criteria and provides a brief description (in the form of a check question), a sample indicator (how the criterion could be measured), as well as the mentioned tradeoffs.

Summary

Criterion Name	Description	Sample Indicators	Tradeoff with
Comprehensiveness	Is the scope of information adequate? (not too much nor too little)	Percentage of pages with more than ten hits per day in an Intranet. Scale of a geographic map.	Clarity Conciseness Timeliness Maintainability
Accuracy	Is the information precise enough and close enough to reality?	Number of digits after the decimal point of figures in a statistic chart.	Clarity Conciseness Timeliness
Clarity	Is the information understandable or compre-hensible to the target group?	User feedback, number of follow-up / help desk questions (product manual)	Accuracy Comprehensiveness
Applicability	Can the information be directly applied? Is it useful?	User ratings, number of downloads (Internet)	
Conciseness	Is the information to the point, void of un-necessary elements?	Number of pages in a report (e.g., a consulting report), percentage of reports with summaries	Comprehensiveness Accuracy
Consistency	Is the information free of contradictions or convention breaks?	Number of convention breaks during an intranet navigation	Timeliness

Criterion Name	Description	Sample Indicators	Tradeoff with
Currency	Is the information up-to-date and not obsolete?	Number of outdated items in a database	
Correctness	Is the information free of distortion, bias, or error?	Number of errors in a document	Timeliness
Convenience	Does the information provision correspond to the user's needs and habits?	Number of necessary process steps to access information online	Security
Timeliness	Is the information processed and delivered rapidly without delays?	Time from creation to publication (e.g., in a journal)	Comprehensiveness Accuracy Consistency Correctness
Traceability	Is the background of the information visible (author, date etc.)?	Percentage of items without author and date indications on an intranet	
Interactivity	Can the information process be adapted by the information consumer?	Number of user options or data views	
Accessibility	Is there a continuous and unobstructed way to get to the information?	Downtime of an information system per year	Security
Security	Is the information protected against loss or unauthorized access?	Level of data encryption, number of required passwords	Convenience Accessibility
Maintainability	Can all of the information be organized and updated on an on-going basis?	Number of required administrator hours per time period	Comprehensiveness
Speed	Can the infrastructure match the user's working pace?	Response time of the server	Security

Table 12: Description of the selected criteria

Sixteen criteria have been included in the information quality framework. They have been divided into four logical levels. The criteria can be categorized into subjective (or judgmental) criteria, (objective) product or intrinsic criteria, process criteria, and infrastructure criteria. We have also seen that they relate either to the time, format, content, or cost dimension of information. Finally, we observed interdependencies between the sixteen criteria in the form of tradeoffs or possible goal conflicts.

Conclusion

We have now analyzed how the sixteen criteria relate to the four levels of the information quality framework. In the next section their sequence in the framework will be explained.

Transition

3.2.4 Steps in the Framework

The four steps in the framework are the result of an amalgamation of phase models on information behavior found in relevant academic literature. These models typically distinguish between three to six phases of information processing, starting with information searching and finishing with the actual use of the allocated and evaluated information. Typical information behavior models were reviewed by Meyer, 1996. He compared the models proposed by Kramer (1965), Hauschildt (1985), Gemünden and Petersen (1985), Hogarth (1987), Kuss and Silberer, Kroeber-Riel (1980, 1992, all cited in Meyer, 1996). Another model has been proposed by Davenport (1997). All of these models stress the identification or selection, evaluation or assessment, transformation or allocation, and application or use of information.

Origin of the Four Steps

The vertical structure of the framework reflects a chronological sequence (or phases) from the user's point of view. For him (or her) information may be the answer he needs to find, understand and evaluate, adapt to his context and apply in the correct manner. Thus, an information system (based on a general understanding of the term) should assist him in identifying relevant and sound information. It should help him to evaluate whether the information is adequate for his purpose. It should assist him in re-contextualizing the information, that is to say understand its background and adapt it according to the new situation. Finally, the knowledge media should provide assistance in making the found, evaluated, and allocated information actionable, e.g., use it effectively for decision-making. The key questions (of an information consumer) to be answered in each phase are the following ones: 1. Where is the information I

Logic of the Four Steps

need? (identification) 2. Can I trust it? (evaluation) 3. Can I adapt it to my current situation? (allocation) 4. How can I best use it? (application).

The figure below illustrates this logic and adds typical activities at every step. It shows that the identification phase consists of locating the information and the domain to which it relates, as well as in finding related sources. The evaluation phase consists of activities which help to better judge the soundness and relevance of the identified information and its source. The allocation phase contains a set of activities that all help to adapt the information to a new application context by reducing or extending it or by converting it into other formats. The application phase finally is where information is put to use, either directly or with prior trials and training. As a result of the application experience, new information needs may arise which in turn lead to the new identification of information. Thus, the cycle is completed.

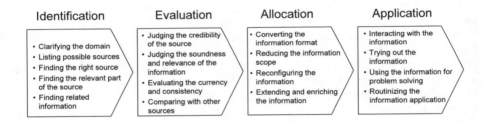

Identification	Evaluation	Allocation	Application
• Clarifying the domain • Listing possible sources • Finding the right source • Finding the relevant part of the source • Finding related information	• Judging the credibility of the source • Judging the soundness and relevance of the information • Evaluating the currency and consistency • Comparing with other sources	• Converting the information format • Reducing the information scope • Reconfiguring the information • Extending and enriching the information	• Interacting with the information • Trying out the information • Using the information for problem solving • Routinizing the information application

Figure 7: The information usage cycle

As stated earlier, the current framework can be used not only as a systematic arrangement of crucial information quality criteria, or as the key questions of users, but also as a systematic problem lens. The four phases of the framework can be used to designate four dominant information quality problems, namely: information *overload* (information is not integrated and cannot be identified effectively), information *misjudgment* (information is not validated and nevertheless believed to be correct), information *misinterpretation* (information is not seen in context or contextualized), and information *misuse* (information is not made actionable).

*Positioning of the
Criteria along
Steps of the Cycle*

The phases described above have been used in the framework depicted in Figure 6 to structure the information quality criteria. Criteria which are crucial for the identification of information are *comprehensiveness conciseness, convenience* and *accessibility*. If a source does not provide comprehensive in-

formation in a concise manner, then information is either missing or it is buried and cannot be identified because too much
time is required to find it. The same holds true for the retrieval
process: if its not designed in a convenient manner, then too
much time is lost identifying the information. If the infrastructure is not accessible, then all other criteria are meaningless
since information cannot be identified at all if the basic information infrastructure (whether it is a closed library building or
an intranet server that is in its backup or revision mode) cannot
be contacted or used.

Criteria which are crucial for the evaluation phase are *accuracy, consistency, timeliness*, and *security* since they all influence the way that information is judged or evaluated. If information is perceived as not accurate, as inconsistent our outdated
by the time it is received, then it will not be accepted by the
information consumer. In consequence, he or she will not allocate or use it for decision-making. This is also the case where
the information infrastructure is perceived to be insecure, in
terms of protection against manipulation, unauthorized access,
or system failures.

The allocation phase affects the *clarity, correctness, traceability*, and *maintainability* criteria. Adapting the information to
a new context should make it clearer (by highlighting the most
relevant aspects and translating the 'jargon' for a new application context) and should reveal, whether the information is in
fact correct for the new context or not. Allocating or contextualizing the information also signifies that its background is made
explicit so that its original context can be retained. This will
also help to maintain (i.e., modify, update, or delete) the information when it is in use.

In the last phase of the usage cycle, information is applied.
The key criterion in this phase is of course *applicability*, that is
to say whether the information can be easily applied and
whether it provides a value-added at this point or not. Other
crucial criteria in this last step are *currency* of the information
and *interactivity*: information is not fit for use if its obsolete or
not adaptable to a changing context, hence the term interactive.
Finally, *speed* is an ever-more important criterion as far as the
information infrastructure is concerned. If such an infostructure
is not as fast as the user needs it to be, then it will be the weak-
est link in the information chain of a user and slow him or her
down. This in return negatively affects the applicability of the
information as a whole (content and media).

The four information cycle steps that have been discussed in   *Preview*
this section provide a powerful logic to structure the information handling on the one side, and the value adding activities on

the other. The next section on IQ-principles shows how these four value-adding steps can be implemented, that is to say, how the four criteria in every step can be improved.

3.2.5 Information Quality Principles

3.2.5.1 The Function of Information Quality Principles

Principium dicitur, quod in se continet rationem alterius.
(A principle is what contains in itself the reason for another.)

CHRISTIAN WOLFF

Functions of the Principles

The fourth and final element of the framework is the set of management principles. As already mentioned, they provide pragmatic help in implementing the framework and achieving the quality criteria contained in it. The principles are also placed vertically along the framework since they follow the same step-by-step logic as the four phases discussed above. Every principle relates to the criteria that are found in the same column as the principle. The integration principle, for example, aims to improve the criteria of comprehensiveness, conciseness, convenience, and accessibility.

Principles as Integral Part of the Framework

The four information quality principles are an integral part of the framework presented in this study. In consequence, the framework can help the analyst to not only think about the crucial information characteristics (the individual information quality criteria) and the inherent conflicts or tradeoffs between them, but also about how these characteristics can be achieved. But what is a principle and how can it be used to resolve information quality problems? These two questions will be addressed in these introductory paragraphs.

Horn's Definition of Principle

According to ROBERT E. HORN, inventor of the information mapping method, a principle is a statement that 1) tells what should or should not be done, such as rules, policies or guidelines, warnings or cautions; 2) seems to be true in light of evidence, such as generalizations or theorems; 3) is unprovable, but implied by other statements such as assumptions, axioms or postulates (Horn, 1986, p. 111).

Merrill's Definition

According to education specialist M.D. MERRILL, a principle is a proven, enduring guideline for human behavior. It is a relationship that is always true under appropriate conditions regardless of program or practice (Merrill, 1987).

From these approaches, we can derive the following working definition of a management principle that is adequate for the context of this study.

> A management principle is a general, instructive, concise, and memorable statement that suggests a way of reasoning or acting that is effective and proven to reach a certain goal within an organizational context.

Definition: Management Principle

The main advantage of a principle is that it summarizes a whole set of techniques, tools, and effective ways of handling a situation through one memorable sentence that leaves room for interpretation and context adaptation. The possible danger in such principles of action is that they can be misinterpreted or applied in the wrong context. To prevent this danger, a principle should be embedded in a certain context and illustrated through numerous examples.

Advantages & Dangers

The above definition of a management principle only reflects one generic type of principles, that of principles of action. There is, however, a whole set of principles that are not at aimed at *action* but rather at insight. These principles do not describe how a problem should be resolved or handled. They focus on *understanding* and prediction, and they outline how something works or can be better understood. These principles typically describe mechanisms that occur over and over again and are difficult to see at first sight. An example of such a principle in the management context is the Peter Principle, which states that people are often promoted until they are overwhelmed by their responsibility and thus ill-allocated.[43] As far as the information quality framework is concerned, there is a focus on action-oriented principles.

Two Main Types of Management Principles

Principles can be broken down into more specific maxims. Maxims are thus more elaborated and specific than principles. They contain specific action steps or rules that should be followed. As principles, maxims require prior knowledge of a domain for their skillful application. They increase our insight, but cannot replace it. (Polanyi, 1974, p. 31). Another related term is that of a heuristic. Heuristics are general rules of thumb or problem solving strategies. They are closely related to prin-

Related Terms

---

[43] For a description of the famous Peter Principle of promotion, see: Peter, L.J. and Hull, R. (1969) *The Peter Principle*, New York: William Morrow and Company. The principle states that, in a hierarchy, every employee has a tendency to be promoted to his level of incompetence.

ciples, but tend to be more domain-specific and detailed than principles.[44] One example of a heuristic is backwarding, e.g., solving a problem by starting with the end-result in mind and working one's way backward to the current situation. Sometimes the term 'law' is also used in this context to designate a relationship that is always true under certain circumstances. In the management context, Parkinson has formulated witty and insightful (yet unscientific) laws of administration.[45] Laws in this context focus more on insight than on action. In order to better understand the benefits and characteristics of principles, the next paragraph presents two examples of such principles.

Examples:
The Pareto or
80/20 Principle

One of the best-known management or effectiveness principles is what JURAN has labeled the Pareto principle. It is commonly known as the 80/20 principle and is sometimes traced back to an insight by VILFREDO PARETO who analyzed the distribution of wealth in 1897 and found that there was a pattern of 'predictable imbalance', namely that twenty percent of the people owned eighty percent of a nation's wealth.[46] This principle has since been applied to a variety of phenomena, from total quality management to time management. In the context of quality management the principle states that twenty percent of all possible failure sources create eighty percent of all the quality defects that a company struggles with. In the time management context, the principle stresses the fact that it's usually 20 percent of all your activities that produce 80 percent of the total result and that you should thus focus on these twenty percent of value-adding activities. As the last phrase illustrates, there can be a connection between an insight and an action within one principle. In general, the 80/20 principle reminds us to pay special attention to the 'vital few' or the drivers of a problem. This function of a reminder can also be seen in another area where principles play a crucial role: negotiation.

A Negotiation
Principle

One often cited principle of negotiation is that of 'moving from positions to interests.' The rationale behind this powerful principle is the following one: In a negotiation context, there

---

[44] This definition is taken from Northcraft & Neale (1990), p. 184. Northcraft and Neale also highlight the potential negative consequences of such cognitive shortcuts.

[45] See Parkinson, C.N. (1980) *Parkinson: The Law*, Boston: Houghton Mifflin Company.

[46] For further information on the history of this principle see: Koch, R. (1998) *The 80/20 Principle: The Secret of Achieving more with less*, New York: Bantam Doubleday. In general terms one can paraphrase the principle as follows: a minority of causes, inputs, or effort usually leads to a majority of the results, outputs, or rewards.

may be irreconcilable differences in terms of the positions taken by two negotiation parties. The trick is to move beyond those positions to the real interests of these parties which may still be reconcilable.[47] The focus on positions will not yield a productive outcome of a negotiation. Thus, a moderator should try to uncover the hidden interests that guide any negotiation. This is an action-oriented principle that suggests a way to resolve a lock-in situation. But as any kind of action principle, it is based on insight. The insight in this example is that negotiations often stop because the involved parties are not able to abstract from their taken positions and consequently compromises cannot be identified.

These two examples show that principles can play a vital guiding role in many complex situations. The list of examples could be extended by such prominent principles as the principle of *subsidiarity* (first used by the Catholic Church and later also adapted by the European Union for its decision-making process), the principle of *parsimony* by William Occham (see for example Goldstein 1999, p. 129 or Flasch, 2000, p. 504), or the *sustainability* principle from ecological economics. All of these principles are based on fundamental insights that have been turned into action guidelines.

What can we learn from these examples about the benefits and characteristics of principles for management? What makes a good set of management principles and what should it achieve? It should have become clear that one major benefit of articulating management principles is to *reduce complexity* and *focus the attention* of employees on crucial value-adding activities. In order to serve this purpose, a principle has to be short, memorable, widely applicable, and unambiguous or self-explanatory. It must be clear, as stated above, where and when the principle should be applied. This can be achieved by providing examples or by describing situations in which the principle has already been applied successfully. In the remainder of this section, we will do exactly that: state information quality principles in a concise and memorable manner and provide examples of how they can be applied. [48]

The Main Functions and Requirements of Principles

---

[47]   For a description of this principle see: Harvard Business Review on Negotiation and Conflict Resolution, 2000 or Fisher, Roger and William Ury (1983) *Getting to Yes: Negotiating Agreement Without Giving in*, New York: Penguin Books.

[48]   For further descriptions of the role and content of management principles see: Wortman and Max (1970). This approach cites division of labor or span of control as traditional management principles. Another, early, approach is that of Megginson (1958). He defines a (management) principle as a general

3.2.5.2 Background and Main Insights of the Four Principles

Development of the Principles

The four principles outlined in the following sections have been developed in an iterative interaction among inductive and deductive activities. Inductively, the principles were gathered by *grouping related value-adding activities* performed by the companies portrayed in the case studies. Deductively, the principles were compiled by *reviewing existing information and communication principles* and by comparing information and communication guidelines and value-adding processes from existing academic sources.

Induction: Value Adding Activities

As far as the inductive compilation of the principles is concerned, I have identified 28 activities in the case studies that were said to increase the quality of the information product. They are categorized and described below.

Integration Activities	Validation Activities	Contextualization Activities	Activation Activities
• Visualizing concepts • Listing sources • Summarizing content • Personalizing content • Prioritizing content • Highlighting aspects • Giving an overview • Eliciting patterns	• Evaluating the source • Indicating the level of certitude / reliability • Describing the rationale • Comparing sources • Examining the hidden interests / background • Checking consistency	• Linking content • Stating target groups • Showing the purpose • Describing the background • Relating to prior information • Adding meta-information • Stating limitations	• Notifying and alerting • Demonstrating steps • Asking questions • Using mnemonics and metaphors; storytelling • Stressing consequences • Providing examples • Offering Interaction

Figure 8: Encountered value-adding activities as background for the information quality principles

Integration Activities

The activities listed in the first group, labeled as integration activities, all focus on making information more easily accessible by aggregating, compressing or integrating it (and its sources). This can be achieved by summarizing it visually (e.g., through diagrams) or verbally (e.g., through overviews and abstracts), by providing a personalized directory of relevant sources in one location (e.g., through a profile-based portal) or by highlighting crucial elements or patterns (i.e., connections or links among elements) that are of high importance or priority to an information consumer.

---

proposition sufficiently applicable to the series of phenomena under consideration to provide a guide to thought. For this definition, he refers to Alford and Beatty's book on *Principles of Industrial Management* (New York: The Ronald Press Company, 1951, p. 30). For a slightly more recent view on the topic see: Ross and Murdick (1977).

The activities grouped in the second section are labeled validation activities because they all aim at analyzing the correctness and consistency of the provided information. This can be achieved by evaluating the source and its interests, by evaluating the information itself or by comparing it with other sources. The information provider can also facilitate this evaluation process by clearly indicating the level of certitude of the provided information and describing its rationale.

Validation Activities

The third group summarizes activities that provide a context for the information. This can improve the clarity of information, as its background becomes transparent. Adding context to information can be achieved by outlining how (including when and by whom) the information was created and how it can be used. One way of doing this is by adding meta-information, such as author, date of creation, or target groups. Another way consists of linking information to related material or clearly stating its limitations.

Contextualization Activities

The fourth group is labeled as activation activities because all measures increase the likelihood that information is acted upon. These activities are: providing the information as it becomes relevant (notification or alerting), showing how it can be used (through demonstration and interaction), assuring that it has been understood by asking questions, providing the information in a format that fosters the retention and subsequent use (such as metaphors, mnemonics, examples).

Activation Activities

While the activities described and grouped above are taken directly from the empirical part of this book, the elements described below have been gathered from existing literature. This approach is based on the premise that information quality principles must not only summarize real life activities that are useful in increasing information quality, but must also take into account already existing principles of information quality management, sense-making, information transfer and communication. Several such principles are discussed below and related to the five categories of information integration, validation, contextualization, and activation. In doing so, we not only discover whether our own principles are plausible or not, but can also learn about the mechanisms which make operational principles effective.

Deduction: Building on Existing Principle and their Mechanisms

In their book on information quality and knowledge, Huang et al. propose four information quality principles (Huang et al., 1999, pp. 19-21) which help to manage information for high quality in the database context. These principles are not explicitly labeled, but they are described as follows:

Huang et al.'s Principles

1. Companies must understand their consumer's information needs.

2. Companies must manage information as the product of a well-defined information production process.

3. Companies must manage the life cycle of their information products.

4. Companies should appoint an information product manager to manage their information processes and resulting products.

While these principles are certainly helpful and provide means of improving information quality on an organizational level, they cannot be used by *individual managers* to increase the value of information that they themselves produce or use. Unlike the approach of Huang et al. the principles proposed here should stress the impact of information quality concepts for the individual knowledge worker and not only for the organization as a whole. Nevertheless, the four principles by Huang et al. highlight key issues, namely that information providers must first understand the needs and expectations of their information consumers, that they must manage information as a product and a process and that accountability is the crucial element in assuring information quality. The first principle of understanding the consumer's needs is reminiscent of the activities grouped above in the integration section, that is to say tailoring the information to the needs of the information user. It is also addressing the first level of our information quality framework, the community level. The second principle can be positioned within the process level of our framework. It is also closely related to the validation activities mentioned earlier (assuring that the information is still relevant or current). The next principle of Huang et al. relates to the process and the infrastructure level of our framework (e.g., the criterion of maintainability). As stated above, the last principle is beyond the scope of our framework and relates to the organizational implementation of information quality.

⇒ *Principles at Various Levels*

What we can learn from these four statements is that action-oriented principles in the context of information quality should not only focus on the organizational level, but also offer specific advice for teams and individuals.

Weick's Sense-Making Activities

Besides reviewing the principles articulated by information quality scholars, we can also look at the field of managerial sense-making and learn from its insights into the nature of valuable information and how it can be achieved. In his analysis of the (potentially negative) effects of electronic information provision and use in the workplace, KARL E. WEICK distinguishes between five crucial sense-making activities that he labels as *effectuating, triangulating, affiliating, deliberating* and *consolidating* (Weick, 1996, p. 214). From these five activities we learn more about what could be done to make information more valuable. These five activities can be related to information quality as follows.

For Weick, *effectuating* signifies seeing what information means in its application or experiencing its consequences in action. This can be related to the simulation or demonstration activities discussed in the activation group earlier. The main goal of effectuating is to see what information means in action. This is also one of the aims of the activation activities described inductively on the previous pages. Their mutual credo is: „To know, you must act."

The second concept Weick employs to describe effective sense-making is *triangulation*. He states that „people learn about an event when they apply several different measures to it [...]" (Weick, 1996, p. 215). This concept can be related to the validation idea expressed earlier, i.e., to compare various sources to validate a piece of information. Both can be summarized with the stanza „to be sure, you must compare."

The third key concept of sense-making is *affiliating*. Weick describes it as 'socializing' information or embedding it in an intersubjective context. It is closely related to triangulation but does not rely on the comparison of written sources, but rather on the opinion of different people. People can provide new perspectives on the same information and validate it based on their prior experience. In terms of our four groups, the concept is related to validation activities. However, through the emphasis on putting information into different contexts it is also related to the idea of contextualization. To sum up this concept in a phrase one could say that „to put information into perspective, you have to run it by various people."

The next activity crucial to sense-making is *deliberating*. It cannot easily be related to our previous activities because it stresses the absence of any kind of activity. Weick views deliberating as a mindful de-acceleration of information processing which enables a reflective reinterpretation of events. Deliberation on the part of the information recipient can be fostered by providing information at an adequate frequency. In this sense, deliberating is related to integrating the information in a way which makes it easier to process by the recipient, i.e., giving him or her time to interpret it and reflect about its meaning before new information is provided. The guideline that one can derive from these ideas is: „For information to be understood, you have to provide time to review it."

The last crucial activity to foster sense-making is *consolidating*. Weick introduces this concept by stating that „people learn about events when they can put them in a context" (Weick, 1996, p. 216). He emphasizes the power of context to synthesize and give meaning to scattered details (p.217):

To consolidate bits and pieces into a compact, sensible pattern frequently requires that one look beyond those bits and pieces to understand what they might mean.

Consolidating as an activity that tries to provide a context for isolated information is very close, if not to say identical, to our concept of contextualization, where background or related material is provided to make information more easily interpretable. That this may also make information more compact is a fact that I have neglected so far, but Weick rightfully emphasizes. We can thus state the following guideline based on this principle: „To make information clear it must be related to its environment."

⇒ *Connections between Principles*

Besides reiterating important activities compiled earlier, Weick's five sense-making activities have helped us to see crucial connections between them. The concept of consolidating, for example, has shown that contextualizing information may also help in making it more concise, thus integrating it.

Alesandrini's Principles

Whereas Weick's principles focus on effective sense-making, the next seven principles by Alesandrini focus on the effective processing of massive amounts of information. KATHRIN ALESANDRINI, a professor of information ecology, has developed a pragmatic approach to prevent information overload encapsulated in the acronym SURVIVE. It summarizes her seven main information management principles, they are: synthesize details, underscore priorities, reduce paperwork, view the big picture, illuminate meeting issues, visualize new concepts and extract the essence (Alesandrini, 1992). All of them emphasize activities that we have summarized in the integration category, such as synthesizing, prioritizing, reducing, viewing the big picture, visualizing and illuminating and extracting the essence.

⇒ *Integration Activities*

⇒ *Relating Principles to Tools, Providing Mnemonics*

There are two things that we can learn from Alesandrini's approach of 'engineering' management principles. First, one must emphasize the tools that can be used to put a principle into practice. Alesandrini offers various mapping tools, intelligent forms or planning templates, co-ordination heuristics, and filing techniques, and she frequently refers to software solutions that can help to apply the principles. Second, Alesandrini has understood that for principles to be operational, they need to be memorable and concise. Every one of her principles can be expressed in two to three words, and all the principles can be summarized in one acronym – SURVIVE. To further activate her tips in the minds of the managers, Alesandrini provides self-tests through which executives can test how well they are already applying the principles of effective information processing (an approach that has also been used in this book).

Chemist and philosopher (and knowledge management's first herald) MICHAEL POLANYI has articulated several 'operational principles of language' in the context of intellectual work (Polanyi, 1974, p. 78). Although the principles are called operational, they are in fact more theoretical (and fundamental) than those proposed by Alesandrini. They relate to the process of linguistic *representation* and to the *operation* of symbols in order to assist the process of thought. Polanyi's principles or laws (he uses the terms interchangeably) are the laws of poverty and grammar, the laws of iteration and consistency, and the law of manageability. Especially the last law or principle is of crucial importance for the context of information quality, as will be shown below.

Polanyi's Language Principles

The laws of *poverty and grammar* state that any effective linguistic system must use a relatively small number of components (e.g., the letters of the alphabet) that can be combined in a systematic way (e.g., the grammar). These two laws have to be combined with the laws of *iteration and consistency* which state that the used words (or utterances) must have a distinct 'gestalt' by which they can be repeatedly recognized as referring to the same concept or idea. While the first three laws refer to linguistic representation, the last law regards the operation of symbols. Polanyi defines this third principle of manageability as follows (Polanyi, 1974, p. 81):

The principle of manageability consists in devising a representation of experience which reveals new aspects of it. […].

We may conclude that linguistic symbols must be of reasonable size, or more generally that they must consist of easily manageable objects. […].

Language can assist thought only to the extent to which its symbols can be reproduced, stored up, transported, re-arranged, and thus more easily pondered, than the things which they denote. (Polanyi, 1974, p. 81).

This principle is obviously closely related to the idea of integrating or compressing information to make it more easily manageable or to reveal new insights. Polanyi provides the example of a geographic map (as Karl Weick, Richard Wurman and others after him have also done) to illustrate this important

⇒ *Relating Principles to Examples*

principle (*ibid.*):

A map is the more accurate the nearer its scale approaches unity, but if it were to reach unity and represent the features of a landscape in their natural size, it would become useless, since it would be about as difficult to find one's way on the map as in the region represented by it.

⇒ *Quality: Reduction in Quantity*

Information quality can thus be closely associated with the (adequate) reduction of information quantity. This insight is embodied by the integration principle proposed in this book. Polanyi's principles not only show the importance of adequate information reduction, but also provide insights into the nature of useful operational principles. Specifically, they reveal that operational principles must be illustrated through numerous examples, metaphors, or parables. The importance of examples is also apparent in the principles proposed by the next author.

Grice's Principles of Conversation

Another important thinker in the domain of linguistic principles is PAUL GRICE. Although he did not intend for his principles to be operational or prescriptive, his insights into the functioning of conversations can contribute to the understanding of high-quality information. Paul Grice has proposed four maxims of conversation which he sees as consequences of the so-called 'co-operation principle'. This regulative principle for functioning conversations can be stated as follows (Grice, 1975, pp. 60f.):

Make your conversational contribution such as is required, at the stage at which it occurs, by the accepted purpose or direction of the talk exchange in which you are engaged.

Clearly, this principle is too broad and general to be of direct use in a conversation. But Grice provides more specific maxims which are based on this principle, namely the maxim of quantity, quality, relation, and manner (Grice, 1975, p. 175).

The maxim of *quantity* is similar to the principle of manageability discussed in the last paragraph. As our 'integration' category, it stresses the conciseness of information by proposing two imperatives: Make your contribution as informative as is required. Do not make your contribution more informative than is required.

The maxim of *quality* can also be expressed in two imperatives, they are: Do not say what you believe to be false. Do not say what for which you lack adequate evidence. These two maxims are reminiscent of the validation category which we have proposed earlier and which states that information should be validated before being communicated.

The third maxim proposed by Grice is the maxim of *relation*. It can be expressed in two words: be relevant. In the discussion of the information quality framework, this idea is represented by the first level of the framework, the community view. It states that information must be targeted to the needs of the community that uses the information. In Grice's view the maxim of relation should force a speaker to say only things which are pertinent to the current conversation context. Hence, the principle also hints at the important issue of re-contextualizing information so that it is apt for a new situation.

The last maxim proposed by Grice is that of *manner*. It consists of four imperatives: Avoid obscurity of expression. Avoid ambiguity. Be brief. Be orderly. This maxim (and its four imperatives) is closely related to our validation category where the prime goal is consistency in format and content. It is also similar (especially in regard to the imperative regarding brevity) to the idea of integration introduced earlier.

The four maxims discussed above are not intended as instructions for speakers on how to behave in conversations; rather Grice states that these maxims are naturally followed in any well-working conversation. Many authors (among others Sperber and Wilson, 1995), however, have pointed out that there are numerous exceptions to this rule and that many well-working conversation contexts violate Grice's principle and the associated maxims. Nevertheless, Grice's insights can be used to highlight crucial issues of information quality in conversations. They can also illustrate the fact that principles should be combined with clear imperatives or rules. Grice's idea of stating one principle that is then divided into four maxims (which in return can be broken down into imperatives) can be taken as a general device to structure operational principles hierarchically.

⇒ Complement Principles with Maxims and Rules

A more instructive set of information quality principles has been proposed by design prodigy CLEMENT MOK. He has articulated four principles that he summarizes as the four C's of interactive information design (Mok, 1999, p. 132). They are the control, consistency, context, and corroboration principles.

Mok's 4C Design Principles

The *control* principle states that the level of interactivity in an information system should be such that the information consumers can control where they want to go (i.e., which information they want to access), how they want to get there, and how they can stop and start.

The *consistency* principle states that all the conventions, symbols and functions used in an information system should follow the same logic and use this logic without exceptions.

The *context* principle states that information (and its design) should always be related to the information around it.

The *corroboration* principle, finally, states that the medium should corroborate the information; the interactivity should

⇒ *Qualities of Useful Principles*

⇒ *Matching of Principles and Reviewed Activities*

Related Principles and Concepts

reflect the nature of the content and foster its comprehension and application.

These four rules are not only good examples of useful management principles because they are mutually exclusive and collectively exhaustive, but also because they are concise and memorable. In addition, the four C-principles of Mok are closely related to the ideas we have already come across. The control principle is related to the integration activities that emphasize the fact that information must be tailored to the needs of the information consumers. The consistency principle is similar to many of the validation activities we have examined earlier that aim at improving the consistency of information and its environment. The context principle is of course closely related to the contextualization activities listed in Figure 8. The main aim of the corroboration principle is very similar to that of the activation activities encountered earlier, namely to ensure that information is understood and applied.

Besides the pertinent principles presented in the previous paragraphs, there are other, similar insights that can be found in the relevant communication, knowledge management, and information science literature. Most of these contributions highlight the central role of information integration, validation, contextualization, and activation activities. In concluding this sub-chapter, we quickly review some of them below.

In their book on corporate knowledge management, Davenport and Prusak (1998) devised a pragmatic and instructive definition of information that reiterates many of the ideas covered so far. They define information as originating and being *applied* in the minds of people, as *contextualized*, categorized, calculated, *corrected* and *condensed* data that make a difference. The central elements of this definition highlight the fact that information must be applicable or activated, contextualized, validated and condensed or integrated to be of value.

ROBERT E. HORN is a professor of information science and the inventor of the information mapping methodology (Horn, 1989), a procedure to improve the layout and the content of technical on- and off-line documentation. He proposed, among various other maxims, the principle of relevance, the labeling principle and the chunking principle. The *relevance principle* can be stated as follows: Include in one chunk ($\cong$ paragraph) only information that relates to one main point based on that information's purpose or function for the reader. This principle expresses the same concern as our activation activities, namely to make information fit for the purpose or function for the reader. Closely associated with this principle is *labeling principle*: Label every chunk and group of chunks according to specific criteria. These criteria are the text block types which indicate the context for a particular paragraph, e.g., whether it is a definition, a procedure, a list of advantages and disadvantages, or an example. The labeling of every paragraph is one way of making the context of information explicit that will be discussed in our contextualization principle. Both the relevance and the labeling principles are based on the chunking principle. It states that information should be divided into short chunks and that each page should not contain more than seven such chunks. This principle is closely related to our integration principle, which emphasizes the reduction of information to accommodate the cognitive limitations of the information consumers.

Famous principles that increase the quality of written communication were also articulated by WILLIAM ZINSSER. He proposed the following four principles of high-quality written information for non-fiction professional writers in his seminal book 'On Writing Well'. These principles are clarity, simplicity, economy, humanity (Zinsser, 1990, p. 153). Stated as imperatives these principles have the following concise form: be clear, keep it simple, keep it short, write in a personal and authentic style. The clarity, simplicity, and economy principles are clearly related to our idea of information integration. The principle of humanity adds the dimension of style and personal tone which we have neglected so far. In my view, however, this can be seen as a sub-element of clarity.

A last, related set of information principles is the one proposed by Meyer in his habilitation on visualization in management. Meyer (1996, p. 81) suggests five principles which – if correctly applied – can increase the value of visual information. They are the principle of minimalism, conciseness, adequate format, consistency, and of closure. As Zinsser, Meyer uses information quality attributes as the main labels for his principles, with the exception of the first and the last one. The first three principles relate to the adequate reduction of information quantity and are thus a variation of our integration theme. The *principle of minimalism* suggests that only the information that needs to be communicated be visualized. The *principle of conciseness* stresses simple and regular patterns to convey information. The *principle of adequate format* articulates the insight that simple figures are more easily recognized as belonging together than more complex ones. The *principle of consistency* is closely related to our validation activities that aim to improve the reliability and internal consistency of information. Meyer's consistency principle states that similar information objects should be grouped together in a similar manner. The *principle of closure*, finally, is derived from Gestalt psychology and finds that closed areas are more likely to be perceived as belonging together than those that are open. This principle is specific to visual perception and is therefore not incorporated into our general approach.

⇒ *Most Sets*
Stress Integration
and Validation

Reviewing these examples of operational principles to improve information, we can conclude that all of them stress the adequate reduction or compression of information and its consistent representation. In comparison to the contextualization or activation principles, the principles of integration and validation seem to resurface more often in existing principles. This fact is illustrated visually in the summary diagram below, which lists the main principles discussed so far and categorizes them according to their fit with our approach.

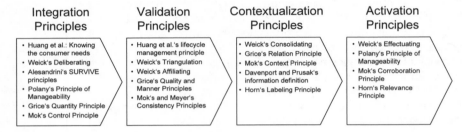

Integration Principles	Validation Principles	Contextualization Principles	Activation Principles
• Huang et al.: Knowing the consumer needs • Weick's Deliberating • Alesandrini's SURVIVE principles • Polany's Principle of Manageability • Grice's Quantity Principle • Mok's Control Principle	• Huang et al.'s lifecycle management principle • Weick's Triangulation • Weick's Affiliating • Grice's Quality and Manner Principles • Mok's and Meyer's Consistency Principles	• Weick's Consolidating • Grice's Relation Principle • Mok's Context Principle • Davenport and Prusak's information definition • Horn's Labeling Principle	• Weick's Effectuating • Polany's Principle of Manageability • Mok's Corroboration Principle • Horn's Relevance Principle

Figure 9: Existing communication principles as background for information quality principles

Rationale of the
Four Principles

The rationale behind these four principles and their sequence is the following one: If a manager is to profit from information, he must first be able to grasp it and see it in its entirety; hence information (or its sources) must be *integrated*. The manager must also be able to trust the information or at least see how reliable it is; hence it must be *validated*. If he can find the information, get an overview on it and trust it, he still has to be able to fully understand it and see whether it fits his (new) context or not. To support this information adaptation process, the information has to be enriched with context (it has to be *contextualized*). Finally – to actually be used by the manager – the information must be provided in a format that facilitates remembering and using it. It has to be *activated* in the mind of the manager by connecting the information with what he already knows or by providing implementation aids that facilitate the application of the information.

There are other relevant principles that are not depicted in this diagram. They will be discussed in the upcoming sections where each of the four main information quality principles is discussed in detail.

Preview

The description of each individual principle follows the same logic: First, a quote illustrates the essence of the principle. Then, the rationale of the principle is outlined, followed by its description and definition. The definition is then applied and numerous examples are provided. As always, each section ends with a conclusion that highlights the main insights associated with each principle.

From the activities encountered in managerial practice and from the principles in existing literature, we were able to gather and categorize various insightful ways of improving information quality. We have labeled them as the integration, validation, contextualization, and activation principles. Every one of these four principles will be described in the subsequent sections.

Conclusion

3.2.5.3 The Integration Principle

Pluralitas non est ponenda sine neccesitate.
(A multitude should not be used without necessity).[49]

WILLIAM OF OCCHAM

One of the most pressing problems which knowledge workers face today is that of information overload which results from the great quantity of information that they have to screen each day (for a survey on empirical evidence of this fact see Eppler 1999). As a consequence of this situation, information must not only be tailored to the needs of information users, it must also be freed from unnecessary elements and the various, dispersed information sources must be made easily accessible in one location (to reduce searching and co-ordination efforts). This is the general premise behind the integration principle.

Introduction:
Occham's Razor

The core idea behind this principle can be traced back to a prominent idea of medieval philosopher WILLIAM OF OCCHAM

---

[49] In the fourteenth century, the Franciscan monk WILLIAM OF OCCHAM coined this sentence, which stresses the value of concise explanations. It has been formulated in similar ways by other philosophers and thinkers including Aristotle, Duns Scotus, and Odo Rigaldus. For an analysis of this principle and its (at times) also negative consequences, see Poundstone, 1988. For further analyses see Flasch, 2000, p.739 or Goldstein, 1999, p. 129.

(1285-1349) who stressed the fact that we need to articulate our ideas in economic ways in order to make our contributions as concise as possible. This idea has become known as Occham's razor (because it cuts away unnecessary complication) or the *principle of parsimony* and it is often used as a methodological imperative, maxim or evaluation criteria when stating laws, descriptions or hypotheses. It suggests that what can be stated in fewer terms and still explain or state the same is of higher quality. To employ this principle in management, we use the term *integration*. This term seems to fit the core idea behind a management principle that aims at improving the conciseness of information without sacrificing its scope or comprehensiveness, and this in a way that is convenient and easily accessible.

Terminological Background

According to Webster's dictionary, the verb integrating means to form, to coordinate, to *blend into a functioning or unified whole*, to unite with something else. It is a synonym of *synthesizing*, blending, *joining systematically*, or unifying and it is closely related to terms such as combining, conjoining, concentrating, *compacting*, consolidating, fusing, merging, organizing, or systematizing. These terms describe the value-adding activities that can be summarized in the integration principle.

Before we define the principle and how it can be applied, we will briefly outline its rationale by referring to similar concepts and ideas.

Key Activity: Content Subtraction

PETER BRADFORD is one of the world's most prominent information designers. He has won over 300 design awards (some of his contributions on information integration can be found in Wurman, 1996, p. 67.) For Bradford, one of the central and most crucial design tasks is that of content subtraction. He writes the following about this activity (*ibid.*):

Content subtraction is a formidable skill; when sensibly compressed and reduced, content becomes a bare skeleton of essential ideas.

To reveal these essential ideas, information must be stripped from unnecessary elements and combined with other items that complement it. This is a highly sophisticated task, especially when performed by information systems and not by experienced individuals. The difficulty of delegating this subtraction process to machines has been pointed out by HERBERT SIMON and by RUSSEL ACKHOFF. Simon has stated one of his design principles as follows: An information-processing subsystem (a computer or new organization unit) will reduce the net demand on the rest of the organization's attention only if it *absorbs* more information previously received by others than it produces – that is, if it listens and thinks more than it speaks.[50] Similarly Russell L. Ackhoff notes the following insight regarding management information systems (MIS) and information reduction:

> My experience indicates that most managers receive much more data (if not information) than they can possibly absorb even if they spend all of their time trying to do so. Hence they already suffer from an information overload. They must spend a great deal of time separating the relevant from the irrelevant and searching for the kernels in the relevant documents.[51]

The Rationale behind the Principle

Unless the information overload to which managers are subjected is *reduced*, any additional information made available by an MIS cannot be expected to be used effectively.

This idea of sensible reduction can also be found in other domains, namely in library science. Below, ROBERT S. TAYLOR outlines his access III idea, which is similar in its central message:

> Access III is a third cut of the information universe in the process of isolating information of use. Its purpose is to provide a summary and/or brief explanation of the content of an item. The function of such processes is to benefit the users *by reducing a large amount of information into a compact item without losing too much information in the process.*[52]

Taylor gives various examples of such information compression processes, such as *abstracting*, providing an *executive summary*, or *maps*, *graphs* and *charts*. We can summarize these activities and ideas in the following principle.

In order to enable information consumers to identify relevant information effectively, information must be integrated, i.e., it must be aggregated and cleansed from unnecessary elements to reveal its most pertinent insights. Dispersed sources of information must be compiled to provide unified access and to provide the information user with a convenient way to identify and access relevant information.

The Integration Principle

Thus, the integration principle states that information has to be provided in a comprehensive and concise, convenient and accessible manner to be of high quality.

---

50   Simon (1971), p. 38.
51   Ackoff 1967, p. B148.
52   Taylor, 1986, p. 60.

*Description of
the Integration
Principle*

The integration principle states that high-quality information has to be condensed or compressed (made comprehensive, concise, convenient, and accessible) in order to give the information consumer an overview before details are presented. An alternative term for this principle would be the aggregation principle.[53] The application of this principle should make it easier to identify relevant and sound information quickly. Means of applying this principle are for example abstracts (content summaries), concise forms of visualization (e.g. maps or diagrams), categorization (e.g., hierarchical content trees), prioritization, or personalization (as in an intranet portal). The main problem that is resolved through this principle is *information overload* (see O'Reilly, 1980, Schick et al., 1990, Eppler, 1998 or Schneider, 1987) or the fact that information is no longer acknowledged but ignored or stored away (and thus looses relevance or impact) when it is fragmented, prolix, inconvenient, or inaccessible.

The case study on getAbstract in chapter four will make it apparent that there are two ways of integrating information, namely micro-integration and macro-integration.

*Two Types of
Integration:*

Single information items can be abstracted and synthesized or a series of related information items or products can be integrated. We refer to the first type as *micro-integration* and call the second one *macro-integration*. What is considered to be one information item depends on the context in which information is used. A single information item may be a definition of a term, a book (or just a chapter), a protocol (or just a part of it), a website (or a segment of it), a report (or just a chapter of it), a newspaper (or just one newspaper article). Related information objects may be books on the same topic, websites by similar companies, reports on the same problem, or product ideas by the same engineer. The main aim of macro-integration is to integrate sources and their main content and context, whereas the goal of micro-integration is to make information from one source more accessible, complete, and especially more concise and convenient. The following diagram shows various possibilities for achieving these goals through specific mechanisms. As

*Micro and Macro
Integration*

---

[53] Aggregated information does not per se lead to a higher decision quality (in terms of accuracy and speed). The empirical findings on the effects of information aggregation on decision quality have been inconclusive (some claiming reduced decision quality because of aggregation, some claiming a higher decision quality). They are compiled in Schick et al., 1990. My conclusion from this fact is that 'aggregation' should not be treated as a black box, but rather viewed as a tool that can be used inadequately or adequately.

the diagram shows, these mechanisms can either be performed automatically (through computer algorithms) or

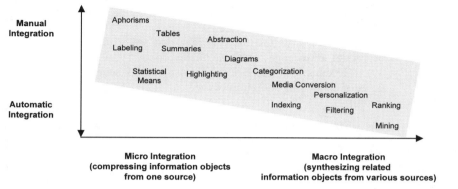

Figure 10: Mechanisms to integrate information

The diagram positions more than a dozen possible integration mechanisms according to their focus (on individual or related information objects) and their most likely form of implementation (either automatic or manual). The shaded, tilted block indicates that integration mechanisms that synthesize a great number of related information objects from many different sources tend to be automatic (because the great complexity can no longer be handled without the help of computers) while the integration of individual information items tends to be manual. These manual and automatic mechanisms can be referred to as *information integrators* which I define as follows:

Application of the Principle

The term information integrator designates any kind of cognitive or automated mechanism that improves the comprehensiveness, conciseness, convenience and accessibility of information by eliminating unnecessary elements, providing an overview, or aggregating information sources.

Definition: Information Integrator

Aphorisms as
Information
Integrators

While I cannot provide a complete list of all possible ways in which information can be integrated, I can provide examples that embody this principle and make it actionable. The following descriptions do not explain the mechanisms in detail, but rather focus on their main idea. Whenever possible references to further information are provided.

KARL WEICK writes that 'the idea that aphorisms could be bearers of knowledge has distinguished roots' (Weick, 1979, p. 39) . He cites FRANCIS BACON, who mentions several advantages of aphorisms and outlines the central benefit of aphorisms (p. 40):

The interesting characteristic of aphorisms is that knowledge is *distilled* rather than deduced, and that it has a developing character much like interpretations in context.

Aphorisms in this sense (like parables or metaphors) are distilled and stimulating knowledge that is reduced to the essence and stated in a poignant way. To formulate an insightful aphorism, a person must not only have extensive experience, but he or she must also have the capacity to sum up this experience in a concise and yet instructive manner. Aphorisms are „*sudden insights*" (Sengle, 1987, p. 4) that are delightful, concise and profound at the same time; in this way they are closely related to proverbs[54], but tend to be more personal. They are convenient in the sense that they are useful in many situations and they are easily accessible (they can be understood without extensive explanations). They are concise – often only one or two sentences long – and comprehensive because they embody a word of wisdom. Two thinkers who have (also) become famous for the aphorisms they formulated or recited are GEORG CHRISTOPH LICHTENBERG and ARTHUR SCHOPENHAUER.[55] Below are given three typical examples of aphorisms (taken from Lichtenberg, 1987) that illustrate their potential to summarize insights:

---

[54]   For an insightful discussion of proverbs and their functions see: Erasmus of Rotterdam (1983) *Adagia*, Berlin: Reclam. In this work of 1500, Erasmus discusses a great variety of famous and lesser known proverbs and reveals their insights and rationale.

[55]   See Lichtenberg (1987) and Schopenhauer (1988). Other thinkers who have used the aphorism format are Blaise Pascal, Friedrich Nietzsche, Ludwig Wittgenstein and Sören Kierkegaard. Nietzsche said the following (in Twilight of the Idols) on this form of expression: "It is my ambition to say in ten sentences what other men say in whole books – what other men do *not* say in whole books."

The most dangerous untruths are truths moderately distorted.

Wisdom's first step is to attack everything. The last one is to live in harmony with everything.

Growth in knowledge that is too fast and achieved without one's own contribution is not very fruitful[...] What you have to invent yourself, leaves in the mind a trail which can be used in other situations.

These aphorisms can be taken out of their original context because they are articulated in a self-sufficient manner. But there is of course also a danger in isolating these insightful statements from their historical context or from the context of the author.[56] Because of their brevity and openness (or as Bacon has called it: their 'developing character') there is a danger of misinterpretation. This may be one of the reasons why their use in management has been quite limited. Nevertheless, one can find a wide variety of management aphorisms in managerial practice and theory. They have the form of corporate proverbs, famous quotes of corporate leaders, or personal management principles. Their systematic and purposeful use is, however, still underdeveloped and their potential to compress knowledge often largely neglected. One company that uses aphorisms heavily in their products is getAbstract (see chapter 4.3). Every book summary that this company produces contains a set of aphorisms taken directly out of the book. Complementary to the review and the written summary, these original quotes embody many of the key thoughts proposed in a book. To close this paragraph on aphorisms as information integrators, we can conclude that they may indeed compress knowledge (e.g., experience, insights, rules) in a stimulating way, but that they require great skill in doing so.

An approach towards integration that is perhaps more compatible with current management practices than aphorisms consists of tables. Tables compress information by categorizing or grouping it according to several dimensions. These dimensions are usually depicted as horizontal *rows* and vertical *columns* that are drawn as lines or simply separated by space. In this way, a table can provide an overview before details on all its elements are presented. Typical examples of such tables are numeric tables, a table of contents, a table of pros and cons (one column listing the advantages, one the disadvantages of a solution), a table of sequential steps (e.g., procedural tables), a table of chronology that lists concurrent events in parallel columns (e.g., schedules), or a table that compares and contrasts various

Tables as Information Integrators

---

[56] For further descriptions of aphorisms, see: Gross, J. (1987) The Oxford Book of Aphorisms, Oxford: Oxford University Press.

options. A table can have the form of a simple list or of a highly structured, multi-dimensional matrix. Tables can be classified, in my view, according to their *content* – whether they contain numbers, text, or pictures –, according to their *format* – simple or nested –, and according to their *use*. As far as the use of tables is concerned, ROBERT E. HORN distinguishes between the following kinds of tables in the management context: tables of content, classification tables, decision tables, parts-function tables, parts tables, (expanded) procedure tables, specified action tables, stage tables, and if-then tables (Horn, 1989, p. 109). When I analyzed the tables used in 32 management reports by Gartner Inc. (see chapter 4.4), by the Giga Information Group (see chapter 4.5), by the Tower Group (an analyst company owned by Reuters), and by the investment and research firm Durlacher Ltd., I found seventeen tables that were used for the following five purposes: First, for *matching* purposes, i.e., visualizing what combinations make sense, as in matching products and sales channels. Second, for *rating* purposes, i.e., ranking options according to certain criteria. Third, in order to *compile and juxtapose pros/cons or strength and weaknesses* of a certain object or strategy. Fourth, to *compare* options or objects according to a set of mutual attributes. Fifth, for mere *listing* purposes, such as listing events chronologically or companies and their descriptions alphabetically, or listing product categories and examples. There were also some tables that combined two of these purposes, such as listing and comparing items in the same table. All of these tables rely on the row/column format to organize and concentrate information. Below I provide a meta-table – a table of tables – that gives an overview on some of the most common uses and forms of tables in the management context as described above.

Table Purpose	Table Content	Table Format	Examples	Generic Structure
1. Matching	*Matches items that should be employed together, such as sales channels and products, or people and tasks, or situations and tools.*	Columns: items Row: items that can complement the items in the columns or should be used together.	Matching products and adequate sales channels, matching people and tasks, matching tools and application situations, matching media and messages, matching target groups and channels, etc.	
2. Listing	*Items that are enumerated and described, such as events, companies, products, actions, services etc.*	Columns: item attributes such as name, size, price, examples, etc. Row: listed items and their names, such as products or options.	Listing the events that took place prior to a merger. Listing the steps to repair a machine. Listing the available products and their characteristics.	
3. Comparing/ Contrasting	*Items that are compared with one another, such as strategies, technolo-gies, compa-nies, people, places, investments, etc.*	Columns: items to be compared to one another Row: attributes by which to compare the items	Comparing technologies, comparing locations, comparing alternative investment opportunities, comparing job candidates etc.	
4. Examining Pros/Cons, Strengths/ Weaknesses	*Items that are evaluated in terms of advantages and disad-vantages, such as strategies, options, products, companies etc.*	Columns: Two columns, one positive and one negative one. Row: the attributes of the object to be evaluated	Evaluating the pros and cons of a merger candidate. Examining the strengths and weaknesses of a technology. Analyzing the reasons for and against a market entry strategy.	
5. Rating	*Items that should be rated according to a set of criteria. Items can be a website, a service, a consumer product, a company's credit risk etc.*	Columns: rating criteria Row: rated items	Rating the quality of websites, rating the health of an industry sector, rating the financial strengths of start-up companies, rating the movies currently playing at your theatre.	
6. Combined Purposes	*All of the above.*	Columns: items or attributes Row: items or attributes	Listing, comparing and rating a set of items in one single table. Another type of combination are if-then tables.	

Table 13: A table of tables from the realm of management

The table summarizes the content and format of the afore-mentioned six types of tables and provides examples from the realm of management.

To close the discussion of this second information integrator, we can conclude that tables are a frequently used information integrator that can provide numerous benefits. Nevertheless, tables can also hurt the legibility and style of a text and they can be difficult to comprehend. Becoming aware of the various types and forms of tables can help to design better tables for use in management.

Labeling as Information Integrator

The key idea behind the next information integrator is to provide informative labels for large chunks of information in order to signal their potential relevance to information consumers before they invest a great amount of time. Labels can be instructive document *headings* or representative book chapter *titles*. They can be the sub-headers of a report that represent the main insights or they can be an e-mail *subject line* that makes clear what has to be done as a result of the content of the message. The crucial quality of a label is its *signal* function. It should not only signal what type of information (e.g., a procedure, a definition, an empirical fact, an order, a conjecture, etc.) is contained in an information object, but also what the reader can expect in terms of content (see Horn, 1989, p. 93 for this point). The art of labeling consists of the skill of choosing adequate proxies for an information object so that the label serves as a *pars pro toto* – a part that stands for the whole.

Summaries as Information Integrators

The most straightforward way of compressing information is to summarize it. As chapter 4.3 discusses this topic extensively, I will only mention it briefly at this point. As an informative label, a good summary knows what to leave out. In the case of an executive summary, this means focusing on the key results of a study and not on its background, motivation, or structure. In the case of an oral presentation, it can mean repeating the main steps that have to be undertaken in light of the gathered evidence. Generally any type of summary will include the main idea contained in an information object and supporting material that complements this main point. A sample template for a summary may be to answer the questions of who says what (to whom), when, where, why, and with what ultimate result or conclusion.

---

[57] There are also software-based automatic summarizers available on the market, such as the solutions of Pertinence, Inxight, Applied Semantics, Lextex, Copernic or Sinope. These summariz-

A good summary should leave out examples, formalities, details, repetitions, minor points, interpretations other than the ones stated, and generally known facts. By eliminating these items, the summary can be considerably shorter than the original information. Additional compression can be achieved by generalizing, finding common elements, or by grouping various pieces of information together.

In the context of scientific information, summaries are often referred to as *abstracts*. An abstract summarizes the contents of an academic article in roughly 200 to 300 words. There are two extremes of abstracts. Informative abstracts are highly condensed versions of the original article and employ the same structure to reveal the central results of an article. Descriptive abstracts do not reveal the results or the key content of an article, but focus instead on the overall topic and its relevance. Descriptive abstracts explicitly discuss the structure of an article while informative ones focus on the main ideas. A scientific abstract usually consists of a (research) context, the main problem(s) discussed in an article, the methodology employed, the main findings, and their implications.[57]

Another 'academic' way of reducing a great amount of data to condensed insights can be found in statistical methods. These can be divided into *descriptive* and *inferential* methods. Both types can be used to aggregate information by eliciting patterns from large data sets. Descriptive methods are used when we analyze a complete data set and inferential methods are used when we only have access to a sample of the entire set. Examples of such methods are (multiple) regressions, cluster, correlation and conjoint analyses, or factor analyses. All of these operations lead to less, but higher order information, revealing new insights or patterns. Through statistical analysis and inference, a large group of registered, codified data can be aggregated into a group, a trend, or a degree of importance.[58]

Highlighting is a much simpler mechanism to give information consumers a reduced view on an information object. This view stresses the most essential elements of a document

Statistical Means as Integrators of Information

Highlighting as Integration

---

ers generate extracts from large texts by applying sophisticated heuristics to identify particularly relevant text items.

[58]   For further insights on the potential of statistical methods to reduce information load and for a sophisticated discussion of 'information statistics' see: Kullbach, S. (1997) *Information Theory and Statistics*, Mineola: Dover Books.

Abstraction as
Information
Integration

by highlighting them visually through colors, larger fonts, underlining, or through flagging icons.[59] By highlighting central elements in a text, a speech, a map, or on a website, crucial information is more rapidly grasped. The attention of the information consumer is focused on the most pertinent part of a document.

A more sophisticated, but also more precarious approach towards information compression is abstraction or the synthesis of information through models and theories. Abstracting information in this sense (and not in the sense of writing summaries) means finding a few general ideas or rules in a plethora of details, occurrences or facts. In doing so, one withdraws from concrete phenomena to what they have in common. This task inevitable involves neglecting minor differences and emphasizing common elements. Because of this, abstraction is a double-edged sword: on the one hand it provides a bigger picture that enables new insights and overviews, on the other side it deletes differences and leads to a less differentiated view of an issue. This tendency towards overgeneralization has been labelled as the problem of induction by KARL POPPER[60] and has been pointed out prominently by (among others) DAVID HUME[61]. But WILLIAM OF OCCHAM already analyzed the risks of abstraction. He stated that abstraction reduces precision. (Goldstein, 1999, p. 123). Our ‚pragmatic'[62] study is not the place to debate the merits and risks of abstraction for the advancement of science.[63] Let it suffice to say that abstraction is a key mechanism to reduce

---

[59] For a detailed description of highlighting see: Kowalski, G. (1997) *Information Retrieval System – Theory and Implementation*, Boston: Kluwer Academic Publishers.

[60] See for example: Popper, K. (1979) *Die beiden Grundprobleme der Erkenntnistheorie*, Tübingen.

[61] For a discussion of Hume's problem of justified generalization see Eisenhardt et al. (1988), p. 57. Another great critique of abstraction was provided by Friedrich Nietzsche who was skeptical about generalizations and abstract concepts since nature does not follow such a logic (see Eisenhardt et al., 1988, p. 56). In this regard, Nietzsche also foreshadowed the anti-representational movement of autopoiesis (constructivist) scholars such as Humberto Maturana or Francisco Varela (see for example Varela, F. (1996) *Invitation aux Sciences Cognitives*, Paris: Seuil, Points Sciences).

[62] As mentioned earlier, I use the term 'pragmatic' in the sense of James and Peirce, stressing that we should make our ideas clear by looking at their practical consequences.

[63] For an in-depth discussion of the role of abstraction for scientific reasoning see Eisenhardt et al. (1988).

information quantity effectively. It is also a mechanism that – when used unreflectively – can lead to wrong results or distorted representations. Consequently, information that is abstracted from original data has to be examined in terms of implicit assumptions and in terms of the neglected details.

One can distinguish three forms of abstraction (according to C.S. PEIRCE, see Minto, 1995, p. 180): *induction, deduction*, and *abduction*. In induction, a great number of real life observations is synthesized to form a conclusion (= the abstraction), such as a rule. In deduction, this conclusion or rule is articulated before the real life observations are made. The observations are then used to see whether the (a priori) abstraction was correct or not. The third type of abstraction, abduction, is the most imaginative one. It requires prior experience in a subject area. Abduction consists of the process of finding and articulating a hypothesis or abstraction that can then be tested deductively.

Modes of Abstraction

These three modes of abstraction contain the same three elements: first, an abstraction (such as rules or general characteristics), second, specific cases or observable facts, and third, the application of the abstract to new cases (using abstract concepts to change or predict specific phenomena). Which mode of abstraction is used depends on the knowledge of the person striving for an abstract representation: if we already have a feasible abstraction (a hypothesis) we can use deductive reasoning to see whether it matches the facts. If we only have a great number of facts, we can observe what they have in common and generate an abstract and hence reduced representation of them (induction). If we successfully describe a case through an abstract concept because of our previous experience (or because of our imagination), we can separate that abstraction from the case and see whether it is also applicable to other cases (abduction). The diagram below visualizes this difference between the three approaches (it is a modification of a diagram used in Minto, 1995, p.181).

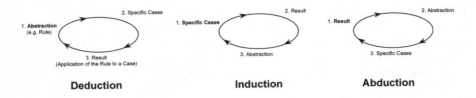

Figure 11: Three modes of abstraction

All of these three modes ultimately (or hopefully) lead to the same end result, namely an adequate (albeit idealized) synthesis of information in the form of abstract rules, theories, descriptions, classifications, principles, formulas, functions, or schemas. In practice, the three models will often be used in combination, one complementing the other.

Categorization as a Means of Integrating Information

Another cognitive mechanism closely related to abstraction, which also reduces the quantity of information – and makes it more accessible – is categorization. Categorization can be seen as a particular form of abstraction (Eisenhardt et al., 1988, p. 96) that focuses on the building of groups of related elements. Hence, it offers similar benefits and risks as abstracting (such as focusing on particular aspects of items for grouping purposes).

In his seminal work on categorization (aptly named: Women, Fire, and Dangerous Things: What Categories Reveal about the Mind), GEORGE LAKOFF states that there is nothing more basic than categorization to our thought, perception, action, and speech (Lakoff, 1987, p. 5). Although we often construct and use categories unconsciously, the attentive and systematic effort of categorizing information hierarchically can reduce its scope and cognitive load and allow for a better overview on a subject area.

In the context of this study we view categorization as the conscious effort to group information items together in a hierarchic manner based on common features[64], family resem-

---

[64]   This is the 'classic' view of categorization. The other elements reflect recent research on categorization that has been pioneered by Eleanor Rosch (see Lakoff, 1987, p. 15). Meyer, 1996, p. 119, argues that there are two ways to categorize: hierarchical and linear. He concedes, however, that linear categorization can only be used for small information sets.

[65]   I have articulated other rules for adequate categorization in Probst et al., 2000, p. 48.

[66]   In his seminal 'Sciences of the Artificial' HERBERT A. SIMON said the following about taxonomies: "An early step toward understanding any set of phenomena is to learn what kinds of

blances, rules, membership gradience, or certain category prototypes (best examples of a group). Such conscious categorizations should meet (as far as possible) the so-called MECE criteria (see Minto, 1995, p.103). MECE is an acronym that stands for mutually exclusive and collectively exhaustive categories. It states that whenever we construct a hierarchy of categories, we should strive to make these categories free of overlaps (i.e., they must be disjunctive or in Lakoff's term non- overlapping, see Lakoff, 1987, p. 287). Furthermore, the categories should fully cover the subject area that they describe when taken together. Otherwise the categorization is incomplete.[65] The result of categorization can be a taxonomy (a structured hierarchy of terms defined by feature bundles). Taxonomies are categorizations that are imposed by a specific purpose, such as providing easier access and storage or improving understanding.[66] Elements in a taxonomy must be distinguished by individual criteria. Typical such categorization criteria are:

- by time (age or chronology),
- by location (or origin)
- alphabetically (categorizing items by their first letter from a to z),
- by (relative) importance or ranking
- by size or scope,
- by information format (e.g., protocols, journal articles, internal reports, presentations, etc.)
- by usage situation (e.g., reference information, templates, archives, etc.), and
- by distinctive or contrasting features (e.g., fictitious versus factual information, operational versus strategic items).[67]

Catagorization Criteria

Although categorization by reference to these or other criteria[68] is primarily a human task, there is now software available that can intelligently generate such categories (visually and in

---

things there are in the set – to develop a taxonomy." See Simon (1981), p. 154.

[67] This list of categorization criteria was compiled based on the insights of Minto (1995) and Wurman (2001).

[68] Aristotle uses the word category to refer to a kind of predicate. In his system, there are ten basic categories: substance, quality, quantity, relation, time, place, position, state, activity, and passivity. See Aristotle (1976), p. 70 and p. 353.

[69] The following examples are taken from Eppler (1998).

[70] See Ewing (1974), p. 108.

[71] See Minto (1995) and Winograd & Flores (1986).

text form) out of large sets of information. Examples of such software applications are Autonomy (www.autonomy.com), Dialog Corporation's Infosort Server (www.dialogue.com), and Aurigin Systems (www.aurigin.com). The first two mine documents and thus generate a system of categories to improve the retrieval of documents, the latter is mostly applied to patent information to screen and group existing patents.

While the categorization criteria above are general and applicable in any domain, there are also pre-defined categories that are tailored to the management context.[69] DAVID E. EWING, former editor of the Harvard Business Review, finds the following in his analysis of management communications:

A surprisingly high percentage of business and professional communications break [sic] down into a *finite list of categories*, despite a nearly infinite range of subject matter. This is because of the emphasis on *analysis, logical differentiation, priorities, evidence, interpretation,* and *recommendation.*[70]

Other researchers have found similar managerial information categories. BARBARA MINTO found six dominant categories (*directives, requests for funds, 'how to' documents, letters of proposal, progress reviews*), while WINOGRAD and FLORES found three dominant category pairs which they labeled 'conversational building blocks' (*request/promise, offer/ acceptance, report/ acknowledgment*).[71] What these categories show is that insightful categories can cut away the clutter in information and enable a manager to see the big picture faster and clearer. The wrong type of categorization (i.e., framing a problem in only one way), on the other hand, can lead to a distorted image of reality and block out possible solutions.

Integration through Visualization: Conceptual Diagrams

One of the most powerful ways of integrating information – making it more concise, comprehensive, convenient, and accessible – is by using images. A picture can summarize a great amount of information in an accessible way. Diagrams are abstract, non-figurative images that convey knowledge by depicting information with its relationships to other pieces of information. Such diagrams offer various advantages, two of which are described in the following quote by EFRAIM FISCHBEIN (cited in May, 1995, p. 303):

Firstly a diagram offers a *synoptic, global representation* of a structure or process and this contributes to the *globality and the immediacy* of understanding. Secondly, a diagram is an ideal tool for bridging the gap between a conceptual interpretation and the practical expression of a certain reality. A diagram is a synthesis between these two apparently opposed types of representations – the symbolic and the iconic. Diagrams are not, generally, the direct image of a certain reality. It is the figural expression of an already elaborated conceptual structure, like any other symbolic system."

The use of such diagrams to create and convey knowledge has also been labeled as *diagrammatic reasoning*. May (1995, p. 300) explains the meaning of this term, which was coined by C.S. PEIRCE:

For PEIRCE, the term diagrammatic reasoning refers to the *construction, manipulation* and *observation* of *(representing objects and their mutual relationships in) diagrams*. Diagrams support the mental models or analogies in the thinking process by *facilitating conclusions and evaluations*.

Gartner, the IT research group, refers to this type of diagrammatic reasoning or information integration as 'strategic visualization' and defines it as follows (Bair, 1998):

Strategic visualization graphically illustrates the *strength of relationships* by the *proximity of objects* on the display. Advanced technology can make a significant difference in users' ability to *interface to large knowledge repositories*. The advances use the distance between objects on the display to reflect the similarity of meaning, similarity of content or other relationships (e.g., association with a group).

The type of strategic visualization discussed in this section typically consists of two levels. The first level represents *individual pieces* of information (such as the terms on the branches of a mind map). The second level provides an overall structure for these pieces in a coherent *framework* (such as the central circle of a mind map and its hierarchy of branches). The elements within such a framework can be distinguished by several features, namely by *size, color, orientation, form,* and *position* (see Bertin, 1973).

Diagrams are thus layered conceptual graphs that visualize either *quantitative* measures or *qualitative* ideas and concepts. In the eye-diagram below, eighteen such diagram types are summarized visually. They are divided into simple ones (on the lower half of the eye) that contain few elements and few interactions among these elements, and complex ones (on the upper half of the eye) that can contain many elements with numerous connections among them. Diagrams on the left hand side are especially suited to represent quantitative information, whereas diagrams on the right hand side can be used to visualize ideas, concepts or qualitative models.

Examples of Diagrams

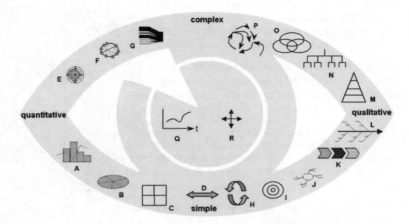

Figure 12: A diagram of diagrams for the realm of management

Diagrams in Detail   The eighteen diagrams contained in the figure above are briefly explained in the table below. The following list does not include all feasible diagrams that can be used to compress information. It does, however, list some of the most frequently used ones, as well as references where they are explained in more detail.

Letter in Figure	Diagram Name	Typical Purpose	References
A	Bar and Line Chart	Compare quantities	Meyer 1996
B	Pie Chart	Show division of a whole	Meyer 1996
C	Matrix/Portfolio Chart	Position and fill in elements according to their characteristics	Bertin 1973
D	Spectrum	Show the options between two extremes	Wahren 1996, Meyer 1996, Eppler 1999c
E	Spider Web Chart/Radar Chart	Evaluate according to multiple criteria	Meyer 1996
F	Synergy Map	Show interdependencies or flows between elements	Bertin, 1973, Eppler 1999c
G	Sankey Diagram	Show origins or division of a whole (e.g. income)	Meyer 1996

Letter in Figure	Diagram Name	Typical Purpose	References
H	Cycle	Show the sequence of reoccurring phases or steps	Wurman 1996
I	Concentric Circles/Spheres	Show the layers of an item	Wurman 1996
J	Mind Map	Visually assemble related ideas & concepts	Buzan & Buzan 1997
K	Process Chart	Show a sequence of steps	Galloway 1994
L	Fishbone Chart	Show the contributing factors of a problem	Evans/Lindsay 1999
M	Pyramid	Show the hierarchy of concepts	Eppler 1999c
N	Tree Diagram	Show the elements of a complex whole	Minto 1995, Mok 1996
O	Venn Diagram	Show the elements of overlapping groups	Meyer 1996, Mok 1996
P	Network Diagram/System Diagram	Show the dynamics of a complex system	Probst & Gomez 1989, O'Connor & McDermott 1997
Q	Time line/Time series	Show a development over time	Eppler 1999c
R	Coordinate System/Cartesian coordinates	Position items according to various criteria	Bertin 1973

Table 14: Diagram descriptions

As mentioned earlier, the above table can summarize only a few of the diagram types that exist. Other, more sophisticated diagrams could be added to this list, such as entity-relationship diagrams (Laudon & Laudon, 2000, p. 242), flowcharts (Eppler, 1999c), distribution charts (Meyer, 1996, p.193), Allen Novak's Concept Maps (see for example Mok 1996), Toulmin Argumentation Maps (see for example Huff, 1990), Lenk's Z diagrams (see Wurman 1996), Gray Scale Charts and Chernoff Faces (see Meyer 1996, pp. 46-51), as well as graphic conceptual frameworks such as Stafford Beer's Viable System Model (see for example Mok 1996, p. 20), Michael Porter's Value Chain model or his visual Five Forces model for market analysis, etc. All of them enable us

Other Diagram Types

Media Conversion

to aggregate a great amount of information in a systematic way so that the patterns inherent in information become visible.[72]

Compressing information can also be achieved by converting content from one medium to another, as in turning a book into a film, a report into an oral presentation, a speech into a written abstract, or a table into an interactive simulation. By using media with higher richness (e.g., channel bandwidth) or greater density, more information can be communicated in less time. This conversion process requires an adaptation of the content to the new medium and can thus not be fully automated. Low quality e-learning applications illustrate this point: When written training material is simply put online or enhanced with multimedia components, the resulting computer based training is usually neither interesting nor truly instructive. The caveat with regard to this information integrator is thus echoing MARSHALL MCLUHAN's famed credo: consider the medium as part of the message and adapt content adequately when changing it from one medium to another in order to save time or increase clarity or convenience.

Indexing as Integration

Another mechanism that is primarily aimed at making information more accessible and convenient is the index. An index is an alphabetical list of key terms and key people or institutions that are mentioned in a document, whether a book, a magazine, a newspaper, or a website. The index summarizes the page numbers on which a particular term is mentioned (or provides a direct link to the term in the case of a site map index). Although the index is a classic device to make information more accessible, new forms can be envisioned, such as a thumbnail index (an index of figures that displays them in a stamp-size format) or a visual index that shows correlations among the cited terms and key figures.

Filtering as an Integration Strategy

A slightly more complex integration mechanism is filtering. The objective of filtering is to shed out irrelevant information so that the information consumer only has to focus on the information items that are relevant to his or her needs. As shown in the diagram below, we differentiate between *cognitive* filtering, *automatic* filtering, and *collaborative* filtering which combines the cognitive filtering of various people through automated mechanisms.

---

[72] For an in-depth discussion of the quality of diagrams and pictures see Doelker (1997). For quality criteria of images in the context of annual reports see Fulkerson (2001). Most of these diagram types are included in the interactive knowledge visualization suites called let's focus (see www.lets-focus.com).

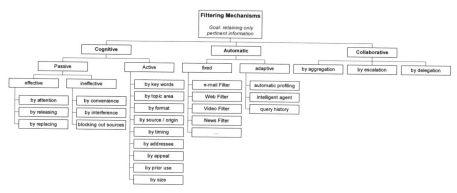

Figure 13: Filtering strategies in overview

Figure 13 lists various strategies to filter out irrelevant information.[73] Personal, *cognitive* filtering strategies can be either used *actively* or they can be employed *passively* without even noticing them. The former ones can operate by filtering out irrelevant information based on key words, topic areas, the format (e.g. e-mail versus letters), the sender or source, the time of arrival or the information's urgency, its addressees, its initial appeal or prior usage experience, or simply by the size or scope of the information. The latter ones can be divided into effective passive filtering strategies, and ineffective ones. *Ineffective* ones try to filter out information that is cumbersome (by convenience), that contradicts already acknowledged information (by interference) or by simply not looking at the information sources anymore (by blocking them). (Mostly) *effective* passive filtering strategies are based on our limited attention and on our ability to release or replace information once it has lost its value.

As far as *automatic* filtering mechanisms are concerned I distinguish between fixed mechanisms and adaptive ones. Filters that are fixed tend to be media specific. E-mail filters for example (as used by Microsoft outlook or Lotus Notes) are based on simple rules or key words to block or eliminate incoming information. Other examples of such filters are web filters (such as Siemens' own Webwasher that filters out banner advertisement on the Internet), or news filters (such as Yahoo's my.yahoo.com service). *Adaptive* automatic filters are still in their early development stage and not as sophisticated as cognitive or collaborative filtering mechanisms.

---

[73] For an extensive discussion of personal information filtering strategies see Meyer, 1996, pp. 99-106.

Most of them are based on automatic profiling, i.e., recording an information consumer's usage patterns and applying them to devise adequate filtering schemes. Intelligent agents can be more sophisticated automatic filters as they continuously learn from the behaviour of an information consumer and actively reach out for new, possibly relevant information. The degree of interaction between the filter and the information consumer is usually higher than in the case of a simple filtering profile or a query history. A query history simply uses the already made filtering requests to adapt the future information triage to the information consumer's needs.

Finally, *collaborative* filtering is, in my opinion, the most sophisticated filtering mechanism. Here, I distinguish between three principal forms of filtering, namely by escalation, by delegation, and by aggregation. Filtering by escalation is already implemented in various groupware applications. It is based on the premise that if many people select a certain document and rate it as relevant, then this document may be also be pertinent to other information consumers with similar (stored) interest profiles. Consequently, the information is also sent to them. The escalation filter uses a mix of social and technical mechanisms to screen and forward information. Filtering by delegation can also be seen as a mix of technical and social mechanisms, although the social dimension clearly dominates. This filter consists of simply delegating one's filtering needs to another person, such as a secretary or a personal assistant. This can be done without IT-support. The critical task in filtering by delegation is whether one can convey one's sense of relevance to another person or not. Collaborative filtering by aggregation is similar to the escalation mechanism. Unlike escalation, where the collective *rating* of a piece of information determines its filtering 'destiny', filtering by aggregation simply deletes information that is not used frequently or not used at all by other information consumers. This type of filtering mechanism also eliminates redundant information, hence the term aggregation filter.

Personalization

The next three integration mechanisms are only going to be described briefly since similar mechanisms have already been discussed and many examples of their application already exist. They are *personalization*, *ranking* and *mining*.

Personalization is a mechanism that reduces information to the needs of the information user based on a once-defined (and continuously refined) profile. It is closely related to profile-based filtering, as discussed above. Typical examples of personalization devices are Internet portals. They aggregate information sources, references, news items, and software applications (like calendars, e-mail or instant messaging) in one screen that is adapted to the information consumer's needs, habits, and preferences. But personalization can also go further than mere aggregating, filtering or customizing (e.g., adapting the layout or arrangement of information).[74] Sophisticated personalization mechanisms can be imagined, which would adapt information to the cognitive and situational preferences of information consumers. In this way, visual types could access information in the form of diagrams or presentations, whereas as auditive types could be able to listen to them.

The next mechanism to make information accessible is ranking. With the term ranking, we refer to the attribution of degrees of importance to information or the classification of information according to quality, relevance, popularity, urgency or priority indicators. This makes it possible to queue information and sequence it more effectively. Typical examples of such ranking mechanisms are hit lists, frequently asked questions (FAQs) or citation indices.

Ranking

A method of integrating information that relies purely on automated processes is mining. Mining is not only a metaphor that describes how information 'nuggets' buried in data mines are brought out to light, but also a detailed method used by large firms to sort and analyze information, to better understand their customers, products, markets, or any other phase of their business for which data has been captured (Jessup & Valachich, 1999, p. 2-106). Data mining tools (such as MIS Alea) enable analysts to graphically drill down from summary data to more detailed data, sort or extract data based on certain (filtering) conditions, and perform a variety of statistical analyses, such as trend analysis, correlation

Mining

---

[74] Gartner distinguishes between personalization and customization technologies, as illustrated by the following quote (Fleming, Phifer, 1998): "At the *administrative* level, it is useful to *structure content* so that the appropriate information can be delivered to the appropriate users. Managed in this fashion, content makes use of *personalization technologies*. At the user level, being able to subscribe to information that is relevant is important. When users can control their own access to appropriate information, they use *customization technologies*. While both sets of functionalities fall under the term "*content personalization*," managing content effectively on an intranet requires implementing functionality for both the administrative and user levels." Leading vendors in this area are, according to Gartner, Broadvision and Vignette.

analysis, forecasting, and analysis of variance (*ibid.*). Data mining in this sense also relies on online analytical processing (OLAP) tools that enable analysts to view information from various perspectives and combine it in manifold ways. Data mining, however, cannot be applied to just any set of information. For data mining to be effective, a basic infrastructure of specialized databases has to be in place. These specialized databases are called data warehouses or data marts. Without this crucial infrastructure, integrating information through mining is a difficult, if not impossible task. Data warehouses in their own right represent an information integration strategy, as Jessup and Valacich (1999, p. 2-107) write below:

> Data warehouses represent more than just big databases. An organization that successfully deploys a data warehouse has committed to pulling together, *integrating*, and sharing critical corporate data throughout the firm.

Examples of such warehouses for knowledge-intensive processes are scanner data repositories for promotion planning, client data pools for the customer relationship management process, or inventory databases for procurement planning.

Other Integration Mechanisms

We have now surveyed more than a dozen of the most widely applicable mechanisms that exist to integrate information. Although they seem quite different from one another (take, for example, aphorisms and mining algorithms), all of them have one thing in common: *they make it easier to identify relevant information quickly.* Many other tools exist which can achieve the same objective. One could mention speedreading techniques, expert systems, intelligent agents, ghostreaders, information brokers, clipping services[75], visual bibliographies and others (see Eppler 1998). The main aim of this chapter, however, was to propose a strong principle and show that there is a variety of ways in which this principle can be applied.

---

[75] An example of a media clipping service that goes beyond aggregating media information, and provides in-depth analysis of media reporting is www.mediatenor.com.

The integration principle suggests that information producers and managers should strive to compress information consistently, to make it more concise and thus more easily accessible. It states that dispersed information sources should be integrated in one location.

Examples of mechanisms that help to apply this principle are aphorisms, summaries, tables, categorization, and various forms of visualization, personalization, ranking, or mining.

Conclusion

3.2.5.4 The Validation Principle

Validity is enhanced when the system provides signals about the degree to which data or information presented to users can be judged as sound.[76]

ROBERT S. TAYLOR

One effect that takes place when managers suffer from information overload is that they become overly confident in their *judgment* (see O'Reilly, 1980, p. 687) and tend to be more credulous towards new information than they would normally be (Shenk, 1997, p. 152). Because of these psychological mechanisms, it is essential for the effectiveness of information-rich, knowledge-intensive business processes that the *validity* of information is assured or at least made visible to decision makers. How this can be achieved is explored below.

Introduction

Validity is a term that – according to Webster's dictionary – is a synonym for soundness or cogency. It is derived from the Latin term *validus*, meaning 'strong'. It refers to the quality of being logically sound (or strong) or, outside the domain of logic, effective in its consequences. A set of information (such as a method) is valid if it is well grounded, internally consistent, and if it produces the desired results. Validity of information is thus threefold: it refers to the creation of information (whether it is well grounded or not), its relationship to itself (consistent or self-contradictory), and its consequences (effective or not).[77] These three aspects of validity are illustrated in the figure below.

Terminological Background

---

[76] Taylor, 1986, p. 64.
[77] Validity also has a legal sense which we neglect here, namely that quality of a claim which renders it supportable in law. Next to the legal sense, there is also a scientific one, where we can distinguish between *internal* (e.g., correct cause-effect analy-

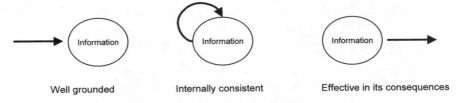

| Well grounded | Internally consistent | Effective in its consequences |

Figure 14: Three main aspects of information validity

Key Activities:
Evaluating &
Checking

In light of the above distinction, a proposition can said to be valid if it is correctly inferred or deduced from a premise, if it does not contradict itself, and if is effective in its (real life) consequences.[78] The term valid can consequently be applied to a variety of information types, such as assertions, arguments, conclusions, reasons, or even to entire intellectual processes (such as the validity of a due diligence analysis).

In order to find out more about the validity of a conclusion, a fact or a method, one has to evaluate it. The key activities that can be described as validating are thus assessing, analyzing, scrutinizing, confirming, auditing, (double-) checking, substantiating, or authenticating. Typical questions that are asked in these activities are:

- Are you sure?
- How do you know that?
- Where's the evidence for that claim?
- What are the assumptions behind this?
- Does it make sense?
- How did that information come about?
- Will we get it soon enough?
- Is the information secure?
- What happens if this information is wrong?
- How credible is the source?
- Can others confirm this?
- Have there been comparable results elswhere?

---

ses) and *external* validity (e.g., correct generalizations), as well as *construct* or face validity (i.e., if the theoretical variables have been operationalized correctly). Related concepts are those of *predictive validity* and *concurrent validity*. See, for example Yin, 1994, p. 33 or Iselin, 1988, p. 157.

[78] This last element (practical consequences) is again a result of the pragmatic view point taken in this study. Still, the dictionary definition of validity also stresses the effectiveness of something valid and gives the example of a valid method.

All of these questions aim at eliciting the degree of validity that is inherent in a set of information, whether it is the information itself, its source, its infrastructure and delivery process, or its consequences. Because this is not an easy task, the principle that is described below provides more specific instructions than the general questions listed above.

Based on these considerations, we define information validity as the characteristic of information to be accurate and consistent, and to be delivered in a timely manner on a secure infrastructure. The rationale behind this principle is thus a more systematic evaluation of the *accuracy, consistency, timeliness* and *security* of a piece or set of information. This seems a reasonable approach towards information validity as others define it in similar terms. CLYDE W. HOLSAPPLE and ANDREW B. WINSTON define validity as the accuracy, certainty, and consistency of some body of knowledge.[79] To operationalize these criteria, two major tasks must be performed: information and its sources must be checked and indicators of their validity must be provided. Below we summarize this reasoning in the validation principle.

The Rationale behind the Principle

> In order to enable information consumers to evaluate information effectively, it must be validated, i.e., it must be checked for accuracy, consistency, timeliness and security. Indicators of a piece of information's validity must be provided with the information to facilitate this task.

The Validation Principle

The validation principle states that high-quality information has to be validated (in terms of correctness, consistency, timeliness, and security) in order to present only justified information to the information consumer. It also states that the validation mechanisms that are behind a piece of information should be made visible. Means of applying this principle are consistency checks on the information itself, comparisons with other sources, an analysis of the primary source of the information (its reputation and competence), and a rating mechanism (based on a rating scale) that makes the degree of validation of the information visible (and gives information consumers the chance to provide feedback on the perceived quality of the information). These mechanisms are described in more detail below. The main information quality problem that is resolved through this principle is, as pointed out in the

Description of the Validation Principle

---

[79] For an online version of their glossary see: http://www.uky. edu/BusinessEconomics/dssakba/dssbook/glossary.htm [15.9.01]

Source & Content Validation

introduction to this principle, *misjudgment* of (incorrect, inconsistent, late, or manipulated) information.

As shown in Figure 15, validating activities examine two distinct objects: the information itself and its source(s). We designate mechanisms that evaluate or improve either the source or the information (or both) as information validators and define the term as follows:

Definition: Information Validator

> The term *information validator* designates any kind of mechanism that provides assistance in improving or evaluating the accuracy, consistency, timeliness, or security of information and thus improves the knowledge about the validity of a piece of information.

Application of the Validation Principle

Several examples of such information validators are provided below. They are summarized in the next diagram and are briefly described in the subsequent paragraphs. The diagram shows that we again distinguish between manual processes and automated ones that can be performed with the help of computers.

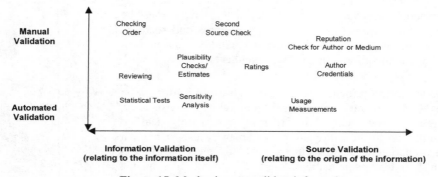

Figure 15: Mechanisms to validate information

Manual and Automated Validation

First, we are going to look more closely at validation mechanisms that work without the help of computers, such as order checking, an analysis of an author's credentials or second source checks. Then, we are going to examine mechanisms that rely at least partially on the help of computers, such as statistical tests, sensitivity analyses or user ratings.

Checking Order as Validation Mechanism

A very simple and yet effective heuristic to evaluate the consistency of information is to look at its structure or at the order that ideas or facts have been given. BARBARA MINTO writes the following on this validation mechanism in her seminal work on logical thinking and writing (Minto, 1995, p. 119):

The point I wish to reiterate is that you cannot tell that nonsense is being written unless you first impose a structure on it. It is the imposition of the structure that permits you to see flaws and omissions. [...] *Checking order is a key means of checking the validity of a grouping.*

According to Minto, the logical ordering of information is a prime signal of its validity. In her view, any grouping of inductive ideas (e.g., ideas that together lead to a conclusion) should come from one source or relate to one concept, such as one process (where the information is ordered chronologically), a structure (where information is organized hierarchically), or a class (where information is ordered according to its ranking). Several symptoms can indicate lacking validity in terms of ordering. The following three questions can give a first indication of the validity of a group of supposedly related pieces of information and they can provide helpful hints on how the validity of a grouping can be improved:

- Do the elements in a group of information have something in common? If their common characteristic is not easily apparent, then the grouping (the organization of information) is probably not valid. The validity check question is: what do all the pieces of information in a group share? What is the same about them? This can be applied to taxonomies, hierarchical concepts, simple bullet point listings etc.
- Are the elements within a group all referring to the same level of abstraction? If very specific items are mixed with rather abstract information, then the grouping is most likely not valid.
- Are there information items that reoccur in several groups? In other words, are there redundancies in the groups of information? If so, then the ordering of ideas or facts is probably not valid.[80]

---

[80] Information redundancy is of course not always a sign of flawed logic. In fact, it can sometimes improve our understanding of ideas or concepts. Also in this study, one can find mechanisms that are grouped under more than one principle (such as the MECE criterion which is used here and in the integration principle). This 'fruitful redundancy' should be distinguished from 'sloppy groupings' that do not foster understanding.

These qualities are reminiscent of the MECE criterion introduced earlier (see the integration principle), referring to a mutually exclusive and collective exhaustive categorization. Here, however, we look at existing information, such as a directory or a table of contents, to find redundancies or inconsistencies as indicators of possible flaws or errors.[81]

Reviewing

One of the most effective validating mechanisms for 'intellectual' or academic information is reviewing. Reviewing is the systematic evaluation of information by various, independent, qualified people. There are several forms of reviewing. One of the most frequently employed review mechanism within academia is the *double blind review* process where typically two to three reviewers evaluate an academic contribution (such as a paper) without knowing (supposedly) by whom it is written. The author of the paper in return does not know who has evaluated his or her paper. He or she only receives the comments of the reviewers which should make the paper clearer and generally of a higher quality. Next to this 'classic' method of reviewing many other forms exist. Typical review formats are through a review board, through the readers themselves[82] (through rating and comment sections), through experts that aggregate their opinions in various rounds (so-called Delphi groups), or through other authors[83] who cite existing work and thus make it more credible and established. The most basic form of reviewing is often referred to as the four eyes principle, stating that any information that has been produced should at least by checked by four eyes, meaning two people.

---

[81] Another way of checking the order and validity of a piece of reasoned information is by applying argumentation schemes or argumentation rules. Such argumentative techniques to evaluate the validity of information are described in: Frans H. van Eemeren, Rob Grootendorst A Systematic Theory of Argumentation. The pragma-dialectical approach. Cambridge University Press, 2003.

[82] For a very effective form of such a 'collaborative reviewing' see for example: www.slashdot.org or www.wikipedia.org.

[83] For a particular, practical, form of this review mechanism see the Giga case study in chapter four.

[84] For a particularly comprehensive review criteria list see: the Procedures for Reviewing Papers for the Annals of Biomedical Engineering:
http://nsr.bioeng.washington.edu/ABME/rev.html. This checklist provides a generic and yet specific and instructive set of criteria which can be used to evaluate contributions critically (especially in regard to the quality of the writing).

An essential prerequisite for a functioning review process is a common set of review criteria that all reviewers understand and apply in the same way. Without such common criteria, the reviewing of 'intellectual information' (information that describes the how and why of complex phenomena) will tend to depend on personal preferences rather than universal standards and will thus become somewhat arbitrary. Benchmarks in the area of criteria-based reviewing are medical journals which often include elaborated lists of criteria by which a paper should be evaluated (for examples see: Baker and Fraser, 1995 or Lionel and Herxheimer 1970). Such criteria typically include scientific standards (such as a detailed description of the used methodology), as well as general standards of good writing (clear language, logical structure etc.).[84]

Reviewing is not, however, a validation mechanism that is only used within academia. Below are two examples from large organizations that use reviewing for the quality control of their internal knowledge bases. Both are taken from a Gartner report by Harris and Flemming (1998):

Examples of Review Processes

Wyeth-Ayerst Knowledge Validation Process: To qualify for inclusion in the knowledge base, a nominated sales practice must have been in use with *documented results*, must represent a common opportunity with *broad applicability*, and must be *current* and *relevant*. Information is captured through a personal interview conducted by a KM team member and must be *validated and approved by the executive staff within sales*. Philosophies and support structures in place to maintain the knowledge content include: 1 *Judgment processes to evaluate, tailor and approve original submissions*. 2. Maintenance processes to update or discard existing content. 3. Subject area *expert* processes providing part-time manpower to *judge* content for inclusion.

World Bank: The entries in the knowledge base are given further weight by including the source's name, how to reach him or her, an automatic expiration date for the entry (which *mandates a review* and *revalidation* to be kept) and the presence of a *second opinion* to provide additional perspective.

The scope of such a review mechanism should be designed to fit the information's potential impact (its criticality) and its urgency (for this point see also Muenzenmayer, 1999). Information that can have a great impact (such as prices or contract conditions), but that is perhaps not very frequently modified, should undergo a more extensive review process than information that is of low criticality and of high urgency (such as the daily cafeteria menu plan in a corporate intranet).

Plausibility Checks
& Rough Estimates

While review processes such as the ones described above rely heavily on other people, the next mechanism can often be performed individually. The information is simply validated with a rough analysis in regard to its plausibility and accuracy. The two key questions of this (common sense-) mechanism are the following ones: Based on my prior experience, can this information be accurate? Using another method, would I come up with the same information?

A more sophisticated version of this mechanism is used in consulting: In order to validate a prediction or an estimation, other methods are used to generate the same kind of prediction. In this way, the results can be cross-validated or their possible range can be determined. Another similar validation mechanism often used in consulting is checking the plausibility of information by looking at its consequences. The key question here is the following: If this information is correct, what would have to follow in light of this evidence (and are those consequences plausible)? While these validation mechanisms are primarily thought experiments, they can sometimes be supported through computer simulations (e.g., through Excel calculation spreadsheets), especially if the information to be validated is numeric or quantitative.

Second Source
Checks

Another direct and simple way of validating a piece of information is to see whether other sources confirm the information and to analyze what reasons other sources give for information that differs. One specific method of implementing this mechanism can be found in the Giga case study in chapter four, where every document includes an *alternative opinion* than the one expressed by the Giga analysts. Reasons for alternative opinions are stated and related to the Giga position.

Ratings

The mechanisms that can be labeled as 'rating' try to make explicit how readers view a particular piece of information or a particular source of information based on a common set of criteria. Whereas reviewing usually improves the quality of information or impedes it from being distributed, rating is the mere signaling of the perceived quality by information consumers. Examples of such rating mechanisms can be found in magazines (through letters to the editor), on the Internet (e.g., Amazon's „did you find this review useful?" question) or on corporate intranets and knowledge bases where peers indicate whether the contribution of a colleague has been useful for them or not. Below, we provide an example of a particular rating schema used in criminal investigations. This particular rating schema[85] applies to both, the information and its source, since they both influence the validity of a claim.

→ Information ↓ Source	1 Certain	2 observed by the source	3 Heard and confirmed	4 Heard but not con-firmed
A reliable	A1: The police officer himself has observed and reported an event.			
B mostly reliable				
C not reliable		C2: An unreliable contact person has directly seen and reported an event.		
X Impossible to judge				X4:An anonymous caller left a message on what she heard about an event.

Figure 16: The information validation schema used by international crime investigators

This rating schema is similar to the probabilities used by the IT-analysts at Gartner Inc. where probability values indicate the certitude of a prognostic statement. Gartner's validation schema is reproduced in the case study in chapter four. The categories of this particular framework should be interpreted as follows:

A   = indicates a very reliable source, such as a police officer who is an eyewitness of a reported event.

B   = indicates a reliable source, such as a police officer of a neighbouring state.

C   = indicates a moderately reliable source, such as an elderly bystander.

X   = indicates that the source is most likely not reliable or that no reliability rating of the source of the information is available. An example may be a partner-in-crime of a criminal.

1   = indicates sound information that has been gathered first hand.

2   = indicates probably correct information that has been directly reported.

3   = indicates possibly correct information that has been commu nicated indirectly.

---

[85]   The rating schema is based on an interview with an agent of the Swiss federal police.

4   = indicates insecure information for which validity cannot be guaranteed.

(5) = indicates improbable information which is believed to be false or implausible.

(6) = indicates that the information cannot be assessed

Example: A1 = sound information (first hand experience) from a reliable source (a police officer)
Criteria limit: B2 is still judged to be valid information.

This rating schema gives international crime investigators a universal code by which they can indicate the validity level of a statement or report. In this way, they condense their evaluation of information into one concise formula. A similar but by far less complicated formula is used by book reviewers, as described in the next paragraph.

Example: Book and Article Ratings

Another way of validating information consists of having qualified journalists or writers produce abstracts of books or articles who also evaluate material according to a list of given criteria. As the getAbstract case study in section four will show, such ratings can be an informative tool for managers. Book abstract services usually rate business books on a scale of one to ten according to criteria such as applicability, innovation, style, comprehensibility, and structure. There are also online magazine databases that have begun to offer ratings. EBSCO host, for example, rates articles based on the following criteria: research, practice, original, readable.

Rating the Medium

The service that book abstract companies provide as a 'side-effect' (their prime value-added activity being the summarizing of books) can itself be a legitimate product that can be extended to other media. In a survey on information quality on the Internet we asked over 670 Internet users what could be done to improve the quality of information on the Internet. 39.8 percent of all respondents indicated that an *online content rating agency* would contribute significantly to a higher quality of information on the Internet. Such online rating agencies could be for content what Standard & Poor or Moody's (the credit risk information companies) are for financial markets, namely a sound and neutral opinion on the quality of an institution.

Reputation Check

The result of (high) ratings is reputation. But ratings are not always easily available. The reputation of a source can be evaluated with other means, such as opinion portals, see for example www.keen.com, online newsgroups (it is possible to search for these through www.deja.com or www.google.com), or through citation databases (such as the one on information technology literature hosted by the NEC Corporation or the database hosted by the Institute for Scientific Information - ISI). Other means of evaluating the reputation of a source are Delphi questionnaires, where experts are asked about their opinion on selected information sources, or the membership of a source in a reputed association or club. This can also be a mechanism to evaluate the credentials of an author. This point is elaborated in the next paragraph.

The credentials of an author or information producers can be used as an indicator of the validity of the information that he or she provides. Credentials are institutional affiliations, prior experience or education in a domain, memberships in selective professional associations, awards or other recognitions, prior publications, prior critique addressed to them, official positions held, etc. All of these indicators can be used to evaluate whether an author is reliable or not.

Author Credentials

I have now described several mechanisms that rely moderately or not at all on the help of computers. The next few validation mechanisms are difficult to imagine without the help of computers. They are statistical tests, sensitivity analyses, and usage measurements.

Besides the above mentioned more qualitative heuristics, there is a whole variety of quantitative, statistical tests that can be used to evaluate the validity of hypotheses, the normality of distributions, or the general characteristics of data sets. This is not the place to discuss tests such as McNemar's Test, the Wilcoxon Test, or simple Sign Tests. Nevertheless, these sophisticated analysis and evaluation tools should not be neglected when discussing issues relating to validity.

Statistical Tests

Another mechanism that can be used quantitatively is sensitivity analysis. The key questions to be asked in this type of analysis (for the context of information evaluation) are the following ones: How much will this information affect our overall result (or our performance) if it is wrong/inaccurate/missing/manipulated? How carefully should we thus be in using or evaluating this information?

Sensitivity Analysis

The reasoning behind these two questions is that the validity of a piece of information is especially crucial when this information has a great impact on our actions. A procedure to determine the sensitivity or the potential impact of (wrong) information is sensitivity analysis and simulation. If a small change in the information results in relatively large changes in the outcomes or consequences, then the outcomes are said to be sensitive to that information. This may mean that the information has to be determined very accurately or that the use of the information has to be redesigned for lower sensitivity (or for greater robustness).[86]

This kind of reasoning can be implemented with the help of (numerical) models and it can be applied to such models. According to Professor HOSSEIN ARSHAM, sensitivity analysis is the study of how the variation in the output of a *model* (numerical or otherwise) can be apportioned, qualitatively or quantitatively, to different sources of variation.[87] This analysis can be performed in a rough, qualitative manner (through estimations) or through rigorous, numerical what-if analysis with tools such as Microsoft Excel.

Usage Measurements

Another informative although crude quantitative mechanism to collect indicators of information validity is usage measurement. Usage measurement tools automatically register how many times a document has been accessed or downloaded and by whom (for example in the Internet context)[88]. While these measures do not give any guarantee of validity, they can signal highly relevant or highly acclaimed content items. Usage measurements that reveal top downloads or the most read articles can also be combined with rankings in order to see whether the information that is most frequently accessed is also the one with the highest rating.

Other Validation Mechanisms

In this section, we have only touched upon the many forms that exist to validate information. Many more mechanisms could be mentioned, such as *forced validation* where information is only registered if it meets a pre-defined, rigid standard. This validation mechanism is often used in online forms where the user is required to enter information in a standardized format; or the use of *cross sums* (cross totals of digits) of numbers to confirm their accuracy. There is also a great variety of *software* available that can be used for validation purposes: tools that check the accuracy of numbers, the consis-

---

[86]   For a similar explanation of sensitivity analysis see:
      http://pespmc1.vub.ac.be/ASC/SENSIT_ANALY.html.
      [10.11.01]

[87]   See: http://ubmail.ubalt.edu/~harsham/senanaly/SenAnaly.htm
      [20.11.01]

[88]   Software tools that measure such traffic or information demand in the context of the Internet can be found at the following sites:
      www.websuxess.com, www.segue.com, www.webtrends.com, www.ebSure.com, www.netgen.com. Some of these tools can also locate format inconsistencies or tagging or code and spelling errors.

tency of layout conventions, the timeliness of information provision processes, or the security of an information server or a communication line. The most powerful validation tool, however, may still be our ability to reflect critically on new information, to look at its background and its assumptions, its possible distortions or omissions, and to think about its consequences. In this way, we can prevent the negligent misjudgment of new information, even when we are under heavy information load.

To summarize some of the mechanisms provided above, I have put them into a simple sequence, resulting in a five step validation procedure that can be used to evaluate information quickly. Five steps for quick information validation:[89]

Quick Validation

1. Examine the *purpose* of the information: Is the purpose of a text, document, website, manual etc. to instruct, to promote, to advocate, to predict, to speculate, to defend, or to refer? Is that purpose clearly signaled or is there a hidden agenda to be expected? Does the information always relate to that purpose?
2. Look at the *author*'s credentials and possible interests: Is the author (or are the authors) knowledgeable and reputed in the domain? What is their relationship to the topic? What is his or her background? Can the author easily be contacted?
3. Look at the *medium* or the environment of the information: Is there a review or control mechanism for the information? Are there restrictions and standards for information producers in that medium? Who is responsible for the medium (the journal, the website, the book, the report, the database)? Is the medium secure and is it delivering information in a timely manner?
4. Look at the *information* itself: is it
    a) current and up-to-date (versus not dated or outdated),
    b) free of apparent contradictions, argumentative fallacies, or errors,
    c) well-balanced (versus only discussing one side of an issue),
    d) well-referenced (e.g., are sources listed),
    e) well-presented (language, structure, layout etc.).

---

[89] For comparable validation procedures (particularly tailored to the Internet context) see for example: www.esu13.org/tech/courses/literacy or www.anovember.com/articles/zack.html. Both of these articles (entitled "Information Validation") provide heuristics such as the ones listed above.

5. Compare the major ideas or 'facts' that are presented with those from other sources. Do they correspond?

If these five elements are considered when surfing an Internet website, when reading an analysis of a problem, or when consulting a database, the subsequent interpretation and use of that information can be more thorough.

Conclusion

The validation principle suggests that information has to be evaluated in terms of its accuracy, consistency, timeliness, and security to be of high quality. The result of such an evaluation should be signaled to future information consumers. Validation thus also signifies to provide (meta-) information on the validity of a piece of information.

Examples of mechanisms that help to evaluate and consequently improve the validity of information are checking its order, having it reviewed by independent third parties, checking second sources, analyzing the source credentials and reputation, applying statistical tests, or performing a sensitivity analysis.

3.2.5.5 The Context Principle

Contextualizing information is a powerful way to increase both the interest of an audience and the audience's propensity to act on information in a certain way.

THOMAS DAVENPORT

Introduction

According to design guru CLEMENT MOK information design makes information understandable by giving it a context (Mok, 1996, p. 46). By providing a context or an environment that acts as the information's background, the information becomes clearer and its limits become more apparent. The traces of the information become visible and it can be more easily updated, modified, or deleted if necessary.

Context helps to avoid the *misinterpretation* of information. Without an adequate context, information is often ambiguous because it can mean many things to many people. Where does this information come from? What is it good for? How should I interpret it? Is this relevant for me? What should I look at next? These are but some of the questions that can be answered by context. But context is not a clearly discernable object, nor is it a well defined term.

The philosopher CARLO PENCO sees context as a set of related concepts rather than one precisely defined term (Penco, 1999, p. 270):

Contexts are not things we find in Nature; there are so many different ways of using the term „context" (in philosophy, linguistics, psychology, theory of communication, problem solving, cognitive science, artificial intelligence) that it would be better to speak of a „family-resemblance" concept. Since Dummett we speak of the „context principle" in Frege and Wittgenstein; we speak of „context of utterance" in pragmatics; we speak of „context sensitive" grammars in linguistics, and we speak also of „linguistic context" and „non linguistic context".

Etymologically speaking, the word context is derived from the Latin verb *contexere* meaning to weave together (i.e., to relate). Akman (2000, pp. 4-5) cites the following dictionary definitions of the term that can illustrate this meaning:

Terminological Background and Context Types

According to the Oxford English Dictionary the term 'context' usually has two primary meanings: (i) the words around a word, phrase, statement, etc. often used *to help explain* the *meaning*; (ii) the general *conditions* (*circumstances*) in which an event, action, etc. takes place. In another dictionary (Collins Cobuild English Language Dictionary), the prevalent meanings of the term include the following: The context of something consists of the ideas, situations, events, or information that *relate* to it and *make it possible to understand* it fully. If something is seen in context or if it is put into context, it is considered with all the factors that are *related* to it rather than just being considered on its own, so that it can be properly understood.

In contrast to these definitions, which stress the aspect of context to relate information in order to make it more comprehensible, the following definition by MAC DERMOTT stresses the 'situatedness' of context. He defines context as a „*place* of action in a *time* of action; with rules of signification which are themselves part of the activity" (cited in Bateson et al., 1981, p. 293).

Another distinction is introduced by Penco (1999). He generally distinguishes between *subjective* (or cognitive) and *objective* context, the former relates to the information consumer's situation, the latter to the surroundings of the information. The subjective context consists of assumptions on the world, such as rules or meanings. The objective context is a set of features of the world, such as time, place, a speaker etc. This distinction is quite close to the one drawn by ANDREW PETTIGREW (1987). He distinguishes between an *inner* (or internal) and an *outer* (or external) context.[90] As BAUR (Baur

---

[90] In the context of organizational action Pettigrew also distinguishes between a *horizontal* and a *vertical* context. The vertical context describes how something smaller is embedded in

Inner vs. Outer Context

2001) notes, this distinction can be applied to information as well.

The distinction between internal and external context is in fact made in information science literature. Barry and Schamber (1998) distinguish between an *internal* (e.g., subject area knowledge), an *external* (search goal), and a *problem* context (e.g., methodology) for information (Barry & Schamber, 1998, p. 222).

The *internal context* of information describes the circumstances of its creation, such as its purpose, its author and date of creation, its format, its underlying assumptions, the number of times it has been revised, its price, or its sources. The *external context* relates the information to its environment. This type of contextual meta-information can refer to related documents. It can indicate who owns the information (who is responsible for its updating) or where the information is located. Other possible (external) contextual indicators are the usage history of the information (how many times it has been accessed and by whom) or its demand (high versus low) and its access rights and usage restrictions or circumstances. The information may also serve another function that its original purpose; clarifying the outer context would thus also consist of clarifying the information's function and how long the information can be judged as correct (its expiration date) for this function. These elements of the internal and external context of information are summarized in the figure below.

something bigger (relating to the scale dimension). The key question to be asked is: how does it relate to the next level? The horizontal context describes how something of now relates to something prior or upcoming (relating to the time dimension). The key question here is: how does it relate to the past/future?

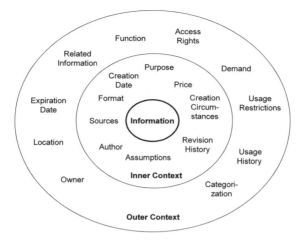

Figure 17: Elements of an information's context

What all of the factors depicted above have in common is that they help to embed information in an environment. The key activities to contextualize information are hence to *embed, position, relate, situate,* or *compare.* The next paragraphs describe why these activities are critical for the quality of information.

Key Activities: Embedding and Relating

One reason why context is important for information in knowledge-intensive processes is that it can provide orientation. Whitaker writes the following on the role of context in knowledge processes (Whitaker, 1996, p. 400):

The Rationale behind the Principle

When the observing system is an enterprise, effectiveness in handling 'context' is therefore a critical element in the process of 'organizational learning.' Contextual information supports *orientation* to incoming data by providing a basis for evaluating coherence and consistency [...]

Similarly, Hanselmann (2001, p. 111) points out the advantages of contextualization (adding context) in the area of product development teams and their sharing of knowledge:

Benefits of Adding Context

The contextualization [of knowledge] supports the *interpretation process* of product development staff and helps them to *evaluate, modify,* and *apply* knowledge content, for both the knowledge giver and the taker.

Next to orientation, context can also provide additional motivation to look at a piece of information (because one can better relate to it) and to act upon it or apply it. Davenport describes this function of contextualization as follows:

Contextualizing information is a powerful way to increase both the *interest* of an audience and the audience's propensity to *act* on information in a certain way. Adding context usually involves detailing the *source* of the information, the *comparative information* available, and the previous *history* surrounding this information (Davenport, 1997, p. 122, my italics).

Based on these benefits of adding context[91], we formulate the contextualization principle as follows:

The Contextualization Principle

> In order to enable information consumers to understand and adapt information correctly, i.e., to allocate it adequately, they need to be provided with the context of that information.
>
> The provided context should increase the clarity of the information (what it is about), the perceived correctness (where it applies and where its leads to false results), the traceability (where it comes from and how it originated), and its maintainability (where and how it can be updated).

Description of the Context Principle

Thus, the contextualization principle states that information is of high quality if the provided context makes it clear, correct (for a new context), traceable and maintainable. It implies that high-quality information is always presented with its context of *origination* and its context of *use*. The main IQ-problem that is resolved through this principle is the *misinterpretation* (and consequently the *misallocation*) of information.

The key questions that are answered by adding context to information are: where did the information come from, why and to whom is it important, and how should it be used? Through meta-information on these questions, the information should become clearer for the target group, because it

---

[91] Contextualizing also has another advantage. It can help learners to de-contextualize their acquired knowledge and use it effectively in new contexts, something which many students find difficult. By making the context of a method, a technique or a theory explicit, the later de-contextualization can be fostered, since the contextual factors can be more easily separated from the information itself. For the phenomenon of knowledge lock-in or knowledge inertia (that can be prevented through contextualization) see: Gerstenmaier, J. & Mandl, H. (1994). *Wissenserwerb unter konstruktivistischen Perspektive.* Forschungsbericht Nr. 33. Institut für Pädagogische Psychologie und Empirische Pädagogik. Ludwig-Maximilians-Universität München.

will become possible to understand the information's background. The target group can also better assess whether the information holds true for a new application context and if it is correct even under different circumstances. The context principle should also assure that the information is traceable, that is to say that its various origination steps can be traced back to the original source (this criteria is also known as *attributability*). Finally, the context principle refers to the infrastructure in which information is stored. This infrastructure should not be neglected, but maintained to serve in future contexts.

Means of applying this principle are adding meta-information (such as author, reviewer, origination and expiration dates, target group, etc.), referring to similar pieces of information or to people who have used the information, and referring to prior information of the same kind. We call these mechanisms information contextualizers or contextualization mechanisms and define them as follows:

The term information contextualizer designates any kind of mechanism that improves the clarity (or interpretability), correctness (or adequacy), traceability or maintainability of information and thus clarifies the information's background and possible applications.

Definition: Information Contextualizer

The mechanisms which are used to add context to information can be derived from our initial distinction of inner and outer context. The following diagram lists several methods through which both types of context can be added to information in order to make it and its background and application clearer. Again, we distinguish between *automated* mechanisms that can be performed (at least partially) by computers and *manually* added context information that has to be compiled and described by a person.

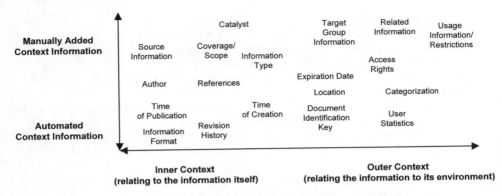

Figure 18: Mechanisms to add context to information

Application of the Principle

These contextualization mechanisms are briefly described below and further references on their functioning are provided. First, the manually added context elements, such as the scope and the original sources, are described. This is then followed by context information that can be generated automatically, such as time of creation or user statistics (i.e., demand). As in the case of the integration and validation mechanisms, not every contextualization mechanism can be clearly positioned as either purely manual or purely automated, since the actual implementation depends on the specificities of the situation (e.g., routine versus non-routine) and of the information (e.g., structured versus unstructured).

Catalyst

As a contextualization mechanism, a catalyst is a short introductory statement that outlines why a certain piece of information (such as a document) has been produced (see the Giga case study in chapter four for a description and examples of this contextualizer). Catalysts express the motivation behind a piece of information. They can be questions, events, mishaps, reports, collaborations, mandates, or orders. A catalyst helps to understand the background of a piece of information and why and for whom it might be relevant. The catalyst goes beyond a statement of purpose, because it also outlines how the purpose became relevant (and for whom).

Target Group Information

The second context-adding mechanism is more widely used than the catalyst. It simply consists of stating the addressees or target groups for a piece of information. A book may state the target groups on its back, a software application may outline its potential user profiles in it its help file, a protocol may start with its distribution list. By knowing the target groups for the information, its potential relevance can be more easily and more rapidly evaluated.

A third information contextualizer is a section that lists related information. The Gartner case study in section four will
show that this section is a vital component in many Gartner
reports. Almost every Gartner briefing ends with a directory
of *prior* reports on the same topic or with reports *from others*
on the same topic, or with reports on *related issues.*

The section on related information may also be referring to
other *people* who have also used the information or information that people who have used this information recommend
(as Amazon's online book ordering service does).

Related Information

The next contextualizer consists of instructions. These can
instruct an information consumer on how to best use the
available information, e.g. where the information should be
applied and where it does not fit, where to be cautious in
applying the information and where a one-to-one application
is possible. This type of usage information or usage restric-
tion is often included in analyst's reports that include legal
disclaimers (see chapter four for examples of such usage
restrictions). These restrictions help an information consumer
to judge the information.

Usage Information/ Restrictions

Sub-mechanisms of usage information are usage situations
or scenarios. This is an effective way of contextualizing information by providing possible scenarios of its use. In this
way, the information user can compare his or her current
situation with the situations described in the information's
context section. A best practice report[92], for example, may
begin with a section outlining the possible application scenarios of the report and by specifically excluding a number of
situations in which the documented best practice should not
be applied (e.g., under extreme time pressure). Listing possible (and unsuited) application situations can help the information consumer in his or her decision to allocate (or not
allocate) a certain set of information to a problem or task at
hand.

Usage Situations as Context

The previous information contextualizer helped to decide
whether information is fit or correct for the current context or
not. The next one can also be used in this manner. By indicating the type of information that a document, a website, a data
base, or a film contains, the information consumer can decide
whether it is correct and clear for his or her purpose. This
type of meta-information (information about information)[93]

Information Type

---

[92] A best practice report is a document that outlines how a proven
way of solving a problem can be applied.

[93] There are various definitions and classifications of meta-
information and meta-data. Bearman and Sochats distinguish

Information Format

does not state the format of the information (whether it is a presentation, a text, a video, a news item, a sound clip, a book, etc.) but the content type or subject area. An information type can be, for example, a project meeting protocol, a manual, a product listing, an instruction video, an event documentation, or an order. Unlike meta-information, which designates the information format, information types must be defined according to the specific context or the specific knowledge-intensive process that they cover. Meta-information that designates the information format, however, can often be used independently of the specific context, by simply differentiating among the various media in which information resides (i.e., text, image, video, sound, multimedia). Information format information can be identified by an information system itself, whereas the classification of a piece of information with regard to an information type often requires human intelligence and local knowledge of a specific context. Human intelligence is also required for the next mechanism, information on the information producer or author.

Author Information

While the author or creator of a document, a database entry or a speech can often be registered and identified automatically, his or her background can usually not be automatically codified. This background information, however, can provide helpful additional insights to better understand the context of a piece of information. Typical elements of this type of contextual information are the education of the author, his institutional credentials (see the validation principle) or his previously held positions, his memberships in associations or committees, his relation to the topic he is writing or speaking about, or his position and function within an institution. Through these and similar indicators, an information consumer can better understand the intention of an information producer and thus interpret and allocate his or her information better.

Source Information and References

The background information on an author described above can be extended by further information about the sources of information that have been used in compiling new information. Information on these sources can make the context of

---

six types of meta-data: 1.Identification and resource discovery meta-data (incl. administrative data) 2. Rights meta-data on terms and conditions of information usage 3. Structure meta-data 4. Context meta-data 5. Content meta-data 6. Meta-data on the "use history" of a document (number of accesses etc.) See: http://www.mpib-berlin.mpg.de/dok/metadata/pots/tsld004.htm [3.08.2001].

new information clearer and more visible. Source information of this kind can have many forms. The most common one is the bibliography or the references, where sources in the forms of books, journal and newspaper articles, or websites are listed. Informative references not only include the author, title and the editor, but also give a brief summary of the content (so- called annotated bibliographies) and thus provide additional context for the cited works. Variations of this form of source information are directories of interviews or directories of consulted organizations. These directories help to position an information product in a community and thus to better understand its preferences, its possible biases, and its hidden agendas (such as the infamous citation cartels in the academic context). Providing source information simply means to reveal one's sources and their characteristics. If the patterns inherent in a set of sources (e.g., the studies cited in an article) are made apparent, the references can become an even more informative mechanism. This can be achieved by highlighting crucial books or articles in the references (as done in this study), by connecting related works visually through lines, or by grouping them according to common themes. All of these mechanisms make the context of the used sources clearer.

Coverage/Scope

The clarity of information can also be improved by providing information about the scope or extent of an information product before the information consumer is required to immerse himself in that product. This type of scope or coverage statement is usually included in the abstract or executive summary. It states the *perspective* that is taken, the *core topics* that are discussed and the *questions* that are answered. It may also state the *limits* of an information product or what is omitted in it. A statement of coverage or scope may finally also make some of the inherent *assumptions* underlying a piece of information explicit.

Access Rights

A statement of scope or coverage is a purely content-related element that is usually defined by the information producer him- or herself. The access rights to that information, however, can be assigned by information producers and by information custodians, administrators or supervisors. The access rights determine who is eligible to access, modify, distribute or delete a set of information. While this may not primarily be a mechanism to add context, it can be used as such: Who can access the information reveals a lot about its criticality. A document that is classified as 'strictly confidential' and reserves access rights to only a few people creates a different context than information that is freely available on the Internet. This contextual dimension of access rights should not be neglected. Many confidential documents thus include explicit qualifiers that clearly indicate the limited access and distribution rights with labels such as 'confidential', 'for your eyes only', 'do not circulate', etc . Not only do they lead to a more cautious handling of the information, they also steer the interpretation process of the information consumer by signaling their potentially negative effect when communicated to other people.

Categorization

Categorization, too, is a mechanism that does not only improve context, but – as we have seen in the section on information integration – also the conciseness or accessibility of information. Providing categories to which information relates is an effective mechanism to create a context for information. As the Giga case study in chapter four will show, a *hierarchical tree of key terms* as a category system can help to 'locate' a document logically within a universe of concepts and terms. How a document, a database entry or a website is categorized can tell a lot about what it can be used for or where it comes from – the two main aspects of context as it is discussed in this section. Categorization provides another benefit for contextualization: Through categorized key words, a document can be related to a *glossary* where an additional explanation of crucial terms is provided, thus further clarifying the context of a contribution. In the overview of contextualization mechanisms in Figure 18, categorization is placed in the middle of the continuum of manually versus automated context information. The reason for this is, as already stated earlier, that there are intelligent algorithms that can automatically generate categories to group information, nevertheless human intelligence is still often needed to make sense of a large of set of information.

Expiration Date

Previously, we have stated that the context of information relates to its origin and its application (e.g., where it came from and what it is good for). As far as the second area is concerned, somebody has to decide how long the information will be considered as still correct, relevant, or current for application in new contexts. This is usually done through adding an expiration date to a filed document, a training application, a data base entry, a regulation, a manual etc. – either manually for each individual information item or through an automated mechanism that assigns a fixed life span to every document type. The expiration date tells an information consumer up to which date information can still be considered as valid. The expiration date thus states the temporal context for a piece of information. It is a vital element of meta-information that is often neglected.

Another potentially relevant piece of meta-information is the location of information. The term location refers to the physical or logical position of a piece of information. In order to avoid duplications, redundancies or version mismatches, it often makes sense to store a piece of information (especially in the case of documents) in only one location and reference it in all others. This location, whether physical (where the document is stored) or logical (where it appears), can act as a surrounding of the information and can contribute to its context. Similar or related information can be placed together in the same location thus facilitating the references to related material. Previous versions of the same document can be stored together thus showing the development of the information. Some information systems highlight this information environment visually by providing a metaphorical environment for the information, such as a garden, a park, an ocean, a bookshelf or a globe.[94] By visualizing information in a virtual environment that replicates contextual factors such as scope, proximity, confidentiality, or age of a document, a great amount of context can be communicated in a very short amount of time. Since we often automatically frame context as a certain space or location, this seems a natural contextualization strategy.

Location

Besides space, another 'natural' contextualizer is time. Time as an element of an information's context has two facets (in the area of knowledge-intensive processes). First, the time at which a piece of information is created. Second, the time when it is released or communicated. The first one is generally referred to as the time of creation (which can be either automatically registered or entered manually), while the second one is the time of publication (which can also be automated). These two contextual elements should be clearly distinguished because they reveal the time lag inherent in many information systems. Many academic journals, for example, indicate when an article was first received to reveal the time lag (and available improvement period) of their published contributions.

Time of Creation and Time of Publication

---

[94] Companies who have developed such visual information environments are: Silicon Graphics (information spheres and globes as well as ports), UBS (information landscape), British Telecom (information garden), and Inxight, a Xerox company (information walls).

Revision History

The next context information also relates to the time dimension: the revision history. It represents a simple mechanism to highlight the origination process of a document. A revision history can often be generated semi-automatically which means that some elements are provided by the information system while some need to be entered by the information producers. It answers the following questions: who has worked in which way and on what parts of a document, a website, a database, a project plan, a spreadsheet etc. Typical elements of a revision history are the names of the authors, the dates of their revisions, the assigned version numbers of the documents or applications, and the titles of the sections which were added or modified. Highly collaborative documents, such as software specification reports or project outlines, often include a table at the beginning of the document which contains a revision history with these elements. Below is a fictitious example of such a table.

Document Version	Date	Changes	Made By
0.5 First Draft	9.3.01	First draft created with chapters one through five	Tony Marsh & Jeff Bride
0.8 Second Draft	13.4.01	Draft appended with chapter six (detail information on timing)	T. Marsh & Amy Quacker
1.0 First Version	18.4.01	Minor changes of chapters one through three incorporated (team suggestions) and layout adapted to corporate identity.	T. Marsh, J. Bridge, A. Quacker, Jeff Gable
1.5 Modified Version	4.10.01	Section 2.5 added on project planning and reviewing	J. Bridge
2.0 Second Version	25.11.01	Adapted to new organization chart for 2002	J. Gable, T. Marsh
2.5 (Planned Revision)	*1.2.02*	*Planned: Detailed adaptation of organization chart*	*Planned: T. Marsh*

Table 15: A typical document revision history

Document Identification Key

The last few contextualization mechanisms have been fairly simple and straightforward. This is not the case for the last two mechanisms which are provided as examples in this section. They are document identification keys and user statistics. Document identification keys (sometimes also referred to as trackers) are alphanumeric labels that are attributed to documents according to a set of rules in order to facilitate their storage and retrieval. They are based on document naming conventions such as in the following example:

TITLE CLIENT PROJECT-NR. DOCTYP DATE VER-SION.doc. This naming convention tells information producers in which way they have to assign file names to their created documents. The naming convention stated above would generate document identification keys such as the following one: ReorganizationStrategy Nestlé 235A internal Presentation 2/2/2001 Version 2.1.doc. Document identification keys can also be purely numeric. In that case, every number is coded and related to a certain attribute of a document. Such a document identification key could be the following one: 13.390.64-102.120901. The first two digits of this key identify the business unit in which the document has originated. The next three digits identify the department. The number 64 that follows identifies the author, and the number 102 designates the document itself with the last six digits identifying its date of creation. While naming conventions are usually easy to devise, they are quite difficult to implement, primarily because of the required discipline on behalf of the information producers who have to adhere to them. Because of this, it often makes sense to assign such identification keys automatically.[95]

User Statistics

User statistics represent contextual information that can be captured automatically. They can reveal insights about the context of information as far as its *application* is concerned. User statistics capture the demand for information items and allow various analyses based on the captured demand information. User statistics can, if adequately processed, answer questions such as these:

- What are the most requested reports by project managers?
- Which patent documents are least referenced? Which are cited the most?
- Which book on project management has been ordered most often?
- What other books have people who bought this book ordered?
- Who has looked at this document? Who downloaded it?
- What is the most popular website on procurement planning?

---

[95] The consulting group McKinsey & Company assigns the document keys through its library team. Every presentation has a unique, highly coded, alphanumeric key that designates the origin of the presentation. These keys are used by the library team to quickly locate relevant presentations.

- What is the demand for this document in relation to all others?

Answers to these questions help an information consumer to find relevant information or to assess information more objectively. User statistics provide additional background on information by showing how (much) the information has been used before. In order to generate user statistics, standard database functions (such as views) can be used within a company, and web statistics tools (such as Webtrends) can be used for the Internet context. For paper-based information, surveys and questionnaires can be employed.

The contextualization mechanisms that we have reviewed in the previous paragraphs should be used carefully and not only cumulatively. This is also true for other means of adding context that have not been described. Additional 'tools' to add context are informative titles or key word sections that reveal the context of a document, annotated bibliographies or web directories that provide further background and links to sources, or *annotating mechanisms* that provide the possibility to append information with personal remarks, interpretations, bookmarks, etc. Giving information consumers the possibility to provide comments or *feedback* (which is visible to other information consumers) can also be a possible way to add context to information.

To summarize the many mechanisms discussed above, let us try to combine most of them in one application that I call *context visualizer*. Such an application could (if implemented) make the context of a document instantly visible to information consumers. It would include the functionalities that are described in the next paragraph.[96]

The context visualizer presents information items as books in a large, colorful (and dynamic) bookshelf on the screen. Document types and formats are clearly distinguished by the backsides of the books (and their colors) which represent documents of all kinds. Documents that are often accessed are slightly pulled out of the shelf while texts that are used seldom develop spider webs.[97] Larger databases or documents are represented through larger books. Documents that have passed their expiration date are visualized as dissolving

---

[96]   The idea of the context visualizer is based on an application developed by the Technical University of Vienna called Libviewer, see: http://www.ifs.tuwien.ac.at/libviewer/.

[97]   This functionality is actually already implemented in the libviewer program referenced in the previous footnote.

books with fading colors. When pulled out, every document reveals its title, abstract, pictures of its authors, and a revision history. The references of each document include a button that highlights all referenced documents that are stored in the virtual bookshelf. Once this reference-button is pressed, all referenced documents blink on the bookshelf. The location of a document in the bookshelf is based on the author's surname and on the main topic discussed in the document. Books that are next to each other are by the same author (as in a real bookshelf) and every level on the bookshelf is dedicated to a topic, project, business unit etc. The bookshelf can also be rearranged to reveal other views onto the documents, such as 'by date', 'by topic categories', 'by rating' (high ratings are indicated by gold ribbons on the book covers), 'by confidentiality' (documents that are confidential are represented as books with chains and locks attached to them). The color coding on the covers of the books can be used for various purposed: books with the same color can relate to the same project, same group, or same department. Books that are on a tray in front of the shelf are being edited and should be considered as checked out.

This type of interactive document interface is but one way in which the important element of context can be given more weight. Another way of emphasizing the importance of context is through *guidelines*. JOCHEN HANSELMANN has explored this strategy for the knowledge-intensive process of product development.

Hanselmann distinguishes various types of context which are crucial when a product development team codifies its experiences (the knowledge derived from the process) and which must be made explicit. Specifically, he mentions the context of the *product*, the *process* context, the *methodological* context, the *organizational* context, the *social* context, and the general or *environmental* context (Hanselmann, 2001, p. 113).

Guidelines: Context Codification

For Hanselmann, the codification of such contextual factors is a prerequisite for effective knowledge transfer. He lists the following key questions as guidelines for *context codification* (p. 114):

- Have all the mission-critical and generally important contextual factors been codified?
- Has the application situation of the codified knowledge been sufficiently described and have critical environmental factors been mentioned?
- Have the basic, almost self-evident, contextual factors

which allow for easier interpretation of the information been mentioned?

- Are the contextual factors described in a way that is comprehensible and clear to others who have been not involved in the original context (explanation of abbreviations and specific terms, background on key people)?
- Can the contextual factors foster the creative interpretation and modification or even further development of the codified knowledge?
- Do the contextual factors that have been described enable inexperienced developers to re-create the application context and thus apply the knowledge more easily?

Through the above guidelines and through the use of contextualization mechanisms as have been described in this section, the contextualization principle can be operationalized. This, in consequence, will lead not only to information which is clearer, but also to information that can be re-used in other circumstances. Mechanisms that foster the use of information are explored in the next section on the activation principle.

Conclusion

The contextualization principle suggests that information producers and managers should always provide a context for their information in order to clearly show what the information is about, how it came about, what it can be used for (and where it doesn't apply), and finally what (and whom) it takes to maintain it.

Examples of mechanisms that help to apply this principle are catalysts (the reasons why a piece of information was produced) typical document meta-information tags (e.g., author, date of creation, target group etc.), expiration dates, user statistics, revision histories, or references to related information. To implement these mechanisms one can use software applications or foster the contextualization of information through guidelines.

3.2.5.6 The Activation Principle

To be of value, information must be acted upon. If it is ignored, it is valueless.[98]

ANDREW P. GARVIN

One of the standard definitions of quality is fitness for *use*. *Introduction*
Information, however, is often difficult to use or apply, even
if it is integrated, validated, and contextualized. It is not
enough to *compile*, *control*, and *contextualize* information for
it to be truly useful and actionable. It also has to be *communicated* in a motivating and efficient way to accommodate the
cognitive and situational preferences of the information consumers. It has to lead them to possible implementation strategies of the provided information by organizing content for
easy application – at least in the context of knowledge-intensive processes. Otherwise information is only collected,
screened, and evaluated, but not acted upon, a phenomenon
that is also known as *paralysis by analysis* (instead of informed decisions and actions). How such a paralysis through
information can be avoided by activating information is discussed in this section.

The term activation (in our context) refers to the fact that   *Terminological*
information as such is often a passive form of codified   *Background*
knowledge that has to be activated in order to be useful.
Thus, the principle that is introduced in this section has been
labeled as the activation principle.

Activation is a term that – according to the Webster's dictionary – signifies *to set in motion* or to *organize* or *create
readiness*, to *accelerate a reaction* or to *convert into active
derivatives*. Activation can also be defined as the *stimulation
of activity* or causing something to have *energy*, to energize.
The term can be applied to anything that is marked by or
involving direct *participation*. Synonyms of activating or
activation are *triggering a reaction* or *setting off an effect*. In
the context of information in knowledge-intensive processes,
the effect that we hope for is an increasing propensity to act
on information (given that the information is sound and relevant). For this to happen, we need to do the things that are
implicit in the verbs listed above, namely organize information so that it is readily available and convert it into an active,
energized element that catches the attention and interest of

---

[98]   Garvin, 1993, p.58.

information consumers. These are some of the key activities that are summarized by the activation principle. Other examples of such activities are described in the next paragraph.

Key Activity:

Organizing Information for Easy Application

Activating information is a complex task and as such cannot be completed by doing only one thing. It is rather a group of tasks that when taken together increases the likelihood of providing useful information. These tasks all revolve around the key idea that information has to be organized for action in order to be useful. It has to be converted into a format that allows information consumers to use it without further transformation (e.g., further reduction, repetition, format conversion, re-interpretation, digitization etc.).

Examples

An example of such an activation procedure is the conversion of a bulky printed software instruction manual into a context-sensitive, interactive (e.g., fully searchable) online help program that is automatically updated to release changes in the software. Another example of organizing information for easy application is the delivery of a feasibility study with a cost simulation program that can be modified by the information consumer in real-time according to his or her personal beliefs and estimates or according to the newest developments. Yet another example of activation was given in the introductory section of this book in the product development scenario. There, a 'dead' mass of project reports was brought alive by bringing together product engineers from various projects and by letting them exchange and *discuss* their lessons learned in a moderated on-site workshop. This workshop used visualizations and structured discussions to exchange the latest insights, ask each other *questions*, and collectively think about possible applications of the discussed findings. Not only did the workshop produce new insights and application ideas, but it also lead to vivid memories for the participants. These personal memories of every participant help to retain the discussed issues longer than just by reading a lengthy report and use them whenever adequate situations arise. These three examples show that there are specific ways in which information can be made *faster*, more *current*, more *interactive*, and ultimately more *applicable*. These adjectives are the four information quality criteria that are most affected by the principle (as shown in the IQ-framework on page 68).

The Rationale behind the Principle

The rationale behind the activation principle is thus to make information actionable for information consumers by catching their attention, accommo-dating their application needs and preferences, and anchoring information in their minds so that it remains available to them for later use.

WILLIAM SANDY (CEO of a productivity improvement company) points out this crucial insight for the context of planning as a knowledge-intensive process, where the plan is the central information product or 'knowledge artifact' (Sandy, 1991, p. 31):

As the plan seeks to *persuade others to action*, there can be a tendency to increase the weight of factual support. And yet the key today is to crystallize information to its essence. Information can be organized for the convenience of the collector or the *usability* of the user. The best way to gear your plan for easy *conversion to implementation* is to *organize* the logic of the plan in a way that *fits the organization of the implementation work to be done*. When you follow that logic, information is available to users in the way that they think and work.

The need for such mechanisms can be illustrated through a short parable by SÖREN KIERKEGAARD, the Danish philosopher, writer, and religious thinker. In the following anecdote he illustrates the changing nature of knowledge once it is applied (see Oden, 1978, p. 38, my italics):

Let us imagine a pilot, and assume that he had passed every examination with distinction, but that he had not as yet been at sea. Imagine him in a storm; he knows everything he ought to do, but he has not known before how terror grips the seafarer when the stars are lost in the blackness of night; he has not known the sense of impotence that comes when the pilot sees the wheel in his hand become a plaything for the waves; he has not known how the blood rushes to the head when one tries to make calculations at such a moment; in short, *he has had no conception of the change that takes place in the knower when he has to apply his knowledge.*

Increasing the fitness for use of information thus implies helping the knower anticipate this change in the state of knowledge once he or she is about to apply information in a critical situation or in a knowledge-intensive process. One way of achieving this (as will be shown below), is by providing the information in an interactive manner that simulates the later application context.

Based on this reasoning, we define the activation principle as follows:

> In order to enable information consumers to use information effectively, it has to be provided in a directly applicable format, in its most current version, in a highly interactive process, and on a fast infrastructure. This assures that information is applied because it is available when needed and because it is easily noticed and remembered.

The Activation Principle

Description of the Activation Principle

The activation principle states that high-quality information provides means of activating the information in the mind of the information consumer and thus renders it memorable and easily applicable for later use. The activation principle strives for greater information *impact* by making the information as applicable and current as possible and by providing it in an interactive and fast manner. Specific means of applying this principle are repetitions of crucial information elements, mnemonics (cognitive shortcuts such as abbreviations), stories (vivid plots which make the information more memorable), metaphoric language and metaphoric visualizations, simulations or animations that make the information come alive and motivate the information consumer to actively explore and use it (these and other mechanisms are described below). The main IQ-problem that is resolved through this principle is often referred to as *paralysis by analysis* or the fact that information is often not stimulating or motivating actions or decisions, but rather delaying them. A generic term for this information quality problem is *information misuse*. Related problems are labeled as knowledge inertia or the *knowing-doing gap* (see Pfeffer and Sutton, 2000). These terms reflect our frequent inability to put acquired information into action or adapt it sufficiently to new contexts.

To operationalize the activation principle, the same strategy will be used as for the other three principles. So-called activation mechanisms or information activators that improve the applicability, currency, interactivity, or speed of information will be presented, discussed and referenced in this section. A common definition for these mechanisms is the following one:

Definition: Information Activator

> The term information activator designates any kind of mechanism that improves the applicability (or usefulness), currency, interactivity or speed of information and its provision and thus makes information actionable and more likely to be used effectively.

Application of the Activation Principle

We distinguish again between mechanisms that can be automated and those that require the presence and the skills of a person (labeled as 'personal activation'). In addition, one can differentiate between activation mechanisms based on optimizing the *format* of information and mechanisms that achieve activation through the way that information is *delivered* (although the two are often interdependent). Some of the most frequently used activation mechanisms are summarized in the figure below.

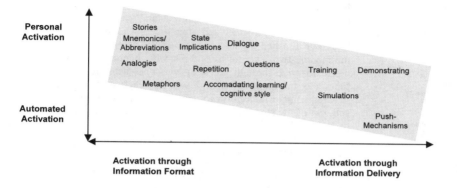

Figure 19: Mechanisms to activate information

The grey tilted band in the figure above indicates that activation through a change in the information format requires more human skills than a modification of the delivery process. While activators that rely on format changes directly influence the content of an information 'package', activation through delivery modifications affects the medium or channel through which that package is conveyed. Although this makes intuitive sense, the two areas of information format and delivery are not completely independent of one another. Sometimes a change in the delivery of information affects the information format of that information and vice versa (as in the case of a printed technical manual that is made available in an online version and consequently changes its format from sequential to a multimedia hypertext). In the short descriptions that follow, we begin with personal or manual activators and then describe activation mechanisms that rely heavily on the use of computers.

Format vs. Delivery

One of the most natural ways of getting and sustaining the attention of knowledge workers and increasing their propensity to retain and use information is through vivid stories. Stories are, as esoteric as they might seem in the context of knowledge-intensive processes, a highly effective, but demanding activation mechanism. Stories make information more salient and interesting by stimulating the curiosity of information consumers. Knowledge management and story-telling specialist DAVID SNOWDEN of IBM (which has pat-

Stories as Activators

ented its storytelling methodology) outlines this effect of stories in the following example (see Snowden, 2001):

In one project, the time taken to complete e-learning modules was halved by a series of stories using „stars" called Tom, Jason and Linda. E-mails were received after the first module saying things like „I've finished module one, here's the assessment, Please send me module two, I've got to find out what happened to Jason." The desire to drive through the story was one factor in the improved timescale; the main one though was that each story had been constructed using a fable form to deliver a precise message, and in the sub-text of the story to prepare the ground for the learning that was to follow. Just as a good teacher provides context to support the content that will follow, so story repopulates an e-learning environment with context to facilitate learning.[99]

Snowden also provides the reasons for this effect. He states that stories deliver complex ideas in a simple, consistent, and *memorable* form. He claims that they can convey a message in culturally diverse situations without loss of meaning if they are rooted in anecdotal material obtained from the relevant communities and if they are rich enough in terms of content and structure. A story typically consists of three structural elements: a *setup* or starting situation, a *confrontation* (a growing crises culminating in a climax), and a *resolution*.[100] The resolution often contains the morale of the story. The morale reveals the core values that are transported through the story. Another crucial structural element of many stories is the existence of one or several protagonists or heroes who are given a certain task that they need to complete.

Next to these components of stories one can distinguish various *types of stories* in terms of their main purpose for knowledge-intensive processes. One can distinguish between mnemonic stories that mainly aim at helping knowledge workers remember crucial process information (such as important locations or steps), failures stories that primarily illustrate how to prevent mistakes, and anecdotes that simply entertain, transport implicit values or illustrate a problem or a solution. A last type of story is the 'pedagogic' application

---

[99] This quote reveals that story telling is also a contextualization mechanism. Again, we find that some of the mechanisms can be discussed under more than one principle, illustrating our approach of fruitful, but moderate, redundancy.

[100] For an analysis of stories and their elements, see for example: Mellon, N. (1998) *The Art of Storytelling*, New York: Harper Collins. Or: Lipman, D. (1999) *Improving your Storytelling: Beyond the Basics for All Who Tell Stories in Work or Play*, August House.

story that outlines how a knowledge-intensive process can be successfully completed. All of these 'practical' story types work if they use the key qualities of stories, such as a rich and specific context (in terms of time and place or setting), a purposeful and challenging task for the protagonist, a sequential logic, and a memorable outcome that contains an element of surprise and one strong main insight or morale.

In order to use stories to activate information, several tools or elements can be used such as fictionalizing or anonymizing the content (a good idea in the case of failure stories), using archetypical characters or groups that have a strong identity (such as the Dilbert character used in management cartoons), or building hyper stories (new, combined narratives) from various anecdotes or anecdote components. This activator is positioned at the upper left hand corner of the overview diagram, because good story telling cannot be automated. Stories can, however, be distributed or delivered to information consumers in a great variety of forms, ranging from e-mail anecdotes, workshop narratives, to multimedia tales.

One of the main benefits of stories is that they make information memorable so that it can be used whenever the need arises. Mnemonics also serve this purpose. Mnemonics are memory aids or mental shortcuts that help to retain a series of terms, steps, criteria, or principles through abbreviations (or other means, see Belleza, 1983). In the context of knowledge-intensive processes, we have used mnemonics to gather lessons learned or knowledge derived from the process (see section 0) in product development teams. Specifically, we used the acronym CORAL to convey to eight groups of product engineers from three companies what it takes to generate useful project reports for their peers. CORAL is a mnemonic abbreviation that stands for critical, original, reliable, actionable learnings (see Eppler & Sukowski, 2000). Those attributes are the characteristics of high-quality lessons learned documents: They are *critical* to the success of a product development project. They are gathered and articulated by the *original* project team members. The documented lessons learned are *reliable* because they have been examined and reviewed by the entire team and one external specialist and they are *actionable* because they can be directly used in future projects. Finally, the documented experiences are true *learnings* because they represent new, insightful know-how, know-why, or know-what. The CORAL acronym also embodies the crucial notion of getting under the surface and going to the 'bottom' of a project problem. Acronyms such as

Mnemonics as Activators

this one have long been used in management. They are highly actionable because they can provide rapid and systematic help in stressful situations. They represent simple rules (see also Eisenhardt, 2001) that have stood the test of time. Below, we have summarized some of these well-known management mnemonics. One has to keep in mind that their purpose is to aid strategic or tactical thinking in turbulent times, not to express universal truths. They should serve no other purpose than to make the information contained in them more salient and easier to recall or convey.

Acronym	Elements	Purpose/Meaning
AIDA	Attention, Interest, Desire, Action	The sequential states of a potential client that a salesperson has to achieve in order to close a sale.
FIFO	First In First Out	The management principle of logistics where the oldest items go first and the newest stay longest (e.g., in a warehouse).
KISS	Keep It Simple and Stimulating	Advice for keeping instructions concise and motivating.
PEST	Political, Economic, Social, Technological [Aspects of the Environment]	The main areas of a company's strategic analysis of its external situation
4P's	Product, Price, Promotion, Place	Four important marketing parameters that need to be coordinated to optimize a product's market success.
SMART	Specific, Measurable, Ambitious, (alternatively: Aggressive or Agreed) Realistic, Time-bound [Goals]	The necessary requirements for effective goal-setting, e.g. the attributes of project goals.
SPIN	Situation, Problem, Implication, Need	Used in sales situations to work with a prospective customer in assessing his needs.
SQ3R	Survey, Question, Read, Recall, Review	The steps of effective text reading.

Acronym	Elements	Purpose/Meaning
7S	Strategy, Structure, Systems, Staff, Style, Shared Values, Skills	Summarizes McKinsey's view on the crucial success factors of a company.
SWOT	Strengths, Weaknesses, Opportunities, Threats	Standard strategic assessment categories to evaluate a company, a product, or a market in regard to future developments.

Table 16: Typical mnemonic acronyms and their purposes

The acronyms listed in the table above are typical examples of mnemonic abbreviations as they are general and as none of them is longer than five characters (which represent terms in a sequence).

Good mnemonic acronyms that help to retain instructions or crucial elements during a knowledge-intensive process have to be well-designed in relation to their format and their content. As far as the format of a mnemonic management abbreviation is concerned, the acronym must be short (two to six letters) and it must be easy to pronounce (a combination of consonants and vowels). It also helps if the acronym has a (at least indirect) relation to its domain, such as the SMART project goals or the SWOT analysis that hints at a rapid procedure. In regard to the content that the acronym represents, it should neither be completely obvious or self-evident, nor too sophisticated or complex. It should express a meaningful sequence of steps or factors that can be followed or that can be applied to judge or improve a situation. The content should also have the quality to be elaborated, that is to say to contain a chain of reasoning based on experience and logic.

Another acronym from our own experience that can illustrate these attributes is called PEAK. Unlike the CORAL mnemonic device that summarizes crucial criteria, the PEAK acronym represents the necessary steps for the **p**rocess-based **e**xchange and **a**nalysis of **k**nowledge in a team workshop: One has to set **p**riority areas, **e**valuate their strengths and deficits, devise **a**ctions to reduce these deficits, and **k**eep the momentum through follow-ups. Besides indicating the purpose and the steps of the workshop, the PEAK abbreviation also contains the important idea of reaching a higher level (i.e., continuous improvement) or making it to the top, the peak.

Our experience in industrial product development and new media project teams shows that team members pick up on such mnemonics extremely quickly and use them as a part of their regular working jargon. In this way, the acronyms become a sort of brand name that makes process and project communication more efficient since everybody knows what a PEAK workshop or a CORAL document is without the need for elaborated explanations.

Analogies & Metaphors

The next activation mechanism can also be used to eliminate elaborate explanations. The use of analogies and metaphors in the transfer of information for knowledge-intensive processes can save time, increase understanding and motivation, and make information more easily applicable. These benefits can be achieved because both mechanisms, analogy and metaphor, act as bridges between what is already known and concepts or ideas that are new to an information consumer. The following quote describes this characteristic and outlines the difference between analogy and metaphor (Gurney 1999, p.1709):

Analogy allows an explanation of an unfamiliar concept by *directly* likening it to a familiar one, whilst a metaphor is an explanation of an unfamiliar concept made by likening it to the *characteristics* of a familiar one.

This characteristic of relating new concepts to familiar ones can be used by information producers to make information more salient and to foster the creative interpretation and use of information. In the case of analogies, entire concepts or concrete entities are *directly* compared or related to one another through stories, comparisons, or parables that explain their close similarities, whereas metaphors use imagery, abstract concepts, and figures of speech to indirectly relate characteristics of an object or idea to those of another.

A short example can illustrate this difference. Saying that the Internet is like the railroad system is an analogy that stresses the characteristic of both to be networks that act as a basic infrastructure for transportation (of people or information). Saying that the power of the Internet is like a two-edged sword (according to one of its inventors VINTON G. CERF[101]) is a metaphor that conveys the notion of something that has advantages and simultaneous disadvantages; in the case of the Internet providing information and misinformation.

---

[101] See his vision statement on the homepage of the Internet Society at: http://www.isoc.org/internet/conduct/truth.shtml [3.1.02]

In order to use analogies as information activators, information producers must know their information consumers and their existing knowledge. They have to know which objects of reference are familiar to their target communities. D'Arcy (1999, p. 33) highlights this important aspect in the following quote on analogies in the management context:

> Though analogies help clarify points, many managers are unsure about how to come up with them. First, manager should think about the situation or idea that they want to describe. Then, they should consider what *common references* in the audience's knowledge base might help them relate to the new concept. These related points create the basis for analogies.

When used in this way, analogies can be a powerful mechanism to bring information to life and assure that it is properly understood and remembered.

The Use of Analogies

While the use of analogies is relatively simple, given that there is prior knowledge about the information consumers and their background, the adequate use of metaphors can be quite demanding. The term 'metaphor' is derived from the Greek verb *metapherein* which means „carrying something somewhere else." As analogies, metaphors provide a path from the understanding of something familiar to something new by carrying elements of understanding from the mastered subject to a new domain. This is why ARISTOTLE calls the metaphor a *tool of cognition*. According to ARISTOTLE, a metaphor provides *rapid* information and is to the highest degree instructive; it facilitates the process of learning. [102]

The Use of Metaphors

There are several forms of metaphors that can facilitate learning in the context of knowledge-intensive business processes. Aaron Marcus (Marcus, 1998), an information design thought leader, distinguishes the following forms of metaphors that can be used for information activation:

Structural metaphors represent functions, objects and elements of an information system with familiar artifacts. An example of this type of metaphor would be the representation of digital documents in the form of folders, envelopes or post-it notes.

Operational metaphors substitute the behavior or process of one information system with familiar procedures form other domains, e.g., representing the deletion of a digital document by moving it into a (virtual) trash can or recycling bin. Operational metaphors are closely related to *pragmatic metaphors* that enable an information consumer to absorb or

---

[102] See Eppler (1999), p. 116 , or Eco (1984), p. 100.

understand procedural information. An example would be using the tape recorder buttons of play, rewind, pause etc. to navigate in a database. Marcus also describes another closely related type, that of *activity metaphors* which can be used to control a process, to communicate or play a game. A well-known metaphor of this kind is the supply chain, where the image of a chain indicates that goods move sequentially from one supplier to the next.

Analogies and metaphors can be used extensively in the context of knowledge-intensive processes to convey complex ideas in salient forms. They can be employed to convey knowledge about the process (procedural knowledge), knowledge used within a process (factual knowledge), and knowledge derived from the process (experiential knowledge). These process-oriented analogies can take on various forms, from mere figures of speech that explain an insight (e.g., running this process is like running a marathon, you need a long breath"), to visual illustrations that document a process (for example as a funnel with various inputs, levels, and one output), to entire software applications that are based on the logic of a metaphor or analogy (such as a lessons learned database that has the form of a chronicle or encyclopedia).

Stating (and Enforcing) Implications

The previous two activators, metaphors and analogies, were complex, varied and demanding. The next one, however, is simple and straightforward. It simply consists of pointing out what the implications of a piece of information are in terms of needed actions, decisions or future developments. Implications or ramifications are the „so-what's" of information. They are the main consequences of an insight, a procedure, or an experience. The research reports of GARTNER INC. and the GIGA group always conclude with such 'action items' or 'bottom lines' (see chapter four). An implication of an insight, an experience or a mistake may be, as Eisenhardt and Sull (2001) point out, that a certain rule has to be followed. KATHRIN EISENHARDT and DONALD SULL suggest that – especially in turbulent markets – simple rules are the best strategy to run a company (as opposed to position-based or resource-based strategies). They suggest that two to seven simple one-line rules (which often include clear criteria) that focus on a key process can help managers find and exploit new opportunities quickly and consistently. This rapid pursue of opportunities is a key characteristic of today's successful companies, Eisenhardt and Sull argue (although one of their illustrative cases for this claim is the recently faltered Enron Corporation).

Clearly stating and *enforcing* the implications of information is a crucial management task. This is true in light of the fact that a great amount of business relevant information is created, discussed, and never applied. Pfeffer and Sutton (2000, p. 54) have found (among others) the following indicators for such a culture where talk substitutes for action:

- No follow-up is done to ensure that what was said or written is actually done and put into practice.
- Planning meetings, and report writing become defined „action" that is valuable in its own right, even if it has no effect on what people actually do.
- People are evaluated on how smart they sound rather than on what they do.
- Complex language, ideas, processes, and structures are thought to be better than simple ones.
- There is a belief that managers are people who talk, and others do.

If information is to be activated, to be used, this type of behaviour has to be discouraged. Pfeffer and Sutton (2000, p. 56) suggest that companies need to avoid the 'talk trap' and foster action, for example by promoting managers who have operational experience in managing processes. Other ways of promoting action are fostering a culture of simplicity that does not reward unnecessary complexity, fostering language and information that is action oriented and establishing follow-up processes to ensure that decisions are not only documented, but also implemented. Another important suggestion of Pfeffer and Sutton regards the reasons why not to use information (p. 57):

Do not accept excuses and criticism for why things won't work or can't be done, but rather reframe the objections into problems to be overcome rather than reasons not to try.

The main message of all these suggestions, from including 'action items' in texts to emphasizing simplicity in style, is that information does not equal action. The implications of information for action have to be made explicit and mechanisms have to be installed that ensure that those implications are followed through.

One of the most powerful ways of turning information into action is through systematic conversations, or more specifically through dialogue. A dialogue can, if properly conducted, motivate employees to not only understand information better, but also to act upon it. A conversation that is lead

Dialogue & Conversation

as a real dialogue (and not as a crossing of swords) can not only be an excellent mechanism for knowledge transfer, but it can also represent a simple way to achieve commitment and consensus on an issue – a prerequisite for effective action in organizations. Dialogue in this sense is a specific form of conversation that respects certain *rules* of conduct and begins with an open, non-judgemental state of mind. Such dialogue rules may include active listening without interruptions or personal attacks, balancing inquiry and advocacy, the confirmation of understanding through paraphrasing, the explicit discussion of basic assumptions, and the suspension of hierarchy (see Mengis 2001 for similar dialogue rules). Conversation researcher and consultant PHIL HARKINS refers to such *action-inducing dialogues* as powerful conversations. In Harkins (1999), he defines a powerful conversation as an interaction between two or more people that progresses from shared feelings, beliefs, and ideas to an exchange of wants and needs to clear *action steps* and mutual *commitments*. In Harkins' view, powerful conversations lead to action, accomplishment, commitment and understanding by moving through these three distinct stages, which are controlled by a team leader. In stage one, the introductory stage of a conversation, the team leader sets up his agenda with an honest feeling, belief or idea. Then, in the second or middle stage, he discusses the issue, probing for the wants and needs of the other person and then clearly states his own wants and needs. In the closing stage three, the leader nails down the next steps and makes sure he (and the other person) got what was wanted out of the conversation.

This 'operational' view of conversations is quite different from the concept of conversation as it is discussed in knowledge management literature. There, conversation is often seen as a vehicle to generate new knowledge through 'languaging' rather than to assure that existing knowledge is applied (see von Krogh and Roos, 1995, for such a 'generative' approach towards conversations).

Although both approaches are quite different in terms of their conception of conversations, both share the belief that true understanding and commitment cannot be achieved by simply giving orders or stating facts. It must be developed in an interactive process of collective sense-making. This sense-making process should not, in my view, be left to chance, as conversations often get tangled up in details or side-issues. It must be actively managed. Von Krogh and Roos (1995) and Weeks (2001) thus use the term 'conversation management' to emphasize the importance of systematic conversations.

Managing conversations can have many forms, none of them should be mistaken for a rigid control of what is said (and by whom). Conversation management can be seen as the enabling of fruitful discussions and the cutting-short of counterproductive arguments (that Harkins calls 'swamps'[103]). It can be supported through numerous tools that visualize conversations streams, document decisions, or help to uncover basic assumptions. Examples of such tools are argument maps, visual protocols, ladders of inference, issue histories, or brainstorming (see Eppler & Sukowski, 2000 or Mengis 2001).

These tools typically foster dialogue as it has been described in the previous paragraphs. While some (such as brainstorming) focus more on the generative potential of conversations, others (such as the issue history) emphasize the application of discussed items. Talisayon illustrates this two-fold nature of conversations as means of knowledge creation and application in the following quote (Talisayon, 2001):

Dialogue requires suspension of judgment and advocacy, trust among team members, willingness to examine alternative viewpoints and facts contrary to one's beliefs, and openness to new possibilities. Dialogue includes reality checks, cross validation of perceptions, inquiry into premises and construction of a *consensus* or shared reality.

Based on this understanding of dialogue we can conclude the following: For conversations to succeed as activators of information (in the realm of management), they must not only be conceived as open, *divergent* discussions or brainstorming sessions, but they also have to be seen as structured and goal-oriented procedures that ultimately lead to a *converging* dialogue on what has to be done next. They require a discussion plan that assures that the debated issues are implemented and that the necessary follow-up actions take place (see also the notes on the knowing-doing gap mentioned earlier). The role of the discussion leader is crucial and cannot be replaced. He needs to plan the conversation, ensure that it proceeds according to the rules of a true dialogue, and he has to shift it from a divergent to a convergent mode once there is suffi-

---

[103] In Harkins (1999) several reasons for such conversational swamps are discussed. They include frequent interruptions leading to a poor exchange of signals and information; unclear, poorly expressed or poorly understood content; unfocused content marked by tangents; or the cramming in of too many facts, concerns, wants and needs.

cient mutual understanding. Another one of his or her tasks is to ask the right, action-inducing questions. This sub-issue of dialogue is explored in the to next paragraph.

Questions as Activators

Asking questions may seem like an unusual mechanism to increase the propensity to use information. Nevertheless, instructive questioning can foster the retention of information and its reflective and creative use by 'forcing' information consumers to examine it more closely.

Asking the right kind of (activating) questions is not an easy task. Skeptical, confusing or intimidating questions can have a contrary effect, namely to delay actions and to foster a paralysis by analysis. Asking the right questions in this context means inquiring in a way that helps information consumers to systematically reflect on information and its possible applications. To develop this questioning skill, information producers must know *which* questions work and *how* to ask them. Substantial management literature is available on both of these issues.[104]

As far as the question types are concerned, various *formats* can be used to activate information consumers, such as questions that require an *evaluation* or *comparison* of information, *hypothetical* questions or questions that regard the *consequences* of information. Examples of such activating questions for the context of knowledge-intensive business processes are the following inquiries:

- Why do you think is this information relevant for us?
- Do you agree with this statement? Why (not)?
- How does this information relate to what we already know?
- What is missing from this information?
- What is the most striking/important/useful element of this information?
- What would happen if we didn't have this information?
- How would you apply this insight? Where would it be useful for us?

---

[104] For an overview on the right kinds of questions see: Finlayson, A. (2001) *Questions That Work: How to Ask Questions That Will Help You Succeed in Any Business Situation*, New York: Amacom. For information on how to ask these questions in the right manner, see: Magruder, J., Mohr, B.J. (2001) *Appreciative Inquiry: Change at the Speed of Imagination*, New York: John Wiley & Sons.

- Who should also know about this?
- Where else could we use this information?[105]

These questions are 'right' because they lead to further probing with regards to the conveyed information. They also need to be asked in the *right manner*, that is to say at the right time (i.e., allowing for reflection), in the right sequence (i.e., moving from easy to difficult questions), in an adequate tone and gesture (i.e., without pressure). To check whether questions are activating or not, an information producer can review them with the following criteria: Do the questions make the information more *meaningful*? Do they motivate the information consumer to make *connections* among concepts? Do the questions direct the attention of the information consumer to the most relevant aspects of the information? Do the questions force him or her to compare, contrast, evaluate or extrapolate information? If one of these criteria are met, then the questions are likely to activate the information consumer.

There are many managerial situations in which the questions mentioned above can be added to information. Typical application areas are project reports that are enhanced with evaluative questions, investment plans that include questions on alternatives, technical manuals that end every chapter with test questions, strategic plans that ask for relevant target groups, or market reports that ask for application areas of the findings.

The next three activation mechanisms do not require extensive explanations as they are already widely used. Training, demonstrating, and simulating are three 'traditional' ways of bringing information to life.

Training, Demonstrating & Simulations

The first method, training, consists of putting information consumers in situations where they need to apply information repeatedly. One such training situation may be an accountant who has to analyze four different balance sheets based on given key ratios and suggest adequate measures within a given amount of time.

Demonstrating usually consists of having information consumers watch somebody use the information in an application context. Such demonstrations may have the form of a screen cam, where a computer user watches how a virtual user operates a software application. A demonstration may also be a guided tour that shows how information has to be consulted,

---

[105] For similar and related instructive questions see also: www.memory-key.com/StudySkills/asking_better_questions. htm.

interpreted, and applied, for example in the case of databases or websites.

Simulation finally is a mixture of the two prior forms. Information consumers can watch how information is applied and replicate the observed behavior in a simulated environment. In this way, the situation of the Kierkegaardian sailor introduced earlier should be prevented, because information consumer know what it feels like to apply the information in more or less authentic situations. Typical simulations include flight simulators or generally complex machine simulators that help pilots or operators remember and apply their instructions. But simulations can also be used in other domains, such as urban planning principles (a famous simulator from this domain is called SimCity), strategic pricing (where various management simulation programs exist), or conflict resolution.

Repetition as Activator

The next activation mechanism is even simpler than the three previous ones. It consists of repeating crucial items of information so that the information consumers are more likely to notice, remember, and apply them. Activation through repetition uses various formats to repeat the same central terms, ideas, problems, errors, concepts or principles. Examples of repetition that are used in this way are technical manuals that repeat crucial user errors at various positions in the manual or product concepts that highlight key advantages of a product idea at various points in the concept. In the context of oral presentations, repetitions are a device that is often used. Typically, the most important elements of a speech are repeated at the end to increase their impact.

Accommodating Learning Styles

Before concluding this section on information activators, we focus on two mechanisms that can be quite costly, but highly effective. The first one consists of adapting the information format and delivery to the cognitive style of the information consumer. The second one will discuss the just-in-time delivery of information based on the information consumer's usage situation.

Adapting information to the cognitive preferences of information users implies that information has to be provided in various formats in order to best suit the cognitive preferences of the targeted information consumers. One typology of cognitive styles that has been used extensively in the management context is the one by PETER HONEY and ALAN MUMFORD (see for example Honey & Mumford, 1982, or

Mumford, 1995). This learning or cognitive style typology[106] is based on the learning cycle of DAVID KOLB[107] and distinguishes among four major learning types: the activist, the reflector, the theorist, and the pragmatist. Honey and Mumford have shown that most people tend to have one dominating style and that this dominating style makes them more or less receptive to various information formats. *Activists* learn best in active, engaging situations and are thus most receptive to information in the form of simulations, games, or trainings. They abhor listening to lectures or reading long tests. *Reflectors* learn best when they have time to reflect on information and if they are presented with information from various perspectives and with additional background or reference material. *Theorists* prefer information in the form of models, theories, and abstract concepts that relate pieces of information to one another. *Pragmatists*, finally, prefer information that is directly linked to a purpose and structured according to the task or the process that is documented. The following table summarizes these preferences.

Learning Style	Preferred Information Formats
Activist	Interactive Information Formats: Checklists, Simulations, Games, Demonstrations
Reflector	Detailed and Varied Background Information: Evaluations, References, Anthologies, Reports, Surveys
Theorist	Synthetic, Abstract Information: Models, Concepts, Visual Frameworks
Pragmatist	Practical Information Formats: Trainings, Process Charts, Guidelines, Question and Answers

Table 17: Learning types and their preferred information formats

---

[106] Honey and Mumford's typology is by far not the only learning typology. It is, however, one of the most practical ones. For an overview on other models of learning types, see for example: DeBello, T.C. (1990) Comparison of eleven major learning models: variables, appropriate populations, validity of instrumentation and the research behind them, in: *Journal of Reading, Writing and Learning Disabilities*, No. 6, pp. 203-222.

[107] Kolb's learning cycle consists of four phases that correspond to Honey and Mumford's four learning styles. The phases are: having an experience (activist), reviewing the experience (reflector), concluding from the experience (theorist), and planning the next steps (pragmatist). See Mumford, 1995, p. 30.

To evaluate the learning style of an information consumer, numerous tests exist. They range from multiple choice questionnaires to a few diagnostic questions that an information producer can ask to better assess the dominating style of his or her information customers. Such diagnostic questions may be whether the information consumer is a perfectionist (an indicator for a theorist or reflector learning style), whether he or she generates ideas quickly (an indicator of an activist learning style), or whether following strict rules is seen as efficient (an indicator for a pragmatist learning style).

Adapting information to the learning style of information consumers can be an arduous task. It may require the adaptation of texts, graphs, interfaces, and sequences. Because of this, it is mostly applied in repeated one-to-one situations, where the information producer can target his information product to the needs of one individual, for example when an expert regularly prepares reports for his or her superior. Hence, this type of activation is a feasible mechanism if there are few information consumers and if their preferences can be assessed easily. Otherwise, this strategy may be too costly to apply. Alternatively, one can choose to provide information for all four cognitive styles simultaneously, that is to say deliver it in four versions. This, however, would require that information consumers are aware of their cognitive styles, which is not always the case. Still, there are many information products (such as several corporate websites) that offer elements that are targeted at activists or pragmatists (such as checklists and question and answer sections) and items that are tailored for reflectors and theorists (background information and visual frameworks). The disadvantage of this approach is that tailoring information to different preferences requires time and results in a direct trade-off with the timeliness and currency of information; and timeliness is often an essential element of information activation. This is fact is highlighted by the last activation mechanism, the just-in-time or push delivery of information. It is described in the next paragraph.

Push Mechanisms   The main idea behind the 'push' activation mechanism is to provide information in the very moment it is needed. In this way, the information consumer does not have to search, store, or remember it. Information is pushed to the user just-in-time whenever the situation requires it. This is especially relevant for time-critical information that has to be provided without delays in the most current version (such as stock prices, news, alerts, complaints, emergencies, etc.). The term *push mechanism* has so far been mostly used in the context of

Internet information services where it designates web content that is delivered to information consumers through dedicated channels with the help of a special markup language. Decina et al. (1999) summarize this view in the quote below.

Push is the *automatic delivery* of content to users' computer desktop; content is organised by topic defined by a publisher and users receive information according to their own pre-defined profile. Three elements thus integrate a would-be complete definition: (1) automatic delivery, (2) content organisation, (3) user profile.

For our context of knowledge-intensive processes, I view push mechanisms in a broader sense, designating all information delivery forms where the information consumer is *automatically notified* about new information that is currently relevant. This can be achieved through various means ranging from e-mails, webcasting, instant messaging, SMS (short messages delivered on cellular phones), to direct personal face-to-face notification. Pushing information can simply mean to notify a specialist who is about to go through a difficult knowledge-intensive process step that there are already codified experiences available that have been documented from previous process runs. It could be as plain as sending an e-mail to a colleague about an expert he has to talk to today. In a more sophisticated form, a push mechanism can be an automated notification that a new document has been published which meets his interest profile. Typical requests of information consumers that can be resolved through push mechanisms are for example: „Notify me when any of my customers has less than two day's supply on hand," „If there is a delay in the project reporting send out warning mails with adequate instructions", or „If there are new reports on labor laws send them to me" (see also http://www.dbmsmag. com/9711i15.html for similar examples).

The activation mechanisms that have been described in this section are just a few of the available tools that can be used to make information more applicable, current, interactive, or speedy. Several other forms exist that can be applied to information in knowledge-intensive processes, such as using emotional triggers, dramaturgy (such as shocks) or frequent examples, assigning priorities, or making information more motivating through real and virtual personalities (such as avatars or chatbots).

The activation principle suggests that information has to be explicitly organized for action, that is to say it must be made applicable and kept current. It must be provided in an interactive and fast manner so that it meets the requirements of the

Conclusion

information consumer's application context.

Examples of mechanisms that help to make information more useful for action are stories, metaphors, mnemonics, simulations, repetitions or push-mechanisms (that provide information when it is needed).

We have now described all the elements of the information quality framework, from the individual criteria and their levels to the principles. In the next section, the framework will be used for several typical application contexts.

3.3 Application of the Framework

My view is that theories are, amongst other things, instruments, but they are not only instruments. The main difference is that I cannot say of an instrument that it is true or false. I can say only that it is a good instrument or a bad instrument and that it is good or bad for a certain purpose.[108]

SIR KAL R. POPPER

Section Overview

In this section, we will put the IQ-framework to use in various knowledge-intensive contexts. In this way, it can be shown that the framework is applicable in a variety of situations and for a variety of purposes. The first subsection demonstrates how the framework can be used as a *diagnostic tool* to analyze, measure and rate information products. The second subsection emphasizes the framework's use as a management and *improvement tool*. In the third section the framework's application in *education, training, and planning* will be discussed.

Three Steps of the Methodology

The three subsections and their sequence can be seen as three main steps of information quality management: First the status-quo and the problems relating information quality have to be *analyzed* and *measured*. Then, *improvement* actions that address the identified problem areas need to be designed and implemented. As a third step, *training* and further *planning* activities should be implemented to assure that the improvements in information quality are sustainable and that the staff understands their logic and importance. The cycle is then completed, or re-iterated, by a new analysis and a measure-

---

[108] Popper, 1994, p. 16.

ment of the achieved improvements. This cycle is similar to the so-called *Deming or Shewart cycle* in Total Quality Management which begins with a planning phase in which quality goals are set and converted into tasks (do), which are then implemented, measured (check) and adapted (act). This generic cycle is summarized in the table below and adapted to the information quality context.

Plan:	The client's information quality expectations and criteria are captured and converted into information product characteristics and tasks. Adequate quality levels are defined by assigning criteria-weights.
Do:	The necessary tasks to develop and maintain a high-quality information product are designed and implemented.
Check:	The compliance of the criteria is checked internally and externally.
Act:	The identified problems are resolved and the tasks are adapted.

Table 18: The PDCA-cycle applied to information quality management[109]

The information quality framework can be used in all of these phases by providing a common reference point and a systematic coordination tool. It can be used to focus all involved parties on the essential elements and levels of an information product.

Using the IQ-Framework

In the planning phase, the IQ-framework can be used to set adequate quality levels and goals, to analyze tradeoffs and devise first action steps. In the „doing" phase, the four IQ-principles and their mechanisms can be used to improve the fitness for use of information products. In the „check" phase, one can use indicators that are derived from the framework and its criteria. In the „act" phase, finally, the framework can be used to split up and assign responsibilities. The next three sections outline how these tasks can be achieved with the help of the IQ-frameworks and its derivatives. For this, however, we do not use the Deming cycle, but the simpler one of analyzing, improving, and sustaining.[110]

---

[109] See Deming, 1986.

[110] A similar approach of information quality management has been suggested by Albrecht (2001). He distinguishes between the assessment phase, the prioritization phase, the re-design and re-education phase, and the re-integration (or alignment) phase.

3.3.1 Analyzing and Measuring Information Quality

Introduction

The application examples discussed in this section focus on the use of the information quality framework as a *diagnostic lens*. First, the framework's criteria will be used as the basis for a questionnaire in order to highlight *perceptual differences* among two groups regarding the current quality status of an intranet. Then, the framework will be used to generate, structure, and apply *indicators* to *evaluate* and *monitor* information products, processes, and infrastructures. As a final application example for the analysis phase, the information quality framework will be used as a *rating* scheme for information products.

1. Assessing Perceived Information Quality

Before information quality can be improved, one has to analyze where the biggest problems arise due to insufficient information quality. In this first diagnostic step, the IQ-framework can be used to identify *perception gaps* (for example between managers and information technology professionals), problem areas, and *improvement needs*.

To assess the current quality level of an intranet (or a website) and its content, the sixteen information quality criteria can be converted into questions. The criterion of comprehensiveness, for example, can be converted into the following question: Do you find that our intranet provides information that is comprehensive enough or are many items incomplete or missing? We have used the IQ-framework in three companies in this way. This was done through an online questionnaire which asked the employees to assess the Intranet according to the sixteen criteria (e.g., is it convenient to use, is it comprehensive, are the entries mostly current, etc.). The (averaged) ratings by the employees revealed, among other things, that perceptions of quality can differ according to the role that an employee has with regard to the intranet. A sample assessment result is represented below. The chart reveals the fact that business customers (e.g. sales staff) assess the quality of the intranet differently than IT-managers of the same company (in regard to various criteria). Generally, the IT managers view the overall quality of the Intranet more optimistically than their internal customers. Their average ratings often achieve the highest score of 5, whereas their customers only rank two criteria as fully achieved (correctness and consistency).

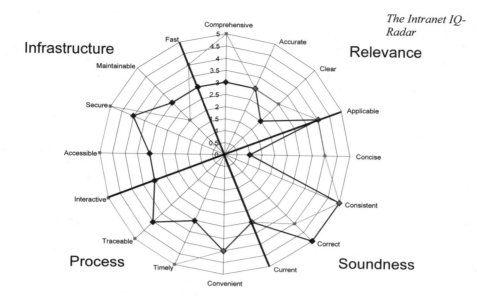

Figure 20: Using the IQ-Framework to make IQ-perception differences visible

The spider web graph, that we label as the IQ-radar (see Eppler & Muenzenmayer, 1999), reveals several discrepancies in terms of the perceived intranet information quality. First, the employees of the information technology department (labeled as IT) believe that they and the information producers or authors provide concise information, when they are in effect overloading the customers who rate conciseness with a score of one out of five points. The customers of the IT department (labeled as Customer), on the other side, are not aware of the maintainability problem that the IT department faces, and that is indicated by the average score of two by IT. Another fact that is revealed by this graphic analysis is that the internal customers may overestimate the correctness of the provided information (since their rating is higher than that of IT).

In terms of the overall assessment, the IQ-radar shows that the process and the infrastructure of the intranet are more or less adequate, while the relevance of the provided information has to be improved. The biggest improvement need is to train authors and information producers to create clearer and more concise information. In the subsequent improvement phase, integration mechanisms (see section 0) have to be implemented.

Interpretation of the Diagram

While the questionnaire-based IQ-radar presented on the previous page can be used to initially assess the overall perceived quality of an information system, such as an intranet, *continuous* quality monitoring cannot be conducted in this manner. Employees simply cannot be asked to fill out a questionnaire of sixteen to twenty questions every week. Thus, automated measurement devices need to be installed. Such measurement tools exist, at least for the Internet and intranet context. With the help of the IQ-framework, they can be matched with all relevant information quality levels and criteria. In the case of Internet and intranet applications, one can distinguish between *site analyzers, traffic analyzers, web mining tools*, and *feedback software*. Site analyzers[111] can be used to assess the quality of the information infrastructure (the lowest level of our framework), while traffic analyzers[112] can measure process quality indicators (such as the convenience and timeliness of information provision). Web mining tools[113] and feedback or questionnaire software can go beyond this and make inferences about information soundness and relevance by recording and analyzing the behavior of information consumers. With the help of these tools and with the structure provided by the IQ-framework, a *quality scorecard* or cockpit can be assembled that provides a concise image of the current state of information quality. As such, the quality scorecard can be used as a management tool to monitor information products, processes, and infrastructures. Below, we provide such as scorecard for an online knowledge base that consists of market analysts reports.

The scorecard is made up of sixteen indicators that are (mostly) measured automatically through the information system. Their color or shade indicates whether the level is above or below a certain desired value (such as seventy percent). In the example represented below, the process indicators are all below the desired level, three of them are very low.

---

[111] Typical site analyzers are Webmaster 5.0 by Coast Inc. (www.coast.com), WebAnalyzer 2.0 by Incontext (www. incontext.com), Watchfire (www.watchfire.com), or Hypertrak Perfor-mance Monitor by TrioNetworks (www.trionetworks.com).

[112] Such as: Hyperion's Web Site Analysis Suite, Netric's Surf Report, Nedstats' SiteStat, Exody's WebSuxess, or Boutell's Wusage product.

[113] Examples of such applications are WebTrends and WebFeedback.

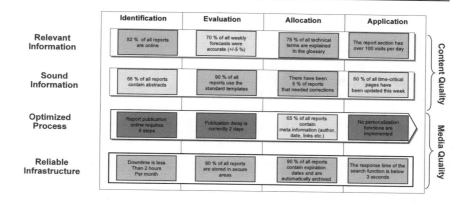

Figure 21: A sample information quality scorecard

By analyzing this scorecard regularly, managers can better know where to focus their information improvement activities. For the present example this is clearly the case for the process dimension where all indicators are unsatisfactory. Indicators such as the sixteen presented in the above figure, need to be specified in terms of (absolute or relative) target values and tested for plausibility. They need to contain a minimal, an optimal, and a warning level as every indicator should be linked to counter-measures that are triggered if a warning level is reached. Besides their warning function, the indicators can also document improvements in information quality, if they are measured regularly.

Description of the Scorecard

Besides the assessment of existing intranets or Internet websites, the IQ-framework can also be used to evaluate the potential impact of a new information infrastructure. Using the IQ-attributes and levels, one can analyze the benefits of introducing a knowledge management system to support knowledge-intensive processes. A knowledge management system is an IT-based software suite that contains collaboration, content management, visualization and aggregation as well as search and retrieval functionalities (see Seifried & Eppler, 2000). In the following table (modified from Eppler, 2001) a knowledge management system is evaluated in terms of its benefits for information quality. In this way, the often nebulous benefits of a knowledge management system can be made more tangible. The first column of the table lists the functionalities of the new knowledge management system (such as computer supported cooperative work and learning, search and filtering mechanisms, portals etc.). The second column indicates which quality criteria are improved through

Evaluating the Impact of a KM-System

the new functionality. The third column lists the software applications that provide the functionalities listed in the first row.

Knowledge Management System Functions	Affected Information Quality Criteria	KM-Applications
Collaboration	Relevance, Optimized Process	Modeled Workflows
CSCW	Timeliness, Applicability, Traceability, Currency	Real-time Virtual Meeting Protocols
CSCL	Clarity, Applicability, Interactivity	Web Based Learning Communities
Groupware	Applicability, Comprehensiveness	Shared Databases, i.e. Lessons Learned Repository
Content Management	Relevance & Soundness	Document and Data Sharing
Document Management	Comprehensiveness, Consistency, Currency	Meta-tagging, Check-in/Check-out
Personal Information Management	Comprehensiveness	Contact Management Software
Group Information Management	Comprehensiveness, Consistency	Contact Tracking Software
Visualization & Aggregation	Soundness	Source Integration and Personalization
Knowledge Maps	Conciseness, Clarity	Knowledge Application Map
Portals	Conciseness, Currency	Employee Portal
Taxonomies	Consistency	Corporate Thesaurus
Directories	Comprehensiveness	Expert Directory / Yellow Pages
Intelligent Search & Retrieval	Relevant Information, Optimized Process, Reliable Infrastructure	Search Engine
Searching	Accessibility, Timeliness	Fuzzy Search Functions
Filtering	Comprehensiveness, Conciseness, Convenience	E-mail Filter
Profiling	Comprehensiveness, Timeliness, Conciseness, Applicability	User Profile
Sorting	Clarity, Applicability	Database Views, Ranking
Push	Timeliness, Convenience	Notification with file attachment
Pull	Accessibility	Notification with link

Table 19: An analysis of the impact of a knowledge management system on information quality

By examining how the functionalities of a knowledge management system affect information quality, management can better assess the potential impact of such a new infrastructure and estimate its cost-benefit ratio. For the system that is assessed in the table above it became evident that the KM-suite lacked functionalities to improve or guarantee the correctness and accuracy of information. It also did not provide sufficient support to guarantee security, maintainability and speed of the system. These IQ-attributes are not directly (or not dramatically) improved through the new system.

Purpose of the Table

The third and final example of using the IQ-framework for assessment purposes is *rating*. The IQ-framework can be used to rate information products much like Moody's or Standard & Poor rate the quality of corporations and their credit risks. Rating in this sense of the term requires a concise and consistent evaluation of an information product based on a systematic set of objective criteria. Rating content in this way is especially crucial for the Internet where traditional quality gates (such as editors or lectors) often do not exist. Some of the existing information quality rating institutions, such as the Internet content rating agency (www.icra.org), focus on self-assessments and aim at clearly designating content that is not suited for all audiences.[114] There are also content rating institutions that evaluate the quality of specialized websites. Such institutions and corresponding rating mechanisms exist for law-related (e.g., the five star legal sites rating) or health-related websites (e.g., the MedCERTAIN Trustmark[115]). While these institutions rate or certify public Internet websites,

3. Rating Information Products

---

[114] Both IT-analyst companies that are described in chapter four offer such rating services. The Giga Group has developed a so-called Website Scorecard and a corresponding rating ribbon to designate sites that have met all its requirements. Gartner Inc. offers a self-assessment tool to evaluate the quality of websites. Neither of the two rating systems has so far gained high visibility outside the IT-sector.

[115] MedCERTAIN states its mission as follows: MedCERTAIN will establish a fully functional self- and third-party *rating system* enabling patients and consumers to filter harmful health information and to positively identify and select *high quality information*. We aim to provide a system allow European citizens to place greater trust in networked information, exemplified in the domain of health information. See: http://www.medcertain.org/english/metadata/overview.htm [13.1.02].

there are also companies that use information quality ratings for their internal information. Organizations with large corporate intranets, such as Deutsche Bank or Reuters, use an Intranet certification mechanism to signal the various information quality levels to their intranet users. The following figure illustrates the rating schema of the Deutsche Bank intranet. It consists of four quality levels that are indicated through star symbols. Each level, ranging form one to four stars, is tied to specific content, technical, and navigation criteria.

Criteria	Number of checkmarks			
	Intranet Certified ★★ ★★	Intranet Certified ★ ★★	Intranet Certified ★★	Intranet Certified ★
Content				
Is there a link to the company's portal on the entry page of the site?	mandatory	mandatory	mandatory	mandatory
Is the content up-to-date?	mandatory	mandatory	mandatory	mandatory
Target group for the site	whole bank	whole bank	Business Division or several hundreds potential readers weekly	
Is the entire content available in English?	mandatory if the target group is global or has a business division scope	mandatory if the target group is global or has a business division scope		
The last update of the site is easily available	mandatory	mandatory		
Is the date of the last update of each page clearly available for the reader?	mandatory			
Technical aspects				
Availability of the site	around the clock, 365 days / year	around the clock	around the clock	
Interactivity / Navigation				
Are the name of the site administrator (Webmaster) and site responsible (Content) given?	mandatory	mandatory		

Figure 22: Deutsche Bank's intranet quality levels

Systematic & Democratic Ratings

These and other rating mechanisms use more or less unsystematic lists of information quality criteria that form the basis for the rating. By using the information quality framework, content rating agencies, especially in the Internet context, can use a coherent set of criteria that clearly distinguishes whether the criteria relate to the relevance of the information itself (i.e., does the site provide the right, relevant information), the soundness or validity of the content (i.e., whether it provides right, correct information), the quality of the information process or service (i.e., whether it provides information right), and the quality of the underlying infrastructure. All of these four levels affect the end-result that is perceived by the information consumer. In fact, the consumer should be involved in the rating process. As indicated in the section on assessment earlier, the criteria of the framework can be converted into evaluation questions. If these questions are asked of information consumers and aggregated, then the rating can incorporate the customer perspective. This can even be done in real-time by providing updated thumbnail ratings on every evaluated page as depicted below.

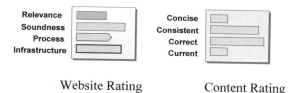

Website Rating   Content Rating

Figure 23: Thumbnail ratings as real-time assessments of information quality

The rating symbol on the left shows that (at the moment of access) the examined website is rated low (by the previous users) in terms of relevance and process quality, but high in terms of content soundness and infrastructure. The rating graph on the right side is placed on a website where the content is rated separately. It reveals that the site's content is rated as not very concise and not very current, but as mostly correct and consistent. This type of real-time rating is already used in various knowledge management systems. The same mechanism can be used for public websites, although there are significant risks of manipulation that have to be addressed first, e.g., avoiding competitors who lower the rating of a website by repeatedly entering low evaluations. A precursor of such a real-time rating can be found in the open reviewing of books at the online bookstore Amazon. There, users can not only rate books they have read, but also the reviews others have written about books.

Explanation of the Diagrams

In this section, we have examined three specific ways in which the information quality framework can be used to analyze information quality problems or assess the current level of information quality. First, it can be used for (collective) *assessments* in order to highlight perception differences. Second, it can be used to *monitor* or evaluate a system. Third, it can be used (internally or externally) as the basis for a *rating* or certification system.

Conclusion

3.3.2 Improving and Managing Information Quality

Introduction

If we are to avoid the problem of paralysis by analysis that has been discussed earlier, specific actions need to follow the analysis of information quality problems. The information quality framework can provide a systematic plan for such actions. Specifically, the framework suggests to focus on improving the relevance and soundness of information, while continually optimizing the provision process and the underlying information infrastructure. For the assessment phase, we have mostly relied on the individual information quality attributes on those four levels. For the improvement, however, we will use the information quality *principles* that simultaneously affect all four levels. The reasoning behind this is that changes on all four levels are necessary to dramatically improve information quality. We can use the four principles to improve information products as diverse as *meeting protocols, project and process documentations, management presentations* or *corporate websites*. In the next few paragraphs we will show how the principles can be applied to these areas. Several real-life examples of such improvements will be provided.

Improving IQ in Meetings

Information plays a crucial role in management meetings, be it real get-togethers, workshops or negotiations, or 'virtual' conversations in the form of videoconferences, desktop conferences, telephone conferences or simple online chat sessions. Information is the basis for the decisions that are made in such meetings. The quality of information is thus a crucial prerequisite for adequate meeting decisions.

Meetings, however, suffer from numerous problems that often lead to inadequate decisions or no decisions at all. Examples of such problems (see Matson, 1996) are unprepared participants, lacking on-site information (which leads to postponed decisions), unfocused and diverging discussions, unclear terms and confusing discussion streams, deviations from the main goal of the meeting, or inadequate timing (i.e., getting lost in details). Increasing the quality of meeting information can reduce many of these problems. By making information more accessible, more current, and more action-oriented, meetings can be improved dramatically. Through the application of the four IQ-principles, we

---

[116] Jerry Rhodes writes on this subject: Making thinking visible in meetings is an important way to assure the quality of thinking that goes on between people who are colleagues and collaborators. See Rhodes (1994), p. 155.

can devise a form of meeting information that 'forces' participants to streamline their meetings and allocate their time more effectively. In the context of the knowledge-intensive process of holding a meeting, the four IQ-principles can be converted into the following imperatives:

- *Integrate* all agenda points, goals, decisions in one chart.
- Have the participants *validate* their statements and the group decisions instantly and not after the meeting.
- Highlight the meeting's purpose by always providing the meeting's *context* in terms of background, timing and goal.
- *Activate* the participants by instantly visualizing[116] what is being said and by showing how much meeting time remains to reach the set goals (this can create a sense of urgency).

Applying these four principles to meetings leads to a radically different type of protocol that can be used to prepare, manage or facilitate, and document a meeting. We have developed a meeting methodology and a software application based on these principles. It is called On*Track* (see Eppler, 2001) and enables teams to generate real-time visual and interactive protocols of their meetings. Thus, the soundness, relevance, convenience, and reliability of the stored information can be improved because the protocol is accessible during and after the meeting (timeliness) and crucial team decisions, argumentation streams, or statements can be quickly identified through the visual cues (conciseness) and zoomed in (comprehensiveness) through clicking on particular statements on the interactive protocol.

The figure below shows a screenshot from a meeting that is about halfway through its agenda. The meeting participants follow the visual agenda through an overhead projector or beamer or through a window in their desktop conferencing system in the case of a virtual meeting (Microsoft Netmeeting in our case since the application was written as a Visual Basic for Application program). In this way the meeting's content is *integrated* in one chart. Additional information can be linked to the individual agenda points or their symbols. The parking symbol at the beginning of the meeting, for example, indicates that this topic has been 'parked' for a later discussion and that more information is available by clicking on the symbol. The statements and decisions are automatically *validated* by all participants as they are able to see (right away) how the protocol documents their statements or the group's decisions. The *context* of the meeting also remains clear as the meeting's goals and agenda points are always visible to every participant. The timer that counts the remaining minutes until the end of the meeting is one device to *activate* the participants. If, for example, only ten minutes are left and the participants see that they have only discussed the first two agenda points, then they will be forced to focus their discussion. In the on-screen version of the application, there is an additional feature that visually shows when participants wander off the main topic. Their statements are written further away from the agenda line, in a darker region (by the protocol writer who manages the software through a simple menu with intuitive buttons). The application also tries to make information more action-oriented by clearly distinguishing discussion elements of the meeting and its main results in terms of key issues and decisions. Decisions that have to be converted into a to do list are visualized in the box left to the discussion and meeting stream.

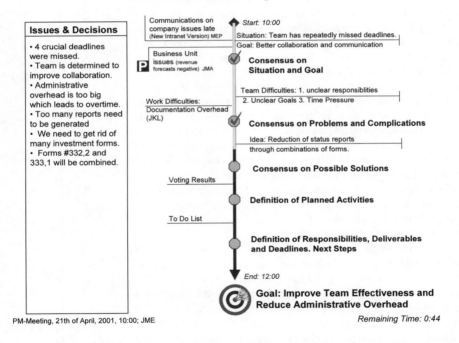

Figure 24: Improving information quality in meetings through a visual protocol

The basic idea behind this approach that can also work with a simple flipchart, is to transform meetings into active information sharing and decision events. This vision is also outlined in the quote below by Eric Matson (Matson, 1996):

Transforming Meetings through Information

The best way to avoid that misunderstanding [that meetings aren't work] is to convert from „meeting" to „doing" - where the „doing" focuses on the *creation of shared documents that lead to action.* The fact is, at most computer-enabled meetings, the most powerful role for technology is also the simplest: *recording comments, outlining ideas, generating written proposals, projecting them for the entire group to see, printing them so people leave with real-time minutes.* Forget groupware; just get yourself a good outlining program and an oversized monitor. [...] „You're not just having a meeting, you're creating a document," says Michael Schrage [a meeting consultant]. „I can't emphasize enough the importance of that distinction. It is the fundamental difference between ordinary meetings and computer-augmented collaborations. Comments, questions, criticisms, insights should enhance the *quality of the document.* That should be the group's mission."

The experiences so far with this approach to meeting information have shown that our application does in fact improve the quality of meetings and their documentation (based on the use in four projects). But the biggest impact has probably been in the preparation phase of meetings. Here, the On*Track* application forces the manager of a meeting to systematically think about the goal of the meeting, the required information and participants, and the logical steps that lead to the meeting's goal. In terms of documentation, we have worked with one company that has put several of these interactive protocols on their Intranet for employees to explore. In addition to using the software to moderate and document meetings, we have also generated meeting templates that managers can use to prepare a meeting (e.g., kick-off meeting templates, conflict or problem resolution templates, information sharing meetings, etc.).

Nevertheless, the application clearly is of limited use if a meeting has many different goals, more than a dozen participants, or a highly emotional content that is best left undocumented. This type of visual protocol may also not be adequate for executive meetings where crucial decisions need to be thoroughly documented in full prose and according to official company guidelines.

Meetings are important catalysts for the conversion of information into decisions and subsequent actions, but they are only moments in time. On a continuous basis, projects and processes are the crucial forms of organizational action. Processes and (time-bound) projects are not only an effective way organizing knowledge work, they are also major instruments of knowledge creation and learning. The documentation of knowledge-intensive processes and projects is thus not only important for controlling purposes, but also for the systematic gathering of valuable knowledge. As discussed in section 3.1.2, there are at least three types of knowledge that should be documented as high-quality information, namely knowledge *about* the process or project (e.g., project management know-how), knowledge used or generated *during* the process or project (industry knowledge or gathered facts), and knowledge derived *from* the project or process (viz. experiences or lessons learned). The four IQ-principles can be used to improve the documentation of all three types of knowledge content. Their application to this context yields the following improvement tasks:

- *Integrating* process and project management documentations from various sources (e.g., applications, legacy systems, personal experiences, manuals, archives, reporting systems etc.) and formats (e.g., plans, courses, guidelines, articles etc.) in one single access point or platform (e.g. through a knowledge management suite) and providing a concise overview on all contents (e.g., through a process portal or a project knowledge map).
- *Validating* information through review cycles and quality gates before it is documented in the project or process repository.
- *Contextualizing* new information by relating it to prior, already documented knowledge. Providing a context for stored information by relating it to the project or process (e.g. at what point in the process the information becomes relevant).
- *Activating* documented knowledge through push-mechanisms or alerts that are automatically triggered once a process or project step is initiated. Clearly highlighting action items in these documents and facilitating

---

[117] This type of interactive project or process documentation can be combined with the visual protocols introduced earlier. By clicking on one of the meeting icons in the project map, one can access the corresponding visual protocol.

their application through training events and personal accounts (success or failure anecdotes). Animating process steps and their sequence and illustrating their critical points through examples.

Using these principles, we can generate a different form of project or process documentation that is highly visible, interactive, current and convenient and that combines knowledge about, within, and derived from a process in one single medium.

A possible starting page for such a platform is depicted below. It shows the main steps of a project, its central activities, people, relations and experiences, as well as the links to important documents and tools. We have implemented two such visual and interactive process and project portals on corporate intranets, one as a project management portal at a new media agency, the other as a key account process portal for a marketing research company.[117] With a third company in the sector of financial services we have used a (Lotus Notes) database interface with the same categories as visualized below (this facilitates the collaborative reviewing of new information). These portals can be used as simple document repositories or as training devices, as they contain not only reports, plans, and calculations, but also checklists, templates, and personal experiences.

While it is too early to evaluate the overall success of all three systems, a higher diffusion of project or process knowledge can already be noted. The main advantage of this form of integrated, interactive documentation is that it is at the same time concise and comprehensive. The criteria that has caused the greatest problems so far is maintainability because changes in the structure of the documentation tend create high modification and maintenance costs, especially in regard to the visualizations. But maintenance is also one of the key challenges in traditional project or process documentations. This is especially true for paper-based (TQM) process manuals that document process know-how. Through our new visual and electronic documentation formats, changes can be detected sooner and their modification can be instantly made visible to all employees.

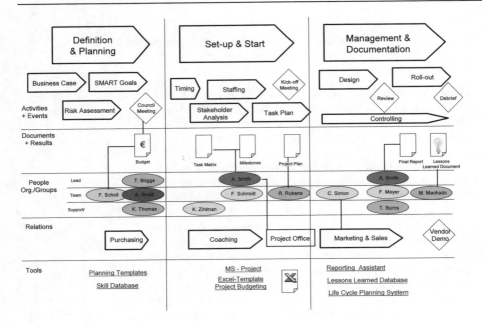

Figure 25: A sample entry page of a project portal

Another, more playful version of this integrated and interactive process map is what I call the process or project underground, a metro-like map of the central steps, documents, experts, and applications needed for a process or a project. The example below is taken from a three year project at the mcm *institute* that is documented interactively with the depicted project map. The main advantages of this type of documentation is that it raises attention, it is based on intuitive conventions and thus easy to use, and it can be appended through new 'metro lines' if needed.

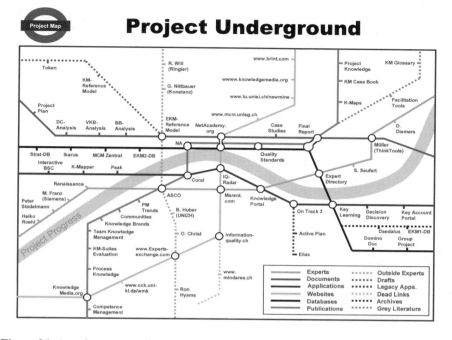

Figure 26: A project map outlining three years of project documentation

While the improvements outlined above can be quite cost-intensive, the next set of measures that are derived from the IQ-principles can be implemented without any additional costs. They simply require some attention. In this paragraph, we focus on a frequently used information product within companies: *management presentations*. Because of the complexity and time pressure of many management decisions, managers often use dedicated specialists to prepare the basis for their decisions. These specialists have the know-how and experience to evaluate options more carefully and present an objective assessment to management in the form of a presentation. The problem, however, that arises from this delegation is one of knowledge asymmetry or knowledge transfer. Specialists often find it difficult to convey their knowledge to managers in a short period of time because the managers do not share the specialist's background, expertise or enthusiasm for a topic. The issue of information quality is consequently of crucial importance for the knowledge transfer between specialists and managers. The symptoms of inadequate information quality in management presentations (that is presentations *to* man-

Improving IQ in Management Presentations

agement) that can be observed are plentiful (see Eppler & Probst, 2001). Specialists tend to overload managers with technical details that are discussed before a sufficient overview on a topic has been given. They often neglect to indicate what consequences their findings have in terms of the practical decisions that need to be made. Many specialists use technical jargon or abbreviations to demonstrate their expertise without ever explaining them. Another frequent mishap in management presentations is that experts run out of time in their presentations because of inadequate planning. Consequently, they cannot repeat their main findings and support them with illustrative examples to facilitate the subsequent decision process of the managers. Many of these symptoms can be avoided if specialists and managers are aware of a few basic principles. Improving the quality of information in presentations requires four major steps:

- *Integrating* the reported findings before presenting them. This means providing an agenda or overview at the beginning of the presentation, limiting every slide to a maximum of seven items (or using diagrams), and clearly emphasizing the main message or insight at the beginning and at the end of the presentation.
- Providing a reasoning that allows managers to *validate* the findings that are presented, e.g., showing how the various recommendations were gathered and assessed and including indicators of certainty or mentioning sensitive areas of an analysis explicitly.
- Establishing a *context* for the presented findings, for example by stressing what is new or surprising in relation to already known findings. The context of the presentation should also be documented: the date, author, event, and location of the presentation should be noted on the slides for future reference or consultation.
- *Activating* the content and the audience by using humour, repeating central ideas, providing frequent examples or by asking thought-provoking questions. Using metaphors and anecdotes and dramaturgy to keep the audience's attention and make the content more salient.

These simple activities can improve the impact of a management presentation because they make it more accessible, more consistent, clearer, and more applicable. In order to assure that his or her presentation to management meets these criteria, a *specialist* must ask him or herself the following questions *before* the presentation:

1. What is my main message and how can I best support it through evidence and examples? Do I give a sufficient overview on the topic before I go into details? (Integration)
2. Do I make clear how my suggestions or findings came about? Do I show the basis of my argumentation and how it could be refuted? Do I highlight areas where I am not a hundred percent sure? (Validation)
3. Do I provide suggestions on how the information has to be interpreted or understood? Do I clearly distinguish between central information and reference information? Do I make clear for whom the information is relevant and why? Do I relate new findings to already existing knowledge of my target audience? (Contextualization)
4. Do I help management to remember and understand the key take-aways of my presentation or am I overloading them with boring details? How can I maintain their interest in the topic through examples? Which information format is most useful for the managers in their subsequent work? (Activation)

The *management* in return can also play an active part in increasing the impact of a presentation given by a domain expert. Specifically, managers can ask the following questions *during* a presentation:

1. What is the main message or insight of this presentation for me and what consequences does it have for my decisions and options? (Integration)
2. How did the expert come up with these findings? Which methods and sources are behind the main insights? Can I rely on them? Does the argumentation make sense? Where can I find further evidence for these claims? Do the other members of management agree with the conclusions? (Validation)
3. How should I interpret the findings? What do I need to understand in detail and where can I just follow the basic line of argumentation? How does this information relate to what I already know about the topic? Can I use this information for other areas? (Contextualization)
4. What do I have to remember for my next decisions? How can I comprehend or use it better? Do I need to convert the findings into other formats so that it can be used better by my colleagues? (Activation).

These questions force a manager to reflect on his or her understanding of a complex presentation. They foster an active elaboration of the presented information and thus increase the propensity of management to act on presented information. The check questions cannot, however, replace the expertise of a presenter or the common sense of a manager, but neither managers nor experts are usually specialists in knowledge transfer or information quality (and they don't need to be). Asking the questions listed above (and finding answers to them), can provide a basic review mechanism for information quality in complex decision processes. In this way, management presentations can become true knowledge sharing events and not just face-offs between experts and decision makers.

Improving IQ in Corporate Websites

Management presentations are mostly internal information products and typically address only a small number of people. One of the most visible *external* information products with a potentially global audience is a company's website. A corporate website is a central point of contact for (potential) customers, employees or investors.

Company websites, however, suffer from numerous problems. They are confusing and inconsistent in terms of layout and navigation, they force the information consumer to wait or register through lengthy forms, they contain obsolete and outdated pages or dead links, and they make information difficult to find by using ambiguous terminology or by employing too many navigation levels.

The root causes for these problems are often internal ones: There is no clearly defined review and publication process or style guide within the company. The responsibilities for the website are not divided properly among the various departments and offices. The content of the website is organized in terms of the internal structure and not according to external needs. The information consumer is distracted by a lot of irrelevant information or by frequent changes in the overall logic of a site. To overcome these and other problems numerous approaches exist (see for example Alexander & Tate, 1999, Clausen, 1996, Belcher et al. 2000, Moore & Wiener, 2001). In terms of the four IQ-principles, they can be summarized as follows:

- *Integrate* the content of the website in terms of processes, infra-structures and interfaces: Use one publication platform (such as Lotus Notes or Vignette Storyserver) and one consistent process design and an enforced set of standards for the website. Make the content easily accessible to information consumers through a portal-type starting page (that is structured in terms of user categories), a comprehensive site map and a search engine.

- Make sure that only *validated* information is published on the website: Install an internal review process for information that is put online. Use different quality gates for different types of information (i.e., according to the timeliness and criticality of the information). Install a feedback mechanism with the web audience by inviting comments and user ratings in order to externally validate the published content. Use web-statistics as an additional point of validation.

- Ensure that all published pages are properly *contextualized*: Every page should contain a 'last updated' section, an author and contact section, and relevant meta-information in the so-called meta-tags of each page (for search engines and web-crawlers, etc). Use expiration dates as internal meta-information to automatically archive outdated content.

- *Activate* the online content through adequate metaphors, people, colors, animations and multimedia elements. Activate the information consumer by giving him or her the choice to select, filter or be notified about changes.

These steps can already improve the quality of a website dramatically. They are, however, easier to list than to implement, as they require a great deal of discipline on behalf of a company's staff. This is true for all the information products examined in this section, whether meetings, documentations, presentations, or websites. Information quality requires a systematic and disciplined approach. If this discipline is neglected, then the achieved improvements are only temporary. This important issue of how the discussed improvements can be sustained is discussed in the next section.

In this section we have looked at ways of applying the information quality principles to improve the quality of information in such diverse fields as meetings, reports, presentations or websites. I have shown that integrating, validating, contextualizing, and activating information are fundamental issues in most information products that are used in knowledge-intensive business processes.

Conclusion

3.3.3 Teaching and Sustaining Information Quality

Introduction

In this section we look at the application of the information quality framework in teaching and communication to foster information quality related skills and behavior on a sustainable basis. First, we examine how the IQ-framework can be used as a *curriculum* and as a tool for information quality courses and seminars. Then, we look at the framework's use as a planning and communication device in the form of an information quality *vision*.

1. Teaching IQ Concepts

If the principles that are proposed in this book should have any sustainable effect on information in knowledge-intensive processes, then it is inevitable to educate and train managers about the importance of information quality. Information quality is not an issue that only involves information system professionals, but one that should be on the agenda of any business school or executive education program. This view is emphasized by the following two quotes from Khalil et al. (1999, p. 57, my italics).

IS students should be exposed to a more detailed elaboration of the *general IQ concepts* and to *detailed methods and techniques* to achieve high-quality information. They should also understand the need for IQ improvement goals to fit the objectives of the organization and the need for integrated, *cross-disciplinary* management of information production, storage, and use processes. This understanding should include both the product and service aspects of information. [...] Faculty initiatives still primarily focus on the product aspects of information quality rather than the service aspects. The more critical issue, however, is to examine what should be taught in both the IS curriculum and the *management curriculum* about IQ.

Topics such as information as a product and service, management and quality control of information processes, should be covered in *non-IS courses*, such as marketing, managerial accounting, and operations. (Khalil et al, 1999, p. 59)

Using Case Studies

The authors, professors at various North American universities, argue that information quality should be a key topic in courses ranging from marketing to operations management. In my view, information quality is first and foremost a general management topic that should be included in most MBA programs, whether as a dedicated course or as an element in quality management, MIS (management information systems), knowledge management or introductory information management courses. Nevertheless, there isn't any literature on how to teach information quality concepts in non-IS (information systems) courses. The case studies that are provided in section four can provide some first steps in this direction. They can be used to sensitize management students to problems of accuracy, applicability, maintainability etc. in business processes. In addition, they illustrate the use of various measures and principles. While case studies are one feasible (and authentic) way of fostering information quality related skills, they are probably not sufficient. As Khalil et al. write, students should also be exposed to *detailed methods* (e.g., organizational measures and quality improvement tools) and to *general IQ concepts,* such as the relevant theories (e.g., on cognition, technology, design, communication) and the specific information quality terminology. For those key tools and concepts, the IQ-framework can provide a generic structure for a management curriculum. Such a curriculum is described in the next paragraphs.

A curriculum on information quality that is based on our framework consists of two overall blocks: first, a theoretical one with a focus on concepts, terms, and (reflected) theories; second, a practical one with a focus on tools, methods, and applications.

Using the Framework as a Curriculum

The *theoretical* block contains five main modules (see the figure below). In the fist module, students examine ways in which information is actually used in management contexts. Various information management cycles are examined in regard to their differences and similarities (as compared in Meyer 1996). Specifically, this module examines how managers identify, evaluate, allocate, and apply information. The module also contains the central information problems that have been examined in this chapter, namely information overload, misjudgment, misallocation and misinterpretation, and information misuse or paralysis by analysis. In the second module, the subjective or relative information characteristics are examined. The concepts of information scope (comprehensiveness), accuracy, clarity, and applicability are examined from various (economic, social, psychological, technological) perspectives. The third module then discusses intrinsic information characteristics, labeled as the four c's, viz. conciseness, consistency, correctness, currency. With the help of several examples, students examine how these attributes affect the overall impact of information. The fourth module examines the content management process and its steps, problems, roles and responsibilities. The fifth and final module discusses the necessary infrastructures to meet the various demands of information producers, administrators, and consumers. The tradeoffs among the various levels and criteria are also discussed in this final module of the theoretical block. The five modules and their sequence are summarized in the figure below.

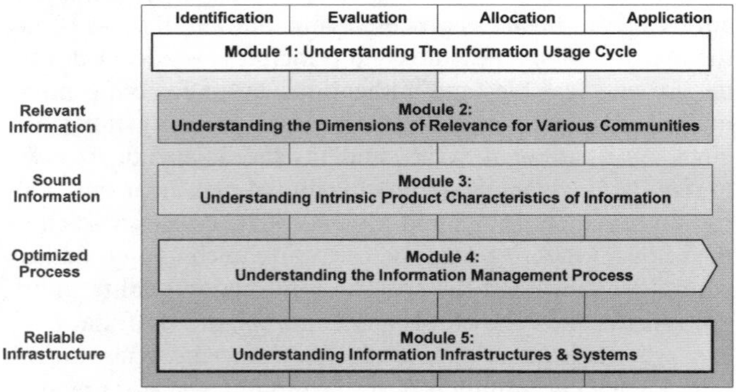

Identification	Evaluation	Allocation	Application

| | Module 1: Understanding The Information Usage Cycle | | |

Relevant Information — **Module 2: Understanding the Dimensions of Relevance for Various Communities**

Sound Information — **Module 3: Understanding Intrinsic Product Characteristics of Information**

Optimized Process — **Module 4: Understanding the Information Management Process**

Reliable Infrastructure — **Module 5: Understanding Information Infrastructures & Systems**

Figure 27: A core curriculum on information quality

The theoretical block depicted above serves as a general introduction to information quality. It should foster a sense of orientation and systematic reflection on crucial information quality stakeholders, terms and problems.

The *practical* block that follows focuses on the development of skills and competences. Specifically, students learn how to *diagnose* information quality problems, how to *improve* information products, and how to *implement* organizational measures to guarantee information quality. How these three competencies can be developed in the context of a general management course is described in the next few paragraphs.

Using the Framework as a Pedagogic Tool

To foster the *diagnostic competence* of current or future managers, the IQ-framework can be used as an evaluation schema. In an information quality course that I teach at the MBA-level, students have to analyze a website, a knowledge management system, a project reporting system, or a technical manual in terms of information quality. Specifically, the students are asked to analyze an information product in terms of the four levels and the sixteen criteria of the IQ-framework. They have to pay special attention to evident tradeoffs between various criteria. After two to three hours, the students present their findings in the form of a rating, as discussed earlier in the section on assessment and rating. Their presentations end with specific suggestions on how the quality of the information product can be improved.

To further foster the *improvement competence,* students must be able to experiment with various improvement tools and mechanisms. The four IQ-principles and their associated mechanisms must be integrated into exercises and case studies. Students must apply these measures to low information quality products and improve them under time pressure. The following table lists some of the tools and techniques that can be used in that context.

IQ-Principles	Relevant Techniques, Tools and Skills to be Taught
Integration	Visualization, abstraction, filtering, categorizing / taxonomy-building, portal technology, media conversion, etc.
Validation	Sensitivity analysis, estimates, source evaluation, reputation check, statistical tests, etc.
Contextualization	Meta-data, adding catalysts, referencing, revision history, usage scenarios, etc.
Activation	Asking instructive questions, story telling, using analogies, metaphors and mnemonics, providing examples, simulation, stating implications or action items, accommodating cognitive styles, etc.

Table 20: Techniques to be covered in the practical block of the course

To foster the *implementation* or management competence, students must be informed about crucial organizational tools that can be used to sustain a corporate information quality program or initiative. Examples of such organizational mechanisms are guidelines, quality circles, quality rewards and incentives, workflows, forms and templates or collaborative problem solving techniques such as Ishikawa diagrams or force field analyses. Some of these tools can be used in a classroom situation. They are briefly summarized in the next table. The table also indicates how the tools can be used in in-class assignments.

Organizational IQ-Tools	Teaching Format
Information Quality Circle	Students work in interdisciplinary teams to work out information quality problems documented in a case study (e.g., in the form of role plays).
Process Redesign and Process Gates	Students analyze a reporting process and devise adequate review mechanisms and gates to improve reporting quality.
House of Information Quality	Students are asked to relate their expectations in regard to the course material to information quality criteria (e.g., what makes their course material maintainable or actionable?).
Ishikawa-Diagram for Information Quality Defects	Students must summarize the problems mentioned in a case study with the help of an Ishikawa diagram (see chapter 0).
Customer Surveys on information satisfaction and visualization of results with Pareto chart	Students are asked to convert information quality criteria into a questionnaire, e.g., on the quality of the university homepage.
Information Quality Monitoring	Let students experiment with monitoring tools, such as site analysers, traffic analysers or web mining tools. Many of them can even analyze public websites.
Forms and Templates	Students are asked to devise a sample form or template for a management manual, a project report, or a department website.
New organizational roles (quality manager, information product manager etc.)	Let the students write sample job descriptions for information quality-related functions (incl. The required qualifications for the task).
Policies and Guidelines[118]	Have students write up guidelines for e-mail and online communication with the help of the UBS case study from chapter four.
Information Quality Mission Statement	Students must formulate an IQ-vision for a company.
Force Field Analysis of Information Quality	The students list positive and negative influences on information quality and assess their impact.
Information Quality Standards & Indicators	Students must find measurable indicators for every IQ-criterion.

Table 21: IQ-Tools and their use in management education

2. Information Quality Mission

One of the organizational tools that is listed in the table above is the information quality *mission*. A mission can play a powerful role in sustaining the momentum for information quality improvements. This is why we look at this particular application of the IQ-framework in more detail. In this final section, we examine how information quality can be fostered on a sustainable basis by other means than teaching. Another way to foster information quality oriented behavior

---

[118] For an example of how to devise information quality guidelines in the source selection context, see Belcher et al. 2000.

is by committing the workforce to a common information quality vision. Such a vision outlines the goals, steps, and criteria that are set for information quality. Several companies have begun to articulate such visions. Below, we provide three real-life examples of such vision statements. Two of them are concise, focusing only on the main goals and tasks, one is more elaborate because it also includes the means and resources that are used to achieve the set goals.

The Swiss bank UBS has articulated an information qual- *The Intranet* ity vision for its intranet and Internet websites that is di- *Quality Vision* rectly derived from the framework developed in this study. *of UBS* It reads as follows:

The target of Web Quality Management is to promote a quality-oriented publishing culture for both bank web and Internet by setting appropriate standards, monitoring tools and initiatives.

Our mission is to install a functioning quality management system (roles, processes, standards, tasks, templates) for the web publications of the corporate center, both externally and internally, to assure that the published *content* is correct, consistent, clear and up-to-date, that the publishing *process* is streamlined and optimized on an ongoing basis, and that the *infrastructure* is accessible, stable and secure.

Another large Swiss bank that struggles with similar prob- *Credit Suisse's* lems is Credit Suisse. The vision of CREDIT SUISSE for its *Intranet Vision* intranet (called Privatelink) is the following one (Muenzenmayer, 1999, p. 34):

Provide readers with a fast, user-friendly intranet containing comprehensive, reliable and up-to-date information. Provide each organizational unit with a state-of-the-art platform for publishing information quickly, easily and cost-effectively.

As we can see, both information quality visions include a number of quality criteria and solution components. A more elaborate information quality vision has been developed at British Telecom. It does not only contain the major goals of the information quality initiative, but also the various means of getting there. It is reproduced in its entirety below. The author of this version is NIGEL H. TURNER of British Telecom, London. Its application scope is so far limited to the IT department of networkBT.

INFORMATION VISION FOR *networkBT*

For *networkBT* to achieve its strategic goals it is imperative that we develop world class network information management capabilities. One of our key strategic objectives will be to apply asset management principles and practices to our information assets, so that we *minimise the costs of failure incurred by poor information* quality and realise the opportunities inherent in the exploitation and management of **high quality information**.

To achieve this goal, all our information improvement activities will be driven by 10 key principles:

1. *networkBT* board members will be given individual responsibility for enhancing the value of appropriate areas of our information assets. *Information quality will be managed actively*, with *explicit criteria* laid down for *accuracy, completeness, accessibility & ease of use*.
2. We will define and enforce *methods & standards* for management of information. We will also set *improvement targets* and measure achievement against them.
3. We will appoint *information stewards* who will act as the dedicated agents of *networkBT* board members and who will be tasked with enhancing the value of our information for the benefit of our customers, our suppliers and our people & agents.
4. We will *educate* all our people to value information as a key business asset. We will recognise and *reward* good stewardship of information and take corrective action where information is not stewarded to the standards expected. We will communicate our information successes and failures to all our people and agents and encourage their input and participation in improvement activities.
5. We will build and maintain effective *feedback mechanisms* so that identified information problems can be fed back to a named individual. On resolution the originator will be informed of the outcome.
6. We will create and sustain a *culture* where we recognise and reward people who share information responsibly across *networkBT*, and outside. We will also lay down the conditions for sharing of information to ensure that the information is shared on the basis of need and adheres to corporate, regulatory and legal requirements.
7. Our business *processes* and supporting *systems* will be designed and operated to ensure that the integrity and quality of our information is maintained and enhanced.
8. We will minimise *duplication* and *redundancy* of information. Where duplication is required for operational reasons we will ensure that master sources of information and defined and managed. Secondary sources will be rigorously registered and controlled.

9. We will build and maintain a comprehensive *inventory* of our information assets so we know what information we hold, where our information is, why we hold it, who is responsible for it, and who uses it.
10. We will provide our people and agents with industry best *tools* and methods to baseline, cleanse, maintain, enhance and audit our information assets. Activities will be automated wherever possible.

As the other two visions, this one commences by explicitly stating the relevant information quality criteria (after having given a rationale for the vision itself). It then moves on to list the activities that are planned to improve these criteria, such as standards, roles, processes, training, methods, cultural issues, infrastructures and tools.

Comments on the Vision

Means as the two discussed in this section have their obvious limitations. Even if employees have the necessary IQ-qualifications because of adequate training, and even if they are made aware of the key IQ-goals through a clearly articulated vision, they may still lack the willingness or the time to care for high-quality information. Information quality is, as so many other issues, a *leadership* challenge. This is one of the reasons why two of the three visions reproduced above stress the aspect of *culture*. Visions and trainings are like water on a hot stone if the corporate culture does not foster information quality on all levels and in all knowledge-intensive areas. They produce a quick sizzle and then evaporate.

Limitations of Trainings and Visions

In this section, we have looked at specific ways in which the information quality framework can be used to foster high-quality information. One such way was a management *course* that consists of a theoretical and a practical block, covering central concepts, theories, tools and applications. Another way of fostering information quality based on the IQ-framework is a clear and concise *vision statement* that outlines the rationale, the goals and the means of a company in regard to its information quality.

Conclusion

3.4 Conclusion: Main Insights of the Framework

Conclusion of the Framework and its Application

The main claims of the framework presented in this chapter have been the following ones: To increase the quality of information, it has to be targeted at a specific community in order to be relevant. It has to be managed as a product (with intrinsic qualities that we call soundness) and as a (continually optimized) content management process. The platform on which information is provided has to be managed in order to be reliable. We refer to this reasoning as the four views or levels of information quality: the *community* level, the *product* level, the *process* level, and the *infrastructure* level.

To manage the quality of information one has to pay attention to the author's, administrator's, and user's point of view and to their specific needs. One has to be aware of the potential conflicts between various information quality criteria and make these constraints visible for information consumers, authors, and administrators.

The information user needs to be able to find and access the information (*identification* phase), he needs to be able to assess the information (*evaluation* phase), he has to be able to see the information in context and adapt it to his specific situation (*allocation* phase), and he has to be able to use the information for decision-making or other applications (*application* phase). In order to assure that this is possible, certain management activities must take place at every one of the four described levels and in every one of the described phases. One can summarize these management or value-adding activities with the help of four principles: the identification, validation, contextualization, and activation principle. These principles make it easier to communicate and implement an information quality improvement program (versus having to explain a great number of criteria).

Repetition of the Main Elements

One of the key principles proposed in this study is the principle of „integration" or content synthesis. This principle argues that the value of information can be increased by providing a concise overview on it. Since this study tries to apply its findings to itself, I provide a brief summary of the main findings of the research up to this point:

1. There is a wide array of research which focuses on the concept of information quality which can be defined as the fitness for use of information for its creators, administrators, and users.

2. The current research can be grouped according to the level of analysis and to the focus of attention.

3. The main problem groups that can be identified as information quality problems are: information overload (information is not integrated), information misjudgment (information is not validated), information misinterpretation (information is not seen in context or contextualized), and information misuse (information is not made actionable).

4. In order to increase the quality of information, it has to be targeted at a specific community in order to be *relevant*, it has to be managed as a product (with intrinsic qualities that we call *soundness*) and as a (*optimized*) content management process, and the platform on which information is provided has to be managed in order to be *reliable*. We refer to this reasoning as the **four levels** of information quality: the **community** level, the **product** level, the **process** level, and the **infrastructure** level.

5. In order to assure the quality of information, certain management activities must take place at every level. One can summarize these management or value-adding activities in **four principles**.

6. The **integration** principle states that high-quality information has to be condensed or compressed (made *comprehensive, concise, convenient*, and *accessible*) in order to give the information consumer an *overview* before details are presented.

7. The **validation** principle states that high-quality information has to be validated (in terms of *correctness, consistency, timeliness,* and *security*) in order to present only *adequate* information to the information consumer and that the validation mechanisms that lie behind a piece of information be made visible.

8. The **context** principle states that high-quality information is always presented or made accessible with its context of origination and its context of use (where did it come from, why is it important and to whom, how should it be used).

9. The **activation** principle states that high-quality information provides means of activating the information in the mind of the information consumer and thus renders it *useful*. Activation mechanisms make information memorable, and thus more easily *applicable*, keep it *current*, make it interactive (to be useful to the specific needs of the user) and assure that the information can be used fast.

Conclusion

In order to be useful, a framework must not only provide a systematic set of categories. It must also provide help how these categories can become meaningful to the people who could benefit from them. Such means are case studies, templates, management principles, or examples.

4. Information Quality Case Studies

In this chapter various real-life examples are presented which illustrate means of analyzing and improving information quality in the context of knowledge-intensive processes. The chapter concludes by formulating propositions and conclusions derived from the six case studies.

Chapter Overview

4.1 Overview of the Case Studies

The following case studies illustrate the application of the framework developed in chapter three. Specifically, the following case studies are used to *highlight authentic problems* of assuring information quality in knowledge-intensive processes (in the problem section of every case), to specify what the quality *criteria* mean in real-life situations (there is a criteria table in every case study), to illustrate effective means of *implementing* the IQ-principles, and to elicit key *success factors* that enable high quality information products. The key success factors are addressed in each case study and they are examined in a cross-case study manner in the last section of this sub-chapter.

Purpose of the Case Studies

The following case studies are all organized in the same way. This will enable the reader to make comparisons between the individual cases. In addition, the 'replication logic' of these multiple cases allows for an easier detection of common themes and topics (or crucial differences) and consequently increases the external validity of the documented research (see Yin, 1994, p. 33). The structure that is used to describe the company cases is as follows.

Consistent Case Study Structure

Every case study begins with a brief description of how the case information has been gathered. Then, the company's context and *background* is outlined. This includes a brief history of the firm and its development, as well as information on its current size and scope. Thereafter, the *products and services* are described and how they are managed to increase the quality of information. After that, the actual production *process* and its *problems* are discussed. The problem discussion is followed by a brief overview on *competitors* and by statements of *customers* on what they like or dislike about the company's information services. To conclude the case study, I outline possible *future developments* and recap the *main insights* regarding information integration, validation, contextualization and activation. Crucial *contextual factors* that foster information quality in the described context are also summarized at this point.

Two Types of Case Studies

There are two types of case studies included in this section to present empirical evidence on the usefulness and applicability of the information quality framework. The first type is *action research case studies*. They have been researched through active participation in the problem solving process at the described company (the first and the second to last case are of this type). The second type of case study material has been gathered through personal interviews, document analysis, and product or service tests.

Company	Key Product in the Case	Problem	Solution	Case Methodology
1. IHA·GfK	Market research reports	Make the reports more useful to managers; offer knowledge, not just data.	Improve the knowledge transfer to the client by activating the information through value-added infor-mation services.	Action research over a period of three years (1998-2001) with the company.
2. get Abstract	Business book summa-ries	The often high time investment to read a business book and under-stand its main ideas and concepts.	Have professional writers produce concise, five page summaries with a consistent rating, structure and style.	Interview with the CEO, several customer inter-views, press analysis, extensive tests of the services, website analysis (June 2001).

Company	Key Product in the Case	Problem	Solution	Case Methodology
3. Gartner Inc.	Research and analyst reports	Increase the value and impact of IT-research reports.	Provide a client extranet and concise research notes with reoccuring elements.	Interview with the Country Manager of Gartner Inc. Switzerland, several customer interviews, test of the services and products, website analysis (August 2001).
4. Giga Information Group	Research and analyst reports	Increase the value and impact of research briefings.	Provide a client extranet and concise research notes.	Interview with the managers of Giga Switzerland, several customer interviews, test of services, website analysis (August 2001).
5. UBS	Financial services	Increase the quality of business-related internal communication.	Establish a set of concise and consistent communi-cation guidelines	Action research over a period of three years (1998-2001) with the company.
6. EIU (Economist Intelligence Unit)	Country Risk Reports	Guarding and further improving the information quality of the expert reports while growing the buisiness strategi-cally.	Recruit highly experienced analysts, install various quality checks and provide versatile interaction with the content.	Interviews with EIU managers and experts, as well as customers in 2003 and 2004. Extensive tests of the services.

Table 22: Overview of the case studies in this section

The six case studies documented in this section highlight information quality criteria, problems, solutions, and contextual factors. They show specific ways in which the quality of information can be improved. The case studies also illustrate why information quality is a decisive factor in many competitive markets.

Conclusion

4.2 Activating Knowledge: The Added Value of Market Research Reports at IHA·GfK

The data business is saturating and becoming a commodity. The knowledge business knows no limits.

PETER HOFER, CEO, IHA·GfK

Case Study Sources

This case study is based on action research with the company over the course of three years. The action research took the form of over fifty personal interviews with employees, numerous workshops with various teams and departments of the company, and an analysis of its products and services. In addition, we analyzed the Internet and intranet sites and evaluated the local infrastructure and working practices. The dominating element of the action research, however, was a bilateral project between our competence center at the University of St. Gallen's Institute for Media and Communications Management (=mcm *institute*) and the company's management. In working together with the company for this project, we analyzed its *information process* (from the client briefing and first offer through survey construction, survey use, survey codification and analysis, to the final survey interpretation and client feedback) as well as samples of the final information *product* (the market reports) and the *infrastructure* (such as the company's client extranets, the local IT-system). Besides these direct sources, we have analyzed a number of competitors.

Company Overview

IHA·GfK[119] (see www.ihaGfK.ch) is the largest Swiss market research company with one of the highest market shares in the national market research and market information services domain. It is part of the international market research group GfK (Gesellschaft für Konsumforschung) which is headquartered in Nuremberg, Germany, and which is the eighth largest market research company in the world in terms of annual sales. The organization in Switzerland has over 300 employees and thus qualifies as a medium-sized company. In addition to its own staff, the company owns several smaller Swiss companies in the area of empirical market and social research. IHA·GfK was founded in 1959. In 2000, its annual sales were 70.9 million Swiss Francs.

---

[119] The company name is an abbreviation which written out translates into "Institute for Retail Analyses / Society for Marketing."

The main products of this company are market research and public opinion studies, market data and statistics, and market and (food, non-food, near-food, pharmaceutical, and media) sales analysis tools, such as media monitoring tools, category management tools or sales analyzer applications. IHA·GfK is a classical market research group that works for multinational consumer good manufacturers, pharmaceutical companies, retail stores, and the media industry (e.g., newspapers, radios, and TV-stations). The Swiss federal government, specifically the federal bureau of statistics, is also a key client of the company. Typical questions that IHA·GfK answers are: 'How many people are watching our program?' 'What does the general public think of our image?' 'Are our clients satisfied with our products?' 'Where is our market going in terms of pricing and promotions' 'How many units have we sold in this region?' 'Where do we lose customers?' or 'What is our market share in the upper price segment?'

The Core Product

Besides the traditional market research services, such as surveys, sales data, store checks or mystery shopping (e.g., analyzing points of sales), customer or employee satisfaction surveys, and focus groups, IHA·GfK also offers *consulting services* that help clients interpret and follow-up market findings. These consulting services often take the form of a workshop or executive coaching. The workshops, which go beyond the mere presentation of market research findings or sales data, try to create new knowledge by bringing together various experts (and sometimes even competitors) from an industry domain. Examples of such additional services are 'prosumer' forums (discussions with customers about product improvements), trend workshops (seminars about future industry developments), or car clinics (where automotive issues are discussed).

Additional Services

Since this company's main products are in fact information products, the quality of information is a crucial competitive component. Until recently, however, the quality of information was mainly viewed in terms of accuracy, consistency, correctness, timeliness and currency (i.e., getting the numbers right). But in 1999 (as market data became more and more of a commodity), the company realized that a higher margin business could only be entered if other quality criteria such as applicability, convenience, conciseness, clarity, or maintainability started to become relevant to them. This, however, meant a change in the available infrastructure and in the qualifications of its staff who –until then – were mostly trained in statistical analysis and not always proficient in information design and effective client communication.

The Crucial Role of Information Quality

The New Strategy

The changing business environment also meant a change in strategy. Simply reacting to customer inquiries and delivering the data they asked for was no longer enough. IHA·GfK needed to re-bundle its market data creatively to generate customer value beyond the mere delivery of sales data. It needed to think about the strategic issues in the markets of their clients. This signified a new role that was often as close to consulting as to market research. It also signified investments in knowledge management to better use the available tools and know-how and make them continuously available to employees and clients. The CEO of the company, Peter Hofer, formulated this strategy as follows:

Flipping the Information Pyramid

We want to keep and extend our market leader position in Switzerland through a professional *project engineering, optimized standard processes*, and through a focus on *added value* behavior, which means that we develop information concepts that help our clients pursue their strategies.

In order to provide such 'information concepts', the company realized that it had to understand the strategies of its clients and adapt its data accordingly, so that the provided information could be directly useful for strategic decision-making. In explaining this strategy to his employees, the CEO used the picture of a pyramid made up of data on the lower, information on the middle, and knowledge on the top level. He called the new strategy a 'flipping' of the pyramid: whereas IHA·GfK used to focus on the lower level of the pyramid, mainly selling data as raw, un-interpreted market statistics, it should now focus on providing actionable advice and market know-how with corresponding analysis tools and techniques. This would not only ensure customer loyalty and competitive differentiation, but, as stated above, also a higher margin business, since the relationship with the clients would consequently evolve from a 'data supplier' to a 'solution partner.'

The CEO summarized this view with the phrase: "The customer defines the rules of the game." How IHA·GfK has reacted to these new rules and how it changed from a *data supplier* to a *knowledge broker* is described in the next paragraphs, where we outline some of the actions taken to increase the quality of information for both the employees of the company and its clients.

Activities to Improve Information Quality

As so often, no single activity is enough to dramatically improve the quality of information and re-position a company as a provider of high-quality content. Rather, a mix of *technological, behavioral*, and *organizational* changes has to be initiated. This was also true in the case of IHA·GfK. There, these changes affected most information quality criteria and improved the perceived value of the offered information products.

As far as *technological* changes are concerned, they deal primarily with the improved *access* of clients, partners, and employees to market information. A key vehicle for this greater accessibility is of course the Internet. Selected clients were given direct access to data analysis tools over a dedicated *extranet* that bundles relevant data and applications. In this way, IHA·GfK was no longer just a supplier of data, but in fact an application service provider that hosted various analysis tools (and their content). With these on-line tools, a client can run individual analyses and use not only the standard market data, but generate individual views on specific market segments. Instead of a finalized and neatly printed market report, the client has the possibility to explore the gathered data interactively and generate views that fit his or her profile and tasks. In consequence, the technological change that consisted of moving data on-line and giving customers access to it with the help of sophisticated applications has also increased the *interactivity* and *applicability* of the information.

Technological Changes: Client and Knowledge Portals

As far as the employees and their access to internal information is concerned, a *knowledge portal* has been created that provides a concise overview on over seventy available internal tools and information sources. This overview on the intranet has the format of an interactive knowledge map.[120] The map is depicted in the figure below. It shows the various tools and information sources that an employee can use when gathering, analyzing, organizing or communicating information.[121] Underlined items are tools or applications that are

---

[120] For the qualities and functions of such interactive maps see also Peterson (1995).

[121] Another element in the knowledge portal besides this map and various links and directories is an *interactive balanced scorecard*. In order to make the vision of the CEO, formulated on the previous page, come alive, we needed to make it more accessible to employees. For this purpose, we developed an interactive, flash-based, application that showed what the strategy meant to employees. With the metaphor of a tree, the four perspectives of the balanced scorecard (a concept developed by Kaplan and Norton, 1992) and their connection to the strategy was demonstrated. The employees had the possibility to interactively explore the strategy in terms of IHA·GfK's know-how (the roots of the tree), its core processes (the trunk), its clients (the leafs), and its financial performance (the fruit of the tree). Every perspective was

directly sold to clients; hence, the map also includes some of the products and services. When an employee clicks on one of the items, he or she can read about the tool's application (when to use it), its functioning (how to use it), and its evaluation (how well it works), as well as who is an expert on the tool at IHA·GfK (the so-called 'tool owner'). The main problem with the map in its current format is its *maintainability*, since a graphic map is not as easy to maintain as a central database. The main advantage is its *conciseness* and *interactive* and *convenient* use. To compile the information for the map, we conducted over thirty interviews with specialists and project managers. The reason for establishing such a map was partly the new strategy (and its emphasis on value added consulting tools), and partly because of the problems that employees had in finding cross-departmental information. We will look at the problems that occur in the knowledge-intensive process of market research after the behavioral and organizational changes have been described and their impact on information quality has been discussed.

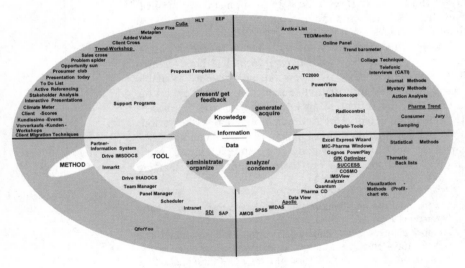

Figure 28: IHA·GfK's interactive knowledge map of tools and information sources

commented through audio by the CEO and linked to specific indicators and goals. In this way, the information on the company's strategy was made *interactive*, *entertaining*, and *understandable*.

The technological changes described above, e.g., the client and knowledge portal, were not easy tasks to get under way. They required systematic co-ordination across various departments of the company. The same was true for the behavioral changes that needed to take place. They consisted of two main elements, namely fostering *consulting* as a key activity to provide added-value information, and using sophisticated added-value *tools* in the process. For the first aspect various training formats were devised and implemented. One of these training formats was closely coupled with real-life consulting projects of IHA·GfK project leaders, where market data was just one element of a comprehensive customer solution. Various team leaders were coached over the course of a year regarding their presentations, reports, and client interactions were concerned. These selected team leaders[122] also had the chance to meet regularly and share their experiences. In these meetings, the sharing of examples of high-quality information was emphasized. The examples themselves came from actual projects of the team leaders and from external consultants who contributed best practices from other companies. Another type of behavioral 'tool' (which was quite close to the first one) was what IHA·GfK calls "clientissimo". Clientissimos are role playing workshops where difficult or critical situations with clients are actively acted out and simulated and then discussed in a group of client managers. Through these workshops, the account managers can anticipate comprehension difficulties or criticism. In this way, the managers can test out their ideas and findings with neutral colleagues that provide them with *instant and direct feedback*. This can help to focus the information and avoid 'overloading' the customer in a presentation on market data.

Behavioral Changes: Consulting Know-how

The third 'behavioral' aspect stressed methods and tools that relied on the combination of data from various sources in new ways. Examples of such methods are national and international market surveys that are coupled with market entry strategies or employee satisfaction surveys that are coupled with measures to improve personnel loyalty. The basic idea behind all of these tools was to combine data with follow-up measures in order to increase the value of the provided information. This higher value or quality of information was the result of a focus on making the findings *actionable*, that is

---

[122] The group of team leaders was limited to a maximum of seven. These team leaders, however, were expected to share their insights with their peers and thus act as multipliers.

to say combining insight with action steps that are tailored to the situation of the client. Although this was quite a new approach for a market research company, the first experiences were encouraging, and after two years IHA·GfK decided to institutionalize this approach with a permanent consulting unit. Other such organizational changes are described in the next paragraph.

Organizational Changes: Consulting Unit, Interdisciplinary Teams, Joint Ventures

Changing an organization is like cooking an elephant: you cannot do it all at once. You need to start with easily separable elements. In the case of IHA·GfK this meant that three experienced senior managers left their departments and formed an interdisciplinary consulting unit, IHA *Consulting*. The team's mission was to provide various departments with the skills and tools to deliver value added solutions to clients. In this way, the quality of information should increase by the deliberate crossing of departmental frontiers. On a less senior level, high-performance teams were given the same mission, namely to combine market data from various departments to solve specific customer problems. The same idea of combining data from various organizational units to increase the value of information for the customers was also applied in the global GfK group, of which IHA·GfK is a national subsidiary. There, management teams were formed to exchange experiences and findings on common topics such as Internet user statistics or the retail sector. Another organizational measure to extend both the comprehensiveness of the offered market data and its added value consisted of various joint ventures, for example in the domain of Internet measurement and media monitoring.

The following table summarizes, how these technological, behavioral, and organizational changes have affected the criteria that define information quality.

Information Quality Levels	Information Quality Criteria	Activities to improve IQ-criteria
Community Level	Comprehensive-ness	In order to increase the comprehensiveness of the information provided to clients, the company created interdisciplinary teams within the company and the global group. It entered various joint-ventures to enlarge its scope of market and user data.
(Relevance)	Accuracy	No specific measures were taken since the present label was seen as sufficient. The company had implemented a (certified) quality management system for its survey processes earlier.
	Clarity	Different layout templates were introduced that should make the information clearer and more easily interpretable. Presentations were introduced to make the information contained in market research reports clearer to the client.
	Applicability	In addition to merely reporting the market data, reports now include interpretations of the data, further analysis and cross references, and recommendations for action. The reports are not only presented, but discussed with the client to determine its internal use. The project managers are trained in consulting tools in order to improve the impact of the gathered information.
Product Level	Conciseness	All reports now include executive summaries. Many reports have the statistical information in the appendix and focus on the key results.
(Soundness)	Consistency	All market reports that a client receives have a similar structure, layout and logic.
	Correctness	No specific measures were taken in regard to correctness.
	Currency	The use of ad hoc on-line surveys was intensified to provide more up-to-date consumer data to clients.

Information Quality Levels	Information Quality Criteria	Activities to improve IQ-criteria
Process Level	Convenience	The market report is not only delivered as a document, but also as PowerPoint slides, as a CD-ROM, and in the future also in an updated form on the client extranet.
(Optimization)	Timeliness	Pre-tests were intensified in order to eliminate time lags or possible errors early on in the process. Through the client portal information is available almost instantly.
	Traceability	A knowledge map was developed and put on the company's intranet which makes it possible to trace back any tool or method to a tool owner or tool specialist.
	Interactivity	Clients are given more opportunities to provide input (via briefings, e-mails, presentations, telephone conferences etc.) during the information gathering process, before the report is finished.
Infrastructure Level	Accessibility	The client extranet can be accessed from any computer with Internet access anytime of the day or night. Employees have access to valuable information in the knowledge portal (supported by an interactive knowledge map).
(Reliability)	Security	The client extranet is protected through a password and a hidden link. The intranet is protected through a firewall.
	Maintainability	Specialized key accountants are assigned to the client extranets where the market reports are updated or cleansed.
	Speed	No specific measures were taken since the available infrastructure was seen as fast enough.

Table 23: IHA·GfK service features and their impact on information quality criteria

As the table above shows, the described changes have affected many information quality criteria. The criteria that are particularly affected by the new strategy are the following ones:

Most Affected Information Quality Criteria

1. Applicability: IHA·GfK no longer just delivers a report with enormous tables of data, but rather helps its clients to interpret the findings and use them for their planning activities. Market data are combined with actionable strategies that take the findings into account.

2. Interactivity: Some of the market data is provided on-line, allowing the customers to interactively explore details that are relevant to their segment of a market. Workshops are another way of making information more interactive, allowing customers to ask questions about the delivered data. For the employees, an information and tool directory was provided as an interactive map.
3. Conciseness: Every market research report begins with an executive summary that highlights the crucial findings of a study. Diagrams are used to summarize central insights. Methodological details are now often described separately in an appendix.
4. Convenience: The report is not only delivered as a print product, but also as a CD-ROM with slides and backup material which may include the actual database files. The convenience of internal information access was improved by installing an intranet-based knowledge portal, where crucial information sources are bundled in a graphic format.

The main added value that results from these activities is that the client does not only receive an amorphous mass of market data, but tailored, contextualized market insights that he can directly apply to make marketing decisions. IHA·GfK defines its vision of 'added value' as the net benefit that results from increased market knowledge for a company. In one of its European managers meetings it defined this value for the customer as follows:

Added Value

$$Value = \frac{Quality \times Service}{Cost \times Time}$$

This formula can be read as follows: the value of IHA·GfK's products for the customer is directly related to the information quality and the level of service it provides and is inversely related to the cost and time investments that the client has to make. This implies that the value for the customer is the bigger the higher the quality of the provided information and the higher the level of service that accompanies the information. In contrast, the value that IHA·GfK provides is lower when the costs and the required time for the provided information increase.

IHA·GfK now understands that providing knowledge is very different from providing data. In order to foster effective knowledge transfer, IHA·GfK has to provide high-quality information that goes beyond mere accuracy or timeliness issues and results in informed decisions. Providing knowledge means activating the information in the heads of the client by presenting it interactively, reducing it to its essence, and showing what the information means in terms of next steps. If IHA·GfK succeeds in this transfer of knowledge, it can ask for higher prices for its market data. The pricing scheme and business model of the company is briefly described in the next paragraph, before we turn to the remaining problems in managing the knowledge-intensive market research process.

The Business Model and Pricing Scheme

Generally speaking, market research prices vary greatly according to their (technology and population) scale and (geographic and thematic) scope. Given the high price levels of IHA·GfK in comparison to the industry average, the strategic move toward value added services and high-quality information seems a logical one (since a price leader strategy would reverse the current image). Thus, IHA·GfK is consciously positioning its services in the upper price segment of market research companies. It can do so because it is the biggest market research company in Switzerland, offering all available marketing research methods and infrastructures (for example the possibility to combine regular panel data with ad-hoc research results). IHA·GfK is also one of the most experienced research companies in the business and has an impressive list of references and long-term key clients.

As far the pricing schemes are concerned, one has to distinguish between on-going multi-client studies (called 'buses'), and ad-hoc single-client studies, where a particular customer inquiry leads to a dedicated research project. The multi-client studies are based on regular surveys in which IHA·GfK clients can include their own questions. The prices for this service depend on the number of questions and the type of questions that are asked (e.g., yes/no questions are cheaper than open questions). Through the 'buses', a client can include his question or test material (e.g., advertising campaign material) in a regular round of 500 consumer interviews. In general, this form of market research is quite inexpensive (a couple of hundred Francs per question) compared to a single-client study that can easily amount to a budget in excess of one hundred thousand Swiss Francs, sometimes even reaching one million Francs (as in a nation-wide health survey or in the calculation of TV ratings). The costs of a single-client study depend on the form of research (a focus group discussion for example can be organized for below 10'000 Swiss Francs), the geographic scope, the length of a questionnaire or interview, the size and availability of the target groups and the form of data analysis (e.g., with or without recommendations). An average business-to-business or business-to-consumer market research project with standardized interviews of fifteen minutes each may amount to a total of 40'000 Swiss Francs, including 300 standardized interviews at a cost of 120 Franks each and an analysis and interpretation of the resulting data. Such a project may reveal qualitative insights such as the purchasing behavior of a target group or quantitative results such as the level of brand recognition.

The key insight that one can derive from the description of the pricing model is that the mere delivery of market data offers a much lower revenue potential than an on-going customer relationship that is based on a variety of services and consulting activities. Hence, the quest for comprehensive, value-added information is also a quest for a more profitable business model.

In spite of the promise of the consulting business, the basis of the IHA·GfK business model is still (and probably always will be) the market research process. How that process works is briefly described in the next paragraph.

The way that IHA·GfK produces a market report depends, as does the price, on the type of assignment, i.e., whether the report is part of an on-going multi-client study or whether the report is part of a special project for one particular client. If a market research study is done for one particular client, the following five steps are usually completed in sequence (see the figure below). *The Report Production Process*

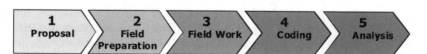

Figure 29: The market research report production process

In the *proposal* phase, IHA·GfK analyzes the information requirements of the client and chooses an adequate set of research tools. It estimates the costs for the chosen research approach and tailors its services to the needs of the client. The result of this step is a 2-10 page project proposal. Once, the client has accepted the proposal, *field preparation* begins. This step involves the design of a survey or an interview series and their pre-tests. The result of this step is a research design that is pre-tested and can yield the desired results. The *The Individual Steps* third step in the process is the actual *field work* where the target groups are questioned and their answers registered (through telephone interviews, group discussions, on-line questionnaires, or written surveys). In the subsequent *coding* phase, the answers are converted into a machine-readable format that can then be analyzed statistically through the help of programs such as SPSS or Systat. These programs are actually used in the last two steps to codify and *analyze* the gathered data and check whether the identified patterns and relationships are significant, reliable and representative, or if they are not. The final step of the production process, the data *analysis*, usually involves the contextualization of the gathered insights, that is to say an interpretation of the findings in light of the customer's situation. Adapting the results to the client's needs is not an easy task and demands a great effort of information filtering and aggregating. One potential problem in this last step is leaving out too much (e.g., not giving the client enough insights), or not leaving out enough (i.e., overloading the client). Other problems that arise in the described process are outlined in the next few paragraphs.

Problems in the Production Process

In six workshops with the company's project managers[123] we gathered and analyzed the challenges in the area of information quality which they saw in this process (and became aware of through their client satisfaction surveys) and we tried to find ways to improve the identified deficits in these five steps. The reoccurring themes or challenges in terms of information quality were the following five issues: First, the *timeliness* of the information that the company provided to its clients was seen as sometimes inadequate (still too many market research reports were not delivered on time). Second, the *accessibility* and *convenience* of the information for clients was judged to be insufficient (it was argued that the new media were not yet fully used for the benefit of the clients). Third, the *applicability* of the information for clients was seen as a great improvement area (here it was argued that more added-value needed to be provided with the market data, such as benchmarks from other companies, comparisons with similar industries, trend analyses, recommendations, consulting services such as workshops etc.). Fourth, finding the right *scope* for information in order not to overload clients was seen as a constant challenge. Finally – because of the relative autonomy of the various units of the company –

---

[123] The first such workshop was held in January of 1999 with about fifteen participants. The last was held in March 2001 with twelve participants.

the project managers considered it a major challenge to provide information in a *consistent* structure and layout. This issue of consistency was also a problem because many clients requested their market reports in a very specific format that at times did not comply with the IHA·GfK standards.

In a separate workshop, twelve IHA·GfK project heads were asked about the most pressing problems of the company (in the context of knowledge work). Fifteen percent of all answers related to information quality issues. In the follow-up to the workshop we categorized these issues into four levels: problems relating to the community of information producers, administrators, and users, problems relating to the information product (e.g., the study, report, CD-ROM, etc.), problems relating to the production and delivery process, and problems relating to the (information technology) infrastructure.

Genuine Information Quality Problems

As far as *community*-related problems were concerned, it was noted that useful documents cannot be highlighted as such by the members of a particular community. There is no rating of the documents, which makes it difficult to identify high-value contributions. In regard to the information *products* there was a general lack of common templates to structure the reports and presentations. Many problems also revolved around the production and delivery process. They ranged from lacking process standards, to inconsistent data storage and file naming conventions. Some participants noted that in the market research production process, not enough quality gates or peer checks on the produced results were in place. The infrastructure problems ultimately related to inadequacies of the used ERP (enterprise resource planning) system for retrieving documents and the lacking context of the documents found in the system. Another major criticism related to the infrastructure's maintainability, which was seen as too time-consuming. Overall, many employees stated that they viewed the lacking quality standards as potential problems and that there was a qualification gap in providing high-value information. Skills such as workshop moderation, visualization, mediation and negotiation, were not sufficiently developed.

These numerous problems were the main reason why IHA·GfK has initiated the technological, behavioral, and organizational changes described above (infrastructure improvements, process standardizations, common templates, training in value-added behavior, etc.). Another reason, however, is the increased competition that IHA·GfK faces in today's market place. In the next paragraph, we briefly describe some of the key competitors.

As far as competitors are concerned, a number of Swiss and international companies offer similar products to similar clients, among them a spin-off of IHA·GfK called Link, the international market research group Nielsen, and the Swiss market research companies Prognos, WEMF, Demoscope, M.I.S. Trend, Publitrend, or GfS. Of all of these companies, IHA·GfK enjoys the highest national market share. It is, however, closely followed by Nielsen. Nielsen can leverage its global network and offer truly global solutions to marketing departments that themselves have an increasingly global horizon.

As a market research company with global reach, and especially in regard to ad-hoc on-line market research, IHA·GfK is thus facing competition from NIELSEN, for example with its NetRatings product line. Nielsen[124] was founded in 1942 by ARTHUR NIELSEN who wanted to measure what people actually did and not what they thought or said they did. Nielsen NetRatings has an explicit information quality policy as far as its Internet-related research is concerned. It defines information quality as a measure of *how valid and reliable data is*.

Nielsen cites the following four minimum standards for high-quality information in the market research context: Information must be free from systematic *bias*, which means the sample must be representative of the population being measured and the resulting data must be projectable. Second, to be *accurate*, data collection must be *consistent* across all computing platforms and be as unobtrusive to panelists as possible. Third, to be *useful*, data collected must be a *complete* picture of online user site and advertising activity. Finally, to be *reliable*, data must be *free from* random *error*. In its on-line presence, Nielsen not only outlines what information quality means to the company, it also provides a checklist of how information quality can be assured. This shows that information quality is not only used as a marketing gimmick, but actually functions as a standard-setting device to improve processes internally. However, unlike its competitor IHA·GfK, Nielsen seems to view information quality only in terms of validity. It does not seem to address the crucial criteria of applicability, accessibility, or conciseness. Nielsen, as a

---

[124] The following statements are based on information provided at Nielsen's net rating website at www.nielsen-netratings.com/ products_IQ.htm [8.2.2000].

global integrated group, does however have a clear advantage over IHA·GfK when it comes to providing comprehensive information. Since IHA·GfK has only recently joined the global GfK network, its global data sourcing is not as advanced as Nielsen's worldwide collaboration and information sharing. The closer collaboration of IHA·GfK with GfK organizations in other countries is in fact one of the crucial future developments at IHA·GfK. Other key developments are described in the next paragraph.

The major future trend at IHA·GfK towards the *knowledge-based business*, e.g., providing clients with a portfolio of value-added services rather than just delivering market data, implies several other developments. These other developments focus on two main aspects, an internal and an external one. Firstly, to further increase the value of the knowledge transferred to the clients. Secondly, to optimize the allocation of knowledge internally. For the first goal, the customer perspective, one of the future goals of IHA·GfK may be to *help its clients improve their information quality,* so that the data generated by the client can be used more effectively in the decision-making process. Having improved its own information quality, IHA·GfK can now use this knowledge to advise other information-intensive companies or departments (such as R&D, marketing, or strategic planning) on how they can get more value out of their generated information. This may also require additional infrastructure which IHA·GfK provides for its clients, such as a hosted market or competitor database. In effect, IHA·GfK would be acting more like an *application service provider* than an external marketing consultant. For some clients, this is already the case today, where IHA·GfK not only provides the data, but also hosts the application that allows clients to directly analyze these data sets.

Future Developments

In terms of the internal focus, IHA·GfK has realized that it requires a more systematic transfer and combination of cross-departmental knowledge. As more inter-departmental processes start to take shape, the capture and re-use of the knowledge *about,* *within,* and *derived from* these processes becomes a crucial task.

We can summarize the main lessons from this case study with the help of the four information quality principles. They highlight crucial activities that IHA·GfK has undertaken to increase the quality of its information.

Case Summary

- Integration: Almost every major market report now contains a concise and systematic executive summary and an on-site presentation where the main consequences of a market study are presented in overview. For key accounts all studies or relevant data are integrated in a client extranet portal.

- Validation: Almost every market research report contains an appendix that explains (in detail) how the data was gathered, analyzed and condensed. The production process is documented in a quality manual and contains various reviews and quality gates, as well as forms for client feedback and the elimination of errors. Various workshop formats help a client manager to validate his findings and his style with peers first, before facing a client.

- Contextualization: Most market reports now refer to related reports or provide links to other available information or benchmarks that may render the information more meaningful by putting it into perspective and enabling comparisons. Besides the actual data, IHA·GfK at times also provides general market data to complement the individual items. This context is sometimes provided personally by a market analyst who presents the findings and relates them to the client's context.

- Activation: Many market reports are now not just sent to the client or just presented in a management meeting, but actually discussed and analyzed in a workshop-like setting where clients can ask questions or probe deeper together with the market research consultants. IHA·GfK has invested heavily in this 'data activation' process, especially in the area of training and tools.

As in other industries, market research companies have begun to understand that merely delivering correct data is no longer a competitive advantage. Convenience, accessibility, and applicability have become crucial quality elements of market insights.

Conclusion

This case study has shown that information quality improvements cannot be achieved by simply focusing on *technological* improvements. The IHA·GfK case shows that *behavioral* and *organizational* changes may play an equally important part in increasing the value of the delivered information. A technological solution for improved information quality is the internet-based client and employee portal that aggregates information and applications in one interface. A behavioral measure may consist of training and experience sharing regarding value-added communication skills and tools. An organizational solution may consist of a task-force that combines information that is usually dispersed in the organization, thus creating high-value insights. Improving information quality not only helps IHA·GfK to increase the margin on its data business, but it could also develop into a separate line of business where IHA·GfK helps its clients to improve the quality of their own information.

4.3 Compressing Knowledge: The Integration of Business Books at getAbstract

We have the biggest and most unbiased information quality control board there is ... the entire Internet community

THOMAS BERGEN
CEO and co-founder of getAbstract Inc.

This case study is based on five sources, the first and most important one being a face-to-face, three-hour long interview with the CEO of getAbstract, THOMAS BERGEN (who is also one of the two founders of the company). The interview was held at the headquarters of getAbstract in Lucerne, Switzerland, on the 12th of June 2001.[125] The second source of information was a collection of newspaper and journal articles that reported on getAbstract. The third source was the company's extensive Internet site and the Web sites of its competitors (see www.getAbstract.com, summary.com, summaries.com, or meansbusiness. com). Another important source was a series of interviews with five individual getAbstract customers, who discussed their experiences with the company's services. Finally, knowledge for the case study was gathered by being an actual customer of the company for four months.

Case Study Sources

getAbstract is a knowledge compression and rating company based in Lucerne, Switzerland with an additional office in Fort Lauderdale, and representations in Paris, Hamburg, Beijing and Hong Kong. It has about 20 full-time employees and a network of approximately 120 part-time collaborators who are mostly professional writers or translators. getAb-

Company Overview

---

[125] The case study was read and checked for accuracy and correctness by Thomas Bergen and by a member of the US management team of getAbstract. Detailed questions concerning the production process were answered by the head of the editorial team.

stract is, according to the company itself, a "leading provider of compressed knowledge" mainly in the area of business books. It states its mission as follows:

To get the latest business trends and knowledge into the hands and heads of executives, managers and business students worldwide through concise Abstracts (summaries) of the newest and most important books on the market.

getAbstract was founded in 1998 by ROLF DÖBELI (formerly a manager at SWISSAIR) and THOMAS BERGEN (formerly a member of management at the banking branch of the retail group MIGROS). The two founders originally conceived getAbstract as a small company with the goal of 200`000- 300`000 Swiss Francs in sales and with a product offering of about one hundred abstracts per year. However, when the organization became incorporated in 1999, it became clear that the initial business idea (summarizing business books) required more legal backing (e.g., formal contracts with the book publishers) and thus a greater investment in terms of financial resources. Since then, getAbstract has received major funding (totaling 14 million Swiss Francs) from two Swiss banks and various institutional and private investors. This has allowed the company to establish a legal department, which has since negotiated agreements with over 120 publishers. This gives getAbstract the legal right to produce summaries of the books offered by these publishers. At the moment, the company is run by the two founders and four other partners. This team of six colleagues (all between 32 and 34 years of age) still holds the majority of shares in the company.

The Core Product   The company provides its (currently about 3,000) private and more than sixty corporate clients or subscribers with concise, five-page summaries of business books, available in four languages (English, German, Spanish, and Chinese) and across multiple platforms (as Adobe PDF files or Palm Pilot files sent by e-mail, as audio abstracts, or in the form of a file repository as part of a company's intranet). The summaries of current and classic business books are written by a network of 120 professional writers and edited by three editors in Switzerland and the United States. These editors also rate each book according to its *overall appeal, applicability, innovation*, and *style*. Every book abstract has the same generic structure: A thumbnail of the book's cover next to the title and the detailed publishing information (sub-title, author, publisher, year, number of pages), a focus table that indicates the overall topic area of a book (such as technology, strategy, or leadership), a half-page of key take-aways in bullet-point format, a rating on a scale of five to ten (books that receive a rating below five are not summarized), a brief review and recommendation of the book, the actual abstract itself (which is about three pages long), and background information about the author(s) of the book. The last two lines of every abstract provide a list of buzz-words used in the book. This generic structure of every book abstract is represented in the table below.

1. **Book Cover Thumbnail**	2. **Book Title**
	3. **Subtitle and Publishing Information**
4. **Focus** area of the book (highlighted in a series of possible areas ranging from corporate finance, marketing, production and economics, to self improvement	5. The main **Take-Aways** (key findings) of the book (about ten main insights of the book on one half-page)
	6. **Rating** of the book (10 is best) in the following categories: Overall, Applicability, Innovation, Style
7. **Review** (including a recommendation for a specific target group)	8. **Abstract** with main concepts and comments on style and implementation guidelines
9. Original **Quotes** from the book in the margins of the abstract	10. **About the Author** (four lines of background information on the writer's position, reputation, and education)
	11. **Buzz-Words** (a short list of new terms coined or frequently used by the author)

Table 24: The generic structure of getAbstract's book summaries

Additional Services

On its Web page, getAbstract provides full access to all abstracts, which are categorized in so-called knowledge channels (or focus areas), such as leadership, self-improvement, strategy, or technology. One can also search the database of book summaries through a keyword search or browse a list of top downloads or new abstracts. The Web site also contains a customization application through which the customer can enter or modify his or her interest profile. In total, the Web server offers a repository of about 1,200 abstracts. BERGEN indicates that this number increases by 500 new abstracts every year.

The Rating Criteria

While getAbstract refers to itself as a knowledge compression and *rating* company, the rating is – as of now – not a very visible part of its services. As mentioned above, the editors of getAbstract rate each book according to four criteria. These four criteria are described as follows on the home-page of getAbstract:

1. Overall Rating /Must Read: How critical is this book to you? Is the information in the book so important that you can't afford to miss it? Have the concepts in this book become so widely accepted that you need to be familiar with them?
2. Innovation: Are the ideas presented in this book new, or are they just the same old recycled clichés?
3. Applicability: How important is the subject matter to your business and personal success? Can you put these ideas to work?
4. Style: How energetic and clear is the writing style? Hey, not everybody writes like Tom Peters!

Impact on Information Quality Criteria

Having briefly outlined the core product and additional services of the company, we can now look at all the services from an information quality perspective. Table three lists the main functionalities of the getAbstract service and shows which information quality criteria are affected by them.

Information Quality Levels	Information Quality Criteria	Functions of GetAbstract.com
Community Level	Comprehensiveness	At the book level: the most important elements of the book are represented in the abstract. At the portal level: most general management books are summarized (more than 8,000 are screened).
(Relevance)	Accuracy	The accuracy of the provided information is determined by the editorial guidelines that are provided to the writers and by the quality of the writers, who are mostly professional journalists.
	Clarity	Only professional writers are hired to write abstracts. Professional editors review the abstracts for clarity and style.
	Applicability	Regular feedback from abstract users is acknowledged and incorporated. The abstracts focus on take-aways and main new terms.
Product Level	Conciseness	Every book abstract is limited to five pages. Reviews are limited to one paragraph per book.
(Soundness)	Consistency	Every book abstract has the same structure: take-away, rating, author, buzz-words. Authentic quotes from the book are included on the side.
	Correctness	Not explicitly addressed.
	Currency	New book summaries are added every week, about five hundred new books are summarized every year.
Process Level	Convenience	The book abstract can be simply clicked on and is directly mailed to the inbox of the client where it can be read as a PDF-file or on the palm pilot.
(Optimization)	Timeliness	New abstracts that fit the profile of a client are automatically sent out by e-mail.
	Traceability	Author and publisher information is always given. However, the reviewer's name is not disclosed.
	Interactivity	The getAbstract customer can interactively edit his account and his interest profile. He can browse various book categories or do a key word search.
Infrastructure Level	Accessibility	All abstracts are accessible all of the time from any computer with Internet access and an e-mail account.
(Reliability)	Security	The getAbstract site is protected by a firewall. The client account is protected through a password.
	Maintainability	The site is continually updated and improved by a team

Table 25: getAbstract features and their impact on information quality criteria

From these information quality attributes, the ones that are affected most by the services of getAbstract are the following five:

Most Affected Information Quality Criteria

1. Conciseness: Every book is summarized in five pages. This increases the conciseness of a book by an average (purely quantitative) factor of about forty.
2. Comprehensiveness: The main elements of the book are discussed. Most qualified and successful business books are abstracted and available on the Web site. The executive can get an overview on a pre-filtered selection of books from a total of about 8,000 business books.126
3. Convenience: The abstract is delivered as a PDF file or for the palm pilot via e-mail. In this way it can be read at one's own convenience either electronically (in mobile situations on the palm pilot) or as a printed page.
4. Accessibility: All of the abstracts are accessible all of the time. The already downloaded abstracts are listed in a profile section and can also be accessed anytime from anywhere. They cannot, however, be directly viewed on-line, but only through an e-mail account.
5. Consistency: All abstracts follow the same structure. Thus, new abstracts can be easily scanned or read in overview and eventually stored in a personal archive.

Added Value

In these five areas, getAbstract clearly provides an added value for its clientele. According to BERGEN, this key value proposition for his clients can be described as follows: getAbstract is a time-saving device and an access point to an up-to-date, electronic library of relevant management know-how. It enables a manager or business student to "get into a new topic quickly." Customer questionnaires issued by getAbstract have actually revealed that a lot of clients subscribe to getAbstract in order to browse new topics or gain an understanding of new trends quickly. Many of them also want to be informed about the bestsellers that are available on the book market. One client, for example, has subscribed to getAbstract, to prime his technical staff on marketing vocabulary and concepts.

---

[126] Nevertheless Bergen acknowledges that this is a weak spot of any abstract service, namely that it can never achieve full comprehensiveness in terms of the summarized books. Because of this, getAbstract will loose or fail to attract customers that look for very specific types of books that focus on a particular industry or a specialized management function.

The next paragraph describes how this added value is turned into a tangible business model.

The revenues of the company are generated through annual subscriptions of 299 US$ per client (this fee provides access to all available abstracts and to one new abstract every week that is automatically sent to the subscriber by e-mail) or through its corporate clients that integrate the service into their intranets. Alternatively, individual book abstracts can be bought at a price of US$9.80 each. Students are also a targeted customer group of getAbstract. They can access the service for US$60 per year. In addition, getAbstract receives a seven percent commission on all books that are ordered through its Web site. With this business model, the sales were in the order of approximately 1 million Swiss Franks for the year 2000 (start of sales was May 2000). *The Business Model and Pricing Scheme*

This revenue side of the abstract business has to be related to the costs that are involved in producing an abstract. The following paragraphs show what it takes in terms of staff resources to produce an abstract. Since getAbstract does not disclose its salaries, one can only estimate the margins of this business model.

In order to produce an abstract, a process which takes up to two months per summarized book, the following twelve steps have to be completed. They are briefly described below. *The Production Process*

1. The first step consists of the book (market) *screening* and the book pre-selection. This step should answer the following question: Which books are relevant to our clients and worth summarizing? The answer to this question is given by a team of three editors in the US and Europe. They screen about 8,000 books per year for potential relevance to their clients. Occasionally, large corporate clients may propose books to be abstracted. An important indicator for a book's relevance or impact is the press echo that it has received or the discussions about it on Internet newsgroups (which are followed by the editors).
2. The second step in the production process consists of clearing the possible legal barriers. The key question in this step is: Can we get the rights for the book in every language? This is very often the case since getAbstract has contracts with over 120 publishing companies.
3. If there are no legal barriers, getAbstract receives a copy of the book directly from the publishing house (mostly for free).
4. The (two) editors in Lucerne (for German books) and the one in Fort Lauderdale (for English books) browse

through the received book and evaluate it for approximately half an hour. If they still think the book is relevant and fairly well written, they decide to abstract it and move to step five.

5. In step five, the editors determine which writer has the free capacity to do an abstract. Every writer writes an average of four book abstracts per year, but this varies greatly from writer to writer, as there are some who may do more if they decide to make their living abstracting books. In order to complete this step, the editors have a comprehensive database of all the books that are summarized, their legal status, and who is summarizing them.

6. If a free writer is identified who may be able to evaluate and summarize the book, it is sent to him or her by the editors.

7. This is the main step in the abstract production process. It consists of the writer reading and summarizing the book. According to BERGEN this is a "black box" process in the sense that getAbstract does not know how or when a writer produces an abstract. There are hardly any guidelines or rules for the actual summarizing of a book. The writer is paid a fixed amount per abstract, regardless of the book's level of difficulty or scope in terms of pages. In the initial two to three months that a new writer works for getAbstract, the abstracts are usually not what they should be in terms of quality, according to BERGEN. They need to be edited heavily by the editors and the writers receive a great amount of feedback from them. The writers do not receive any specific training material, just examples of some very good abstracts. In general, the writers are encouraged to write more than the required five pages, this way the editors can still edit the abstract for its final version. In terms of tools, the writers are provided with a word template. The reproduced original quotes from the book are selected by the abstract writer. He or she also compiles and forwards the list of buzz-words that are added at the end of the abstract. In the future, the writers may even work with a template with XML-tags so that the later retrieval can be enhanced and the abstracts can be more easily integrated into a corporate intranet or document repository.

8. In the next process step, the editors go over the received abstract and decide where changes or cuts are needed. The end rating of the book is also done by the editors in Lucerne or Fort Lauderdale at this point.

9. When the abstract is complete, the legal department once again checks the rights on the book and whether the abstract is in accordance with those rights.

10. The abstract document is then tagged (through XML-technology) with keywords that indicate its subject, date, author, etc. This will enhance the future use of the abstract as an element of a document repository or in the conversion to other formats, such as Adobe PDF files or Palm Pilot files.

11. and 12. The final two steps in the production process of an abstract consist of making a layout for the summary document (either in-house or externally) and putting it online or sending it to clients via e-mail.

In the future, getAbstract plans to add yet another step to this process, namely that there will be feedback mechanism so that readers can indicate what they liked or disliked about an individual abstract.

As can be expected, some of the biggest problems in this process reside in steps two, five, and seven.

Problems in the Production Process

The problem inherent in step two is basically a coordination and time problem. It consists of overcoming the entry barrier of lacking contracts with publishers. This involves a great amount of negotiation and relationship management. Once established, however, these legal agreements between getAbstract and the publishing companies can prove to be a distinctive competitive advantage that is difficult and time-consuming to replicate. For the CEO of getAbstract, this also represents one of the biggest barriers of entry into the book abstract market. He cites examples of companies that have entered the abstract business without proper legal contracts and have since been sued by publishing companies.

The problem inherent in step five is finding enough high-caliber writers who can continually and consistently provide well-written abstracts that reflect the relevant content of a business book. getAbstract's approach to this problem has mostly been by word-of-mouth, networking, Internet monitoring, and by asking for recommendations. In this way, new writers were identified and won through up-front payments. BERGEN points out this crucial challenge in the following quote:

It was a very difficult task to find these business journalists; they are all professional writers. They were found via networking over the Web, then talking to opinion-leaders and working with them, and then through word of mouth. Our staff is a Web community. It is very important to treat them fairly because of this virtual relationship.

Because the relationship to the abstract writers is at the same time crucial for the success of getAbstract and purely virtual, the management gives special attention to their remuneration and to their own working styles. The abstract writers receive a generous flat fee for every produced abstract. In addition, getAbstract is very flexible it its coordination with the writers. One writer, for example, does not deliver her abstracts electronically but by fax, which getAbstract accepts due to the high quality of her summaries. The company is also very flexible in regard to how many abstracts a writer would like to produce in a given time span.

For the abstract writing itself (step seven), the main problem was and still is to achieve and sustain a unique and consistent writing *style* (that BERGEN describes as spicy and entertaining, yet to the point). The solution to this problem relies on the in-house editorial team that uses an internal style guide to make the abstracts more alike (in the sense of a typical getAbstract style). A second solution element in regard to style is the fact that only professional writers are hired as abstract producers and that they are explicitly asked to write in a light and entertaining manner. A third possible improvement in regard to a consistent style comes from customer feedback. According to BERGEN, a number of clients (and sometimes even book authors or publishers) do send feedback on specific abstracts and thus help the company to improve its style and services.

Customer Opinions   In telephone interviews with six getAbstract clients[127] from three different companies, additional information was gathered that reflects the current strengths and weaknesses of the book abstract idea and its implementation at getAbstract.All of the six questioned customers indicated that the abstracts were mostly of good quality and helped them to decide whether a book merits further attention or not. The six customers all said that they were surprised by the consistent high quality of the abstracts and that they greatly appreciated the systematic and fixed structure of the book summaries. However, all of the interviewed customers also said that they

---

[127] One of the interviewed customers was at the same time a client of a getAbstract competitor, namely Soundview's summary.com. He did not, however, stress major differences between the two services (except for the fact that getAbstract also summarizes books in German).

frequently read abstracts that did not meet their expectations (because of style or content). All of them indicated, that they would like to have a bigger choice of book topics (and not just general management books), as well as more or better value-added services, such as a true full-text search, a more sophisticated user profile, links between related book abstracts, a more informative rating system, more topic-categories or sub-categories, or summaries or streams of related books.

Some complaints were voiced regarding the comprehensiveness of the abstracts and their clarity or applicability. Two out of the six customers indicated that when they read an abstract of a book that they knew, they did not always agree with the abstract writer on what were the most important points. One customer said that the quality of translations was at times insufficient in book abstracts that were translated from English to German. This customer also felt that some writers were not knowledgeable enough in the topics they covered and did not always seem to understand the terms that they were using. Another customer, however, thought that the writers did an excellent job at picking the right quotes and knowing where to paraphrase the book text.

As far as the content of the book abstracts was concerned, two customers indicated that they would like to see one or two key charts from every book included in the abstract in order to facilitate the reading and make it more memorable. This issue has in fact already been discovered by getAbstract (also through customer feedback). In the future, getAbstract may include figures and illustrations in its abstracts, if it can process them efficiently and no legal problems in reproducing book charts arise. When asked why getAbstract has so far not compressed knowledge visually or through diagrams, BERGEN gives the following answer:

Until now there have been no abstracts with graphic information because the production process is much more efficient with pure text. You need a graphic specialist if you want to include charts, because the look and feel of the abstract has to be consistent. You cannot just do a scan. We would have to redraw the graphic in our style. We would have to reduce the complexity of the graphic illustration to live up to our promise. We will now test it with a book abstract. Nevertheless, I am sceptical about including charts because our vision is complexity reduction and we would have to do the same with the charts, which will complicate the production process.

Another point that BERGEN acknowledges as an improvement area (as indicated by the clients) is the profiling of customer needs. Here, Bergen states that "We have to get better at evaluating the requirements of our reader. Right now we only provide categories and a profile. In the future, we will learn more about our customers and their needs and let them benefit from this knowledge."

Clearly, a set of only six customers is not representative. Nevertheless, these comments can be seen as valid suggestions for future improvements and getAbstract's reaction to customer feedback shows that it is willing to continually optimize its information processes and infrastructures.

In order to complete the view on getAbstract, the last segment of this case study will portray competitors of the company and outline possible future developments for getAbstract and for the abstraction or summary business in general.

Major competitors of getAbstract are meansbusiness.com, SOUNDVIEW (www.summary.com), and manageris (www.manageris.com) although the last one mainly focuses on the French market and only produces two book abstracts per month (it is thus not further discussed below). MEANSBUSINESS has a significantly lower number of book abstracts in total, but also provides concise summaries of content *across* various books in its so-called concept suites. A concept suite is a summary of book chapters from various books that deal with the same topic (such as information overload, knowledge management, or managing the workplace). Hence, Meansbusiness.com also integrates business books on a macro-level, by summarizing important aspects or concepts across various books (usually four to six books per topic). MEANSBUSINESS only offers abstracts in English.

SOUNDVIEW, a US-based company based in Pennsylvania owned by Clement Communications, offers an "executive book summary" service at its Web site www.summary.com. Each book abstract requires about 20 minutes of reading, according to the company. Summaries are also made available as audio CDs or audio tape cassettes. The text-based summaries of SOUNDVIEW have a scope of eight pages and differ in terms of their structure and style from the abstracts produced by getAbstract.

A SOUNDVIEW executive books summary begins with a thumbnail reproduction of the book and its full title. It contains a one-page *brief summary*, and a seven page *complete summary*. On the front page of a book summary there is a table of contents of the summary. On the second page, information on the book's author(s) is provided. Whereas getAbstract uses a very sober page layout (with only one font, one column, and highlighted sentences that are underlined), SOUNDVIEW uses various sizes of fonts, and bold sentences for crucial phrases or terms. It divides every summary into various topic-oriented chapters. The complete summary is often interrupted with shaded areas that contain short case studies, checklists, examples, or questions. Summary.com offers thirty book summaries each year for a price of US$159 (179 dollars for the audio version). It has agreements with over 30 book publishers (mainly from the United States).[128]

At the moment, new competitors are entering this dynamic industry. Other contenders include summaries.com which offers its business book summaries at only 1.92 dollars a piece. It follows a similar model as getAbstract by sending out one new abstract every week and by offering various subscription models. Unlike the other three players, summaries.com also includes diagrams in its book abstracts. *New Competitors: Summaries.com*

As far as the potential of the book summary business model is concerned, various new directions can be imagined. BERGEN sees four areas in which growth is possible and likely for his company. They represent getAbstract's growth axes and are briefly outlined below: *Future Developments*

---

[128] Besides these commercial competitors, getAbstract faces a number of competitors who also summarize business books or business magazines, but provide these summaries free of charge (as traffic generators or as customer service). Examples of such competitors are www.mwonline.de (a German site that provides summaries of business magazine articles), www.strategy-business.com/books, a site provided by Booz, Allen & Hamilton, or ww.brint.com (which provides book summaries and book discussions through its community members, a model that a number of sites have chosen, which does not guarantee high-quality summaries, however). Another category of competitors are book abstract producers who do so illegally (without the consent of the publishers). Finally, there are specialized abstract services such as MCB University Press that produces abstracts of personnel and training articles with its Anbar Abstracting Journals. MCB publishes abstracts of up to 120 articles twelve times a year.

[129] Another domain, where knowledge compression or book abstracts are already a major business is in the academic sector. Two of the more famous companies in this sector are Cliffs Notes and Random House. The first company produces so-called Cliffs Notes (named after the founder of the company Cliff Hillegass) which are essentially summaries of classic works of lit-

1. The first growth axis is *technology* or the media in which abstracts are provided. getAbstract is already experimenting (as summary.com) with audio abstracts, in which a book summary is read aloud to the executive on a business-class flight or in a car. Future applications may include video summaries that are enhanced by charts, animations, and film clips. A possible trend for the future may be multimedia abstracts that are more interactive and put a greater emphasis on learning and knowledge transfer than current abstracts. As far as technology is concerned, BERGEN also intends to extend the on-line services that are available on the getAbstract Web site. A new service that will be added soon can refer customers to other book summaries that might interest them (e.g., "people who have downloaded this abstract, have also downloaded these abstracts").

2. The second growth area is an expansion of the *languages* in which the abstracts are offered. One logical next choice, besides the existing English, German, Spanish, and Chinese (the latter two are only translated, not originally written) is Japanese. Offering abstracts in a new language can mean access to an entirely new market, either directly by producing abstracts in the foreign language or by licensing the getAbstract brand and the necessary infrastructure to local providers.

3. The third growth axis consists of offering entirely *new products* or services. This means applying the abstraction principle to different types of content, such as speeches or presentations. getAbstract refers to this service as speech abstraction. It has already offered speech abstracts at the

---

erature for college students. The summaries include background information on the text and the author, a two page synopsis, a list of the characters, and a longer summary by chapter, as well as explanatory comments. A book such as Milton's Paradise Lost is usually discussed and summarized on sixty to eighty pages (on the inside cover of every book summary, Hillegass writes that the notes should not be a substitute for the reading of the original). Whereas Cliffs Notes rely purely on text to summarize a book, Random House uses 'plot diagrams' (a variation of Novak's concept maps) to depict the story of the book and its central characters. A Random House "Keynote" summarizes a classic book on only six pages (which makes you wonder what kind of warning could justify this kind of literary text compression). Like meansbusiness.com Cliffs Notes does not only integrate individual books, but also series of books that relate to the same topic, such as books on mythology, or Roman and Greek classics.

ST. GALLEN MANAGEMENT CONFERENCE ISC, and at the SWISS ECONOMIC FORUM. Other similar new services are feasible, such as offering on-demand abstracts for client-requested books, reports, studies, etc., or training executive assistants on how to write high-quality abstracts.

4. A fourth area for growth that BERGEN foresees for the very near future, is in new geographic markets that can be addressed with the existing content, such as Scandinavia, England or India.

5. A fifth and final growth area may lie in addressing entirely new content domains beyond the traditional business books. For this option, getAbstract has already acquired the rights to summarize books such as Harry Potter and the Tiananmen Papers. Other feasible areas may be in the domain of science books, market studies, legal norms and codes, or company profiles.[129] Recently, getAbstract has already begun to offer select summaries of classic literature, ranging from the Bible to Alice in Wonderland.

This list of growth opportunities shows that the book abstract business has many promising perspectives. However, these new applications also confront the suppliers of abstracts with considerable information quality problems (in terms of convenience, consistency, currency, timeliness, security, and many other criteria). Thus, it seems important to install a functioning information quality system right from the start, in order to learn about quality assurance for intellectual information products and leverage the gathered insights in other domains. This is, in my view, an untapped potential of current book abstract services. They can no longer afford to treat the summarization process as a black box that is entirely left to the writers themselves. Rather, they need to install guidelines and tools that "force" the writers to contribute abstracts that meet certain minimal standards in terms of content depiction, style, and structure.

In conclusion, one can say that the biggest entry barriers *Case Summary* for this type of information quality service are the legal obstacles (getting publishers to agree to the book abstraction) and finding enough qualified writers who can provide consistently instructive abstracts over a long period of time. The biggest improvement area lies in the consistent writing style that captures the essence of a business book, as well as in making the information process more convenient and the offering more comprehensive. Possible measures that can be implemented to improve the quality of the provided information are writer guidelines and more elaborate templates that provide hints and examples for the writers to follow. The greatest untapped potential can be seen in relating book abstracts to one another and thus integrating them on a macro-level, as well as providing a more useful and informative rating schema.

We can summarize getAbstract's major benefits or innovations with the four information quality principles:

- Integration: getAbstract integrates on two levels: every book is reduced to five pages, and a great number of books is integrated and made accessible in one Web site.
- Validation: getAbstract pre-selects and filters new business books and rates them according to a defined set of explicit criteria.
- Contextualization: getAbstract provides information on the author and his or her background, it states possible target groups of a book, and it will add references to similar books or to books others have found to be useful.
- Activation: getAbstract stresses the key take-aways of every book and provides them through a push-mechanism to the reader (based on a user-defined profile).

The principle that is most visibly exploited by getAbstract is the first one: Books are integrated or compressed by professional writers in a pre-given format.

Conclusion

The getAbstract case study has shown that high-quality information (in this case especially in the area of conciseness, comprehensiveness, and convenience) may be considered as a growing industry in its own right. The case study has also shown that a framework like the one presented in this study can indicate possible future market niches, such as the one discovered by getAbstract to increase the conciseness of business knowledge in the form of books.

4.4 Putting IT into Context: Gartner Advice and the Difficult Scaling of Knowledge

The main problem in transferring our knowledge to the client is what I call 'the last mile': How to get our information into the heads of a client's project team that needs it.

PETER MÜLLER
Country Manager, Gartner Inc., Switzerland

This case study is based on four sources. The most important one is a 90 minute interview with the country manager of Gartner Switzerland, PETER MÜLLER, as well as several follow-up e-mail 'conversations' with him. Second, the case study is based on the experience of being a Gartner client and using its research reports on a regular basis. Third, it is based on interviews with five Gartner clients from three companies. Finally, the case study is based on an extensive website and document analysis of Gartner Inc. and some of its main competitors.

Case Study Sources

Gartner (formerly known as the Gartner Group) is the largest IT market analysis company in the world. It was founded by the former Wall Street analyst GIDEON GARTNER. Currently, Gartner employees over 1,400 analysts and consultants (about half of this number are analysts). According to Gartner Inc., its analysts advise over 1'000 executives a day across 75 countries. In total, Gartner advices over 10'000 clients. The average amount spent by each client is around 81'000 US dollars. The revenues of Gartner for the year 2000 were 858 million US dollars (509.8 million from the research business alone). The net income was 25.5 million dollars. In terms of national scale, Gartner Switzerland employs a staff of fifteen people: three consultants, three administrative assistants, and nine sales representatives. Since Gartner emphasizes its 'one opinion' on crucial information technology topics, it does not deploy analysts to every country, but rather pools them in a few central locations in the Unites States, England, France, and Germany. Gartner has been in Switzerland for nine years and has a market share of seventy percent among Switzerland's biggest 100 companies.

Company Overview

PETER MÜLLER, the country manager responsible for Gartner's operations in Switzerland, describes the core competence of Gartner as follows:

We understand the IT-sector better than any other company because of our high number of vendor and client interactions. The customer benefit is the advice we can give our clients based on these frequent and informative interactions.

The Core Products: Research

Advice is in fact Gartner's main business. Gartner's services and products can be categorized into four types of activities that all leverage the central competence of information technology advice. The first product group comprises the various *research products* (such as strategic analysis reports, research notes or newsletters), as well as the inquiry services, where customers can ask IT-related questions by e-mail, fax, or phone and receive a tailored answer by one of the Gartner analysts. A part of this product group is also made up of quantitative vendor or market data, provided by Gartner's own DATAQUEST group. Dataquest focuses on sales statistics and related information. A new research product that has just been launched by Gartner is 'G2.' G2 bundles Gartner intelligence relevant for top-management and focuses on advice for CEOs on growth strategies through information technology. While Gartner's research products typically target CIOs (chief information officers) and IT-product or project managers, this new product is aimed at general top managers and their strategic information needs.

Events

Events are a second large domain of Gartner's offerings. Gartner organizes regular conferences where it presents its research findings and brings together various members of the IT-community for discussions and debates. Today, Gartner is the largest IT-conference organizer in the world.

Consulting

A third type of activity that Gartner pursues with great success (in terms of growth) is *consulting*. Gartner consultants advice their clients on issues ranging from total cost of ownership of an IT-system to the strategic IT-implications of a corporate merger.

Measurement

The fourth and last product group focuses on *benchmarking and measurement*, particularly in the domain of cost efficiency. Here, Gartner assembles crucial indicators, compares them across industries or companies and finally advises the clients how to increase the effectiveness and efficiency of their IT department.

Case Study Focus: Research Products

In the present case study, we will focus on the first type of Gartner products, namely research reports and inquiry services. In this field, Gartner delivers 'pre-canned research information' as PDF-files or entire Lotus Notes data-bases that can be easily accessed, searched, or browsed. Gartner acts as an 'outsourced research department' and provides a company with advice on all aspects of its information technology strategy and infrastructure.

The main categories of research products are *research notes* that can be up to five pages long, *executive briefings* (also about five pages), a monthly research *review* with current news and an overview on new research studies, and *strategic analysis reports* on companies, products, technologies, general trends, or markets, which are usually more comprehensive and up to eighty pages long. All of these reports are sent directly to subscribers via e-mail (based on their interest profiles) or they can be accessed through Gartner's information portal at Gartner.com. Although these research reports are the most visible part of Gartner's research activities, they are not necessarily the most important one. According to Müller, most Gartner clients rely much more on direct advice from Gartner analysts through the so-called *inquiry services* than on the research reports themselves. According to Gartner's customer surveys, this form of direct questioning and answering is seen as more efficient by many executives than the reading of research reports.[130] Müller states this fact in the quote below:

If I am a CIO and I invest a million dollars in Gartner, I want to use it 20 percent of the time on research reports, 70 percent on direct inquiries on vital IT-issues, and ten percent on events such as Gartner conferences or symposiums.

Inquiry Services

Through Gartner's inquiry services a customer can ask specific questions to a central phone number or e-mail address and receive direct feedback from one of the analysts from Gartner's pool of researchers worldwide. The identification of the relevant expert and the forwarding of the question is handled centrally by Gartner. Usually, a response may include a reply with advice tailored to the specific situation of the client, relevant reports, and suggestions for action, as well as links to other information sources. The response time for such inquiries ranges from a few hours to a few days. This service is also provided by most of Gartner's competitors in a similar format.

---

[130] This may not always be the case. The interviews with customers and the Giga case study will show that there is also the typical customer need to keep abreast of new developments or trends and get a general overview on the industry. This need is better fulfilled through the reports and newsletters than through direct inquiries.

Research Documents

Although the direct inquiries may often dominate a customer's use of Gartner, one cannot neglect the crucial role of the research reports. They are a key resource for clients (and for Gartner analysts themselves) and they play a substantial part in building the company's credibility and reputation. The reports are also examples of high value content products that are based on considerable expertise and on a well-designed production process that focuses on adding value to information. Below, we look at the various types of research reports, their structure and main benefits, as well as their production process and its problems.

As mentioned above, Gartner offers various formats of research information, the most important ones being research notes and strategic analysis reports.

Research Notes

Research notes are concise summaries of an analyst's opinion regarding a current business issue, a technology, a company, or an entire market or industry. They are typically divided into four sections: the core topic that is discussed, the key issues or questions that are addressed, the main text (incl. various sub-notes or key facts), and the bottom line (or consequence) of the note. There are several types of research notes (that are clearly labeled) such as decision frameworks that help to make sense of a complicated domain, tutorials that explain a new concept, technology notes that examine new technological tools or platforms, or guidelines that suggest an effective course of action.

Strategic Analysis Reports

Strategic analysis reports, the second major type of Gartner research reports, can range from twenty to a hundred pages. They are more complex in terms of structure than the relatively 'flat' research notes. Every SAR (strategic analysis report) begins with a management summary that consists of key issues and key findings in a bullet-point format. The key findings consist mostly of suggestions what may happen in the future and how to best react to those developments. Every chapter in a SAR begins with two bold lines of key issues (in the form of a question) which are discussed in the chapter.

Whereas research notes contain few diagrams, SARs make great use of conceptual charts. These abstract graphics depict networks of companies or market constellations, timelines, product portfolios, or hierarchies of concepts. A particular and unique type of diagram that is used in these reports is what Gartner calls a 'magic quadrant'. A magic quadrant is a central device to aggregate a great amount of market information (and analysis) in one single chart.

A magic quadrant is a matrix that divides a market into four segments and positions competitors in those segments according to their strategic vision regarding the domain and their implementation or execution ability. Gartner defines a magic quadrant as follows (Bradley & Braude, 1995, p.1):

Magic Quadrants as Information Integrators

Gartner Group's "Magic Quadrants" are graphical Strategic Planning Assumptions that position vendors in a market sector going forward.

The figure below shows a typical example of such a quadrant for the computer aided software engineering (CASE) market (Bradley & Braude, 1995, p. 1). It positions the major vendors in this market according to their strategic plan and its alignment with major industry trends (completeness of vision) and according to a vendor's ability to implement this strategic plan (ability to execute). The ability to execute is rated based on a company's management, its financial strength, the existing sales channels, the research and development capacity, its network of alliances, and a number of other factors determining operational excellence.

Figure 30: An example of a Magic Quadrant for the CASE market (Source: Gartner)

As stated in the definition above, a magic quadrant can be seen as a visual strategic planning assumption. Strategic planning assumption are a central information block type in most Gartner's reports. They designate qualified predictions about an industry's future development. A strategic planning assumption may be that by the year 2003, eighty percent of all large multinational organizations will have implemented

Strategic Planning Assumptions

Probabilities as Validity Indicators

an intranet portal with personalized content (0.8 probability). The bracketed probability number at the end of the statement is an integral part of every strategic planning assumption. Since they are assumptions, every such statement is qualified with a probability indicator that designates the level of certainty that is associated with the prediction. In order to make various levels of confidence explicit, Gartner has devised a rating scale for these assumptions. The scale ranges from 0.1 to 0.9. Since the scale is a validation mechanism (it allows readers to evaluate the information more carefully) it is outlined in detail in the next paragraph.

The Rating Scale for Gartner Predictions

Below, Gartner's own description of the rating scale is reproduced (Allen, 1994, pp. 1-2). Gartner has made this description available to customers because it believes that it is crucial that its clients understand the various validity levels of predictions and can interpret and evaluate the information accordingly.

0.9: This will definitely happen, barring an act of a god or war. We would be shocked otherwise. Moreover, we are almost certain of timing.

0.8: This will happen barring exceptional circumstances. We would be *quite* surprised if it did not happen, but a degree of uncertainty exists. Clients should plan on something close to it. In addition, we have a good idea of the timing. We use a 0.8 probability when the largest issue is timing.

0.7: There is good reason to believe this will be true, but there is a decent chance it will not be true. We would be surprised, but not shocked, if it did not happen. The details may change. Moreover, the timing is soft, and it may vary from our estimates. Clients should include this in their strategic plans.

0.6: This is a general direction – better than a rumor or a guess, but not necessarily by a lot. If a client needs to make a decision and asks for our advice, this is what we recommend the client use. This probability is particularly well-suited for time frames greater than two years. Most likely, we do not have a firm idea of the timing.

0.5: A tossup. It would not surprise us if this happened, or if it did not. Clients should include neither this nor its complement in their strategic plans.

0.4: This will probably not happen, but we would be neither surprised nor shocked if it did. We would argue, but not fiercely, with a client who is planning on this event.

0.3: There is good reason to believe this will not happen, but there is some chance it will. We would be surprised, but not shocked, if it occurred. In either case, we would not be sure of the timing. We would argue hard with clients who include this in their strategic planning.

0.2: This will not happen, barring exceptional circumstances. We would be *most* surprised were it to happen, but it is not totally implausible. We would argue fiercely with clients who include this in their strategic planning.

0.1: This will definitely not happen, barring acts of a god or war. We would be shocked if it did happen, and we would make every possible effort to identify the error. We would be disappointed if a client's strategic plans assumed that it is going to happen.

The list above shows that Gartner's main criteria for the distinction between various levels of probability are the *likelihood* of something to happen, and the *time scale* of an event (i.e., how soon something will happen). Gartner suggests that clients use these probabilities in a comparative manner in their IT-strategy development and planning activities (Allen, 1994, p. 2):

Gartner's Probability = Likelihood and Time Scale

We recommend that clients not only use the Strategic Planning Assumption with the highest probability, but that they create a scenario that responds to the lesser Strategic Planning Assumption(s). This is particularly true for Strategic Planning Assumptions with probabilities between 0.3 and 0.7. This ensures that the user will not be caught off-guard should a less-likely event happen, and that the user has a backup plan if and when that less-likely event occurs.

These indications provide help in interpreting (and weighing) the researched information provided by Gartner. While the legal disclaimer at the end of every report is not intended for that purpose, it can also be used to evaluate the quality of the content. Inherent in the disclaimer (which is similar to the one used by other research companies) are central information quality criteria that we have encountered in chapter three:

Sideline: Information Quality as a Legal Issue

The information contained herein has been obtained from sources believed to be *reliable*. Gartner Inc. disclaims all warranties as to the *accuracy, completeness* or *adequacy* of such information. Garter Group (sic!) shall have no liability for errors, omissions or inadequacies in the information contained herein or for interpretations thereof. The reader assumes sole responsibility for the selection of these materials to achieve its intended results. The opinions expressed herein are subject to change without notice.

Information Quality Disclaimer

Besides integrating information in magic quadrants (or other conceptual diagrams such as pyramids, coordinate systems, or cycles) and indicating its validity through probability ratings, Gartner also aims at activating information for the read-

Action Items as Activators

ers through the highlighting of *action items*. Action items describe what companies ought to do in light of the evidence gathered by Gartner. They are – like strategic planning assumptions – especially marked with italic typeface. Often, however, these action items are quite general and need to be broken down into more specific actions by the reader him- or herself. Below are three examples of such items taken out of a Gartner strategic analysis report:

- Action Item: Enterprises should plan on TCP/IP being the digital glue binding together disparate networks.
- Action Item: Enterprises should:
  - Expect to make significant investments in digital asset management tools
  - Expect false starts in designing intuitive dynamic, interactive environments
  - Seize opportunities to become part of the content aggregate
  - Use interactivity to develop a dialogueue with end users.
- Action Item: Enterprises should seize the opportunity to become part of the content aggregation of portal sites and develop actionable content applications that instill confidence within decision-focused interactions.

'Bottom line' as Activator

Another way of activating content (anchoring it in the reader's mind) is through 'the bottom line.' Every Gartner research note ends with a concise paragraph of two to eight lines that summarizes the main insight of the note and its application. Below is an example of such a bottom line taken from a research note on business intelligence and knowledge management:

Bottom Line: Decision-making and knowledge sharing can be optimized when BI and KM are practiced in concert. Enterprises should review existing BI and KM strategies, evaluate the intersection of these processes, and adapt their approaches to enable KM with BI and BI with KM.

Consistent Use of Text Elements

While *magic quadrants*, *strategic planning assumptions*, *probabilities*, *action items*, and *bottom lines* are not major analytic inventions or breakthrough formats, they do help the reader to locate and interpret relevant information quickly. From a management perspective, Gartner exploits this potential through rigorous guidelines that regulate the use of these 'text tools.' This consistent use of certain text elements, enables Gartner to 'condition' or train its readers to its own style and format and consequently to make the reading process for them more efficient. All of the five interviewed Gartner customers acknowledged that this improved the quality of the provided information. One manager of a Gartner competitor, however, pointed out that tools like magic quadrants also have a 'dark side'. Often the methodology behind such an aggregation device is unclear and the individual positions of companies that are placed in such a matrix are highly debatable. Nevertheless these devices have stood the test of time and make Gartner reports clearly recognizable as such.

In addition to the core products described above, Gartner offers various additional information tools, such as document templates, forms or analytical tools (e.g., Excel models or rating tools) that IT-managers can use in their daily work. A possible template may be a generic service level agreement contract. An example for an analytical tool is a Microsoft Excel-based rating spreadsheet for the comprehensive evaluation of a website.

Additional Services

Having described the various information products of Gartner and their features, we can now summarize the activities that Gartner pursues to increase the quality of those products. They are listed below next to the quality criterion that they affect most.

Impact on Information Quality

Information Quality Levels	Information Quality Criteria	Activities to improve the IQ-criteria
Community Level	Comprehensiveness	Gartner employees more than 700 analysts to provide comprehensive and in-depth coverage on most IT-related issues.
(Relevance)	Accuracy	Vendor data is usually compared and cross-checked through other sources, such as vendor suppliers (e.g., chip producers). Reports are checked internally by peers.
	Clarity	Editorial guidelines on language use and peer reviewing stress clarity of language and vocabulary. Glossaries, abbreviation directories, and side-notes and definitions provide additional means of clarification.
	Applicability	Every Gartner document contains strategic planning assumptions that are especially marked (in italic) and can have direct influence on a manager's decision or options. Action items are also highlighted and state ways of implementing the findings. Every research note ends with a bottom line that contains the main suggestions.

Information Quality Levels	Information Quality Criteria	Activities to improve the IQ-criteria
Product Level	Conciseness	All research notes are limited to a maximum of five pages. All strategic analysis reports are limited to a maximum of hundred pages. Long reports include executive summaries. Magic quadrants and conceptual diagrams are used to synthesize content.
(Soundness)	Consistency	All documents of one type (research notes or strategic analysis reports) have the same overall structure. In addition, the same visualization schemes are often used, such as the magic quadrants matrix or process charts.
	Correctness	All documents are peer-reviewed before publication and checked by a topic-'champion'.
	Currency	Most topics are updated on a monthly basis through research notes by the topic owner or his team.
Process Level	Convenience	The documents can be easily downloaded from the Internet or they are sent automatically to a user by e-mail (based on his interest-profile). Inquiries can be addressed to one central phone number or e-mail address where they are forwarded to the relevant experts. The experts will contact the client in the medium that is most convenient to him or her.
(Optimization)	Timeliness	Answers to questions in the inquiry service are given within a couple of days. New information is automatically sent to subscribers with a matching profile.
	Traceability	Prior reports are usually referenced and hypertext-linked. Author information is limited to the name and a list of prior reports.
	Interactivity	Subscribers can customize their Gartner portal and personalize the content selection. Gartner events and consultants provide the opportunity for physical interaction.
Infrastructure Level	Accessibility	The Gartner reports are accessible anytime from any Internet terminal. Inquiries can be placed by phone, fax, or e-mail.
(Reliability)	Security	The Gartner site is protected by a fire-wall and every account is password protected.
	Maintainability	The content updating is delegated to topic owners. The infrastructure is maintained by dedicated web masters.
	Speed	The Gartner infrastructure is highly developed with high performance in terms of access and retrieval speed. The search engine delivers instant results.

Table 26: Gartner service features and their impact on information quality criteria

From the list in the above table, the criteria that seem to be affected most by Gartner's approach are the following four:

Most Affected Information Quality Criteria

1. Comprehensiveness: the large pool of analysts guarantees advice on all IT-relevant issues. As Müller states "our analysts are more specialized than at most other IT-research firms, simply because we have more of them than any other company." The business model of Gartner has changed recently in that respect. Now, all of the research services or topics can be accessed by all subscribers (a model that was introduced by Giga, a Gartner competitor).

2. Consistency: Gartner research notes and reports follow the same format all over the world. In addition the same visualization schemas are often used. Gartner also claims to provide one consistent opinion on most IT-related issues.

3. Clarity: the analyst boot camp (the base training for Gartner authors), the analyst guidelines, and the frequent client interaction and feedback help to assure that an analyst writes in a clear and comprehensible language. Since many Gartner clients are not English native speakers, simple and clear English is of high importance to the management.

4. Conciseness: the research notes and the research newsletters compress crucial findings and the analyst's experience and interpretation to a few pages. The feedback from analysts to client questions is usually very concise (1-3 pages) and tailored to the context of the client.

The added value that these characteristics provide can be described as fast, authoritative and tailored advice on all IT-related strategic issues. Due to this, Gartner has become a reliable and reputed source for IT-professionals. Four out of the five customers whom I have interviewed have indicated that they use Gartner information to not only prepare their decisions but also to defend them in their teams. In this way, Gartner becomes a proxy for objective, reliable information. The added value lies not only in the information itself, but also in the fact that it can bring endless discussions among IT-professionals in a project team to an end through a reliable outside opinion. In next sections, we look at the price tag for that outside opinion and how it is actually generated.

Added Value: Objectivity, Believability and Reputation

Subscribing to Gartner is not a low-cost investment. While Müller acknowledges to be more expensive than competitors such as Giga Information Group, he argues that the hefty price tag on Gartner is backed by unparalleled research re-

The Business Model and Pricing Scheme

sources. The subscription rates vary greatly according to the number of licenses that are bought by a company. One can say that every employee that uses the Gartner services will cost a company a couple of thousand dollars per year. This fee includes an unlimited access to all reports and as many inquiries as requested by the client (within reasonable limits). However, events such as conferences or seminars are not included in this price.

The Production Process

The Gartner research process follows the same, iterative 'answer first' logic as the research process of most business consulting companies (see Minto 1995): The analysts start with a scenario and a hypothesis of where a market may be going. Then, they collect evidence and opinions to prove or modify their initial hypothesis. In this way, they continually revise their hypothesis and add evidence to validate their strategic planning assumptions. The following six steps are Gartner's official description of how a strategic planning assumption is researched and written (Allen, 1994).

1) **Scenarios:** Develop scenarios (five-year forecasts for market dynamics, winners and challengers and technology breakthroughs) and Strategic Planning Assumptions. Key Issues are developed as part of the scenarios; they are questions that have no definitive answers, on which user and vendor strategies are determined for the five-year planning period. Strategic Planning Assumptions, the guidelines or best working answers that can be applied to the Key Issues, are given probabilities ranging from 0.1 to 0.9.

2) **Search:** Search for written material (e.g., vendor announcements and financial analysis) that is relevant to the Strategic Planning Assumptions.

3) **Data Collection:** Survey vendors, users and other contacts in the industry to refine the Strategic Planning Assumptions.

4) **Pattern Recognition:** An ongoing and integral part of the research process on which Key Issues and Strategic Planning Assumptions are developed or modified. This requires constantly surveying and checking the validity and relevance of Strategic Planning Assumptions.

5) **Stalking Horses:** Create a "stalking horse" Strategic Planning Assumption – a tentative Strategic Planning Assumption – when more data is needed. This "stalking horse" elicits comments and stimulates the research network.

6) **Document:** Publish the scenario, as well as *Strategic Analysis Reports* and *Research Notes*. This documentation is a vehicle to further "survey" the user and vendor network.

Before a research report is actually published in step six, it must undergo a brief evaluation by a group of analyst peers knowledgeable in the topic of the report. After the reviews of the peer community have been incorporated into the text, the final draft is cleared for publication by the 'topic champion'. The topic champion is an analyst who is responsible for a domain of related IT-topics (such as knowledge management, data warehouses, networks, etc.).

Quality Control through Peers

Besides peer reviewing, Gartner relies on two other means of fostering quality in the produced reports, namely guidelines and training. The authoring guidelines, however, are not very extensive. They focus on the *size* (e.g., maximum number of pages for a given report type), *style* (e.g., the choice of words), and *structure* (e.g., report templates) of Gartner reports. There are no editorial guidelines about the content of the reports because the management does not want to interfere with the analyst's opinions in regard to vendors or products. Here, the neutrality and objectivity of the analysts is the main concern. In terms of training, the analysts go through a basic 'analyst boot camp' at the beginning of their career. The courses at this camp focus on essential writing skills and on the typical Gartner information elements discussed above (e.g., how to use magic quadrants and probabilities). Later training events focus on knowledge sharing between analysts.

Guidelines and Training

Since the series of steps described above is in effect a knowledge-intensive process, the problems that occur in producing a report are mostly related to the identification, interpretation, and communication of complex information. When asked about the problems in the research process, Müller indicates six areas of potential concern. First, there is the danger of not covering the right 'hot topics' soon enough. Gartner tries to sense such topics through close contacts with its clients, vendors, and with other research institutions. A second problem that all IT-research companies are facing is that of assuring accuracy and reliability of the provided data. Gartner tries to overcome this problem by gathering evidence from a variety of sources including vendors, consumers, suppliers, and government agencies. A further problem in the report production process is reviewing. As of now, this process is not highly standardized. Earlier in this case study, it was indicated that the reviewing is mostly done informally by sharing a report with colleagues before its publication and waiting for feedback or suggestions.

Problems in the Production Process

The next problem is, in Müller's view, the most important one at the moment. The crucial question behind this problem is how to assure a timely and competent response to all inquiries that Gartner receives every day. This is both a logistics and a knowledge management challenge that involves the following issues: How can the right (i.e., competent and available) analysts be allocated to the right kind of questions and how can they re-use already given answers if similar questions are addressed to them? How can they manage their time effectively so that urgent questions can be answered quickly, yet more profound research is not neglected? How many questions should one analyst answer in a given day? Until now, these questions have not been fully resolved. It is mostly up to the analyst how he or she handles the heavy work load. The customer interviews I have conducted indicate that longer response times and less specific answers are indeed symptoms of this problem. According to Peter Müller, Gartner is acutely aware of this 'scope' problem: "We invest heavily in organizational structures for simpler, more direct and more speedy replies from the analyst to the client."

The last two problems refer both to what GIDEON GART-NER has labeled 'collaborative research'. They are a direct result of Gartner's size and research scope which at times makes it difficult for analysts to brief or inform one another about their work. The resulting problems consist of adequately cross-referencing and linking related or prior research reports and assuring that Gartner has one consistent opinion on most IT-related issues. The solution to these problems lies in the powerful information platform that Gartner uses and continually improves. Through the classification and indexing of the reports, new documents can easily be identified, retrieved, and linked. This classification, however, requires a lot of discipline on behalf of the analysts in classifying their work on a daily basis and adding relevant meta-information to their reports. While linking reports to related material improves the traceability and coverage of a topic, it can also be the source of frustration. Too much cross-linking between reports can distract the reader from the flow of the argumentation and make it more difficult for him to concentrate on the core topic. This is one of the findings from the customer interviews that are summarized in the next section.

Customer Opinions   On the basis of five customer interviews some of the problems described above can be better understood and evaluated. All of the interviewed customers were quite content with the information provided by Gartner. All of them indicated that they appreciate the clear and consistent structure of the reports and the way that they summarize crucial developments and trends (as in the magic quadrants that provide overviews on vendors and their strengths or weaknesses). The responsiveness problem was confirmed by two of the customers who indicated that they sometimes had to wait several days for a response. One customer indicated that the answers tended to be rather US-centered and that information on European companies was more difficult to get.

As far as the Gartner on-line infrastructure is concerned, all five clients said that they appreciated the ease-of-use, the good search engine, and the mostly adequate alert service that automatically informed them about new relevant information by e-mail. Two customers also commented that the life events were worthwhile, but costly. The high costs of the service were generally mentioned by all customers.

A long-term client indicated that the positions taken by Gartner were less courageous or visionary than they used to be. He found that the Gartner analysts were more provocative in the past and that nowadays, they were much more diplomatic. This concern resonates with Müller who also aims for crisper and more provocative research reports:

Our information is not crisp enough yet, it has to be more to the point to highlight our position. We are also less courageous than we used to be in our positions. We don't cause as many wow-effects anymore as we used to and we definitely need to become more provocative.

The main concern of this client was a different one, however. He found that the size of Gartner – which is usually a competitive advantage – also has its negative sides. This relates closely to the second challenge described in the problem section above, namely managing the increasing size and scope of Gartner (in terms of logistics and knowledge management). The scaling of Gartner's knowledge is a crucial challenge that is not easy to manage. One client who used Gartner for more than seven year had the following to say about this issue:

It used to be that there was small number of analysts who you would know personally and it used to be we had more contact with these analysts. Now, there are so many more analysts, there is less continuity in terms of staff and topics. There are also too many reports on every topic. Less would be more in this case. The same holds true for the events. The symposiums used to be better, they are just too big now. They didn't present too many new facets and they had less product presentations. We don't need an IT-expo at Gartner. They should focus on a few core issues at every conference.

This 'scaling problem' seems to cause other issues, for example in regard to the website, where a growing number of reports has to be made accessible. One customer indicated that he was confronted with too many reports and that he was no longer able to get a quick overview of all the *new* reports. He also mentioned that the frequent links among reports didn't help him, but rather distracted him and lead to a hunt for information in various reports. In conclusion, he found that there were too many redundancies in the reports.

While Gartner competitors also use linking and cross-referencing to inform customers of related research material, Gartner uses hypertext links not only at the end of every report, but also in the text itself. In next section, we will find out who these competitors are and whether they pose a threat to Gartner or not.

Competitors

Being the number one research company in the IT-sector, Gartner faces a number of aggressive competitors. Nevertheless, the competitive threat to Gartner seems not very significant, since Gartner has a "quasi-monopoly" on the market and many companies cannot afford to loose its information or opinion. In addition, many companies need to subscribe to at least two analysts to get a balanced set of expert opinions, and Gartner is usually one of the two.

Gartner faces distinct competitors for its various activities. As far as research is concerned its main competitors are Giga Information Group (described in the next case study), Forrester and Meta Group. For the quantitative market research performed by Dataquest major competitors are the International Data Corporation (IDC) and the Yankee Group. For the consulting domain the competitors are obviously Accenture, Ernst & Young, Boston Consulting Group, McKinsey & Company and other similar companies. The measurement branch of Gartner does not have major competitors, according to Müller. He mentions Compass as one company who is also active in the benchmarking and measurement sector. Next to these major players, there is also a large number of smaller IT-research companies that cannot gain a large part of the IT-research market due to their limited resources. Examples of such smaller companies are the Delphi Group, Ovum, Burton, Butler, Computerwire, Tower Group, Aberdeen, Seybold, Hurwitz, Zona, or Durlacher. These smaller competitors do not face the same scaling problem as Gartner, but due to their limited resources, they often have to focus on market niches, such as IT-outsourcing or IT in the financial sector. As in other sectors, market niches can be an attractive future industry sector. The last section of this chapter addresses other future developments in this context.

When asked about the biggest development imperatives in the IT-research domain in general, and in regard to content quality and value in particular, Müller refers to the 'last mile problem' in analogy to the telecommunications industry where the last mile to the consumer is still a crucial problem.

Future Developments

The big problem we have is what I call 'the last mile': How can we get the knowledge we have actually into the projects of the client who is under a lot of time pressure, but who would actually need our advice for his tasks. In the future, we will hence work more personally with the client in physical interactions. For example: we deploy a Gartner consultant at the client's site who works in the project team with the client over a longer period of time. We have had a pilot like this. The Gartner consultant can bring our input directly into the project team. To summarize: in IT-research, it is more important what you get across, than what you have in store.

As the next case study will show, getting the attention of the customer is a crucial challenge for external knowledge sources such as Gartner. This is especially true as more and more content sources compete for the attention of a CIO or manager (such as e-mails, Intranet publications, trade journals, consultants, universities, internet portals, etc.).

The limited processing capacity or attention of managers and executives can also be an impediment for future growth. As we have seen with the scaling problem, more reports may not necessarily mean more business. Thus, Gartner's growth strategy is only moderately based on additional revenues in the research domain. Mostly, Gartner strives for new business in the areas of benchmarking and measurement, where the annual growth rate is currently at 25 to 30 percent. This seems reasonable, given the fact that numbers are both more concise and easier to compare than qualitative opinions. Besides benchmarking, Gartner has invested heavily in its consulting branch. This three-year investment has resulted in a growth rate in this area of above fifty percent per year. Another important element in Gartner's growth strategy consists of tailoring its research knowledge for other target groups, specifically general managers and CEOs who are interested in using IT for the growth of their company. As mentioned earlier, Gartner has launched this service under the G2 brand.

Summarizing these activities, one can say that a sustainable growth strategy in this sector needs to focus not only on quantitative, but also on qualitative growth. It has to focus on improving the interaction with the client and at the same time expand its client base. That this can lead to management challenges has been demonstrated with the issues surrounding the scaling problem (e.g., assuring that more information does not result in less actionable advice; this point will also be discussed in the next case study).

Gartner is one of the oldest, largest and most respected business research institutions in the world and co-ordinates over 700 information technology specialists and their documentation. In order to do so, Gartner has recognized the crucial importance of what it calls 'knowledge content quality' (see Harris and Flemming, 1998). It manages its own content quality by enforcing strict format standards, by fostering collaboration among its analysts, and by continually optimizing the internal and external information management process and its infrastructure.

We can summarize Gartner major benefits or innovations with the four information quality principles:

- Integration: Gartner makes information more concise and accessible by using a consistent format and re-occurring text elements that stress the key messages of a report. These elements are executive summaries, bottom lines, action items, magic quadrants, and strategic planning assumptions. In addition, Gartner provides a comprehensive overview on its in-formation through a state-of-the-art Internet portal.
- Validation: Probabilities indicate the level of certainty and the time scale that is associated with every strategic planning assumption. To validate vendor data, Gartner uses multiple sources (such as suppliers or census data). Client feedback is also used a validation indicator.
- Contextualization: The Gartner analysts contextualize information by commenting on vendor's data based on their background and based on other (insider) sources. Thus, they are able to see behind the data and look for intentions and relate them to one another. In terms of retrievability, the analysts add vital meta-information to their reports to make cross-comparisons easier and quicker. The purest form of re-contextualization occurs in the inquiry services, where the analyst has to apply his expertise to the specific situation of a client.
- Activation: Through direct interaction between analysts and customers at telephone conferences, meetings, or conferences, Gartner brings its expertise and advice to live and thus increases its impact. The reports contain various action-oriented text blocks such as action items, bottom-lines or planning assumptions.

The principle that is most visibly exploited by Gartner is the third one: Data and information is put into perspective through the careful analysis and comparison of sources and developments. It is tailored to the context of a client and his or her questions and problems.

The market leader in IT-research has established a high-standard in a classical knowledge-intensive process, namely market analysis and advisory. In doing so, it has created high-quality information formats such as the magic quadrants, or strategic planning assumptions. The scaling of this process, however, remains a crucial challenge for a company as dependent on direct client interaction as Gartner.

Conclusion

4.5 Making Research Relevant: GiGA Information Group's IdeaBytes

Our biggest competition isn't another company, it's low usage: How can we get people to actually use the knowledge they have at their fingertips?

MARTIN ABEL,
Giga Country Manager, Switzerland

The following description of Giga's information products and services is based on a two hour interview with the country manager for Switzerland, MARTIN ABEL, and with the Senior Account Manager for that region, ADRIAN SCHÖN. As far as the quality assurance of the research process is concerned, the case is based on a thirty minute telephone interview with PAUL DE LIGNY BOUDREAU who is the chief research officer of Giga Group. Additional sources were five telephone interviews with customers of those services. Finally, the case study is based on the experience of being a test-user of Giga's products and on the analysis of its website and company and product documentation.

Case Study Sources

The Giga Information Group is a relatively young research company that was founded in 1995 by GIDEON GARTNER who left the first company he founded (Gartner Inc.) to start a new IT-research approach that was based on what he called 'collaborative research' (stressing the cooperation of analysts from various domains). Gideon Gartner was at the time discontent with Gartner's business model of compartmentalized research products that were offered individually to clients. In founding the Giga Information Group, he stressed the unlimited access of clients to all of its research products. In addi-

Company Overview

tion, he conceived the company's research products as Internet-based services that were highly inter-connected and interactive.

The Giga Information Group has since grown rapidly and has now annual revenues of almost seventy million US dollars (it is now part of Forrester Research). It has nine offices in the USA, and 18 in Europe. It has over 1,200 clients worldwide and 350 of Europe's biggest companies are Giga customers. Total subscriptions amounted to 68,7 million US dollars in 1999. Giga employs over a hundred researchers in various locations. In addition, Giga manages an expert net of over 1,200 independent subject matter experts that collaborate with Giga on an ad-hoc basis. Recently, Giga has been acquired by Forrester, another major IT analyst company.

As of September 2000, GIGA GROUP is a European spin-off of the Giga Information. It employs 45 people and focuses on the distribution of Giga products in Europe (with the exception of Germany, Austria, Scandinavia, and England). Besides the international analyst pool, Giga Group has its own staff of European analysts. Currently, there are twelve such analysts who are mainly based in Paris. The company's following mission statements outline its vision of the IT research business:

GigaGroup provides customers with objective advice about harnessing Information Technology (IT). In particular, GigaGroup helps clients make strategic and tactical decisions about the IT technologies, people and processes needed to excel in business.

Giga's mission is to enable you to investigate, make, and verify strategic and tactical IT investments by providing: results ready IT intelligence and advice.

Giga helps organizations manage the developments as well as reduce the risk associated with investing in and deploying new technologies (source: Giga company presentation).

These statements clearly indicate that Giga focuses on research regarding information technology markets and products. When asked about Giga's core competence MARTIN ABEL (who has been with Giga for several years) refers to Giga's ability to give unbiased advice on information technology in a comprehensive, responsive, and hands-on manner. As we will see later on in the case study, responsiveness is indeed one of Giga's distinctive features (as perceived by customers), hence timeliness of the delivered information is one of the key quality attributes highlighted in this case.

Giga's main activities can be divided into three major areas, of which the first one clearly dominates. They are advisory services (mainly ad-hoc research), consulting, and events (conferences and round tables). This case study will focus on the first area and how Giga improves the quality and impact of these research reports. In terms of content, the reports focus on six IT-related domains, namely information management, application development, IT management, computer platforms, communications and networking, and software applications and solutions. The two major types of research products that Giga offers to its clients besides the inquiry services (i.e., asking direct questions to analysts by e-mail or phone), are *IdeaBytes* (reports that are up to two pages long and answer a specific question) and *Planning Assumptions* (which are up to ten pages long and argue a position or opinion about future developments). Besides these two formats Giga also offers *Research Digests* which summarize a large number of research reports in newsletter-type format of roughly one hundred pages, and so-called *Salons*, which are essentially web-areas dedicated to a particular topic or issue such as supply chain planning or data warehouses. Another Giga product are *Flashes* which provide abstracts of new research reports via e-mail. Although Giga's research activities are categorized into a number of research domains, the access to these areas is not restricted. This is due to the belief that IT-problems do not neatly fit into pre-defined categories, but rather cross disciplinary boundaries. Abel describes this view in the following quote:

The Core Products

The times when information was segregated are over. Today information is much more connected. It does no longer make sense to offer just a few of the research services. Thus, Giga provides its client with access to *all* research areas. Analysts may also collaborate intensively to resolve a certain question. We refer to this approach as 'collaborative research'.

In spite of this collaborative approach, pre-defined research areas still exist. They are called Orbits and represent a group of roughly fifteen analysts that work on similar topics. Every one of the thirteen orbits is managed by an orbit leader who is also the final reviewer of every paper published on a particular issue within the orbit's topic domain.

The main research products of Giga, the IdeaBytes and the Planning Assumptions, both follow a consistent structure. For the Planning Assumptions, that argue a specific Giga position in a four to ten page document, this structure consists of the position statement, proofs to back the position, an alternative

Document Structures

view that outlines another possible position, and findings and recommendations for actions based on the taken position. Every planning assumption ends with references and links to related research reports.

The shorter IdeaBytes center around a specific question that was raised by a client, or triggered by an industry event. Every IdeaByte begins with the 'catalyst', i.e., how the question that will be addressed in a document originated: whether from a client inquiry or through analyst collaboration or a specific event. After the catalyst the actual question is stated and the answer to it is described. Again the document ends with references with related material.

Additional Services

Besides the two main types of research documents, Giga offers two software applications which can be used to run evaluations or analyses. These applications enable Giga customer's to better analyze their own situation in comparison to a general industry standard. As we will see in the 'future developments' section of this case study, software applications are a lucrative way of scaling a knowledge-based business such as IT-advisory services. The applications increase the *interactivity* and *applicability* of the offered information and they allow calculations or ratings based on the customer's specific context (the thus provide means of contextualization).

The two software applications that Giga offers are the Web Site ScoreCard that can be used to analyze website effectiveness and Total Economic Impact which helps clients to assess and measure the value of their IT programs.

Impact on Information Quality

How Giga's various infrastructure and process features increase the quality of its information product is summarized in the table below.

Information Quality Levels	Information Quality Criteria	Activities to improve the IQ-criteria
Community Level	Comprehensiveness	All Giga reports can be accessed by all clients all of the time. The Giga Knowledge Center provides assistance in locating the relevant expertise.
(Relevance)	Accuracy	Information is cross-checked by peers and by the topic owner. Giga analysts are usually experienced specialists in their domain.
	Clarity	Every IdeaByte has a clearly formulated client question or an event as a starting point. The document structure is simple and logical. Longer documents distinguish between Giga's position, the proofs, and alternative opinions.
	Applicability	All research notes are either based on a client question or an important event in the IT-industry. The analysts are constantly asked to align their research with the short-term needs of their clients. Every research report is evaluated in regard to its propositions, metrics, and answers. Software modules are provided.
Product Level	Conciseness	Research notes are limited to 1-2 pages. Planning assumptions are less than ten pages. Quarterly research digests provide overviews on new research documents.
(Soundness)	Consistency	All research notes or reports have the same exact structure.
	Correctness	Analysts are independent from sales and must sign a declaration of neutrality. There is a four-level quality assurance process.
	Currency	Salon owners update their topic area on a regular basis and purge outdated material.
Process Level	Convenience	The Knowledge Center automatically directs inquiries to the relevant and available experts and ensures that the contact is established.
(Optimization)	Timeliness	Answers to inquiries are given within several hours. Relevant information is forwarded automatically to subscribers based on their profiles.
	Traceability	The research digest provides background information on senior analysts (research focus, prior position, etc.). Prior reports or other sources are usually referenced at the end of a document.
	Interactivity	Various on- and off-line life events are organized periodically, from telephone conferences to an annual client symposium.

Information Quality Levels	Information Quality Criteria	Activities to improve the IQ-criteria
Infrastructure Level	Accessibility	Knowledge salons group document around topics, knowledge tree serve as a taxonomy to make the files more accessible. Full access is provided to all clients.
(Reliability)	Security	The gigaweb.com site is fire-wall protected. The account is protected by a password.
	Maintainability	The topic owners are responsible for the updating of their research 'salon' and there is an overall web master who maintains the Gigaweb.
	Speed	The search engine delivers instant feedback on the made queries. Access to the website is immediate. Linked documents are retrieved instantly.

Table 27: Giga's service features and their impact on information quality criteria

Most Affected Information Quality Criteria

From this list of attributes, four clearly stand out. In talking to customers, Giga managers and researchers, it became clear that great attention was given to the applicability, conciseness, timeliness, and consistency of the provided information. Here again, Giga's way of managing these attributes:

1. Applicability: Because most research notes are triggered directly by client questions, the applicability or relevance of the research is assured, also by the fact that every document ends with specific recommendations for actions. The internal review process also stresses applicability: Staff evaluations by Giga managers focus primarily on the applicability of the produced research reports and how well client questions have been answered. In addition, software applications can be used which can be applied to the IT-program or Website of the customer. Finally, Giga also monitors the actual usage of its services and may ask clients who do not use Giga frequently why they have not done so.

2. Conciseness: Giga stresses compressed information in all its facets. Research notes (clearly branded as IdeaBytes) are usually only one page long and planning assumptions rarely exceed five pages. In addition, services such as the research digest or the salons provide summaries on all research products. Giga tries to reduce information overload for its clients by only offering two formats of reports and by limiting the number of reports per topic.

3. Timeliness: As confirmed by the customer interviews below, one of Giga's most distinctive features in comparison to its competitors is its responsiveness. Most customer inquiries are answered within hours and most customers indicate that inquiries are usually handled in a very timely and personal manner.

4. Consistency: As stated earlier, there are only two structures for Giga reports, the IdeaBytes and the Planning Assumptions. Both do not vary in terms of maximum size or structure and hence assure a consistency in terms of format. Consistency in terms of content is assured through the weekly telephone conference that all analysts attend and where Giga positions are discussed.

The added value that is generated through these attributes is fast, reliable, actionable and easy-to-use advice that is tailored to the problems of the Giga customers and organized for action. According to Giga, this advice focuses primarily on tactical issues and middle management strategic decisions (unlike FORRESTER that also emphasizes advice on high level strategic issues). In order to track the value that Giga generates for its clients, user statistics are closely monitored. If usage of a customer is consistently low, Giga may call up the client and ask for possible reasons. It may even suggest to reallocate the services to another person where they can provide more value. According to one Giga customer, this value often resides in the alternative (and neutral) views and options that are offered or the hidden risks that are made visible by Giga analysts.

Added Value

In line with its 'collaborative research' philosophy, Giga's business model does not limit the access to a restricted number of research domains, but offers access to all material to all clients. It does distinguish, however, between premium members who have access to additional services, and pure on-line users who can only read the stored reports. The 'members' pay a license of 14,000 US dollars each which gives them the right to attend all Giga events and ask as many inquiries as they want. These members use Giga frequently and profit from its roundtable discussions, analyst sessions, and the yearly GigaWorld conference. Typical members are chief technology officers or corporate IT-architects. Users, the second subscription model, only pay 1,400 US dollars for a one year subscription to Giga's on-line content, support through Giga's KnowledgeCenter, and access to local events. All other services that users may want to use cost extra (such as the inquiry services or the conferences). Nevertheless, a

The Business Model and Pricing Scheme

The Production
Process

minimum total subscription amount of 42,000 US dollars is usually a prerequisite for such licenses.

Throughout this case study, the 'collaborative' nature of Giga research was stressed. Now, we will examine in how far this collaboration is visible in the research process itself.

The production process of Giga research documents is often triggered by an external event or a client inquiry. More seldom, an analyst collaboration or Giga's own research agenda (called thematic planning assumptions) may trigger a research report. The following four steps describe the series of activities that lead to a research publication in the Gigaweb site.

1. If a customer inquiry has been answered in a way that the analyst judges it to be relevant to a large number of Giga clients, the analyst rewrites his or her answer to the original question for a more general appeal. In doing so, he collaborates with his peers within the same orbit (i.e., practice group), asking for comments or feedback on his or her answer.

2. The analyst then produces an abstract of the IdeaByte or Planning Assumption (if several IdeaBytes have been combined in a larger piece) and submits this summary (e.g., two to four bullet points and two to three sentences) to the central, worldwide research coordinator. The coordinator will screen the abstracts on a regular basis. Abstracts that are relevant to many analysts will then be discussed in the weekly global telephone conference with almost all hundred analysts. In this way, the analysts receive feedback on their ideas and knowledge is shared in a global 'conversation'.

3. If the report has the format of a longer piece, a planning assumption, the orbit leader will review the document with the author and release it for publication. The research leader may also contact other research leaders or analysts in case that additional clarifications are needed. The orbit leader is the thought leader of the analyst within a give topic, and not the direct superior.

4. After the report has been published, user statistics measure how many times a piece has been downloaded. The orbit leader then grades every report on a scale of one to ten with a 'quality scoring' (see below). The top thirty percent of all reports are rated again centrally by the head of research.

The four steps show that the production process of Giga reports is neither complicated nor highly standardized. It is however, complemented by a research guide that comprises the rules of authoring. These rules are clear and simple, but strict in terms of document length and structure. The same applies to the quality management that was mentioned in steps three and four. Below the four levels of this quality assurance process are described in more detail.

At present, there are four levels of quality assurance at Giga. The first one is an informal one that is triggered by the analyst. It consists of an informal collaboration with peer analysts, e.g., sending a draft to various other analysts who may be interested in a particular topic. The second level of quality assurance also occurs prior to publication. Before a document is published on the Gigaweb, it has to be reviewed by the relevant orbit leader. Once the document is published, the orbit leader will again review it. This (monthly) review will then become a part of the analyst's yearly evaluation. For this third quality 'scoring' Giga has devised a common set of rating criteria. They consist of the following five questions: Is the (client) question answered? Are there metrics or guidelines for measurement? Are quantifications provided or suggested that help the customer judge a situation or a development internally or externally? Are there conclusions and (actionable) practical recommendations at the end of the text? Is there a specific Giga position that is articulated in the text?

Four Levels of Quality Assurance

There is also a fourth, global quality scoring system that highlights the top contributions of Giga analysts in a given period. It is done centrally by Merv Adrian, Giga's senior vice president for research. Based on the highest evaluation scores, the top thirty contributions are clearly labeled as such and marked in the Gigaweb to signal their outstanding quality to the clients.

Besides these four quality mechanisms, there is an additional one for new analysts. New analysts are continuously monitored by their orbit leader and everything that a new analysts publishes will be reviewed by a superior.

Although the quality management for Giga reports is systematic and elaborate, it cannot solve all the possible problems that arise in the production of research reports. When asked about the main issues that the management faces in the production process, ABEL and SCHÖN mention two major challenges.

Problems in the Production Process

First of all, the issue of how to manage the heavy *work load* and time pressure for their analysts. Since freedom and time to reflect are essential to the analyst's work, a heavy load of client inquiries can actually interfere with the analyst's productivity. According to Abel, analysts tend to be overloaded with client inquiries and often work over twelve hours a day. This may of course lead to a danger of burn-out. Especially the 'star analysts' are overbooked. Finding the right balance between reading, reflecting, and writing is thus one of the biggest challenges for analysts working at Giga. PAUL DE LIGNY BOUDREAU, Giga Group's Chief Research Officer, refers to this challenge as the switch between the absorption mode and the production mode which is not always an easy transition for many analysts, as he points out below:

An analyst needs to pump out findings fast and frequently. In any case enough to get feedback. I call this the 'constructive loop': as he writes more, he becomes well known, and hence receives more inquiries.

DE LIGNY BOUDREAU acknowledges that this virtuous cycle can also turn into a vicious one, as more and more inquiries need to be answered quickly and thoroughly. Re-using already written answers thus becomes an important issue for which tagging, categorizing, and indexing are crucial prerequisites. At Giga, it is still an unresolved question who should do this tagging or indexing. The analysts would be more competent in classifying their work, the editors or the technical staff would be more inclined to do so. However, additional administrative tasks such as indexing or classifying use up more of an analyst's already scarce time. Interestingly enough, Giga's present knowledge management system (based on the Vignette Storyserver application) is almost identical for analysts and clients.

A second problem inherent in the production process of research as Giga pursues it, lies in its focus on short-term issues. Since most research reports are answers to client questions, the research agenda focuses on present or short-term issues. Consequently, Abel sees a danger in overlooking important (long-term, e.g., more than two to four years ahead) trends because of this close client contact and the focus on operational and planning issues. In order to avoid this danger, Giga also pursues research that is not directly triggered by client questions, but these independent research activities amount to a small percentage of the total research underway at Giga. This is due to Giga's core commitment to actionable and timely research that focuses on the current questions of its clients. This illustrates the tradeoff between timeliness and comprehensiveness that was discussed in chapter three.

In spite of the problems discussed in the previous section, Giga customer satisfaction is at a high level (this can be illustrated by the fact that Giga has a yearly re-subscription rate of over eighty percent). The responsiveness and competence of the Giga analysts was confirmed by the sample of five customer interviews. One client said that of all twelve IT-research companies that they had subscribed to, Giga had the quickest and most reliable response time. He indicated that Giga analysts usually answered inquiries in a matter of hours rather than days. This client also referred to the limits of an analyst's impact and pointed at one major problem of knowledge-based services, that of context:

Customer Opinions

Knowledge transfer cannot be ordered. The complexity and decision scope has increased exponentially. *It becomes ever more difficult for an analyst to understand the specific context of a client.* Often, I would have to brief the analyst for three weeks about what we do, before we can use his advice. So, for a win-win situation, you have to update an analyst for quite a long time. Linking him into the context of the company is difficult.

This crucial issue can only be resolved partially through the inquiry service, where a client states his context and asks for advice tailored to a specific situation. It is a disadvantage of the analyst model versus the consultant's way of working where a steady relationship ensures that the consultant understands more and more of his or her client's context. Giga nevertheless believes that no analyst should spend more than thirty percent on consulting engagements in order to remain open for client questions from a variety of contexts.

When asked for the reasons why he used Giga, one customer indicated that the full access to all topics over the Internet was one reason, combined with the fact that 'you actually find what you are looking for'. The typical questions that this client was able to answer with the help of Giga are related to products and companies, e.g., what products are in this market, who are the major players? For these types of questions Giga usually provided high-quality information. For more complicated questions, e.g. how is this technology going to evolve and how will it affect us, direct inquiries are necessary. This is especially true in regard to the concise IdeaBytes. One customer indicated that "we don't like IdeaBytes because they are superficial", pointing at the limits of this approach to conciseness. The same customer indicated that he preferred the longer planning assumptions, since they were more profound and well written. He also indicated that Giga didn't offer planning assumptions on all relevant IT-issues. He felt that Gartner and Meta (two main competitors) had more documents on the same topic than Giga. This, however, was not necessarily seen as a disadvantage, but rather as a way of limiting information overload, as he states below:

We told them [Giga] not to produce more documents per year. Otherwise we drown in them. This is the paradox: If they produce more, the people will read less.

One other client indicated (as the only negative point) that he was sometimes overwhelmed by the amount of information available on Giga's homepage and that it became difficult for him to prioritize the reports. Another important issue regarding not only this overload problem, but also the applicability of the research information was raised by three interviewed Giga customers. One indicated that he especially appreciated the conceptual summary *diagrams* that were sometimes provided. They enabled him to use the Giga expertise in presentations and meetings as simple slides that summarized a whole topic. He felt that "diagrams can be more easily used internally and adapted for presentations and briefings." A second interviewed customer independently indicated a similar preference for diagrams. He found that "the graphics are simple; we can use them with non-technical people and we incorporate them into our presentations." A third customer also indicated that "we use 'cut and paste' to assemble interesting charts from the reports for our own documents." These diagrams are ways of activating the information contained in the reports. Another way to bring the information to life is of course through events. The interviewed customers indicated that they appreciated the opportunity to meet the analysts in person and talk face-to-face to them about their problems or questions. Many customers stressed the 'real dialogueue' that takes place between Giga and its clients. One client indicated that this dialogueue went as far as being called up every month by Giga's staff. In these phone calls, Giga's managers would ask about the satisfaction with the service and about the issues that were on the manager's mind. This type of real dialogueue was seen as a unique form of activating not only the information, but also the company's relationships with its clients.

Overall the five questioned customers stressed the conciseness of Giga's research reports and the above average customer service. They indicated that they liked the frankness of Giga's reports while still presenting alternative views. The only negative views were on the company's overly strong focus on e-business and its at times inadequate search function on the website. Both issues were only raised by one customer.

Although the IT-market research arena is quite competi- *Competitors*
tive and many companies produce IT-research information, the biggest competitive threat that Giga faces does not primarily reside in other companies, but – according to Abel – in the limited attention of managers. "We loose clients because of low usage, not because of competitors, that's why we monitor usage to closely and follow-up on low-usage costumers." Another reason why Giga may loose clients are mergers and acquisitions. There is only one client where there used to be two.

In terms of specific competitors, Gartner, as a market leader, clearly stands out. While it is true that Gartner Inc. is one of the biggest competitors of Giga, many of the larger companies that subscribe to IT-research companies cannot afford to rely on just one opinion. In consequence, they subscribe to two or three IT-research services and chances are high that Gartner and Giga are among the two (with Forrester or Meta Group being the third one). To win Gartner clients, the Giga sales force stresses the lower price, the comprehensive access model, and the high responsiveness of its analysts.

As a major trend regarding competition ABEL and SCHÖN see the rise of 'research boutiques', that is to say specialized market research companies that focus on a specific niche, such as IT-outsourcing or IT in the financial services industry. Giga will keep its focus on e-business as one factor that distinguishes it from competitors.

Besides the trend of 'nichification' of market research, *Future*
ABEL and SCHÖN see a number of other developments in *Developments*
their sector. Below, we look at some of these trends in more detail.

One mega-trend of market research is to make IT advice more actionable by packaging it as consulting. This offers not only higher margins, but also more intimate customer contact. SCHÖN and ABEL are nevertheless skeptical about the promises of consulting for their activities. While they acknowledge the growth potential of IT-consulting, they see a number of risks associated with this domain. One asset that may be at stake if Giga emphasizes its consulting activities is credibility. As analysts, Giga experts are considered neutral and independent. This may change if they are more and more involved in client projects. Another asset that may be at risk if the consulting activities are further developed is depth. According to ABEL analysts need to keep abreast of many developments and market trends. This would become increasingly difficult if they are involved in operational projects on a day to day basis. Consequently, Giga does not stress consulting as much as other companies in the domain of information technology research. Instead, it focuses on standardized solutions out of its research competence that are highly scalable, e.g., software-based methods which can be used in various contexts to solve customer problems. These software tools are mostly diagnostics instruments, such as questionnaires, simulations, or calculation sheets. They help an IT-manager answer questions such as 'where are we strong and where are we week and what can we improve to increase our performance?' The main advantages of these tools are that they can be used independently of the analyst's availability and that they can be customized to the client's situation. Many other trends that influence this type of business are also triggered by technological innovations. ABEL mentions the Gigabots which are profile-based agents that notify customers about new research that fits their interest profile. Also, new interaction forms between analysts and customers can be envisioned, such as desktop conferences or on-line chats (which are already in use at Giga). A final industry trend that can be envisioned at this point is the closer *integration* of Giga and its customers in terms of a common infrastructure: Giga's knowledge base can now become an integral part of a company's intranet, so that an IT-manager can research the Giga reports in his or her familiar environment. This service is called IntraGiga.

Case Summary   Looking back at Giga's products and services through the lens of the four information quality principles, *integration* and *activation* clearly stand out. Giga has made considerable efforts to ensure that its advice is concise and actionable. How the four principles can be applied to this case is outlined in the four paragraphs below. They summarize the main findings of this case.

- Integration: Giga provides various means of compressing information. First, through the IdeaBytes that are limited to two pages. Second through the limitation of Planning assumptions to a maximum of ten pages. Third, through

---

[131] An interesting new business field of Giga Information Group is website certification. With this service, Giga validates whether a corporate Internet homepage meets its core criteria in terms of contact and company information, clarity, tools (such as a site map), page design and navigation, and privacy policies.

the Research Digest that provide a summary of all published research. Fourth, through the Giga Flashes that provide abstracts on new research reports. A final means of integration is provided through the research salons, which bundle documents, experts, and events that relate to one IT-topic.

- Validation[131]: The most prominent validation mechanism at Giga consists of four levels of quality control and reviewing. In addition, there are ethical guidelines for the analysts that should assure their objectivity and neutrality.

- Contextualization: The background of a research report is often explicitly stated in the 'catalyst' section that describes how or why a certain report was written. At the end of every report, related reports or references are added that provide an additional context for the presented information.

- Activation: Giga emphasizes the activation of its information for clients in various forms, the most evident ones are the recommendations at the end of every report and the fact that every IdeaByte answers a specific customer question. In addition, answers to client questions are usually given within hours and can be used immediately. The currency of the information is also assured by the Gigabots that automatically forward new relevant research to the customer via e-mail. The software applications also make the stored information more interactive and applicable to the context of the client. As a last way of activating the information, Giga provides various events, such as conferences, telephone conferences, or live chats.

Conclusion

This case study has stressed the fact that information must be organized for action in order to be useful for managers and specialists. Organizing for action means answering specific questions, offering metrics, or stating the organizational implications of a trend in a timely, clear and concise manner. It also means using the same consistent structure in every communication. The case study has also highlighted various tradeoffs, e.g. between timeliness and comprehensiveness, between conciseness and applicability, or between applicability and objectivity (as illustrated by the analyst versus consultant discussion).

4.6 Communicating Quality: Guidelines and Quality Criteria at UBS Financial Services Group

It's not enough to provide our employees with new communication tools. We must also equip them with the necessary skills and methods to use them effectively.

MARKUS SCHÄRLI
Head of Employee Communications,
UBS Financial Services Group

Case Study Sources

This case study is based on an action research project of the author with UBS' corporate center and its employee communications staff. The described work on guidelines was part of a larger project. The guidelines work started in 1999 and ended in 2000. The main workshops, where the discussed guidelines were developed took place on May 16th of 2000. Over 25 people participated.

Company Overview

UBS is the largest Swiss bank, a result of the merger of Swiss Bank Corporation and the Union Bank of Switzerland in 1998. It is headquartered in Zurich and Basle and has almost 71'000 employees. UBS is a universal bank in the sense that it provides a wide range of financial services, from investment banking, retail banking and asset management, to private banking. Operating income for the year 2000 was in the order of 36 billion Swiss Francs, resulting in net profits of over 8 billion Swiss Francs.

The corporate center, which provides the context for this case, has a staff of over one thousand employees. The center is home to the group's central services, such as the legal department, the communications and marketing departments, the finance and risk office, and human resources-related staff. The corporate center acts as the central entity of the bank, which coordinates group-wide activities and strives to identify possible synergies among the various business units.

Guidelines as Way to Foster Information Quality

As a global bank, UBS realizes that new media have become an important communication channel for its staff, for top-down and client communication, as well as for bottom-up and lateral information flows. There are many guidelines that have been elaborated to help employees use these new communication channels effectively. There is, however, a plethora of such guidelines on the corporate intranet (and in printed training documents) ranging from e-mail standards to on-line chatting etiquette. These guidelines are often very *long*, they have *different structures* and different styles, as well as *different key messages*. Employees often ignore these guidelines or they are confused which of the many guidelines they should follow. The head of employee communications at UBS is aware of this problem and determined to do something about it. He is pondering the following questions:

What makes a good e-mail, chat session, memo, website, or management briefing? Are there common criteria on which we can all agree that improve communication in these settings? Are the guidelines easily applicable by our staff in their current format? Can we come up with one consistent structure for all guidelines so that we can communicate them more effectively?

In light of these questions, the head of employee communications, DR. MARKUS SCHÄRLI has decided to unify the various communication guidelines and calls together all employee communication officers worldwide. In a full-day workshop with communication staff from all geographic regions, a set of quality criteria is developed and applied to the various communication means, such as e-mail, chat, meetings, intranet publications etc. In this way a consistent and concise set of guidelines is developed.

The main purpose of these guidelines is to provide staff and management with one set of instructive suggestions on how to use a specific communication tool most effectively and create high-quality information. In the present form, however, the various guidelines do not always meet this goal. Below, we describe how a new set of guidelines solves this problem

The Purpose of the Guidelines

The set of consistent guidelines was developed in a one day workshop which involved a number of communication professionals from various sectors of the bank. Prior to this workshop, communications managers were asked to screen and review existing communication guidelines. In addition, all participants were provided with a package consisting of relevant literature and examples.

The Process: How the Guidelines Were Established

On the actual workshop day the following steps were completed. In a first step, I presented the importance and consequences of effective communication guidelines for high-quality information. Then, the workshop participants agreed (through a moderated, pinboard-based discussion) on the UBS core values as they are stated in official UBS documents. This step included agreeing on the most essential values and having a common understanding of their interpretation. In this way, the participants agreed on a total of seven core UBS values, namely professionalism, client focus, security, innovation, integrity, community and cost effectiveness. The next step consisted of applying these values to the communication behavior of UBS staff and the various communication channels. Again, I presented examples of such communication principles and rules on how they should be devised, before we addressed every single UBS value and derived communication principles from it. The rules for the design of the principles that all team members had to adhere to were the following: First, there should not be more than six or seven communication principles in total (so that they can be memorable). Second, every principle has to be relatively self-explanatory and easily applicable. Third, the principles need to be, as far as possible, mutually exclusive (i.e., non-overlapping) and collectively exhaustive (i.e., cover the main aspects). [132] Fourth, the communication principles should focus on content (e.g., topics), format (e.g. style and length), and context (e.g., time, security) of communication in a specific medium.

This rule-based procedure led to five communication principles that were only reworded slightly in the follow-up to the workshop. The resulting principles are described in the next paragraph. One sub-team was given the task of briefly describing every one of them so that the other sub-teams could use them in their writing process. In this way, the working groups had some sort of meta-guidelines to use in their medium-specific guidelines.

The Quality Principles

The agreed-upon communication principles are based on the core values of the bank, namely: professionalism, client focus, security, innovation, integrity, community and cost effectiveness. They set universal standards for each type and channel of communication within the bank and are applicable throughout the hierarchy. Their main goal is to enable the creation of high-quality information in business-related communication. The wording of these definitions is identical to the released 'meta-guidelines' which briefly describe every single principle that is applied in all communication guidelines. As you can see below, the title of every principle is at the same time an information quality criterion.

Principle 1: Targeted
Communication must address the right audience (i.e. for whom the information is relevant). In addressing the audience the most appropriate communication channel should be

---

[132] See Minto (1995) for further explanations of these criteria.

used, taking into consideration cost efficiency, credibility, risk/confidentiality and the characteristics of the content. Content, format, style, language and terminology should be mapped to the needs, context, existing knowledge and the expectations of the audience.

Principle 2: Concise and Clear
Clear, concise communication is cost efficient, demonstrates respect for the time of the audience and helps to reduce information overload and avoid misunderstandings. Clarity can be achieved by taking into account the existing knowledge and information needs of the audience, by focusing on the relevant topics and on key messages, by using a systematic and logical structure (e.g. Who? What? When? Where? Why? How?), by keeping the language simple, avoiding technical terms and abbreviations if possible, and by giving figures if meaningful and available. Conciseness means keeping communication as short as possible to avoid superfluous information and as long as necessary to be clear.

Principle 3: Accountable
Each individual at UBS is personally responsible for his or her communication with others and must be aware of the risks and consequences that this entails. In particular, the owner/author of information is responsible for its authenticity, correctness and compliance with all directives and guidelines including the choice of the right/secure media by which it is communicated. Content, format and style must be in line with our values and principles and must not jeopardize the image or business of UBS.

Principle 4: Respectful
This principle addresses the ethical dimension of communication within UBS, specifically our core values of community and integrity. It means that our communication is as open as possible within the obvious limits set by our business, our strategic goals and the personal integrity of employees, clients and other third parties. Further, this means that our communication is honest (no lies). We are proactive communicators because we respect the professionalism and the needs of our audience. As a general rule we aim to communicate internally prior to externally or at least at the same time. In communicating bad news, we inform those directly concerned first. Finally, the tone and style of our communication is encouraging, motivating and promoting, but we do not

oversell or gloss things over. In language and style the emotions and values of the audience should be taken into consideration.

Principle 5: Timely
We work in a constantly fast-moving business environment where timeliness and speed are of outmost importance. As professionals we cope with this challenge by communicating up-to-date information and by communicating promptly when the information is available and required. If appropriate, we communicate in stages if the whole of the information is not available. In choosing the communication media we ensure speediest delivery if necessary and appropriate.

*Document
Structure of
the Guidelines*

After the core principles were defined, the team had to agree on a common structure or layout for the guidelines in order to assure one consistent look and feel. This was done in a plenary session based on a generic document structure that I provided. It was decided that every communication guideline should follow the same structure and logic: The first item of information after the title of the guidelines is the *target group*, that is to say for whom the guidelines are relevant. Team briefing guidelines, for example, are only relevant to team leaders, whereas e-mail guidelines are relevant to everybody that sends e-mails on a regular basis. After the target group, a short *summary* outlines the purpose and content of the document. Then the *principles* and their application for the specific medium are discussed, followed by background information, such as *references* to related material. Every set of guidelines ends with contact information for *feedback* or questions. This identical structure assures that the guidelines themselves are consistent.

Examples

Below, we provide two examples of the developed communication guidelines. The first set of guidelines relates to team briefings. Team briefings are important communication means since they are used at UBS to communicate strategic top-down information to employees through their team leaders. These guidelines are hence addressed to team leaders and managers who use them to structure the information meetings with their teams. The second example describes guidelines for e-mail use. Since e-mail proliferation or e-mail overload is a problem that many employees struggle with, the guidelines should assure that e-mails are of high-quality and can be read efficiently.

Communication Guidelines: Team Briefing

| All Managers (Team leaders) | *Target Group* |

The team briefing guidelines help all managers to effectively prepare and give team briefings. Team briefings are a leadership tool to inform the members of a team **regularly** on central developments (progress, policy, people, products and points of action) affecting the team. They are a **central** medium to cascade information top-down and receive feedback. The guidelines below are based on the UBS communication principles *targeted communication, clarity* and *conciseness, personal responsibility, fairness/respect* and *timeliness.*

Summary

Principles	Guidelines
1. Targeted	1.1 In a team briefing the manager has to select the key issues affecting the team and its context and communicate those in a manner that is easily understood by the team members and can be related to their own work.
	1.2 A team briefing consists of company-wide as well as local information and relates the two for the team that is being briefed.
2. Concise / Clear	2.1 Every team briefing begins with the overall purpose or agenda of the briefing and the key information (e.g., who, what, when, why, where).
	2.2. The team briefing should consist of the five P's, that's to say news on: progress, policy, people, products, and points for action.
	2.3 Every team briefing ends with a summary of the main facts and, if necessary, resulting actions and responsibilities.
	2.4 Team briefings ought to be limited to one hour.
	2.5 The team briefing minutes should be limited to two pages.
3. Accountable	3.1. Team briefings should always be given by the line-manager who in turn has been briefed by his or her own manager.
	3.2 The manager has to communicate the level of required confidentiality (and accuracy) of the information that is being presented at the team briefing.
4. Respectful	4.1 Every team briefing is minuted and the minutes are made available to all team members.
	4.2. Every team briefing should allocate at least five minutes for feedback, comments, and questions of the team members.
5. Timely	5.1. Team briefings are held on a regular basis (at least monthly) and following a major event or a rumor in order to clarify the facts.

Reference	For further communication guidelines (e.g. on chat, e-mail or publishing) see: http://bw.ubs.com/guidelines.
Feedback	For questions or comments on these guidelines please contact or give feedback to group-employee-communications@ ubs.com.

Communication Guidelines: E-mail

Target Group	**All employees**
Summary	The aim of these guidelines is to help UBS employees optimize secure and efficient use of e-mail. It highlights how e-mail can help to save time and how an overflow can be avoided while attracting more attention to each message. *'Less is more... is the motto'.*

Principles	*Guidelines*
1. Targeted	1.1. An e-mail is addressed to a limited number of persons who are directly concerned by a specific issue. For information addressed to a large number of people, please contact your communications department for advice on other message media (e.g. intranet/desk drop).
2. Concise / Clear	2.1 The subject field should contain a clear title or key words summarizing the content of the e-mail.
	2.2 The message should be friendly, clearly structured, brief and succinct. Instructions / actions to be taken must be clear and explicit.
	2.3 Abbreviations should be at least explained once.
	2.4 Attachments should be as small as possible (compressed files). E-mail attachments sent outside the bank should be in pdf format only, and carry the relevant disclaimer if the information is of a "market sensitive" nature. Bear in mind that pdf attachments can only be read if the recipient has the corresponding software.
3. Accountable	3.1 Content: One should always be aware of the consequences that the content of an e-mail may have. In sensitive cases the sender may require authorization and sources should always be checked.
	3.2 Security: Auto-forwarding of e-mail to less-secure networks (whether internal or external) is not permitted. Incoming external e-mails need to be checked carefully with regards to viruses. No communication with external e-mail addresses may be sent without the written agreement of the client. E-mail, like any form of written communication, is considered under the law to be a legal document and, as such, is discoverable in a legal action.
	3.3 Costs: To avoid storage costs, clogging the network, and slowing down the system only selected e-mails should be saved in a personal folder or printed.
4. Respectful	4.1 In an e-mail, one should treat others as one would like to be treated. If there is potential for disagreement, a telephone call can avoid misunderstandings (this includes avoiding blind copies sent to third parties).
5. Timely	5.1 An e-mail should be answered within two days.
	5.2 If an action is needed, an e-mail should be sent well in advance and a clear deadline given.
	5.3 In case of a prolonged absence, the auto reply function should be used.

References	For a detailed version of this document, we refer to the group e-mail guidelines http://bw.ubs.com/ceo/gec/mailguide_e. htm.
	Guidebooks for the use of e-mails: **Outlook 98 on XYZ**: http://bw.itux.it.ubs.ch/upload/ge/229/Guidebook_d.doc (German only, other languages to see) F
Feedback	For questions or comments on these guidelines please contact or give feedback to group-employee-communications@ubs. com

How UBS' communication guidelines – themselves information products – meet the criteria that define information quality is summarized in the table below. The table emphasizes the fact that communication guidelines should not only be of high-quality to improve their acceptance and application, but should also to set an example and thus increase their legitimacy and credibility.

Impact on Information Quality

Information Quality Levels	Information Quality Criteria	Activities to improve the IQ-criteria
Community Level	Comprehensiveness	All most widely used communication channels are discussed in the guidelines (meetings, team briefings, intranet, e-mail, and chat). In addition to the short version, there is a detailed version of the guidelines available upon request.
(Relevance)	Accuracy	The accuracy of the guidelines was cross-checked between division representatives and with existing (internal and external) communication policies.
	Clarity	The guidelines were checked by regular employees for clarity and comprehensibility, in addition to a review by several communication officers.
	Applicability	The guidelines focus on how to actually use communication channels effectively. Many provide a step-by-step procedure. The relevant target group of the guidelines is stated at the beginning.
Product Level	Conciseness	Every guideline is produced in a short and a long version. The short version is limited to one to two pages.
(Soundness)	Consistency	All guidelines have exactly the same structure and rely on identical principles.
	Correctness	The guidelines are based on existing policies and they were validated with other communication professionals.
	Currency	The guidelines were formulated after all media were already in use for quite some time. They were thus based on current insights into how they were being used. A regular update (e.g., once a year) is envisioned.
Process Level	Convenience	The guidelines can be accessed over the intranet (as HTML files or word files) and printed out.
(Optimization)	Timeliness	Answers to inquiries regarding the guidelines are usually given within one day.
	Traceability	The document owners are indicated at the end of the guideline with an e-mail address.
	Interactivity	The employee communications department can be contacted for comments or feedback.

Information Quality Levels	Information Quality Criteria	Activities to improve the IQ-criteria
Infrastructure Level (Reliability)	Accessibility	All guidelines are accessible over the intranet by all employees of the bank.
	Security	The intranet is fire-wall protected although security is not of a great concern for simple guidelines. The guidelines stress security aspects, e.g., in e-mails.
	Maintainability	There are only six guidelines and since all have the same structure, maintenance is relatively easy.
	Speed	The guidelines can be accessed immediately through the intranet search engine. They are converted to HTML to improve the speedy access to them.

Table 28: Features of the guidelines and their impact on high-quality communication

Most Affected Information Quality Criteria

In terms of the guideline's own quality, the following criteria were particularly stressed in the formulation of the documents:

1. Consistency: The structure of all six guidelines is the same and they all use the same five communication principles.
2. Conciseness: All guidelines are limited to a maximum of two pages. Most guidelines consist of only one page. The total number of communication principles is only five.
3. Applicability: The guidelines provide clear instructions on how to proceed and what to avoid.
4. Interactivity: The document owners of the guidelines are indicated and can be directly contacted for feedback and comments or questions.

Remaining Problems

Although the redesign of the communication guidelines has resolved many of the issues that were identified (e.g., inconsistency, length, redundancy, etc.) various problems still remain. The remaining problems relate to the *adherence* to the guidelines and to *medium-specific standards* that are insufficiently discussed in the guidelines.

The former problem mainly consists of actually getting employees to use the guidelines in their daily work. Here, training events or applications need to familiarize employees with the characteristics of each communication medium. Ideally, the guidelines would pop-up every time an employee uses a communication medium inadequately. Still, the impact of written guidelines on communication behavior can only be limited. They have to be complemented by other means (such as training, frequent feedback, or on-line assistants).

The latter problem consists of extending the guidelines to other areas, such as technical standards. As of now, the guidelines focus only on the main issues that arise when a new communication channel is used. This assures that they remain concise and to the point. Complex communication channels, however, such as the intranet, require additional rules (e.g., design conventions, process elements, and specific roles). These complex regulations cannot be included in a one page document. They may require extensive style guides and manuals which run the risk of overloading the readers. A feasible solution for this problem may be found in electronic publication templates and automated workflows that incorporate the guidelines intelligently and seamlessly.

In terms of future developments, two issues seem particularly critical. The first relates to new communication media, the second to the just-in-time delivery of the guidelines.

Future Developments

As other communication media become readily available to UBS employees, such as WebTV, instant messengers, or virtual reality environments, new guidelines will need to be devised that help employees use them to their full advantage. As already mentioned by many communication professionals, it is a greater challenge to implement the guidelines (that is to says to get the employees to actually use them) than to devise them. This will become an even more significant problem as more media are available for communication. Which brings us to the second issue of just-in-time delivery. Ideally, communication guidelines should be 'pushed' to the employee whenever he or she makes a mistake in the handling of a communication channel. New monitoring systems could provide such automated, context-sensitive help functionalities.

This case study has focused on one particular information product that is vital in many large organizations: the guideline. The examples that have been included are management tools that can be used to foster high-quality information since they provide hints on how communication media can be better used. The guidelines have been designed using a specific methodology that stresses a consistent and concise structure and guidelines that are easy to use. Specifically, the following four principles have been applied:

Case Summary

- Integration: all communication guidelines can be found at one single location in the company's intranet. They are all limited to a maximum of two pages. Every guideline document contains a brief summary.
- Validation: The guidelines have been developed in consultation with almost all relevant communication staff from all geographic and divisional areas. They are based on a set of agreed-upon principles and these in turn have been derived from the company's core values. The specific guidelines were then developed in working groups and presented to the plenary session and revised. Prior to the work of the team, external benchmarks were provided to validate the new guidelines.
- Contextualization: The purpose and background of the guidelines are stated in the purpose, references, and feedback sections. The references also provide the possibility to access further details and background on the information by linking to extended versions of the guidelines.
- Activation: The guidelines focus on how and when a particular communication channel should be used and what steps should be taken. Because the principles are limited to less than seven, they should be easy to recall in every day work.

Conclusion

This case study has introduced both a tool for information quality management and an example of a high-quality information product: communication guidelines. It has highlighted the fact that guidelines need to be made consistent (both in terms of structure or layout and in terms of content, e.g., principles), concise, and applicable in order to be useful information. In this way, the guidelines can in return foster a culture of high-quality communication.

4.7 The Multiple Views on Country Risk Intelligence –Communicating Analyst Knowledge at the Economist Intelligence Unit

With all the available information on the Internet and with the overload of information we are facing, customers turn to us to have an opinion, an informed opinion on a specific country.

ANDRÉ ASTROW
EIU Deputy Editorial Director

The following case study[133] is based on interviews with André Astrow, EIU Deputy Editorial Director and Catherine Sealey, EIU Regional Sales Manager for Central and Eastern Europe, as well as on a number of interviews with EIU customers and frequent users. Further interviews included competitors of the EIU. Additional information was acquired through use of the EIU website and through the product documentation provided by the company. The four products described in the case study were all tested on a two week trial.

Case Study Sources

The Economist Intelligence Unit, part of the Economist Group, is a company active in the field of country intelligence. Over the last fifty years (the company was founded in 1946) the business intelligence division of the Economist Group has established a network of country analysts and country experts, presently 650, most of them based in the countries that they cover. The company can presently rely on a team of 80 economists, based in London, producing in-house risk and forecasting models. Besides the London office, which is the head office, the Economist Intelligence Unit has two major regional offices in New York and Hong Kong and 32 editorial and sales offices around the world. The EIU has currently over 500,000 clients: among them companies of every industry; financial institutions such as investment banking and insurance companies, investors, governments and business schools. The mission of the company is that of providing trustworthy intelligence on the worldwide business context, as outlined on the EIU website:

Company Overview

"Our mission is to help executives make better business decisions by providing up-to-date, reliable and impartial analysis on world-

---

[133] This case study contains material gathered by L. Musacchio.

wide market trends and business strategies. We continuously assess and forecast political, economic and business conditions in almost 200 countries, and provide insight into how companies are responding".

The Core Products

The EIU provides *country intelligence* in different forms that range from raw statistical data, forecasts, indicators, ratios, tables and charts to qualitative reports and risk ratings. The focus is on both the context of the worldwide marketplace and on the associated opportunities and risks for investors. Event-driven briefings are available through the Viewswire or Business Newsletters and provide the latest worldwide developments in business and politics. Economic and geopolitical analysis is also provided regularly in two products called Country Reports and Country Profiles. The three products Country Risk Service, Riskwire and Risk Model provide risk assessments, early warning indicators, ratings and assessments, while data and forecasts are provided trough Country Data, Market Indicators and Forecasts and trough Woldwide Cost of Living.

Operating Conditions and Regulations

In addition to these products, the EIU offers a series of international business guides on business regulations and on changing financial operating conditions, tax laws, and investment opportunities.

Management Strategies and Executive Development

Another group of products focuses on management strategies and executive developments. *Executive Briefing* and *Which MBA?* are the two main products in this group. So-called 'strategic intelligence' is provided trough regular manager surveys, best-practice insights and benchmarking, overviews and case studies.

Industry Trends and Developments

A fourth type of intelligence provided by EIU regards industries. Eight major industries are assessed: automotive, consumer goods and retailing, energy and electricity, financial services, food, beverages and tobacco, health and pharmaceuticals, telecoms and technology, travel and tourism.

Case Study Focus: Country Intelligence

This case study will focus on the first group of products, namely products focusing on the context of the worldwide marketplace and on the opportunities and risks involved. The EIU provides this kind of intelligence at different levels and through different forms. Four main information services will be discussed: *Viewswire, Country Reports, Country Data and Country Risk Service.*

Event Driven-Briefings

Viewswire is an Internet portal where the users can find useful information about the political, economic, commercial, financial and operational worldwide daily events and on their impact on business. The portal is updated every day with a large number of events that the EIU staff judges to be the most important ones. The users can either choose to obtain updates on a single country (from a choice of about 200 countries) or list the worldwide major events of the day.

Five main channels are offered to the users and include: Politics, Economy, Business, Finance and Regulations. Through this portal, the user can have access to information and insights at several levels through background information, updates and standardized reports.

The *Country Intelligence* database consists of three main publications: the country reports, the country profiles and the country forecasts. *Country reports* are provided for 181 countries every three months (full report) and updated every month (update report). The product has the form of a structured report and contains political, economic and financial developments and analyses. The reports contain both information on the political and economic structure of the country and an outlook for the next two years containing expectations on the political, economic policy, economic and financial environment. The focus is on political, economic policy, domestic economy, foreign and trade payments events and on their overall impact on the country risk.

Country Risk Service provides an assessment and an early warning system on the political, economic policy, economic structure and liquidity risks for 100 emerging markets and six main geopolitical areas (Africa, Americas, Asia and Australasia, Eastern Europe, Middle East and North Africa, Southern Europe). Risk assessment is provided also for specific investment risks, namely currency risk, sovereign debt risk and banking sector risk. Risk is evaluated on a time horizon of two years and its assessment is updated monthly via the Internet subscription and quarterly in print. An overall rating is provided together with a brief review of the major short term risk events as well as a political, economic and financial outlook. Separate sections are devoted to a more detailed assessment of these three (political, economic and financial) axes of analysis. These sections are: political outlook, domestic finance and economic outlook, external finance and credit risk (containing specific investment risk ratings, namely currency risk, sovereign risk and banking sector risks). A final risk rating summary explains the overall assessment. Statistical appendices present the economic variables used in the country risk assessments on a seven year basis with three years of actual figures, one year estimates and two year forecasts.

The risk ratings provided by the *Country Risk Service* come out of a risk model developed by the EIU. The Risk

Economic and Geopolitical Analysis

Risk Assessment and Early Warning

Risk Model

Model is accessible over the Internet (eiuresources.com/ras) and provides risk ratings for 100 emerging markets and six major geopolitical aggregates. Broad risk is divided into Political Risk, Economic Policy Risk, Economic Structure Risk and Liquidity Risk. The broad risk is based on 77 indicators ranging across 13 different risk categories. For each of the 77 indicators it is possible to show the question that lies behind the specific assessment and the relations between the score and the assessment (see the figure below). Lower scores are associated with lower risks.

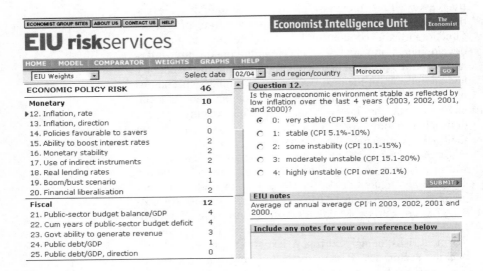

Figure 31: EIU risk model – inflation indicator

Once all the points for each indicator are added up, it is possible to associate each score with a rating. In the EIU rating model the label A is associated with the lowest risk and with a score ranging from 0 to 20, B is associated with a low risk and with a score ranging from 21 to 40, C is associated with moderate risk and with a score range from 41 to 60, D is associated with high risk and a score ranging from 61 to 80 and finally a high risk E rating is associated with scores that range from 81 to 100. This rating is provided for the overall country risk but also for each of the risk categories: political risk, economic policy risk, economic structure risk, and liquidity risk. The scoring of these four categories is provided also for the specific investment risks namely currency risk, sovereign debt risk and banking sector risk (see next figure).

Compare risk summaries for one country over multiple dates				GRAPH ▶	EXCEL ▶
Morocco ▾	08/03 ▾	10/03 ▾	12/03 ▾	02/04 ▾	GO ▶
Broad risk					
Political risk	64 D	66 D	70 D	68 D	
Economic policy risk	45 C	46 C	42 C	46 C	
Economic structure risk	38 B	34 B	32 B	30 B	
Liquidity risk	20 A	20 A	20 A	18 A	
Specific risk					
Currency risk	40 B	39 B	36 B	39 B	
Sovereign risk	40 B	39 B	38 B	36 B	
Banking sector risk	42 C	43 C	41 C	41 C	
Summary					
Overall risk	41 C	41 C	41 C	40 B	
Moody's scale	Ba1	Ba1	Ba1	Baa3	
Fitch/S & P's scale	BB+	BB+	BB+	BBB-	

Figure 32: EIU risk model – country risk break-down for Morocco

Country Data consists of a huge database provided online trough the website of Bureau van Dijk (http://countrydata. bvdep.com/) and enables the users to access and manipulate the data with a great flexibility. The users can choose the country/countries they want to focus on from a database that covers 117 countries from the Americas, Asia and Australasia, Eastern Europe, Middle East and North Africa, Sub-Saharan Africa, Western Europe and 40 regional aggregates that can be used as a benchmark to evaluate the performance of one country against the group. For all the 280 series, annual data are available and for some of them quarterly and monthly data are compiled. The reference years go from 1980 to 2008 with a distinction between actual figures, estimates and forecasts (different colours). Forecasts for the 117 countries are updated monthly. Through the three main axes of analysis (country, series and year) the user can aggregate and compare data in a number of ways through graphing functions, screening functions and segmenting functions. There is also a possibility of downloading data into Excel spreadsheets.

Data and Forecasts

Tailored intelligence and research is also provided by EIU in the form of executive surveys and sponsored white papers. Conferences and seminars are also organized for both current and potential new customers.

Additional Services

Added Value
Usable, Up-to-date
and Reliable
Intelligence

The added value that EIU generates is that of providing usable, up-to-date, and reliable country intelligence. These aspects are crucial to decision making. Visualization and aggregation capabilities of *Country Data* allow the user to combine and compare information in a number of ways and thus help in setting up preferences for alternatives while representing information in a new and flexible way. One way of getting to reliable decisions is that of understanding the implicit relationships between the different forces and systems operating in the environment. In country intelligence, this is a particularly difficult task as the analysts have to cope with very unsteady and complex environments and have to account for the different logics and implications involved. They have to detect both the continuities and the breaks of the systems. They have to focus on the hidden relationships within the system in order to obtain the necessary insights to formulate their view. In this sense, *Country Report and the Country Risk Services* help in matching information with the user objectives and the strategic decision to be made. This can be illustrated with the risk modeler of the EIU. The *Risk Model* is an interactive model whose main characteristic is adaptability. The score given by the analysts can be changed by the user. He or she can assign new weights to the various indicators. (see Figure 33)

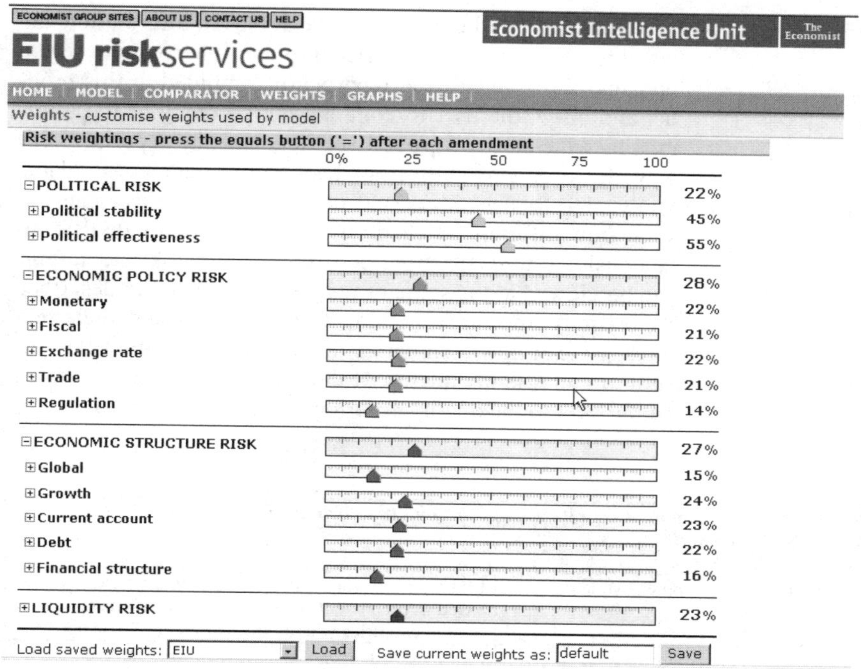

Figure 33: EIU risk model – risk weightings

The user is able to understand how the score is computed by
looking at the question that lies behind every score. With
these two interaction features, the user can adjust the weightings and the scores of any of the 77 risk indicators. The score
is then calculated based on the needs of the users as they
choose weights and scores that better suit the prospected task.
By changing the assumptions and providing the possibility to
see the consequences of such changes, the user is able to
reconstruct knowledge, to give meaning to the knowledge
provided by the service, thus adapting it to the decision situation. Beside this powerful functionality, the model allows for
comparisons of the indicator scores over time, across countries, or across time for a single country. These functionalities
enhance comprehension by generating new visualizations and
combinations and allowing the user to compare data. What is
also interesting about this product from a knowledge perspective is the rating tool: the exposure to risk can be quantified
with a skilful mix of qualitative and qualitative questions.
Another, related feature in this product group is *Viewswire*.
Timeliness is the major feature of this product. Trough the

Viewswire portal the user can have access to information and insights at several levels. Background information, recent updates, and standardized reports are combined in this product and allow the user to combine the currency of the information with the background sections and the reports. Inthis way the user can shift from background and consolidated knowledge to new ideas and news alerts. Here we can observe how different levels of information are provided simultaneously: raw data, structured reports, outlook and ratings can be viewed at the same time by the user. Having described the various information products of the EIU and their features, we can now summarize the activities that the EIU pursues to increase the quality of those products. They are listed below next to the quality criterion that they affect most.

Information Quality Levels	Information Quality Criteria	Activities to improve the IQ-criteria
Community Level	Comprehensiveness	EIU relies on a network of experts in the field based in each country and thus provides information on countries where information is very scarce.
(Relevance)	Accuracy	Information sources are selected and examined carefully by the analysts; forecasts are produced by experienced analysts and are based only on in-house analysis. Reports are checked both internally and externally.
	Clarity	Editorial guidelines on language use and reviewing stress clarity of language and vocabulary.
	Applicability	Products are relevant for the decision tasks to be performed; the country intelligence provided is applicable to business investment decisions in foreign countries. Special attention is paid to emerging and exotic markets where information is difficult to find for executives.
Product Level	Conciseness	Reports such as those of the Country Risk Service provide a great number of information in not more than 15 pages.
(Soundness)	Consistency	Every series of reports follows a standardized structure. The reader is able to find the same structure for all of the country reports provided.
	Correctness	Reports follow a five step review process before being published. The EIU is a completely independent company. No other company has stakes in the EIU nor are they tied to any government or corporation. The EIU does not participate in the financial markets and thus holds no financial interests.

Information Quality Levels	Information Quality Criteria	Activities to improve the IQ-criteria
	Currency	The analysts constantly monitor political and economic development in almost 200 countries and constantly update their intelligence. Information provided is updated with the latest events. All the information is updated daily for the wire services, daily briefing and alerting services or monthly for the full text reports. This updating includes the whole report and not just parts of it.
Process Level	Convenience	Reports can be easily downloaded from the Internet. Data can be easily downloaded as in excels spreadsheets. Inquiries can be addressed to one central phone number or e-mail address where they are forwarded to the relevant experts.
(Optimization)	Timeliness	Each month, the country view is revised as well as the model that is used to generate a new economic forecast in order to catch the deteriorating or improving trends and set up effective early warning systems.
	Traceability	No author names are given, but the main sources of all data are revealed. Revisions are indicated.
	Interactivity	All customers can speak directly to editors to resolve any queries. There is a number on the report that customer can ring up to get extra information, or ask any question. Events are organized in the form of seminars and presentations for existing and new clients. Many of the EIU products have customization capabilities like country risk services and country data. This means that they are adaptable to different circumstances and different contexts. The risk model can be used in a very flexible way. Customers can change both scores and weights.
Infrastructure Level	Accessibility	EIU clients are offered different electronic delivery methods to access the products. Customers can opt for a print or electronic channel that includes CD-ROM, Lotus Notes, online database…The access is either via IP, password or via intranet and extranet.
(Reliability)	Security	Every account is password protected.
	Maintainability	The portal is updated daily and there is a great effort in its development.
	Speed	The EIU websites and applications react almost instantly to queries or changes in entries. The download time of reports is adequate.

Table 29: EIU products and services features and their impact on information quality criteria

From the list in the above table, the criteria that seem to be affected most by EIU's approach are the following three:

- Comprehensiveness: The EIU provides country intelligence on nearly 200 countries trough a large network of experts (about 650) who contribute information on recent economic and political events, comment on the business environment and legislative changes, and give their views on political, economic and social trends. A global reach is provided as information is also available on countries where it is difficult to access statistical information (i.e., emerging markets).

- Interactivity: Interactivity is provided at different levels. As Catherine Sealey, Regional Sales Manager Central and Eastern Europe at the EIU, states: "*All our clients can ring up our analysts in London anytime*". In this way they can ask questions to resolve unclear issues. Interactivity is also provided through customization capabilities of the online products. In *Country Data,* for example the user can visualize and aggregate information in different ways trough graphing, screening and segmenting functions. In the *Risk Model* interactivity means that the user can change the score given by the EIU analyst for each of the 77 indicators and customize weights according to his needs.

- Timeliness: As written in the EIU Publications and Services Catalogue "*Our clients need timely forecasts and analysis, so our process is designed for speed*". The global environment is monitored daily by the network of country analysts and experts who cover the latest events and trends.

- Accuracy: At the EIU, the sources of information are attentively scrutinized by the analysts. The five step production process and the quality checks show a major commitment to accuracy and reliability of information. Forecasts are based on in-house analysis and the forecast models are continuously revised by a team of economists.

The added value that the EIU generates is that of providing usable, up-to-date, and reliable country intelligence. These aspects are crucial to investment decision making. Visualization and aggregation capabilities of *Country Data* for instance allow the user to combine and compare information in a number of ways and thus help in setting up preferences for alternatives while representing information in a flexible way. One way of getting to reliable decisions is that of understanding the implicit relationships between the different forces and systems operating in the environment. In country intelligence, this is a particularly difficult task, as the analysts have to cope with unsteady and complex environments and have to account for the different logics and implications involved.

Subscribing to the EIU is not a low-cost investment. Prices vary depending on how much the customers buy, as the more they buy, the higher the discount., The price depends on the type of institution (non profit and academic institutions, corporates or banks), the number of users, and the number of countries subscribed. For a typical customer, the price for the full set of 146 countries is around 35.000 dollars for five passwords to the Country Reports.

The Pricing Scheme

The intelligence provided by the EIU results from the collection, processing, aggregation, assessment and interpretation of information concerning countries or areas. Analysts involved in this process produce country intelligence out of raw data and qualitative information. EIU intelligence is based on regular contributions from a global network of more than 650 specialists. Experienced in-house analysts assess how political and economic developments and produce detailed two-year forecasts. This intelligence is then edited into a common format and offered through print or electronic channels. The company relies on a hundred country analysts who are permanent staff members, most of them based in London, although some analysts are in the two main regional offices in Hong Kong and New York. The production of country reports follows a five steps process:

The Production Process for Reports

1) **Writing:** Country Reports are written largely by experts in the field and sent to London.

2) **Editing:** Country experts in London integrate the manuscript with their own inputs on what is likely to happen in the country. They check it by running all the forecasting numbers to make sure that they are consistent with the company's global view and regional view. Their final task is that of putting everything together and structures it in a consistent and standardized way.

3) **Second check:** Once the manuscript has been edited and finalized by the primary editor, it is passed on to a more senior person to look trough it. During the review, the senior editor reads the manuscript to makes sure that the forecasts make sense and that the whole report is sound. His task is that of catching any error or inconsistency that there may be in the manuscript within the analysis or between the analysis and the tables and numbers. Once that is done, the second checker will get together with the editor and go trough any problem, asking a number of questions to improve the report. Once everything has been changed, the manuscript goes to a sub-editor or a copy editor.

4) **Sub-editing:** Subeditors or copy editors are very rigorous. It's not just a matter of making sure that the manuscript is in good English, but also to ensure consistency and accuracy. Subeditors do a lot of fact checking and ask questions about any kind of inconsistency that may still be in the manuscript. Once everything has been proofread and checked by the subeditor, then the manuscript is ready to go to production.

5) **Production:** The production team will take a final look at the manuscript to make sure (from a production point of view) that everything is correct and properly coded and styled properly. Then, the manuscript is sent on to New York for electronic distribution and to the EIU printers in the UK.

Problems in the Production Process

Since the series of steps described above is in effect a knowledge-intensive process, the problems that occur in producing a report are mostly related to the collection, processing, aggregation, assessment, interpretation and codification of available information concerning foreign countries or areas. The main factors that can affect this type of process are: quality of the sources, consistency of the analytical frameworks used and the available expertise.

The importance of the quality of information is stressed in the EIU guidelines: *"No matter how good the model or how deep the analyst's expertise, building an accurate forecast is impossible when the underlying data are wrong. So we spare no effort to procure the best and latest data available for the 195 countries we cover".* In countries (like OECD economies) where electronic databases providing national statistics are available, the EIU subscribes to them. In a country where this supply is not complete, the EIU holds direct subscription arrangements with statistical offices and central banks. For the less developed countries (where it is particularly difficult to get information) the EIU relies on a large network of people who contribute information and data released by the statistical offices and central banks. Additional sources are the World Bank, the International Monetary Fund, the United Nations, the OECD, and the EU. Data are selected and scrutinised by the analysts following quality criteria such as timeliness, accuracy and consistency. National statistics are the preferred sources, but when quality criteria are not met, the analyst may choose a better alternative, such as the aforementioned sources or come up with their own estimates.

Data are processed trough a series of proprietary forecasting *models*. These models ensure consistency by applying the same methodology and assumptions. For the Risk Model, this consists of a particularly skilful mesh of qualitative and quantitative assessments. Numerical scores must be assigned to factors that are difficult to compare, and this in a structured way that allows for comparison across countries and time. But as written in the aforementioned EIU publication:

"We never lose sight of the fact that even the best models are an approximation of the real world making our analysts' judgement a crucial factor."

In providing country intelligence, *expertise* is in fact the crucial aspect: forecasts and analyses depend largely on the ability of the analysts to understand the environment of the countries, the different forces that can affect the business, and how to relate them to the decision tasks to be performed. Country experts are people who have had at least 5-7 years experience, who have worked and lived (for a number of years) in the country or region that they cover and can speak local languages. All of them have a university degree and most of them have advanced degrees such as an MBA, Masters or PhD. Their background and experience is mostly in economics, but it also ranges from political science to international relations. The most frequent previous experience is in the banking sector, in research institutes and in multinationals insitutions. Each of the analysts is in charge of very few countries (two, maximum three countries) and visits them regularly, ensuring up-to-date and focused expertise. In addition to local country expertise and experts in the main offices, the company can rely on a team of 80 experienced economists who are in charge of building and testing risk and forecasting models.

We had five interviews with EIU users in two major Swiss banks. Their analyst reported that they use EIU experience in gathering and assessing data at different levels: as an input to in-house risk assessment processes, as a second opinion compared to credit agencies such as Moody's or Standard and Poor's, or simply as a source of information. EIU products allow them to save time in reading newspapers, magazines and doing detailed research. All the interviewees agreed that what they mainly look for are the qualitative aspects, like for instance political stability or fiscal policy; qualitative aspects that need to be quantified in order to be included in a decision model. They all reported that this is a crucial aspect that involves comparisons with other indicators or information, the weighting of different factors, the choice of the indicators that best suit the prospected decision. This ultimately leads to the customisation and personalisation of the provided information. As an analyst from a bank's Collateral Rating Office indicated:

Customer Opinions

"EIU products help us getting a homogenous vision for a decision. They provide data and information, but it is our duty to interpret them and interpretation always holds a high level of subjectivity."

Asking the customers what they particularly like about this product, we gathered a number of positive feedbacks. Consistency seems to be one of the most appreciated features.

"When you go from one report to another you always find the same sections and the same methodology behind each one of them, and this make it very user friendly. Once you are accustomed to use one of them, you can very easily jump from one country to another and this is very useful for me because I am not an expert in many of the countries that I work with, and so at least I can acquire a certain level of knowledge in very short time"

reported an economist at a large Swiss bank. Decisiveness is also valued as he said

"You always find an opinion stated. It is never neutral in a sense; this is what I like about it".

Focus and conciseness are also rated highly. As the responsible for the Risk Analysis and Rating for Africa and Near & Middle East at a large Swiss bank stated

"if you already have a quite sophisticated knowledge about the country, then you are happy to have a report which is very focused on the really important things and it is not talking at length... reports from other providers are well done, but they are long and they are not focused and sometimes they are hesitant about a political judgment and so for me they are not that helpful".

Finally interaction is recognized as plus of the products:

"The good thing is that you can also talk to the analysts in London. When I am going to London I am usually going to see the analysts who are responsible for my region and then you get a better idea of how they are getting their information and how this information is processed and why they are coming to certain conclusions".

Despite this positive view, the interviewees reported that one of the problems of the product is accessibility

"What I don't like so much is the accessibility. Sometimes you have to shift through a lot of papers until you find the latest thing that has happened. If I am interested only on the fiscal development in the country it takes me quite a lot...it is not very user-friendly, so I would like to have a search function with a database of all these reports that would be very helpful for example"

said an economist. Accessibility problems comprise difficulties in downloading the data, as some of the users reported that it could take very long to download a wide series of data. Completeness is also a major concern.

"You don't have the same data for all countries, which is sometimes confusing. In some countries I have seen GDP forecasts until 2005 while for another country you can't find it"

said the responsible for the Data and Management Support at a large bank. Also the quality may differ from one product to another as

"The quality differs, you have different analysts and of course you have different levels of quality"

said the Responsible for the Risk Analysis and Rating for Africa and Near & Middle East at a multinational bank.

When asked about the competitors Oxford Analytica was mentioned for country intelligence services, Standard and Poor's, Moody's, Fitch for ratings, the Institute of International Finance for its country reports on emerging markets, and Bloomberg for daily data.

Country Intelligence is a very broad market as a number of *Competitors* companies provide different intelligence products and services. We can distinguish between full competitors of the EIU and competitors only on certain services. The two major competitors of EIU are Global Insight and Business Monitor International. Global Insight (www.globalinsight.com) is a worldwide operation with offices in 12 countries. It employs over 450 persons between analysts, researcher and economists and offers country intelligence products and services that support corporates, banks and governments in developing strategies, monitoring risks and making successful decisions. The broad range of products offered comprises country analyses, forecasts, economic data, risk services and consulting expertise. Over 200 countries are covered by the services as well as a number of industries. It is a true competitor of the EIU as it can be compared to it in terms of its size, the broadness of coverage and the type of products provided. Business Monitor International (www.businessmonitor.com) is also a major player in the country intelligence market. It offers specialist business information on global markets to financial institutions, multinationals, government and academic institutions. Print and online services comprise country analyses, forecasts, risk ratings and repositories of foreign companies and industry sector data. A smaller company that can nevertheless be compared to the aforementioned two is Oxford Analytica (www.oxan.com). It provides analyses on worldwide political, economic and social developments to both governments and international institutions and manufacturing and financial firms. It relies on a worldwide network of over 1000 experts. Daily briefing services are provided covering both world and regional economic and political developments of major significance. Consultancy and customised research are also offered like country risk and sectoral analyses or monitoring services.

Beside these three major competitors there are other institutes that provide different kind of data, information and risk ratings.

The Institute of International Finance (www.iif.com) is a global association of financial institutions. One of the goals of this institute is to provide members with data, analysis and prospects on economic and financial developments in emerging market economies. Services include Economic Reports, Monthly Economic Reviews, Short Briefing Notes and Key Indicators for selected emerging economies. The Political Risk Services (www.prsgroup.com) provides both country reports, country data and has developed the International Country Risk Guide a political, economic and financial country risk model based on the assessment of 13 political indicators, 6 economic indicators and 5 financial indicators. Political risk letters and country forecasts are also available. Other providers of worldwide information and risk assessments are Euromoney (www.euromoney.com), Business Environment Risk Inteliigence (www.beri.com) and Credit Risk International (www.crimag.com). Regarding the rating the three major rating agencies are Moody's Investors Service, Standard and Poors and Fitch. They are recognized statistical rating organizations. They provide an informed opinion on the creditworthiness of an entity and the financial obligations (such as, bonds, preferred stock, and commercial paper) issued by an entity by assigning a credit rating. Credit ratings used by these agencies are worldwide recognised and follow a scale (specific for each agency) that distinguishes between investment grade and non-investment grade.

Bloomberg is a major information provider of real-time and historical financial data. Through the Bloomberg Professional Service central banks, investment institutions, commercial banks, government offices and agencies, corporations and news organizations can access more than 3.6 million financial instruments and interact with a worldwide financial information network. In this sense Bloomberg is a competitor of EIU only regarding data and not the qualitative intelligence. Another competitor in this sense is Reuters.

Besides these international competitors, the EIU also faces

competition on a more regional level. The German FAZ Institut (www.faz-institut.de), for example, has a Country and Industry Service that provides country reports and investments guides for about 40 countries that are relevant for German investors. It is a small company with 11 employees and a number of free-lancers which targets medium size enterprises. Its added value results from its focus on the impact of country risks on commerce with Germany.

The Economist Intelligence Unit is now a major player in the country intelligence providers market. During the last years it has undergone a process of transformation to an electronic business (see Figure 4) that allowed for cost reduction and market growth. Growth opportunities are envisioned also in terms of services provided and in terms of scope. The EIU wants to keep up with the growing demand for customized research (such as tailor made research for banks and corporates) and increase the industry and country coverage. There is a strategic focus on growth, both through an extended sales network and through a growing product range.

Future
Developments

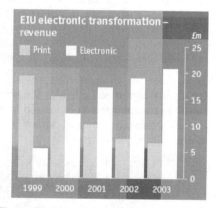

Figure 34: Electronic transformation revenue (source: EIU annual report)

EIU is one of the major and most respected country intelligence providers in the world and co-ordinates over 650 country intelligence experts worldwide. The EIU organization is particularly interesting from an information quality point of view as it is characterized by both knowledge intensive production processes and knowledge intensive communication processes. The first refer to content (what type of knowledge is conveyed) while the latter refers to interaction (how the knowledge is conveyed). Information quality principles influence both processes. We can summarize EIU major bene-

Case Summary

fits or innovations with the four information quality principles:

- Integration: EIU codifies and standardizes information by applying a strong analytical framework and a consistent format to carefully selected information. Formats may vary from one product to another: and includes raw data, indicators and forecasts figures as well as qualitative reports, structured reports and ratings.
- Validation: Validation is achieved trough the strong commitment on information source quality, trough continuously revised models and trough the number of checks and the expertise of the reviewers.
- Contextualization: Customers can interact with the knowledge provided by changing underlying assumptions within the models or trough the interactive views provided by the products. In this way they can adapt and personalize information.
- Activation: The provided intelligence is made actionable through various means, one of which is that customers can speak directly to analysts and participate in conferences and events organized by EIU. The applicability of the provided information is facilitated as customers can download data into excel spreadsheets and work with them in their own models or applications.

The principle that is most visibly exploited by EIU is the first one: data and information is aggregated and compressed in a skilful way that leads to clear and determined views and analysis on complex and unsteady environments.

Conclusion

The Economist Intelligence Unit has established a high standard in a knowledge intensive process, namely country risk intelligence. This has been achieved trough a skilful mesh of aggregation and compression abilities to codify knowledge and through rigorous validation and a commitment to currency and timeliness.

4.8 Conclusion: Cross-case Insights

In this section, we compare the problems, solutions, and contextual factors that were discovered in the six case studies. This will enable us to make inferences about information quality characteristics and their systematic management. It will also generate new propositions that can be tested in further investigations. First, the recurring information quality problems will be discussed. Then the practical meaning of the criteria will be briefly reviewed, followed by applications of the four IQ-principles and contextual factors that tend to foster high information quality.

Goal: General Characteristics and Propositions

The case study material has shown that the dominant problems relate to the information production and delivery process (e.g., keeping it timely and interactive), the characteristics of the final information product (e.g., assuring its consistency and relevance), and managing the often high volumes of information and maintaining them on an adequate infrastructure. We have seen that meeting customer expectations consists of two dimensions: first, in regard to the delivered content, and second in terms of the medium through which this content is delivered.

Resurfacing Information Quality Problems

From the case study descriptions and their problem sections, we can see that the four levels of the information quality framework can help to make sense of these problems and that they can be used to devise counter-measures: Whenever information is seen as incomplete, inaccurate, unclear or difficult to use, it is not targeted at the user group. The kind of information that is provided must be altered. This requires *line managers* to take action. Namely, they have to inform the authors and IT-managers about the true needs of the target communities. Whenever information is not concise, consistent, correct, or current, the *authors* themselves need to take action to improve the information they provide. They either need to seek assistance, receive training or use guidelines and templates to produce information that is to the point, contains no errors, and is based on the latest available data. The *IT-process managers*, usually the staff that is responsible for the deployment and management of software, need to take action if the way that information is produced or delivered is seen as inconvenient, not timely, untraceable, or not interactive enough by information produces or consumers. They need to optimise the authoring, query, and navigation process to meet these criteria. Finally, whenever information seems generally difficult to access or unsafe to store,

Different Responsibilities for Different Problem Types

hard to maintain or slow in its response, the *IT-infrastructure managers*, responsible for hardware and network software, need to take action. They need to improve the available infrastructure to meet the increasing demands of information consumers and producers.

The Practical Meaning of the Information Quality Criteria

Besides the insight on problem types and possible solutions, the case studies also provided an opportunity to look at information quality criteria and what they actually mean in real-life settings. In the six case studies, the following eight criteria were especially prominent.

Conciseness of information seemed to be an important characteristic of information in all five contexts, due to the heavy information load of most managers. Conciseness was the raison d'être for getAbstract and it was the distinguishing factor of Giga who produced no report of more than ten pages. It was also one of the most innovative aspects of UBS' communication guidelines since they were limited to one page only. The EIU, finally, paid particular attention to providing synthetic tabular information in all its reports.

Almost contrary to conciseness is *comprehensiveness*. This criterion was also discussed at various points in the case studies. Gartner was proud of its comprehensive coverage of IT topics (as was the EIU of its scope of covered countries), due to its large pool of analysts. GetAbstract claimed to cover most important business books with its abstracts. However, full comprehensiveness was seen as an illusion by most interviewed managers. In fact, some customers of getAbstract, Giga, and Gartner claimed to suffer from too much coverage ("if they produce more, we read less").

A third "magic c" was *convenience*. All companies in the case studies understand that it is not enough to just deliver information. It has to be communicated in an easy-to-use manner and format that reduces transaction costs. This could mean helping the recipient store and organize the information for later use (as IHA·GfK and getAbstract do for their clients through customer portals). Or it could mean providing information in a number of formats, depending on the customer's situation. GetAbstract delivers its abstracts as PDF-files, palm-files, mp3 sound files and soon also as PowerPoint slides. IHA·GfK not only delivers printed marketing reports, but also provides a CD-ROM with the database, an online platform to run additional analyses, or interactive workshops to interpret the information with the help of experts. The EIU offers its models as Excel files that can be modified by each customer. Other forms of 'information convenience' were discussed in the cases: Gartner and Giga will identify relevant experts and call back managers who have posted questions on their websites. GetAbstract automatically sends out new abstracts to managers, based on their job profile and preferences.

Another one of the "c"-criteria that came up frequently in the interviews was *consistency*. At the Swiss bank UBS, consistency meant that all communication guidelines were based on the same principles and that all of the documented guidelines followed the exact same format and layout. This was also true for getAbstract, Gartner, and Giga, where consistency was seen as imperative as far as the document structure is concerned. All book summaries at getAbstract contain the same elements (from the rating to the buzzwords), as do the reports at Gartner, Giga, and at the EIU.

At Gartner, consistency also relates to the used text items, such as probabilities or magic quadrants that are always used in the same way (and ensured through guidelines, trainings, and reviews).

In all interviews with managers and customers that were conducted for the case studies, there was one credo that - almost like a mantra - was cited over and over again. Namely, that information does not have a lot of value unless it is applied. So it came as no surprise that *applicability* was often given special attention. At UBS, the guidelines only focused on what one actually needed to do to improve communication. Giga even evaluated the performance of its analyst according to how well clients were able to use their answers. IHA·GfK changed part of its business model to increase the applicability of its data. It launched IHA Consulting to assure that the market findings were put into actions.

It also became clear that *accessibility* has become one of the essential prerequisites of information services today. Customers simply expect that information is accessible all of the time, from anywhere, at anytime. They expect an infrastructure that is easily accessible yet highly secure. IHA·GfK, getAbstract, Giga, Gartner and EIU provide this infrastructure through simple web-based logins to most of their services.

The somewhat vague term of *interactivity* has also become more tangible through the case studies. Providing information in an interactive way does not only mean providing a starting page on the web that can be adapted to one's personal preferences. It means being able to explore information interactively and run simulations with it; it means asking what-if questions that were perhaps not anticipated by the information provider themselves. Interactivity also implies a repackaging of knowledge and experiences into software applications. Giga has used its know-how to provide clients with the Website Scorecard, an interactive questionnaire for real-time website evaluations. The EIU has introduced a graphic slider interface through which criteria weightings as basic assumptions in each model can be modified. IHA·GfK has discovered that one of the most interactive formats is not necessarily the Internet, but on-site workshops with clients. Similarly, Giga and Gartner have started to deploy their analysts on-site so that customers can interact with them on a personal basis.

Finally, it seems that in these hurried times, answers are needed faster than ever. *Timeliness* has become a crucial information quality criterion. Giga has realized this and strives to answer any inquiry within hours rather than days. GetAbstract has started to summarize books which are not even published yet, assuring a timely delivery of the abstracts once the book is on the market. IHA·GfK has streamlined its research process and moved online to accelerate the data gathering, analysis and delivery process.

Nevertheless, timeliness can also have adverse effects on information quality. It can negatively influence other criteria such as accuracy, correctness or comprehensiveness. This danger was also seen by several of the interviewed managers and clients.

IQ-Principles in Action

The criteria discussed in the previous paragraphs already highlight some 'good practices' with regard to information quality. When we review the tools and techniques we have encountered in the six case studies, we can detect general, insightful ways of improving information quality. Specifically, we can summarize a number of ways in which information can be compressed, validated, contextualized, and activated.

As far as the *integration* of information and sources is concerned we have encountered one key technology, namely portals, such as the client and knowledge portals installed by IHA·GfK. A portal bundles various information sources and applications in one browser-based interface. The compilation of sources and applications in a portal is ideally personalized, i.e., based on the specific needs and preferences of the user. Other forms of compressing information that were frequently encountered were conceptual diagrams, such as Gartner's Magic Quadrant matrix. Another effective way to compress (prescriptive) information is principles. In the case of UBS, principles were used to represent a number of guidelines and norms.

To *validate* information, to judge its soundness and consistency, various mechanisms were discussed. One very elaborate arrangement is used at Giga, where information is evaluated at four different levels (through peers, superiors, clients, and one global research head). Many companies analyzed in the case studies rely on different sources for the same information as a way of assuring its validity (the EIU for example relies on statistical data provided by national banks in emerging markets, but also gather its own primary data). Other mechanisms for information validation included benchmarking (as in the UBS case), feedback loops (IHA·GfK), and an explicit rating of content, as in the case of getAbstract (the book rating schema) or Gartner where probabilities are used to indicate the level of certainty associated with a prognostic statement.

That information *contextualization* is a vital component of increasing information quality was highlighted by various case studies. Giga's catalyst section in every document is a direct result of the importance of context. A catalyst clarifies the background of a specific question. It tells the reader why a certain question is important and for whom. This 'catalyst' function was also encountered in getAbstract's book summaries. Providing background information was generally seen as an effective way of contextualizing information. In the case of getAbstract's book summaries this background consisted of a book author's credentials. In the UBS case the background consisted of a link to a more elaborate version of the guidelines. In the market research area of IHA·GfK, contextualization means adding general market data to specific findings, in order to relate them to one another and facilitate interpretation. Other effective ways of providing context are topic trees that locate a document in relation to the key terms in a thesaurus, listing the buzzwords contained in a book, or providing links to prior or related reports.

We have also come across various ways to make information actionable. One type of *activation* mechanism consisted of specific text block types that stress the implementation of insights and findings. These text blocks had labels such as Bottom Line, Action Item, Strategic Planning Assumption, Recommendation, or Key Take-Away. They were consistently and repeatedly used to highlight the consequences of information for action. Other key mechanisms of activating information were personal dialogues (e.g., between an analyst and a client), events such as conferences or expert chats, direct question and answer sessions (as in the Giga and Gartner cases), or through workshops, simulations and close collaboration over time (as in the IHA·GfK case).

In the final section of this cross-case study analysis, we focus on the contextual factors that contribute to information quality. The term 'contextual factor' refers to general organizational parameters that influence the quality of information indirectly.

Contextual Factors that Contribute to Information Quality

The first such contextual factor is direct, immediate, and frequent *feedback* from information users to information producers and administrators. In this way, they can quickly adjust their information products to changing needs or detect errors in their analyses. All of the five companies portrayed in the case studies provide feedback mechanisms, either through an electronic channel, e.g., via e-mail or user statistics, or via direct face-to-face feedback from colleagues, superiors, or clients. Sometimes the feedback is informal and spontaneous (such as the feedback that getAbstract sometimes receives from book authors or readers), at other times it is based on a defined set of criteria and given on a periodic basis (as in the Giga quality reviews or in the EIU customer surveys).

Other contextual factors relate to the knowledge workers themselves. In the case of getAbstract and Giga, the writers do not have heavy *administrative overhead* and can focus on their field of expertise. Also, in the case of Giga and Gartner, there is a great degree of (formal and informal) *exchange* between them, through telephone conferences, meetings and conferences or simple e-mail lists. A factor that (among other things) facilitates the exchange among information producers and increases the quality of information is a minimal set of common standards and methods. By creating a common set of (taught and enforced) methods, *standards*, or guidelines to which all information producers must adhere, a company can create a common language that fosters comprehension both internally and externally.[134] These standards were evident in all cases except that of getAbstract, where the management team has acknowledged that it will have to implement such guidelines in the future.

The last crucial contextual factor is *recognition*: for quality to count in a company, high-quality contributions need to be recognized. The quality of information has to be made

---

[134] McDermott describes this factor as follows: "When knowledge workers have common key focus areas and standard methods, enough convergence in thinking between individuals is created that valuable, detailed discussions can take place." (McDermott, 1995, p. 77).

visible to all information producers and outstanding contributions have to be recognized. In this way, there is an additional incentive to provide high-quality information besides satisfying customer expectations, namely to win the respect of peers and superiors.

These contextual factors have not been empirically tested in terms of correlation to information quality. They have only been illustrated through five exploratory case studies. Further research would have to analyze these factors in more rigid ways, e.g., operationalize them and divide them into measurable constructs.

Propositions: Key Success Factors for Information Quality

Proposition 1: If an information provider has institutionalized feedback mechanisms that are in place between information producers and consumers, then it will tend to have higher levels of customer satisfaction than providers that do not have such simple feedback channels.

Proposition 2: The less administrative overhead for information producers in a company, the greater the satisfaction of the information consumers with the information products of that company.

Proposition 3: The greater the institutionalized exchange between information producers, the higher the satisfaction of the information consumers with the information products.

Proposition 4: Information producers that have a minimal set of guidelines and standards create higher customer satisfaction than those who do not have (and use) any such standards.

Proposition 5: Information providers that officially recognize and acknowledge high-quality contributions of their authors, will have higher customer satisfaction in regard to their information products than those who do not.

All of these propositions have to be viewed under the condition of ceteris paribus (i.e., all other things being left unchanged). They are, as of now, highly speculative and only based on a sample of five companies. Whether they are in fact correct or not, can be tested through a survey among a larger number of similar information providers, such as IT-analyst companies.[135] The contextual factors described above

Measuring the Impact of Context

---

[135] There are numerous companies which could be potential candidates for such a survey. They all focus on IT analysis and advisory services and they all produce market reports on information technology. They are: Forrester Research, Emplifi, Telcordia, Metamor, TSC, CGI, CMG, Keane, Ciber, RSM, Sapient, Computer Science, Logica, Answer Think, Kennedy Information Group, Tower Group, Radicati Group, Meta Group, Ovum, Ber-

should be measured for each one of these analyst companies and then be correlated to the values of the customer satisfaction surveys.

Conclusion

The case studies have shown that the four information quality principles can be used as an analytic lens to examine the information value adding activities of companies engaged in knowledge-intensive processes. They have highlighted methods of dealing with crucial information quality problems, such as eliminating obsolete or outdated information, avoiding information overload, or keeping a consistent information format. They have also shown effective ways of fostering information quality, such as highlighting outstanding contributions or bringing information producers and consumers together. The case studies have shown what information quality criteria, such as accuracy or convenience, mean in specific contexts.

4.9 Beyond Corporate Case Studies: Information Quality in e-Government

In the previous sections, we have focused on the description and on insights on managing information quality in the profit sector. In this new section, we would like to focus on an emergent information quality practice: that within and among government agencies and their effort to supply citizens and other agencies with high quality information.

4.9.1 The Relevance of Information Quality for e-Government

e-Government ≠ IT

The provision of relevant, timely, consistent and reliable information to citizens is at the core of many e-government initiatives. In fact, the improvement of the quality and quantity of information provided to citizens is frequently cited as one of the main motives for e-government efforts (Grant and Chau 2005, 4-6). The basic belief behind such initiatives is often that information technology by itself can increase the quality of information provided to citizens (ibid, 7). While interactive online government services, such as e-government portals, public service search engines, online forms, or notifi-

lecon, Butler, Burton, Delphi Group, Hurwitz, Tech Republic, Sema Group, Aberdeen, Durlacher, IT Lab, and Computerwire.

cation services, can indeed increase the accessibility, convenience and timeliness of governmental information, they cannot ensure that the retrieved information is accurate, informative, current, or comprehensive. This may lead to frustrations and unfulfilled expectations on behalf of citizens wanting to complete a certain task or researching relevant public information. As the channels of e-government become more and more of a commodity that citizens take for granted, there is a need for a shift from a management focus on the delivery mode (electronic government) to the essence of the provided service, which is content. This new focus on information requires more than just deploying state-of-the-art information technology. It calls for clear information-related *roles* and responsibilities, for reliable review *processes* and for an information- and citizen-centric service *culture*. In this chapter we outline some of the reasons why the mere reliance on information technology is not enough to warrant high quality information in e-government. We do so with a clear focus on government-to-citizen relationships, although many of the discussed insights can be equally applied to government-to-government or government-to-business relations.

Following this rationale, it is surprising that e-government is an area to which the information quality perspective has not been applied yet, although it offers many fruitful approaches to improve e-government services.

The main premise of this chapter is that only an explicit and systematic effort of managing the quality of government provided information can lead to successful and sustainable e-government services. This systematic effort involves various professional groups (Eppler 2003) within government agencies that need to agree on common quality standards regarding information content, format, delivery process, and infrastructure. If these groups – ranging from managers, content experts, administrators to IT staff – do not cooperate and do not agree on an explicit and common standard for information quality, problems like the ones listed in the following table ensue.[136] The problems in the table below are typical effects of low information quality in e-government websites. They can be detected by employing online satisfaction surveys or conducting online focus groups with citizens from different age groups and with differing professional backgrounds. Although these problems may seem unrelated at first sight, they can all be traced back to a missing informa-

Problems of low IQ in e-Government

---

[136] For similar, authentic citizens' complaints regarding e-government sites, see for example Barnes and Vidgen 2003.

tion quality policy that assures that the right information is made available at the right time, in the right format, through the right communication channels, to the right people, at the right costs.

- Citizens discontinue to inform themselves via online government platforms in order to participate in democratic processes because the public information online is *irrelevant, outdated,* of *unstated origin* or *inconsistent.*
- Citizens cannot find relevant information because the interaction process with a government website is *complicated* and *unintuitive.*
- Citizens cannot comprehend how to proceed to complete a certain administrative task because of *unclear* information. They need to phone in and ask for additional instructions – this in return leads to additional costs in terms of agency staff time.
- Citizens loose valuable time in gathering necessary government-provided information because it is *dispersed, incomplete,* or not well *organized* (i.e., based on a citizen's life situation).
- Citizens do not entrust their personal information to virtual government applications because of unresolved *security* issues (information is not properly protected.)
- Citizens loose interest in public issues because of *lengthy* information that is not concise and does not provide an overview.
- Citizens or their representatives seek legal action against a public institution because influential, but *inaccurate* information that concerns them has been made accessible online *too early* and resulted in negative publicity or reputation impact.
- Citizens cannot participate actively in political processes, because the necessary information is not online on time, due to an *inefficient* publication process and too many bureaucratic barriers.
- The budgets of public ministries can no longer keep up with their growing websites, because *maintainability* issues have not been addressed early and the allocated funding is not sustainable to maintain the online information base.

Figure 35: Problems resulting from low quality information in government-to-citizen e-government

To address and prevent such problems[137], we propose first steps towards an information quality management framework for e-government applications. This chapter is organized as follows: First, we define information quality in the context of e-government. Then, we outline specific ways to manage and assure high-quality information in e-government websites. In the last section, we describe some of the constraints that make information quality improvements difficult to achieve in many e-government settings. We argue that it's useful to view information quality management (IQM) as an innovation for the public sector, as it requires significant changes in the habits and routines of public servants. As an innovation, IQM is subject the typical innovation diffusion barriers, elicited elegantly by communication-based approaches of studying innovation. These barriers, and possible ways of overcoming them, are discussed in the final part of this chapter.

4.9.2 Defining Information Quality for Government to Citizens Relations

In a recent study on government-to citizen e-government initiatives, West states that "there is no agreement on appropriate benchmarks or what constitutes an effective government Web site" (West 2004, 18). In order to develop such benchmarks, we can employ the rich definitions and metrics that exist on the notion of information quality. These definitions can be applied to the e-government context.

As discussed in previous chapters, information quality designates the characteristic of an information product (Wang et al. 1998, Eppler et al. 2005) or service, e.g., a set of information bundled for a specific purpose, to meet or exceed the

---

[137] Accenture's 2004 global e-government survey finds that there are now new efforts to integrate e-government sites vertically across national, state/regional, and local government levels. In this integration process, reliance on the quality of information between the various levels becomes crucial for the effectiveness of the overall system. Thus, large scale e-government integration may be another driver that raises the importance of the information quality issue in government-to-government contexts. In the current paper, as mentioned, we focus primarily on government-to-citizen applications, but it seems obvious that high quality information among government agencies is also one pre-requisite for information quality provided to citizens.

[138] See Barned and Vidgen 2003 for this use of information quality in e-government.

requirements of its stakeholders. The stakeholders of an information product or service are its consumers, creators, custodians (or administrators), direct or indirect content providers, intermediaries, and regulators. High quality information is information that is *fit for use* and of *high value* to its consumers, as it is *free of errors* or other deficiencies. The notion of value in this context is a multi-dimensional one. Besides stressing different quality dimensions (such as content or format) or *attributes* (such as accuracy or timeliness), IQ definitions also highlight different information *stakeholders* (including their value expectations or specifications) and their different *uses* of information. An information quality definition for the e-government sector can combine these elements and specify them for the public service context. The result of this amalgamation is the following definition of information quality for e-government:

Information provided by public agencies to citizens can be considered to be of high quality if the information and its medium meet or exceed citizens' expectations and regulators' specifications and if the information is of high value to citizens because it is fit for their various uses. Information quality can be further defined with attributes that relate to the time, format, content, and media dimension of information (such as timeliness, relevance, conciseness, or convenience).

From Definition to Management

In spite of the merit of such definitions (for example to facilitate the development of metrics for e-government effectiveness and benchmarking[138] or to articulate a quality mission statement), it is obvious that it is much easier to define information quality than to actually assure and manage it. Nonetheless, an explicit systematic definition of what a public institution considers to be high quality information can be a first important step towards more valuable online information. For that purpose, however, the typical IQ definitions are still too general. As we have seen earlier, information quality can be described more specifically with the help of information attributes or structured criteria lists that categorize information characteristics into several meaningful and manageable dimensions. Among the numerous existing information quality frameworks (see chapter 2.3) very few use categories that can be used directly for management purposes, i.e., for assigning responsibilities to specific professional groups. Our framework (presented in chapter 3) offers such attribute categories. They can directly be used to assign specific areas of responsibility for information quality factors in a government agency.

On the highest level of abstraction, the framework distinguishes between content and media quality, i.e., the message and its channel, or information government (defined by content) versus e-government (defined by the channel). The main logic behind this framework is a pragmatic one: the categories help to assign responsibilities for different prerequisites of information quality within a public agency or institution. This is illustrated by the following figure that shows the four levels, labeling them according to the professional group that is responsible for each set of criteria. The main responsibility for providing the right (relevant) information is with the line managers or department heads. The responsibility to see that this content is right (sound) lies with an agency's content providers themselves, usually subject matter experts. The responsibility for a convenient interaction process lies with the information technology managers (who should not interfere with the content-related matters) and the usability engineers (Nielsen 1993, 2000). The responsibility for a reliable and speedy infrastructure, finally, lies with the IT hard- and software specialists (either inside a public administration or with an outside partner). The main plan how each set of criteria is consistently met is referred to as a policy. Each policy is briefly described below.

The IQ-framework Revisited

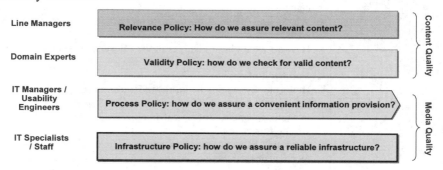

Figure 36: Roles and policies derived from the IQ framework

In order to implement an information quality function in a e-government context based on the above framework, a public agency needs to institute four kinds of IQM policies:

A **relevance policy** based on a profound understanding of the real information needs of citizens. The goal of this policy is to assure that the information that is provided is relevant and comprehensive enough, accurate enough, clear enough, and generally applicable for the targeted citizens.

A **validity policy** that outlines how information is reviewed internally in order to avoid information deficiencies, such as documents that are too long, internally inconsistent, incorrect, or outdated.

A **process policy** that describes how the interaction process remains usable for various types of citizens. Usable in this context means convenient to use, with timely information delivery that can be adapted to one's needs and where the sources of information are visible.

An **infrastructure policy** that describes the necessary preventive measures to assure that the information hard- and software remain reliable. Reliability in this context refers to the requirements of the citizens (they expect an easily accessible infrastructure that is safe and fast), but also to the constraints of the public agency (which must assure that its level of spending for the infrastructure is maintainable in order to offer the services in a sustainable manner).

Table 30 provides a sample checklist with some of the key questions that should be answered by each of the four policy documents in a public agency.

---

1. Relevance Policy[139]
- What are the main expectations of our citizens with regard to content?
- Which are (derived from the expectations) our main content areas?
- How do we monitor changes in the relevance system of the citizens?

2. Validity Policy[140]
- How and by whom is influential information double-checked before publication?
- Is there an appeal process that citizens can employ to rectify wrong information?
- Does published information have a perish date or what other mechanisms are there to insure regular updates of information?

---

[139] Two current studies that illustrate the urgent need for such a policy are Dawes et al. 2003. These authors illustrate that governments are often not sensitive to the information needs and relevancy systems of their citizens.

[140] These suggestions are based on the guidelines issued by the US office of Management and Budget with regard to the implementation of the federal data quality act which requires each federal agency to install an information quality process for its influential publicly released information. See for example: http://www.whitehouse.gov/omb/fedreg/final_information_qualit y_guidelines.html (last accessed July 5th 2005).

---

3. Process Policy

- Have the navigation trails to find information been tested with user groups and with different user scenarios?
- Is the navigation behavior of the users of the e-government analyzed? Are log-off points registered and navigation trails improved accordingly?
- How can citizens suggest improvements to the interaction process?

4. Infrastructure Policy

- Is there a backup system for the infrastructure?
- Is there a strategy on how to scale the system's capacity in case the information demand by citizens increases?
- Is there a rights management and a security software installed?

Table 30: Key questions addressed by the four information quality policies

How these policies and responsibilities are implemented is the object of the next section.

4.9.3 Managing Information Quality in e-Government through Roles, Processes, Tools, and Training

The four levels that were previously introduced can now serve not only to distinguish among different *roles* for information quality, but also to distinguish key *processes*, *tools* and *training* areas that are needed to make high-quality information a reality in e-government websites.

In terms of *roles*, we have already distinguished among staff that is responsible for content selection (content directors), for content validity our soundness (reviewers or content managers), for the interaction processes (usability engineers, webmasters, etc.) and for reliable base infrastructures (IT specialists, platform managers).

With regard to key quality *processes*, we can – again using the four categories – distinguish among feedback processes that validate whether the provided information is indeed relevant to the citizens, review processes that help to validate information before it is published, interaction processes that make the information more easily accessible to citizens, and infrastructure maintenance processes that guarantee the smooth functioning of the underlying hard- and software. Ideally, each such process is assigned to a process owner who oversees its functioning.[141]

As far as information quality management *tools* are concerned that can be used to improve and assure information quality in e-government applications, our prior distinction leads to the following types of instruments: For the relevance dimension, we need tools that help us to survey and monitor the citizens use of the e-government applications in order to see what kind of content is most frequently accessed and which areas of an e-government site is barely used. There is a great variety of such tools available on the market.[142] Many of them can be easily adjusted to the e-government context. For the validity dimension, there are so-called workflow tools that help to organize a review-based publication process that includes quality checks and update mechanisms. With regard to process quality, monitoring tools similar to those discussed for relevance purposes can be employed. They can be used to analyze the log files of citizens' visits to an e-government website in order to detect deficits in the current interaction process. The last group of (mostly technical) tools consists of system monitoring and maintenance tools that help to prevent security issues or system fallout. Examples of such tools are security software (firewall, anti-virus), code parsers (which detect source code compliance with accessibility standards) or site performance improvement software.

A last vital, but often overlooked element of implementing information quality management in an e-government context is the *training* of public administrators. Training with regard to information quality ranges from generally educating public officers about the most pressing information needs of their citizens, to the technical training in running websites, or training information managers about usability issues. Whereas the training related to the relevance and process dimension focuses on the expectations (in terms of content) and use (in terms of interaction) of the citizens, validity training consists of instructing public officers in how to operate review or control processes for information. Infrastructure training, finally, prepares the technical staff for security con-

---

[141] All of these processes rely, of course, on the smooth functioning of the underlying administrative processes. Becker et al. (2004) show in their recent study of processes in e-Government that this is still a major challenge.

[142] Commercially available tools that provide such functionalities are for example www.opinionpoll.com, www.lets-ask.com, www.infopoll.com, www.websurveyor. com, www.webtrends. com, www.analog.cx, www.nedstat.com.

cerns or for fall-out scenarios.

If these areas are considered beyond just focusing on the information technology, then information quality improvements stand on a much broader base. Public policy makers and public officers, who strive to improve the quality of the information provided to citizens, still face, however, many barriers. These barriers are analyzed in the next section with the help of innovation diffusion theory.

4.9.4 Constraints and Barriers for Information Quality Management in G2C Relations

So far we have focused on the factors that contribute to information quality and foster information-quality oriented behavior. For a realistic assessment of the management of information quality in e-government, however, we should not neglect the many restrictions that make information quality improvements difficult, and sometimes even impossible in the public sector. In order to systemize and categorize such possible potholes in the road to information quality, we rely on prior findings from innovation diffusion theory (Rogers 1995)[143]. In order to qualify as an innovation, a novel practice must meet certain characteristics (ibid, 15); first and foremost of course that it offers advantages vis-à-vis older, established practices. These factors influence the rate of adoption of a new practice either positively or negatively. In Rogers's seminal study[144] on innovation these five factors are: the *complexity* of the innovation (i.e., how difficult it is to master it), the *compatibility* with prior practices (i.e., the

---

[143] For a similar application of diffusion theory to e-government (from the citizens' adoption point of view) see Carter & Belanger 2004.

[144] A communication approach, such as Rogers', towards innovation seems a fruitful perspective to understand possible limitations to information-quality induced changes in e-government for two main reasons: First, conceiving of information quality improvements as an innovation diffusion process helps *to be prepared* for possible negative reactions that occur when current processes or habits need to be modified (it is thus a particularly realistic approach that is sensitive to people's resistance to change). Second, the communication approach to innovation diffusion is, as Rogers has shown (Rogers 1995, 78), open to analyzing *any type* of innovation with the help of proven conceptual tools. In that respect, Roger himself has used many *public sector initiatives* as case studies for innovation diffusion.

degree of change necessary to adopt it), the *observability* of the new behavior (i.e., how easy it is to recognize it), the *trialability* of the new behavior (i.e., whether it is possible to test the innovation first), and the relative *advantage* of the innovation for the people affected by it (i.e., the benefits brought by the innovation). These innovation characteristics are examined for information quality management in the table below.

Innovation characteristics...	...and their manifestation in information quality management (IQM)
1. *Relative advantage*: the new practice is perceived as better than current practices.	IQM dramatically reduces information scrap and re-work (English, 1999) and increases citizens' satisfaction with e-government services.
2. *Compatibility*: the new practice is consistent with existing values, past experiences, and needs.	IQM requires the acquisition of new skills, the design of new processes, the purchase of new tools, and the definition of new roles and may thus often be inconsistent with current habits.
3. *Complexity*: the difficulty of applying the new practice	The roles, processes, and tools of IQM are indeed complex, as they consist of numerous, interrelated elements, but they can be mastered trough differentiated, focused responsibilities (i.e., splitting content and media quality tasks) and through adequate training activities.
4. *Trialability*: the possibility of experimenting with the new practice on a limited basis.	IQM can be gradually introduced, for example by first focusing on particularly influential information.
5. *Observability:* the results of a new pratice are visible to others.	Through citizen surveys and focus groups the changes in information consumer satisfaction can be measured.

Table 31: IQM and its innovation characteristics

IQ as Innovation

The above table illustrates that systematic information quality management qualifies as an innovation. Nevertheless, the table also highlights the problematic compatibility dimension of IQM, as it requires many changes in order to institutionalize information quality management. As public administrations are typically geared towards continuity and consistency with previous practices and rules (as their dominant logic), we must address this issue in more detail (see Tornatzky and Klein 1982). In the e-government practices that we have observed (see also the contribution by Lorenzo Cantoni for this issue), there are often compatibility problems with regard to five areas:[145]

1. Existing **rules** or regulations: Establishing new processes and roles requires at times new regulations or modifications to existing ones.
2. Existing **skills**, expectations or routines: Implementing the aforementioned policies requires new skills (as indicated in the section on training) and sometimes new attitudes from public workers
3. Existing tools and **infrastructures**: Some of the existing infrastructure might not be able to support information quality management and thus has to be replaced.
4. Existing **resources**, such as staff, budget and available time: Providing high-quality information is just one of many goals of public agencies, thus this objective might be incompatible or at least in conflict with other objectives that require time, budget, and effort.
5. Existing **reference points** – such as official benchmarks or values, established institutional networks, or predefined standards of higher level public agencies – may lead to mental limitations or biases in the perceptions and attitudes of public servants.

The fifth group of compatibility constraints includes elements that are highlighted in Rogers' theory of innovation diffusion, namely previous practices (for example of citizens or government officials), or norms of the social system (for example regarding security issues) (Rogers 1995, 163). As Rogers states in one of his insightful case studies:

Compatibility Elements

"An important factor regarding the adoption rate of an innovation is its compatibility with the *values, beliefs, and past experiences* of individuals in the social system" (ibid, 4). Following this logic, any type of initiative that aims at improving the quality of information provided to citizens must take into account *how to change current reference points* in a way that is not in extensive conflict with the norms of the social system. In the following diagram we have summarized these compatibility constraints visually. The main implication for e-government managers is thus to reflect whether their information quality policy is actually *fundable* (in terms of

---

[145] See also OECD 2003, 13: "Legislative and *regulatory* barriers, *financial* barriers, *technological* barriers and the digital divide, among others, can impede the uptake of e-government".

the budget allocated to assuring high quality information), whether it is *allowable* (in terms of the existing regulation), whether it is *doable* and *conceivable* with the existing skill base and infrastructure and how it will influence the relationship with existing *reference points*. Pro-actively changing these reference points, for example by comparing an agency's information quality level with that of a comparable agency in another country, is one effective way of confronting these limitations and motivating public servants for information quality improvements that lead to truly *competitive* e-government services.

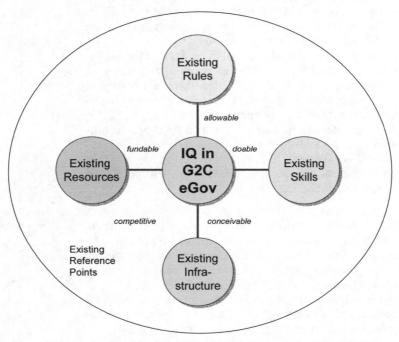

Figure 37: Compatibility constraints for information quality improvements in e-government initiatives

4.9.5 An e-Government Study: Italy's Ministry for Public Administration[146]

This case study illustrates a number of instruments that can be used to analyze and improve information quality in eGovernment websites. It presents a pilot experience of the *Italian Ministry for Public Administration* in collaboration with other parties, aimed at building a *culture* of user-centred website design and management among public administration officers. An operationalization of the information quality model has been developed and tested in two different administration bodies, and then made available to all the others through the diffusion of a CD-ROM, a website and dedicated training programs.The case shows how design, evaluation and improvement of public administration websites can fit into an information quality model, and how its operationalization can lead to a sustainable virtuous circle of continuous improvement.

The Italian law requires that public administrations of a certain kind or size run a Public Relation Office (URP: Ufficio per le Relazioni con il Pubblico). URPs are ruled by a national law: n. 150 (7 June 2000). The goal of information governance is clearly defined in its first article, stating its objectives and application scope. Its goals are: to illustrate and to foster the knowledge of norms, to illustrate the activities of institutions, and their functioning, to foster access to public services, to promote a wider and deeper knowledge about issues of relevant public and social interest, to help internal simplifying processes of procedures, and to help the modernisation of apparatuses, to promote the image of administrations.

While in the 2000 law the use of digital means was listed as a possibility among many others (art. 2, 2), Italy has further progressed in the way toward information governance through e-government means; in particular, it has adopted a law to promote the access of disabled persons to IT tools (9 January 2004, n. 4) and a Code of the Digital Administration ("decreto legislativo", 7 March 2005, n. 82) stating that all the messages foreseen by the 150 law have to be made available also trough websites (art. 54, 1, e). At the beginning it declares that: "The State, Regions and local autonomies ensure information availability, management, access, transmission, preservation and usability in digital form, organise themselves and operate toward this end using information

---

[146] This case experience has been provided by Lorenzo Cantoni.

and communication technologies in the most apt ways" (art. 2, 1).

In recent years, many URPs have published websites in order to improve information accessibility, and to offer various interactive services. While both citizens and operators wanted to enter the web, in a context where the Internet was conceived as being a must, the lack of previous experience and knowledge of the field, together with the will to go immediately online, without careful planning and testing, were the main reasons for low quality online services. Moreover, limited budgets did not allow for a careful quality analysis, aimed to maintain, evaluate and refine the services, hence yielding problems in information currency, accuracy, comprehensiveness (coverage), and others.

After the first hype, the URPs have been considering that simply having a running website is not enough. They have become aware that citizens require high-quality online services that provide high-quality information; moreover, they have started to learn from each others' strengths and weaknesses.

In this context, the Usability CD project was born, promoted by the Italian Ministry for Public Administration (www.funzionepubblica.it), the URP consortium (www.urp. it), the City of Modena (www.comune.mo.it) and the Regione Campania (www.regione.campania.it). The TEC-Lab, Technology Enhanced Communication Lab of the University of Lugano (www.tec-lab.ch) assisted the project in designing, running and evaluating the research activities, as well as in producing educational materials to help government officials improve their information quality. The output of the project was the production of a CD-ROM to be distributed to Italian URPs. The CD-ROM contains a tutorial on website usability issues, a detailed description of two cases of usability analysis and improvement, as well as many additional related materials. Due to the many requests, the content of the CD-ROM has been made available also through a website (http://cpusabile.officinedigitali.it), also a dedicated training program has been designed in collaboration with the CSI, Consortium for IT Services, (Turin) and successfully tested with about fourty Italian public administration officers (12-13 September 2005).

In order to assess the quality of URPs' websites, two cases were chosen: a website run by the city of Modena, called Unox1 ('one by one') and that of the Campania region.

It should be emphasized that "usability", in this project, has to be understood in the context of information quality, refering also to content usability/usefulness; in fact, content usability is becoming an important and challenging usability issue, as stated by Jacob Nielsen (in the preface to Cantoni et al. 2003): "Unfortunately, it is more difficult to study the usability of communication than the usability of navigation. It is pretty clear-cut whether the user can find something or not. *It is more difficult to test the quality of information.* But it can be done. It's an open research question how to improve the methods for evaluating content to make them as efficient and easy to apply as the mainstream usability methods we recommend for testing the usability of websites, intranets, software, and most other user interface designs".

Available data about websites' actual use (usages) were analysed mainly through log files (answering questions like: how many users are there? which areas/services do they access most? What time do they enter the website? How much time do they stay on it? etc.), mailing lists sub-scriptions/un-subscriptions and received e-mails, all these data helped to better understand what kind of information users were interested in (relevance dimension). In one case, the results of a research conducted through telephone interviews were used, to assess the level of satisfaction of citizens with respect to public administration communication activities. Front office personnel was interviewed, and focus groups were run, in order to further focus on what is relevant for citizens in their interactions with those public administration online services. *Analysis Results*

Thanks to these analyses, user profiles have been identified, recording age, profession, Internet access type, goals and expectations of different kinds of users. A distintion had to be made between novice and expert users of the concerned websites, in fact, they have quite different approaches and fruition patterns: information that is needed the first time to understand the service offered by an eGovernment website and its "coverage", could become useless and even annoying for frequent users.

Once the user profiles of the eGovernment websites were defined (13 different profiles for one website, 16 for the other one), user scenarios were developed with the help of all concerned stakeholders. User scenarios are task-oriented vivid descriptions of envisioned use of the eGovernment application, expressed in narrative form, as stories of typical users using the site, with their motivations, goals and expectancies. Inspections have been conducted, in order to assess if user scenarios could be effectively conducted, as well as to measure how easy or difficult it was to conduct them (efficiency); a list of recommendations has been compiled for each of the concerned websites, which have been eventually modified and refined.

Recommendations for improving the websites have been divided into the areas of *content quality* and *media quality*.

Content quality recommendations for improvement ranged from adding missed content, to rephrasing it, to update it, to make it more suitable for the intended target public, etc. Media quality recommendations covered navigation, layout and graphic design. Closely connected to both areas, also the work-flow / processes needed in order to accomplish certain procedures as well as the labelling system (how active parts / links are labelled, how pages / sections are titled) were tested, and recommendations given to make them more useful and sound.

An analysis conducted applying Nielsen's heuristics (Nielsen 2000) and user testing activities complemented the profiles and scenarios strategy.

These two cases have been documented and presented, together with a tutorial and otrher related material, in a CD-ROM presented at the ComPA and ForumPA, the most important Italian events in the field of public administration communication and management. The CD-ROM has been distributed to Italian URPs and made available on a dedicated website, inviting its users to follow the same steps and to enter a continuous information quality improvement process. To complement the CD-ROM self-learning model, also a two-days seminar has been designed and tested, aimed to increase the awareness of the information quality issue among URPs' personnel, to equip them with cognitive and operative tools, as well as to give them hands-on experience in the field, and the opportunity of meeting colleagues with similar interests and problems.

Lessons Learned   Among the many lessons learned during the project, the following ones are worth to be mentioned:

- A continuous improving process needs a strong commitment by the involved public administration offices, hence the importance of having evangelists in URPs, and to offer them a common forum where to get in contact; for this goal, the training experience has proved to be very successful.
- URPs have a quite frequent personnel turnover: hence clear and simple steps are to be proposed, which can easily be followed by people who were not involved in the process from its very beginning.

- A *pass or fail* approach does not seem to be viable; instead, a virtuous circle of continuous information quality improvement seems to be more apt, effective and efficient.
- Working on similar cases greatly helps people to better understand procedures, as well as to feel more at ease and to become committed.
- Considering the law not as a constraint, limiting possibilities, but as a departure point, opening opportunities, greatly helps operators in devising and running an information quality improvement project.
- The IQ model for eGovernment presented in this book contributes to understand this case; let us see how in the following points.

Regarding the restrictions to information quality, they apply in this case, as the following list illustrates:

- *Regulation, Laws, Codes*: URPs are ruled by a national law, and regulated according to local regulations; they require that URPs improve public administration transparency and accessibility.
- *Skills, Expectations, Routines*: on the one hand, poor websites' quality depended mainly on the lacking experience of the operators, hence the opportunity to provide a simple framework, together with actual cases to all URPs by the national Ministry; on the other hand, citizens ask for more and higher quality online services.
- *Tools, Bandwidth, Infrastructure*: the availability of technologies by the administration and by citizens has always been considered in evaluation activities, in order not to produce a digital divide. This also meant not always suggesting the best technology available on the market, if at an early stage of adoption.
- *Budget, Time, Staff*: limits in all of them suggested to reduce expensive analyses (e.g.: user testing), while adopting a sustainable approach, which could be easily iterated and implemented in a continuing quality improvement process.
- *Benchmarks, Initiatives, Networks*: the Italian government has taken the initiative, but public administrations of different levels are involved; there has been a continuous attention to what other URPs have been doing.

Regarding information quality itself, the previously presented conceptual framework highly clarifies this experience, both from the *content quality* and the *media quality* viewpoints:

- *Relevant information*: citizens require *applicable* information, *accurate* (as needed by a public administration), *clear*, so that every citizen can understand it, and *comprehensive*, covering all the range of G2C information flow.
- *Sound information*: web communication requires that information is particularly *concise*, different sources have to provide *consistent* information, *correct* and *current*.
- *Optimized Process*: *interactivity* is the main keyword, while *convenience*, *timeliness* and *traceability* are also concerned, again, in many cases also due to legal requirements (e.g.: in order to identify the information provider and its authority).
- *Reliable infrastructure*: *accessibility* is required to avoid or reduce digital divide, while *security*, *maintainability* and *fastness* are needed both from the point of view of the public administration operators, and from the point of view of citizens/users.

Conclusion

This case study has illustrated that the distinctions introduced in this book help to organize information quality improvements systematically. It also illustrates that improvements in information quality cannot just rely on technological or process innovations, but require dedicated training and education.

4.9.6 Conclusion: Extending IQ to e-Government

This sub-chapter has been based on the premise that the rich field of information quality research and practice can be productively applied to the area of e-government, or rather information government. Especially in government-to-citizen relationships, the quality of the provided information is a key success factor for e-government initiatives. This is the reason why information quality approaches can be and should be applied to this important area. We have argued that a systematic management of information quality must address at least four levels: content relevance, content validity or soundness, the interaction process, and the underlying infrastructure. Clear responsibilities must be assigned to each of these areas within an agency and management processes should be designed and deployed accordingly. These processes can be supported by a variety of tools and facilitated by targeted training. In this way, information quality improvements can be iteratively achieved, for example by first focusing only on highly influential or sensitive information. We have also highlighted that public leaders need to take into account the often considerable barriers to information quality improvements. The factors highlighted by innovation theory, especially the compatibility with past practices, can be useful indicators in that endeavor. To overcome these barriers, government officials must create incentives and competitive reference points to motivate and mobilize public servants to improve their information quality online. Beyond that, they must provide adequate funding, tools and training so that this motivation can ultimately lead to an information government that does not just focus on the electronic channels through which it provides information, but on the actual information itself and its value to citizens.

5. Conclusion and Outlook

The final chapter of the study summarizes the main findings and provides future perspectives on the topic. Implications of the findings for various management levels (top, middle, and line managers) are discussed.

Chapter Overview

The information quality framework presented in chapter three of this study has several benefits, but also numerous limitations. While the main benefits are illustrated in chapter three and include orientation, coordination, measurement, and information product improvement, the limitations are more subtle. One obvious limitation, as far as its applicability is concerned, is the framework's complexity. It contains four phases and sixteen criteria on four levels. Because of this drawback, the information quality principles have been introduced to summarize the many criteria in four simple concepts. Another limitation of the framework in terms of application is its generic nature. Because it is designed to be used for a variety of purposes and for many different knowledge-intensive processes, it is not tailored to one specific situation. It must consequently be adapted to the local context or problem at hand to unfold its full potential. Although the framework is generic, it cannot be applied to all circumstances. As pointed out in chapter three, pure data quality problems may be easier to resolve through dedicated models of data quality (such as the one by Huang et al, 1999). Besides these limitations in the application of the framework, there are further limitations in regard to its elements. The tradeoffs between the information quality criteria that have been identified are based on common sense reasoning and evidence from the documented case studies. In order to solidify these findings, quantitative research should examine these tradeoffs more systematically (through experiments or surveys that examine each tradeoff individually). Another limitation of the framework, which derives from its intended use in management education regards the number and the arrangement of the information quality criteria along the four phases of the in-

Limitations of the Framework

formation consumption cycle (from identification to application). Some of these criteria positions are arbitrary in the sense that a criterion could also be positioned within another phase of the cycle. Every view of the framework could also be extended by including further quality criteria. Because of pedagogic reasons, every phase has been associated with only one criterion on each level. This makes the framework more symmetric and easier to convey. Nevertheless, this can create the impression that the framework is 'definitive' and that every criterion can only have one position in the information cycle. That this is not necessarily the case has been outlined in chapter three and must be said every time the framework is presented to students or managers.

5.1 Implications for Management

There is no such thing as genuine knowledge and fruitful understanding except as the offspring of doing.

JOHN DEWEY

Implications at Various Management Levels

The implications for management of the findings presented in the previous chapters are considerable. They need to be differentiated according to the relevant *levels* and the relevant *areas* of management. Specifically, we can distinguish between implications for top management, line or middle managers, domain experts or specialists, IT managers, and IT support staff. Below, we outline the main implications for these professional groups.

Overview

Before addressing each individual group separately, let us quickly review the information quality framework presented in chapter three and examine how different managerial areas are affected by different levels of the framework.

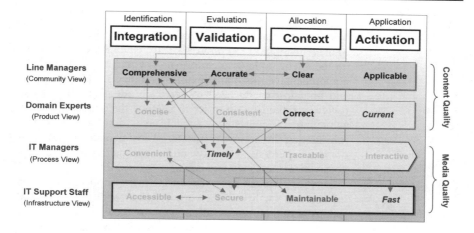

Figure 38: Implications of the framework for different management levels and areas

As the diagram indicates, the tailoring of information to the needs of the community (the top level of the framework) is primarily a responsibility of general managers or line managers. They have to ensure that their staff provides internal and external clients with information that is comprehensive, accurate, clear and applicable for the intended purposes. In other words, management must provide training, standards, and instruments to its employees to enable them to integrate, validate, contextualize and activate information. In the context of knowledge-intensive processes, those employees who are also information producers will most likely be subject matter experts. They will have to pay attention to the four intrinsic qualities of information abbreviated as the four C's, namely conciseness, consistency, correctness, and currency. In doing so, they need to be supported by their IT support staff and by the IT management. The managers of information systems must (in coordination with the business managers) provide, administrate and continually optimize a content management process that is convenient for the domain experts and their clients. This process must enable information producers to deliver information in a timely manner and it must allow them to trace back prior information to its sources, all of this in a highly interactive and flexible manner. The IT support staff, finally, has to focus on activities that make the underlying infrastructure continually available and assure its accessibility, security, maintainability, and speed.

All of these groups need to collaborate closely in order to balance key tradeoffs between information quality criteria. Management and IT support staff, for example, need to agree on the adequate level of information volume to optimize the comprehensiveness-maintainability tradeoff. IT managers and domain experts need to agree on adequate control and review mechanisms in order to balance the conflict between achieving full consistency (which takes time) and providing information in a timely manner. Line managers and their domain experts need to agree on the optimal level of comprehensiveness, accuracy and conciseness.

Having given an overview on the main implications of the information quality framework for the various professional groups within an organization, we now focus on the key role of top management, line managers, and IT managers.

Implications for
Top Management

A recent literature review (Xu et al. 2001) on the factors influencing data quality found that the issue that has received the greatest attention in the relevant literature from 1981 to 1999 is the function of top management (six of ten surveyed publications mentioned this issue, followed by the role of quality managers, training, policies, process management and evaluation). These findings can also be applied to the domain of information quality, as top management plays the important part of agenda-setter and role model.

Top management has two core responsibilities as far as information quality in knowledge-intensive processes is concerned. First, it must *identify* the processes and areas where information quality is of *strategic importance* because it can constitute a sustainable competitive advantage or because it directly influences the key drivers of the business, such as cost-effectiveness and productivity or the satisfaction of key customer segments. Second, it ought to make information quality a priority in these key areas by clearly articulating its *expectations* and *goals* to the responsible business units and line managers and *track* if those expectations are being met.

For both areas, deciding where information quality is a strategic asset and making it a tracked priority, top management can start by asking the following diagnostic questions:

1. In which areas of our business are information products a crucial asset for our company either as input or output factors of our value chain?
    – What are our most knowledge-intensive processes which require professional expertise, information transformation (identification, evaluation, allocation and application) and knowledge codification?

- What are our most important and most visible information products (reports, client extranets, presentations, databases, manuals, e-mails, etc.)

2. Who are the internal and external clients for those information products and what are their general requirements and expectations?
   - How do they use the information? What is their core process?
   - What are the key criteria by which they evaluate information products?

3. Are we consistently meeting these requirements or not?
   - Is the current level of information quality in those areas above or below our competitor's level (or the expected value)?
   - If below, why is there a deficit? If we are above the competition, are we exploiting this advantage?

4. Who is responsible for the deficit/advantage? How can their improvements be made visible (i.e., be qualified and quantified)?
   - Who are the key players and how can we provide them with an optimal environment?
   - What are informative indicators we can measure and use as early warning signals for inadequate information quality levels?
   - How can we foster and reward exceptional quality levels?

In addition to these diagnostic starting questions, several others are provided in the self-evaluation form in the appendix of this study. The questionnaire can give a first assessment of the state of information quality in a company's knowledge-intensive processes. When this questionnaire is used in in-house seminars on information quality, the level of agreement among employees is usually quite high. The differences in terms of status-quo perception nevertheless become evident when their view is compared with that of top managers of the same company who generally have a more optimistic view on their information quality (this experience, however, is based on individual cases and cannot be generalized).

The questions outlined above represent a strategic view on information quality. Top management, however, should not neglect the *tactical* issues, especially with regard to internal communication, that can influence the level of information quality in an organization. Based on the insights derived from the case studies in chapter four and from the problem analysis

Caveats for Top Management

in chapter three, top managers should be aware of the following three pitfalls:

First, do not make information quality the 'flavor of the month'. That is to say, do not introduce it as a new initiative, a strategic project, or a new improvement campaign, but rather present it as a *fundamental business issue* that is vital to the success of any knowledge-intensive firm and that affects all information producers, custodians and consumers.

Second, do not let every team or department find its own information quality definition, but strive for a *(general) common understanding* that is based on the exigencies of the customers. The framework presented in chapter three can be used to organize relevant information quality criteria in a meaningful way and monitor its progress.

Third, do not view information quality as a *purely technological* problem that can be resolved through infrastructure improvements. As the case studies on Gartner, getAbstract, Giga, UBS and IHA·GfK have shown, an adequate IT-infrastructure is only one element of a functioning knowledge-intensive process that leads to high-quality information. Issues such as staff qualification, authoring training, incentives and rewards, as well as standards, guidelines, and process design are equally important factors that need to be taken into account.

If top management asks the right questions and avoids the pitfalls outlined above, improvements in information quality can act as catalysts for advances in a variety of fields, ranging from process design and skill development to internal and external communication.

Implications for Line Managers

While the impact of top management decisions on successful information quality management is certainly high, the most direct impact can be expected from line managers, or in other words, from middle management. The middle managers are responsible for the knowledge-intensive processes that eventually lead to information products. As outlined earlier, it is middle management which must assure that the produced information is as complete or comprehensive as required for the intended purposes, that it achieves the required degree of accuracy and that it is clear and applicable for the internal and external clients. Members of middle management (e.g., team leaders and heads of departments) negotiate explicit information quality standards with information producers, administrators, and consumers. In order to succeed in this regard, line or middle managers must ask a number of fun damental questions. Some of these are outlined below (others can be found in Appendix J, which is addressed to all levels of management):

1. Do all members of a team or department share the same *understanding* of what constitutes high-quality information and where it is of crucial importance? If not, how can such an understanding be developed?
2. Is there a possibility for information consumers to provide direct *feedback* to information producers or custodians so that expectation mismatches can quickly be detected? If not, is there a way to institutionalise such feedback loops?
3. Is there a *review* mechanism for information before it is published or sent to clients? Are there any quality gates or checks that have to be passed? If not, does the middle manager have to look at every piece of information going to clients or can there be a system of peer-reviewing?
4. Are there standardized *templates* or design formats for the different information and publication types in order to assure a consistent format of the published information? Does everybody know them adhere to these formats?
5. Is there a process in place, which *eliminates* outdated information or notifies authors about necessary updates? If not, can the IT department be asked to design such a periodic cleansing process?
6. Are the information producers *content* with their information technology infrastructure and with the their administrative process or do they regularly complain about issues such as IT-support or administrative overhead?
7. Are there official and generally known minimal *guidelines* or rules that regulate the maximum length of a publication, its ideal structure, and preferred style?

These few questions can – if thoroughly answered – lead to a number of positive changes in terms of process design, infrastructures, and policies. As far as policies and guidelines are concerned, two areas of concern should be highlighted. First, knowledge workers generally abhor rigid controls or regulations (see Schultze, 2000). Rather than dictate strict norms and standards top-down, line managers should *actively involve* information producers in setting adequate information quality standards, templates, and guidelines. This will not only lead to more realistic standards, but also to a higher commitment to these standards later on.

A second area of concern is the use of traditional quality improvement and measurement tools, such as quality circles,

Caveats for Line Managers

house of quality, process manuals, Pareto analysis, or statistical controls. As mentioned at several points throughout this book (and probably representing the most controversial or debatable element of it), many quality management techniques and principles may *not* be applicable in the area of knowledge-intensive processes because they follow a different mind-set and because knowledge-intensive processes are often non-routine events that depend on individual style and expertise. The production process for intellectual information products – such as research reports, risk assessments, trend analyses, product concepts, vendor evaluations, or trade journal articles – tends to be highly subjective and is often based on idiosyncratic procedures (see Polanyi, 1974 or Schultze, 2000). While the end-result of a knowledge-intensive process must meet certain well-defined standards, the regulation and ultimate certification of intellectual information transformation processes may not be a fruitful strategy. A practitioner quote from the context of the knowledge-intensive process of underwriting (i.e., risk assessment in the insurance and reinsurance business) can illustrate this point. It is taken from a workshop I conducted in 2001 with a large Swiss financial services group. In this workshop, I stressed the advantages of documenting process knowledge and received the following counter argument from one of the participating underwriters:

In the process of underwriting, that is to say when I need to evaluate a potential risk that we may want to insure, and that I need to 'convert' into a written analysis and recommendation, I tend to look at very particular criteria and not necessarily at those foreseen in my checklist or process plans. This has led to rather different decisions than if I had followed the guidelines. So far, however, these decisions, which are initially based on my intuition and gut feeling, have lead to better decisions than if I had followed the documented process guidelines.

This insightful statement can lead to the following conclusion: While the knowledge *within*, *about*, and derived *from* a process may be codified, stored, and re-used, the skills and intuition of the knowledge worker will remain *the* crucial component, which cannot be codified or standardized. Applying traditional quality metrics and tools would mean neglecting this personal component of knowledge. Instead, 'softer', relatively open heuristics need to be applied, which will give knowledge workers the opportunity to apply their own skills and techniques. Such heuristics have been proposed in section 3.2.5 of this book in the form of four guiding principles that focus on the compression (integration), control (validation), context and cognitive anchoring (activation or captivating communication) of information.

Earlier, I stated that the impact line or middle managers can have on the quality of information is strong and immediate since they manage the knowledge-intensive processes that eventually lead to information products. While this is certainly true, one should not neglect they key role of IT managers (and their staff), as they are responsible for the implementation and administration of the underlying *support processes* and *infrastructures*. These two components have been labeled as *media quality* in our framework (as opposed to the content quality that reflects the relevance and soundness of the information itself). As the production process of information depends more and more on the adequate support through information technology, this group of managers gains importance. Based on the experiences documented in chapter two and four, IT managers must focus on three critical information quality dilemmas.

Implications and Dilemmas for IT Managers

First, they must design and implement a content management *process* that is convenient and efficient for the information producers, administrators and information consumers. The key challenge in this endeavor is finding the optimal balance between the, at times, conflicting needs of these three stakeholders. Here, IT managers can and should act as neutral mediators who strive to find pareto-optimal solutions[147] amidst the various time- and resource-related constraints.

Second, they have to design and implement an information *infrastructure* that optimally supports the content management process and is reliable and secure as well as being fast and efficient. Again, IT managers must strike a balance, namely between flexibility and rigidity, openness and isolation. They must provide a flexible infrastructure that can be adapted to the various local and future needs, but also one rigid enough one to assure maintainability and cost-effectiveness. They must design the infrastructure in a way that permits information sharing and incorporating external sources, but that also ensures confidential information is protected.

Third, and perhaps most importantly, IT managers must instruct and educate their specialized IT *staff* to understand

---

[147] A solution is pareto-optimal if nobody's situation can be improved without worsening the situation for somebody else. If a solution is not pareto-optimal, then there is still room for improvement that is mutually beneficial.

the needs and constraints of the business side. They must hire business analysts or business engineers who can bridge the gap between information technology know-how and business understanding. Because they understand both the technological limitations and the business needs business engineers can find the optimal balance between various conflicting information quality criteria.

Implications for Knowledge Workers

Next to these management areas, one should not forget the main protagonists (and sometimes antagonists) of information quality: the actual producers and consumers of information, who – in the context of knowledge-intensive processes – are mostly highly qualified domain experts or, in other words, knowledge workers. With regard to information quality, knowledge workers have to ask themselves two key questions:

First, am I *receiving* high-quality information, that is to say, do I have access to relevant, sound information that is provided to me in a convenient process via a reliable infrastructure? If not, what can I do to increase the quality of information that I use as my input? Do I need to talk to my superior (the line manager), to my support functions (IT management), or to the information producers themselves? Or do I need to change the sources and media I use?

Second, am I *producing* and distributing high-quality information, that is to say is my information really relevant to my clients? Is it sound and delivered in an optimal way? If not, what do I need to do to improve this quality? Do I have to examine the needs and habits of my information consumers more closely? Should I make greater use of the internal review and validation mechanisms? Should I complain about an inadequate information delivery process and infrastructure?

As far as the first group of questions is concerned, knowledge workers need to assess their information *sources* and see whether these fit their information needs and preferences. They need to think about how they can judge the relevance and validity of information they use for their knowledge-intensive processes. As far as the second series of questions is concerned, knowledge workers need to assess their own skills critically and determine whether they really have mastered professional ways of making information concise, consistent, correct, and current.

Information quality in knowledge-intensive processes can represent a distinct competitive advantage to an organization. In order to exploit this advantage, top management must designate areas where information quality is a strategic priority. It must develop certain minimum standards and convey these to middle management, which in return assures that they are properly understood by the information producers. Middle managers must also ensure that their staff are involved in the standard-setting process, and that they understand the notion of information quality in a consistent way. On an operational level, line managers must ensure that review and feedback mechanisms are in place to continually optimize the level of information quality. To achieve this purpose, line managers must closely collaborate with their information technology department to align the content management process and infrastructure to the needs of the information producers, administrators, and consumers. The managers of information technology must not only design and implement these efficient processes and infrastructures, they should also mediate between the various stakeholders and the technological, resource, and security restrictions. They must ensure that their employees understand the needs of the business side. The knowledge workers themselves, finally, must constantly review their information in terms of input and output quality and reflect on their own needs, preferences and qualifications.

Conclusion

5.2 Overall Conclusion

There is a well-known anecdote about a man searching for the keys he lost outside a tavern. This parable may be an adequate summary of some of the main insights of this study. The man is crawling on the pavement underneath a street light which illuminates the dark alley. A second man comes out of the tavern, sees the man desperately searching on the ground and asks him what it is he is looking for.

"Leaving the restaurant, I dropped my keys," replies the man. The other man kindly offers his help and asks: "Do you remember where you may have dropped them?" "Of course I do", replies the other man, still crawling near the street light. "It was over there in that dark corner." The other man looks at him in bewilderment. "Well, why are you searching over here then, and not over there?" The man on the floor looks

The Story of the Lost Keys

up, hesitates, and calmly replies: "Because the lighting over here is much better."

It seems to me that the information quality discussion has more in common with this anecdote than one may think. Information has lost its value and we are searching for this value in many wrong – but better lit – places. When information doesn't tell us what we need to know, we look for more information, often aggravating the original problem or at least delaying its solution. When information doesn't help to communicate what we wish to convey, we provide more of it, again aggravating the problem (of information overload) instead of solving it.

In this book, we have looked at information quality from both a theoretical and a practical angle. In doing so, I have tried to shed light onto the dark corners of information quality, highlighting four ways in which value can be added to intellectual information products. The research tools used for this purpose were more like flashlights than street lamps. The case studies, focus groups, interviews and surveys focused on particular problems in specific application contexts and neglected many other contextual factors. This has enabled us to concentrate on proven practices that are used by information professionals to make information sound and useful. It has not given us a ready-to-use and fully developed methodology, but it has resulted in a clearer understanding of some of the decisive factors of information quality.

Based on this understanding, various methodologies that are tailored to specific contexts, such as web publications, market research, consulting, or product development can be envisioned.

Answer to the Initial Research Question

1. The main research question of this study regarded the factors determining information quality, or as originally stated: What determines the quality of information in knowledge-intensive processes? The resulting answer to this question is fourfold:

2. The quality of information is determined by the management of information on *four levels*: the target community level, the information product level, the content management process level, and the infrastructure level.

3. The quality of information is determined by a number of at times conflicting *criteria* and the matching of *criteria weight*s between information producers, custodians and consumers.

4. The quality of information is determined by the application of four principles or four *value-adding activities*. They are the integration principle (aggregating and compiling information), the validation principle (checking and evaluating information), the context principle (showing where information came from and what its purpose is), and the activation principle (making the information actionable).

5. The quality of information is determined by a number of contextual factors in the *workplace* of information producers, administrators, and consumers. These factors include training, coordination, infrastructure, and communication among these groups.

Outlook

While these results may be preliminary (as so often in the applied social sciences), I am confident that the topic of information quality is not, and that it is an issue that is here to stay. There are few research topics that are as pervasive and yet as fragmented as this one. A consolidation of information quality research can certainly be expected in the coming years. It is to be hoped that this book has contributed its small part towards such a consolidation.

Conclusion

This book has shown that the information quality field is of great relevance for many knowledge-intensive business processes. It has merely opened a door onto a research domain that will gain additional importance as information is multiplied, diluted, and commodified via the Internet. One possible counter-strategy on a personal, team, and organizational level is to create high-quality information by aligning it to the needs of the target communities, by assuring its intrinsic characteristics, by continually optimizing the content management and delivery process, and by providing a reliable information infrastructure. Specific and systematic ways of achieving relevant, sound, optimized and reliable information have been explored in this study.

5.3 Outlook: Moving beyond Data and Information Quality

The Importance of a Differentiated Vocabulary

It is a common practice in the main stream literature on information quality to use the terms data quality and information quality interchangeably. The main reason given for this lack of differentiation is that it makes problem-focused dis

cussions easier and less complicated and helps to avoid debates on definitions. In our view this is indeed true at times.
Nevertheless, if the future aim is to manage data, information
and knowledge systematically and consistently *to improve
decision making* in organizations, one cannot view these
terms as identical. In fact, one must extend the management
focus to include such functional notions as knowledge quality
and communication quality.

*Managing Quality
along the Entire
Information Value
Chain*

By doing so, management can differentiate and pinpoint
specific improvement areas and responsibilities along the
entire **information value chain** (Glazer 1993), which starts
with the *origination and processing of data*, continues with
their *aggregation and transformation into information*, and
finds its end in the *communication of information that leads
to insights* – knowledge – which enable adequate *decisions*.
In this outlook chapter we[148] will thus argue that the distinctions among these terms are decisive and make a difference
in terms of the effective management of the information
value chain. Specifically, we will distinguish among the concepts of data quality, information quality, communication
quality, and knowledge quality and show how these notions
inter-relate from a management point of view. In order to
illustrate these useful distinctions, we report from a real-life
case study on customer information management in a global
reinsurance company and show how these distinctions help to
reduce a number of problems.

*Definitions and
beyond*

In order to make the distinctions introduced earlier more
accessible and show their interdependencies, this section
defines each one briefly and gives examples of problems on
each level and relevant quality attributes for each of these
constructs.

Data Quality

Data quality is the characteristic of data sets to meet or to
exceed the requirements of the data creators, administrators
and data consumers in terms of data content, format, time,
infrastructure, process, and cost. Data that are of high quality
are an accurate, complete, and current representation of real-
life transactions or states that are accessible in a reliable,
timely, convenient and secure manner.

*Information
Quality*

Information quality designates the characteristic of an information product or service (e.g., a set of information bundled for a specific purpose) to be of high value to its users
and to meet or exceed the requirements of all its stakeholders.
The stakeholders of an information product or service are its
consumers, creators, custodians (or administrators), direct or

---

[148] I am grateful to Andreas Neus of IBM for input on this chapter.

indirect content providers, intermediaries, and regulators. High quality information is information that is fit for use and of direct, high value to its consumers, as it is free of errors or other deficiencies and meets certain functional criteria, as well as *aesthetic, economic* and *ethical* standards.[149]

Knowledge quality is the characteristic of an insight, skill, method, procedure, or experience to be proven, widely applicable and state-of-the art for a certain purpose. The quality aspect of knowledge relates both to its production process (e.g., whether the generated knowledge is validated and elicited, see Mengshoel & Delab 1993) and to its application process (whether it can be used in many contexts, by many people or not) This distinction of knowledge with regard to information and data can be found in the main stream literature on knowledge management (for example Davenport & Prusak 1998): Whereas knowledge answers how and why questions, information answers what, how many, who, and where questions.

Knowledge Quality

A fourth concept that is useful when examining the prerequisites of high quality decisions is communication quality. *Communication quality* is the characteristic of an interaction process among humans (but incl. computers as intermediaries) to meet or exceed their expectations with regard to the exchanged messages and with regard to the process of doing so. Communication quality influences how well high-quality information can be transformed into high-quality knowledge and how high-quality knowledge can be transferred from one person to another.[150] In Wong & Dalmadge 2004 for example, communication quality is defined along the dimensions of interactiveness (including coordination, timeliness and feedback), richness and precision.

Communication Quality

Based on these distinctions, we can examine different quality issues along the information value chain more systematically, as demonstrated by the table below that lists typical DQ, IQ, KQ, and CQ problems. They are structured into meaningful management dimensions, namely content aspects (relevance and soundness of content) and media aspects (the interaction process and infrastructure).

Problem Types

---

[149] In our main discussion of information quality, many aesthethic, economic and ethical issues have not been explored in depth. For a discussion on information aesthetics see: Doelker 1997 or Frownfelter-Lohrke, Fulkerson 2001 or Meyer 1996. For a discussion on the ethical attributes of information see Gasser 2000.

[150] See also the UBS case study on communicating quality in section 4.6.

Quality Dimension	Data Quality Problems	Information Quality Problems	Communication Quality Problems	Knowledge Quality Problems
Relevance	Data is missing (empty data fields)	Information is irrelevant to the tasks at hand	The communication partners are not the right ones.	Know-how is not relevant for the solution of pressing problems
	Data is incomplete (fragmented data fields)	Information is not directly applicable	The communication is not tailored to the target groups	Knowledge is limited to a narrow application scope
Soundness	Data is incorrect (wrong values entered)	Information is not concise, but rather wordy and lengthy	There are implicit misunderstandings among the communicators	Know-how is outdated, not state-of-the art
	Data fields are defined differently (inconsistently)	Information is difficult to understand	There is no feedback cycle	The explicit part of the knowledge is not documented well
	Data fields are duplicate/ exist more than once	Information sources are not traceable	There are distractions and interruptions in the communication	Knowledge is speculative and unsure to work in the context
Process	Data is not kept current	The information is not updated regularly	The communication is not timely, but lags behind action	The knowledge is not transferable in time to make decisions
Infrastructure	The database infrastructure is not scaleable	The information infrastructure is not secure	The communication infrastructure is difficult to use	The knowledge management infrastructure cannot be maintained

Table 32: Quality problems along the information value chain

Different Quality Attributes

These problems relate to different quality attributes in each area, some of which are similar or even identical, wile others differ radically as one moves from data to knowledge. The pivotal quality attributes for each such conceptual area are listed below.

One should note that it is possible that certain attributes are productive and useful at one step in the information value chain, while they are counter-productive in another step. This is for example the case for attributes such as redundancy or ambiguity: While redundant or ambiguous data are clearly signs of quality problems, this need not be the case for communication, where redundancy eases understanding and ambiguity may lead to creative tensions and new ideas.

Quality Dimensions	Data Quality Attributes	Information Quality Attributes	Communication Quality Attributes	Knowledge Quality Attributes
Relevance	Complete	Pertinent	Reciprocal	Proven
	Defined	Applicable	Targeted	Widely Applicable
Soundness	Accurate	Concise	Honest	State-of-the Art
	Consistent	Consistent	Authentic	Shareable
	Unambiguous	Interpretable	Fair	Justified / Reviewed
Process	Current	Up-to-date	Timely	Conducive to learning
	Determined	Interactive	Balanced	Contextualized
Infrastructure	Accessible	Fast	With Feedback possibility	Customizable
	Reliable and Secure	Ergonomic	Without interruptions	Usable
	Accessible	Adaptable	Without distortions	Traceable

Table 33: Examples of pivotal quality attributes of the four areas

How these attributes can be improved in a specific application context in order to avoid the problems listed in the table above is explored in the next section, where a case study from the financial services area is presented. The main objective in the case study is to improve decision quality by sequentially improving data quality, information quality, communication quality, and knowledge quality. In this section we illustrate how critical the drawn distinctions can be in real-life settings. For this purpose, we briefly summarize the problem that an (anomymized) international reinsurance company faced two years ago in managing its customer information on a global scale and aligning its client management decisions according to this globally aggregated information.

A Case Study on Connecting the Different Quality Conceptions

ReInsurerCorp has a divisional organization structure where the business is divided into U.S. Operation and Global Operations. The Global Operations are further organized in four business units, namely Property Casualty, Catastrophe, Life, and Specialty Lines. The Property Casualty is finally subdivided in various geographical regions. The *Property & Casualty* business is *the* traditional reinsurance business

(Property, Third Party Liability, Personal Accident, etc.). It is characterized by a lower profit margin, is not volatile, but has a more long-term oriented vision of their client relationship. The *Specialty Lines* include reinsurances in more specific fields, as for example in Agriculture (crop hail, forestry etc.), Aviation/Space, Marine (Hull, cargo), etc. In general, these businesses are more volatile with high risk exposures, low premium and a customer behavior that is quite opportunity driven. The underwriters active in these lines are specialists in the field. They are usually not worried about the relationship with the client, but more about the bottom line of their business. Many Specialty Line clients behave in quite an opportunistic manner and are not always long term oriented. The *Catastrophe* business is another traditional business of ReInsurerCorp and is highly volatile. Therefore, it has to be strictly controlled by a careful risk management. The *Life* business is a non-volatile business, with the traditional characteristics of long-term client relationships (i.e., contracts often last beyond the usual one year period). There are usually low profit margins; nevertheless ReInsurerCorp wants to strengthen its position in this market.

In relation with these organizational divisions there are two important functions at ReInsurerCorp; the one of the underwriter and the one of the client manager. The client manager is responsible for a geographically defined market. He has therefore a good territorial knowledge and is responsible for the continuity of the relationships with the clients. Moreover, he has underwriting capabilities for the Property and the Casualty businesses, but not for the Specialty Lines. In this latter business there are specific underwriters for every Specialty Line. Underwriters are specialists in their respective area (e.g. aviation) and typically do not have a business background, but one of the technical field, e.g. airplane engineering. This type of organization results in the situation that ReInsurerCorp's multi-line clients, i.e. clients which could or would sign reinsurance contracts in various lines of business, are not managed by one but by various officers of ReInsurerCorp and *a common client data, information and knowledge base and subsequent strategy was at that point not possible.* This is also due to another organizational issue: the flexible part of the rewarding system results in the fact that underwriters are in the first place interested in their Specialty Line whereas client managers mainly care for their geographical region. As a result, underwriters want to underwrite contracts with the clients only when a certain profit margin is predictable *within their business line.* Client managers instead adapt a more global vision on the client. Because of this effect, a few clients that were extremely important to the company were lost, because there was no company-wide assessment of their importance and no co-ordination to offer an improved and balanced contract.

In order to have a more integrated perspective on the clients ReInsurerCorp created a Global Client Centre. This centre was an initiative of the CEO and pursued the following goals:

- identify areas in which the clients are active but yet do not have contracts with ReInsurerCorp and thus represent areas where ReInsurerCorp could develop their business
- manage internal conflicts with regard to clients more effectively: have an overall strategy for clients and get a signed agreement from the various parties involved in a customer relationship.
- improve the skills necessary for an optimal client relationship and achieve a common standard in this regard in order to achieve a certain consistency in dealing with clients.

The Global Client Center developed two instruments to achieve the listed aims. One was the client matrix database, which lists the various clients of a certain geographical region and shows in which businesses ReInsurerCorp has contracts with the single client, where it could develop the business, and who established the contact. The client matrix permits to realize aim number one in combination with the client center. The Global Client Center organized meetings with all the officers engaged in the client relationship management for each geographical area to discuss the matrix and to achieve a global vision on the client (goal 2). The second instrument was a set of skills workshops for employees in direct contact with ReInsurerCorp's clients and should attain the third goal.

The Fragmented Client

In order to solve this problem of the 'fragmented client' and make the right decisions on which clients to keep and which to let go, ReInsurerCorp had to not only improve the data quality on its client (i.e., unifying customer data fields, unifying measurement systems, aggregating regional information,), but also the customer information quality (aligning the reporting categories, frequencies, styles, and layouts), the communication quality among the client managers (by having them have regular conference calls, meeting in a workshop context, and bi-laterally negotiating client parameters), and the knowledge quality (by training client managers on how to interact with customers to detect their negotiation style, their true motives, and their affinity to the company). By relying on a common, consistent customer database, that lead to consistent, timely client reports, which were then discussed personally and interpreted jointly in a high-quality communication process to gain high-level insights into the client's overall importance for the company, the Client Center was able to improve its decision making and keep the right clients. The following table summarizes the different implemented improvement measures and the quality attributes they affect:

Improvement Area	Improvement Measures	Improved Quality Attributes
Data Quality Measures	Make all customer data fields consistent Align customer data definitions Align measurement metrics and methods	Consistent, Complete, Accurate Unambiguous, Defined Reliable
Information Quality Measures	Align reporting categories Align reporting periods Align reporting layout Align reporting style Improve information aggregation process Improve aggregated information presentation (matrix)	Consistent Up-to-date Comprehensive Applicable Interpretable Interactive Concise, Fast, Ergonomic, Adaptable
Communication Quality Measures	Connect managers of same clients in different lines of business Bring those client managers together in common workshops Facilitate the communication visually by merging customer experiences and perceptions.	Targeted, Reciprocal, Fair Timely, Balanced, with Feedback, Without interruptions or distortions
Knowledge Quality Measures	Train client managers in interaction skills with customers Document decisions including the decision rationale (reasoning)	State-of-the Art, Applicable, Conducive to learning Customizable Shareable & Traceable

Table 34: Implemented improvement measures along the Information Value Chain

As a specific example of one of these improvement measures, the following screenshot shows how based on the existing customer data (that the client managers brought to the joint workshop on Excel sheets), information was visually integrated in real time (via a laptop connected to a beamer) and then applied to a common rating of each client through a visual ruler we developed. The documented decision was then captured visually through the same ruler communication tool and appended with explanatory comments to capture the rationale of the taken decision. In this way, the gathered client managers could not only aggregate data into common information, but also visualize it to represent their understanding and common insight into a customer on a company-wide level.

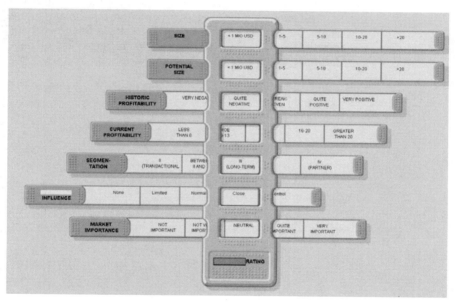

Figure 39: A joint, real-time customer rating based on aggregated global customer information

Merely improving data quality would in this case not have helped to significantly improve decision quality. For that purpose, the entire information value chain had to be examined, starting with improved data entry and capture and ending with explicitly documenting the taken decisions based on elicited and visualized new collective knowledge.

Conclusion

In this outlook chapter we have argued that treating information quality and data quality as synonyms forgoes the opportunity to improve the quality of the entire information value chain and thus ultimately to improve decision quality. We have added other distinctions to this triad, by introducing the notions of communication quality and knowledge quality. We have shown which problems are unique to each level and what kinds of attributes are crucial for each of these notions. We have also shown specific improvement measures in each area, based on a real-life case study from the reinsurance industry. We hope that this first step towards a more differentiated vocabulary can help to sharpen the focus and at the same time extend the scope of information value chain improvements. In our view, a rich, differentiated conceptual language is an important prerequisite for effectively improving and managing the modern information value chain. In this sense, the *quality of terminology* is a critical (theoretical and practical) prerequisite for the quality management of data, information, knowledge and communicaition.

Appendix

Overview

The Appendices contain a collection of all discussed information quality frameworks, and a glossary on central terms. It also contains additional material on the case studies (the study questions). The last section contains a self-test for managers to assess their current level of information quality management.

A. Information Quality Frameworks Survey

Lesca/Lesca (1995):

Information as product	Information as process
• usefulness	• trustworthiness
• comprehensibility	• accessibility
• relevancy	• objectivity
• completeness	• credibility
• adequate representation	• interactivity (feedback)
• coherence	
• clarity	

Königer/Reithmayer (1998):

Dimension	Criteria
1. Intrinsic Quality	Preciseness, Objectivity, Trustworthiness
2. Access Quality	Accessibility, Security
3. Contextual Quality	Relevance, Added value, Timeliness, Information content
4. Quality of Presentation	Interpretability, Understandability, Conciseness, Consistency
5. Quality of the Meta Information	Existence, Appropriateness
6. Quality of Structuring	Existence, Appropriateness, Understandability

Alexander/Tate (1999):

Criteria	Explanation
1. Authority	validated information, the institution behind the information is visible
2. Accuracy	reliable, free of errors
3. Objectivity	information is presented without personal biases
4. Currency	updated content
5. Target group orientation	clearly signaled target audience
6. Interaction & navigation design	Intuitive understanding of elements and their functions

Ruß-Mohl (1994/2000):

Criteria	Examples
Objectivity	Interests of author are revealed
Comprehensibility	Abbreviations are explained
Relevance	Geographic and social proximity to readers' interests
Currency	Fast, but validated information
Reduction of Complexity	Background reports
Transparency / Reflexivity	Clear editorial guidelines (mission) and a corrections corner. Reports about the media industry and about the editor's work
Interactivity	A neutral newspaper "referee". participation possibilities for readers (forum, phone numbers, clubs), a comprehensive website

Wang, Strong (1996):

Category	Dimension
Intrinsic IQ	Accuracy, Objectivity, Believability, Reputation
Accessibility IQ	Accessibility, Security
Contextual IQ	Relevancy, Value-Added, Timeliness, Completeness, Amount of Information
Representational IQ	Interpretability, Ease of Understanding, Concise Representation, Consistent Representation

Redman (1996) :

Perspective	Dimension	Criteria
Conceptual View	Content	Relevance, obtainability, clarity of definition
	Scope	Comprehensiveness, essentialness
	Level of Detail	Attribute granularity, precision of domains
	Composition	Naturalness, identifiably, homogeneity, minimum unnecessary redundancy
	View Consistency	Semantic consistency, structural consistency
	Reaction to Change	Robustness, flexibility
Values		Accuracy, completeness, consistency, currency / cycle time
Representation	Formats	Appropriateness, interpretability, format precision, format flexibility, ability to represent null values, efficient use of storage
	Physical Instances	representation consistency

English (1999):

Dimension	Criteria
Inherent Information Quality	• Definition conformance
	• Completeness (of values)
	• Validity or business rule conformance
	• Accuracy to surrogate source
	• Accuracy (to reality)
	• Precision
	• Nonduplication
	• Equivalence of redundant or distributed data
	• Concurrency of redundant or distributed data
	• Accessibility
Pragmatic Information Quality	• Timeliness
	• Contextual clarity
	• Derivation integrity
	• Usability
	• Rightness (or fact completeness)

Evaluation of seven prior frameworks:

Models: / Criteria:	Lesca / Lesca 1995	Koniger / Reithmeyer 1998	Alexander / Tate 1999	Russ-Mohl 1994/2000	Wang / Strong 1996	English 1999	Redman 1996
1. Definitions	All criteria are defined.	All criteria are defined.	All criteria are defined.	Definitions of certain criteria are relatively open (i.e. objectivity, reduction of complexity).	All criteria and dimensions are defined	All criteria are extensively defined	All criteria are defined.
2. Positioning	Positioned within internal communications for target groups students and managers	Positioned as a generic approach to information quality within the context of unstructured information.	Framework is positioned within usability and web design literature.	Framework is positioned within existing literature on quality in the mass media sector	Clearly positioned within existing information quality literature in the information technology context	A focus on data quality (and data warehouses) from a TQM (total quality management) perspective.	Positioned within database literature
3. Consistency	IQ dimensions are process and product perspective. No contradictions.	IQ- dimensions on the information product level only. No direct contradictions.	No dimensions are given, just a pure criteria list.	Not all criteria are operationalized in the framework.	Overall concise. Some criteria are quite similar such as interpretability and ease-of-understanding.	Not very consistent since different frameworks are used, not one consistent model.	Model is not always represented consistently.
4. Examples	Many short cases are provided	No cases or extended examples are provided	Many examples are provided.	Some US-based examples are provided.	Many examples are provided.	Short illustrative examples are provided	Many examples are provided.
5. Conciseness	12 criteria 2 in dimensions	18 criteria in 6 dimensions	6 criteria, no dimensions	7 criteria, no dimensions	16 criteria in 4 dimensions	15 criteria in two dimensions	27 criteria in 9 dimensions
6. Tools	Simple checklists and matrices are provided as conceptual tools	One simple checklist is provided	Checklists are provided	No management tools are provided	A comprehensive tool (questionnaire with software support) provided.	Extensive survey of available tools provided Many checklists included	Abstract step-by-step methods are provided.
Conclusion	Generic, practical	Generic, theoretical	Specific, practical	Specific, theoretical	Generic, balanced	Specific, practical	Specific, theoretical

B. Other Information Quality Frameworks

Taylor's (1986) Model of Value Added Information Services in MIS:

User Criteria of Choice	Interface (Value Added)	System (Value-added Processes: Examples)
Ease of Use	Browsing Formatting Interfacing I (Mediation) Interfacing II (Orientation) Ordering Physical Accessibility	Alphabetizing Highlighting important terms
Noise Reduction	Access I (Item identification) Access II (Subject description) Access III (Subject Summary) Linkage Precision Selectivity	Indexing Vocabulary control Filtering
Quality	**Accuracy Comprehensiveness Currency Reliability Validity**	**Quality control Editing Updating Analyzing and comparing data**
Adaptability	Closeness to problem Flexibility Simplicity Stimulatory	Provision of data manipulation capabilities Ranking output for relevance
Time-saving	Response Speed	Reduction of processing time
Cost-saving	Cost-saving	Lower connection-time price

The Financial Accounting Standards Board (1980) Hierarchy of Normative Information Qualities of Accounting Information

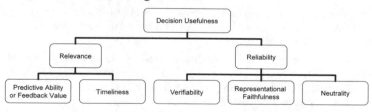

C. Information Quality Glossary

The following glossary provides a collection of helpful definitions. The definitions of the terms have to be interpreted in the context of this book. They are based on the concepts which are developed in the text and on a compilation of eleven knowledge management related glossaries, documented in Eppler, 1999b.

A

Abstraction: The process of moving from the specific to the general by neglecting minor differences or stressing common elements. Also used as a synonym for summarization.

Accuracy: Degree of conformity of a measure to a standard or a true value. Level of precision or detail.

Activation: A term that designates activities that make information more applicable and current, and its delivery and use more interactive and faster; a process that increases the usefulness of information by making it more vivid and organizing it in a way that it can be used directly without further repackaging.

Abstract: A concise and systematic summary of the key ideas of a book, article, speech, or any other kind of relevant information. See also: knowledge compression.

Accessibility: Capable of being reached, capable of being used or seen.

Aphorism: Concise, stimulating and self-sufficient words of wisdom that express a profound truth in a personal and yet accessible way; usually no more than two or three sentences long.

Applicability: The characteristic of information to be directly useful for a given context, information that is organized for action.

B

Believability: The quality of information and its source to evoke credibility based on the information itself or the history or reputation of the source.

Bias: In this context, an unconscious distortion in the interpretation of information.

C

Case study: An empirical inquiry that investigates a contemporary phenomenon within its real-life context; careful and systematic observation and recording of the experience of a single organization.

Categorization: Here, the conscious effort to group information items together based on common features, family resemblances, rules, membership gradience, or certain group prototypes (best examples of a category).

Context: A specific situation that defines the environment in which a piece of information originates or is interpreted.

Contextualization: The act of adding situational meta-information to information in order to make it more comprehensible and clear and easier to judge.

Clarity: Void of obscure language or expression, ease of understanding, interpretability.

Comprehensiveness: The quality of information to cover a topic to a degree or scope that is satisfactory to the information user.

Conciseness: Marked by brevity of expression or statement, free from all elaboration and superfluous detail.

Consistency: The condition of adhering together, the ability to be asserted together without contradiction.

Context: Here, the sum of associations, ideas, assumptions, and preconceptions that influence the interpretation of information; the situation of origination or application of a piece of information.

Contextualization: A term that designates activities that make information clearer, allow to see whether it is correct for a new situation, and enable a user to trace it back to its origin (in spite of system changes); a process that adds background to information about its origin and relevance.

Contextualizer: A mechanism that can be used to add context to a piece of information and thus increase its interpretability.

Correctness: Conforming to an approved or conventional standard, conforming to or agreeing with fact, logic, or known truth.

Communication: Here, the interchange of messages resulting in the transferal or creation of knowledge; the creation of shared understanding through interaction among two or more agents.

Convenience: Here, the ease-of-use or seamlessness by which information is acquired.

Criteria: Standards by which alternatives are judged. Attributes that describe certain (information) characteristics.

Criteria of information quality: They describe the characteristics that make information valuable to authors, administrators, or information users.

Currency: The quality or state of information of being up-to-date or not outdated.

D

Data: Raw, unrelated numbers or entries, e.g., in a database; raw forms of transactional representations.

Data deficiency: An unconformity between the view of the real-world system that can be inferred from a representing information system and the view that can be obtained by directly observing the real-world system.

Design: Here, the rendering of content in a communication medium; design is concerned with how things ought to be in order to attain goals and to function.

Disinformation: See misinformation.

Document identification keys: Concise alphanumeric labels that are attributed to documents according to a set of rules in order to facilitate their storage and retrieval.

E

Ease-of-use: The quality of an information environment to facilitate the access and manipulation of information in a way that is intuitive.

Evaluation: The activity of assessing the quality of a system or the information it contains.

Expert: A knowledge worker who has a high degree of domain specific knowledge and a high heuristic competence in the field of expertise.

Extranet: Semi-public TCP/IP network used by several collaborating partners.

F

Falsity: The characteristic of information not to correspond to facts, logic, or a given standard.

Fact: A statement that accurately reflects a state or characteristic of reality.

Frameworks of information quality: They group information criteria into meaningful categories.

Focus group: A market research technique where five to nine people discuss a topic with the help of a moderator in order to elicit common themes, problems, or opinions.

G

Generic information quality criteria: Attributes of information that are relevant regardless of the specific context, such as accessibility or clarity.

Gossip: Unsubstantiated, low-quality information that is passed on by word of mouth.

Groupthink: Occurs when the members of a highly cohesive group lose their willingness to evaluate each other's inputs critically. It is a phenomenon (coined by Irving Janis) that describes the negative effects that can take place in team dynamics, such as excluding information sources; a tendency in highly cohesive groups for members to seek consensus so strongly that they lose the willingness and ability to evaluate one another's ideas critically (see Northcraft & Neale, 1990, p. 377).

GUI: Graphical user interface; the visual component of a (typically operating system) software application (e.g., Macintosh's System X or Microsoft Windows).

H

Highlighting: Stressing the most essential elements of a document by emphasizing sentences or items visually through colors, larger or different fonts or through flagging icons.

Hypertext: This term refers to the computer-based organization of information by way of linking related (associated) information.

House of Quality: A standard quality management tool that consists of a matrix which relates customer requirements to technical specifications or functionalities.

I

Information: Information can be defined as all inputs that people process to gain understanding. It is a difference (a distinction) that makes a difference, an answer to a question. A set of related data that form a message.

Information Overload: A state in which information can no longer be internalized productively by the individual due to time constraints or the large volume of received information.

Information Quality: the fitness for use of information; information that meets the requirements of its authors, users, and administrators.

Information administrator: Person who is responsible for maintaining (see also maintainability) information or keeping an information system running.

Information consumer: Person who is accessing, interpreting and using information products, see also: knowledge worker.

Information producer: An author who is creating or assembling an information product or its elements.

Information value: Information quality (or alternatively: benefit) in relation to the acquisition and processing costs of information; potential of information to improve decisions by reducing uncertainty.

Informative: Imparting knowledge, instructive.

Interactivity: Being a two-way electronic communication system that involves a user's orders or responses.

Integration: A set of activities that makes information more comprehensive, concise, convenient, and accessible; combining information sources and aggregating content to ease the cognitive load on the information consumer.

Interpretation: The process of assigning meaning to a constructed representation of an object or event.

Interactivity: The capacity of an information system to react to the inputs of information consumers, to generate instant, tailored responses to a user's actions or inquiries.

Intranets: Internal company networks designed to provide a secure forum for sharing information, often in a web-browser type interface.

Ishikawa diagram: A chart that can be used to systematically gather the problem causes of quality defects. Sometimes referred to as the 5M- or 6M-chart because most causes can be related to man (e.g., human factors), machine, method, material, milieu (i.e., the work environment), or the medium (the IT-platform).

J

Judgmental quality criteria: Criteria based on personal (subjective) judgment rather than on objective measures (e.g., relevance, appeal).

Just-in-time information: Current information that is delivered in a timely manner (at the time of need), for example through a (profile-based) push mechanism.

K

Knowledge-intensive process: We define a knowledge-intensive process as a productive series of activities that involves information transformation and requires specialized professional knowledge. They can be characterized by their often non-routine nature (unclear problem space, many decision options), the high requirements in terms of continuous learning and innovation, and the crucial importance of interpersonal communication on the one side and the documentation of information on the other.

Knowledge: Justified true belief, the know-what/-how/-who/-why that individuals use to solve problems, make predictions or decisions, or take actions.

Knowledge compression: The skillful activity of extracting the main ideas and concepts from a piece of reasoned information and summarizing them in a consistent and concise manner.

Knowledge management: The conscious and systematic facilitation of knowledge creation or development, diffusion or transfer, safeguarding, and use at the individual, team- and organizational level.

Knowledge worker: Highly skilled professionals who are involved in the non-routine production, interpretation, and application of complex information.

Knowledge work: Knowledge work is human mental work performed to generate useful information. It involves analyzing and applying specialized expertise to solve problems, to generate ideas, or to create new products and services.

L

Labeling: Adding informative and concise titles to information items so that they can be more easily scanned, browsed, or checked for relevance. Labels should indicate the type of information (e.g., definition, example, rule) and its content (e.g., safety issues).

Learnability: The quality of information to be easily transformed into knowledge.

M

Maintainability: The characteristic of an information environment to be manageable at reasonable costs in terms of content volume, frequency, quality, and infrastructure. If a system is maintainable, information can be added, deleted, or changed efficiently.

Management Principle: A general, instructive, concise, and memorable statement that suggests a way of reasoning or acting that is effective and proven to reach a certain goal within an organizational context.

Metadata: Data which provides context or otherwise describes information in order to make it more valuable (e.g., more easily retrievable or maintainable); data about data.

Mining: A detailed method used by large firms to sort and analyze information to better understand their customers, products, markets, or any other phase of their business for which data has been captures. Mining data relies on statistical analyses, such as analysis of variance or trend analysis.

Misinformation: Information that is uninformative and impedes effective and adequate action because it is incorrect, distorted, buried, confusing because it lacks context, manipulated or otherwise difficult to use.

N

Nichification: A market trend that describes the strategy of incumbents or existing market players to consciously focus on specialized business models or business areas in order to distinguish themselves from competitors.

Non-quality costs: The costs that arise due to lacking information quality.

O

Overload: See information overload.

Objectivity: Expressing or dealing with facts or conditions as perceived without distortion by personal feelings, prejudices, or interpretations.

Origination: The source or author of a piece of information (may include additional origination parameters, such as date, institution, contributors etc.).

P

Paralysis by analysis: When timely decision-making fails to occur because too much low quality information (irrelevant, detailed, obsolete, or poorly organized) is readily available.

Personalization: The act of modifying content or an information system to customize it to the needs and preferences of an information consumer.

Pragmatic (information quality dimension): The characteristics that make information useful or usable.

Pragmatism: A school of thought pioneered by C.S. Peirce and William James that emphasizes the practical consequences of ideas or theories as a criterion of their adequacy.

Principles of information quality: They describe how the quality of information can be increased by focusing on crucial criteria and crucial improvement measures.

Process: A group of sequenced tasks, which eventually lead to a value for (internal or external) customers.

Q

Quality: The totality of features of a product or service that fulfill stated or implied needs (ISO 8402). The correspondence to specifications, expectations or usage requirements. The absence of errors.

Quality Management: See Total Quality Management. Generally speaking, the systematic on-going effort of a company to assure that its products and service consistently meet or exceed customer expectations.

R

Rating (of information or of a source): The (standardized) evaluation of a piece of information or its source according to a given scale by one or several reviewers or readers.

Redundancy: Here, the provision of information beyond necessity.

Reliability (of an infrastructure): Here, the characteristic of an information infrastructure to store and retrieve information in an accessible, secure, maintainable, and fast manner.

Reputation: Here, the characteristic of a source to be consistently associated with the provision of high quality information.

Response time: Here, the delay between an initial information request and the provision of that information by the information system.

Reviewing: Here, the systematic evaluation of information such as articles, papers, project summaries, etc. by at least one independent qualified person according to specified criteria (such as relevance to target group, methodological rigor, readability, etc.).

S

Salience (of information): The quality of information to be interesting or intriguing.

Security (of information): Measures taken to guard information against unauthorized access, espionage or sabotage, crime, attack, unauthorized modification, or deletion.

Sensitivity analysis: A procedure to determine the sensitivity of the outcomes of an alternative to changes in its parameters; it is used to ascertain how a given model output depends upon the input parameters.

Stability (of information): The quality of information or its infrastructure to remain unaltered for an extended period of time.

T

Tacit knowledge: Know-how that is difficult to articulate and share; intuition or skills that cannot easily be put into words. The term was coined in the 1950s by MICHAEL POLANYI.

Timeliness: Coming early or at the right, appropriate or adapted to the times or the occasion.

Total Quality Management: A management concept (and associated tools) that involves the entire workforce in focusing on customer satisfaction and continuous improvement.

Total Data Quality Management (TDQM) cycle: The TDQM cycle encompasses four components. The definition component of the TDQM cycle identifies IQ dimensions, the measurement component produces IQ metrics, the analysis component identifies root causes for IQ problems and calculates the impacts of poor-quality information, and finally, the improvement component provides techniques for improving IQ. See Huang et al. (1999).

Tradeoff: Here, a conflict among two qualities of information that tend to be mutually exclusive.

Traceability: The quality of information to be linked to its background or sources.

U

Usability: The characteristic of an information environment to be user-friendly in all its aspects (easy to learn, use, and remember).

Usefulness: The quality of having utility and especially practical worth or applicability.

V

Validation: Evaluating and checking the accuracy, consistency, timeliness, and security of information, for example by evaluating the believability or reputation of its source.

Visualization: The use of graphic means to represent information.

W

World Wide Web: The graphical user-interface of the Internet based on the http and TCP/IP protocol and the HTML code language.

Warehouse: In the current context a common metaphor to describe an electronic data repository.

X

XML: A generic mark-up language that can be used to structure on-line documents meaningfully.

Z

Zero-faults or zero errors: Here, the quality of information to be one hundred percent correct.

D. Study Questions for the Information Quality Cases

The goal of this appendix is to provide readers, especially students, with discussion questions on each one of the six information quality case studies provided in this book. This can enable a more systematic reflection on the topics discussed in the various cases. The study questions can also be used in a classroom-context to bring the research topic to life through interactive sessions and problem discussions. Some of the questions have been provided by the case protagonists (e.g., issues that they are currently struggling with), but most of them have been formulated by the author.

Goal

1. How can IHA·GfK improve the impact of its Market Reports?
2. What are feasible growth strategies for the company? How can the research competence be leveraged?
3. Which may be new competitors for IHA·GfK? What strategic threats does the company face (and from whom)?
4. What can be learned for other contexts from these reports? How do you generally make information more concise?
5. Use the four IQ-principles in this case to show the strong and weak points of IHA·GfK reports.

IHA·GfK Case Questions

1. Which are the entry barriers for this knowledge-based business?
2. Why is the book abstract production process a knowledge-intensive process? What typical knowledge work problems can be observed?
3. What is the biggest improvement area in the knowledge compression process at getAbstract?
4. Which measures should be taken to improve the current knowledge compression process and the offered services and infrastructure?
5. Where do you see the potential of this business idea? Where would the compression of knowledge make sense elsewhere? Outline two brief scenarios for knowledge compression in the business context.
6. Which characteristics of knowledge have not been adequately dealt with in the book abstracts? Where do you see dangers of relying on compressed knowledge instead of a full business book?

GetAbstract Case Questions

7. In what aspect is getAbstract a virtual knowledge network and where does it lack knowledge networking? Outline current strengths and weaknesses of the company in regard to the effective use of collective knowledge.

Gartner Case Questions

1. How can Gartner improve the impact of its reports? Which criteria are not addressed properly as of now? What can be done to improve them (in regard to process, infrastructure, community orientation, etc.)?
2. What are feasible growth strategies for the company? How can the research competence be leveraged in other areas?
3. Which may be new competitors for Gartner? What strategic threats does the company face (and from whom)?
4. What can be learned for other contexts from these reports? How do you generally make information more consistent and accurate? What would be other generic diagrams such as the Magic Quadrants?
5. What could be done to improve the probability rating schema? What can make it more useful and valuable to customers?
6. Use the four IQ-principles in this case to show the strong and weak points of a Gartner competitor (Meta, Forrester, Giga).

Giga Case Questions

1. What are the main benefits and disadvantages of Giga's quality management system? Should it be modified and if so, how?
2. How could the impact of Giga's advice be further improved? What would be other feasible ways of activating the content of Giga for its clients?
3. Outline how IdeaBytes should be aggregated to larger documents, such as Planning Assumptions. How should an analyst proceed in compiling larger documents from smaller ones?
4. How can the idea of a 'catalyst' be used in other contexts? Where would it be worthwhile to add a catalyst section to documents?
5. How would you make the documents more easily accessible? What are feasible ways of indexing, categorizing, or mapping the IdeaBytes?
6. How would you assure that obsolete or outdated IdeaBytes or Planning Assumptions are removed from the knowledge base? List four specific ways of cleansing the repository.
7. What can IT advisory companies generally do to win the trust of current and potential clients? How can they as-

sure neutrality and independence and signal those values to the market?

1. What can be done to improve the impact of the communication guidelines? *UBS*
2. Which areas should additionally be covered by communication guidelines?
3. Analyze the described method to devise the guidelines. What other ways exist to come up with useful guidelines? Was it really necessary to invite so many communication managers?
4. Research e-mail and meeting guidelines on the Internet and compare them to the guidelines in the case study. What differences can you detect?
5. Which alternative means exist to change the communicative behavior of employees to produce high-quality information?

1. How can the EIU grow its business? Which strategic *EIU*
   directions do you suggest to leverage its content and expertise?
2. How can the sponsorship issue impact the information quality provided by the EIU?
3. What other online interaction features could improve information quality attributes, especially applicability?
4. What other general improvements can be made regarding the information quality of the country risk reports?
5. Which of the EIU mechanisms can be used by other companies? How?

E. Information Quality Assessment – A Self-Test for Information Providers and Knowledge Workers

Use of the Test

With the following short test you can analyze the information product that you provide to your clients and information consumers. This diagnostic self-test reveals whether your information is likely to meet customer expectations or not.

Do you provide value-added, high-quality information?

Overview

Please respond honestly to all of the following twenty questions. Your answers should always be either yes or no. The interpretation of the results is given at the end of the test.

		YES	NO
1.	Is there a simple and direct way for information consumers to give feedback to information producers? (For example: from readers to authors, from users to administrators)	☐	☐
2.	Is all the information that goes out to a client double-checked by at least two people?	☐	☐
3.	Do all the information producers adhere to the same content guidelines and templates? Do all documents share the same look and feel? (In other words, do the authors use consistent templates for their information or does everybody do his own thing?)	☐	☐
4.	Is there a summary or synopsis for all information that exceeds one page?	☐	☐
5.	Does every information include background material such as author information, version, sources, and further references.	☐	☐
6.	Does every information product contain a date of creation or last update?	☐	☐
7.	Do you systematically and visibly highlight information that is of crucial importance among the rest of the information?	☐	☐
8.	Is there a regular, direct exchange between all of the information producers? Do they see each other's work and can they criticize their contributions mutually?	☐	☐

9. Are high-quality contributions rewarded? Is there an explicit incentive for information producers to excel? Is value-added information explicitly encouraged or acknowledged (price, mentioning, part of the job evaluation or the MBOs)? ☐ ☐

10. Do you explicitly tell the customer how to use the information you provide? Are there action items, implementation aids, or 'bottom lines' in every document that help to put the information into practice? ☐ ☐

11. Do you assist the customer in storing or organizing the information that you provide to him? ☐ ☐

12. Do information producers/authors spend less than ten percent of their time on repetitive administration tasks? ☐ ☐

13. Are your clients automatically notified when the information that you have provided to them earlier has changed or needs to be corrected? ☐ ☐

14. Do you explicitly indicate the level of certitude associated with your information? In other words, do you clearly indicate when information accuracy is not a hundred percent guaranteed? ☐ ☐

15. Does the client have the possibility to directly contact the producer (or author) of the information and ask follow-up questions? ☐ ☐

16. Do you deliver the information in a technical format that is directly usable by the customer and his applications (or does the customer have to convert the information first)? ☐ ☐

17. Is there a way to interactively explore the information you provide to clients? (For example: can they zoom in to get more detail, or can they change the format; can they directly access further sources or modify elements and see the consequences) ☐ ☐

18. Are the expectations of the customer in regard to information made explicit and documented (in terms of scope, timing, level of detail, etc.)? ☐ ☐

19. Do you know of all ways in which the customers use the information that you provide? ☐ ☐

20. Do you generally include illustrative examples in the information you provide? ☐ ☐

Please add now all the questions that you have answered with NO. How many times did you answer negatively? If you have answered less than ten times with a no, then the quality of your information may already be quite high. You only suffer of a few symptoms of deteriorating information quality. The hints provided below may help you to overcome them and further increase the value of your information for customers and business partners.

Interpretation of the Results

No < 10

No >= 10

If you have answered ten or more questions with a no, the quality of your information can be significantly improved to meet customer expectations more consistently. Below you find four specific ways in which you can increase the value of your information for your clients.

Four Ways to Foster Information Quality

- **Integrate** or aggregate information to make it more concise and speed up the search process. Provide summaries, abstracts, or overviews before going into details.
- **Validate** or check information before it goes to the client. Check for internal consistency and review the credibility of your sources. Check whether the information is still up-to-date and if all numbers or facts are accurate. Make sure the information meets customer expectations in terms of scope, timing, language, and technical format.
- **Provide a context** for the information. Explicitly state for whom it is important and why. Explain how it originated and where (and when). Outline the specific situation in which the information can be applied and point at its limits. Provide the background of the information in terms of the sources and contributors.
- **Activate** your information in the heads of the information consumers. Use metaphors, repetitions, anecdotes, examples, pictures, and questions to ensure that the provided information can be transformed into personal knowledge. Link new information to what the audience or target group already knows.

References

The following bibliography lists all cited works in alphabetical order. Entries that are printed in **bold face** in the left margin are especially relevant to the domain of information quality research as it is examined in this book.

Accenture 2004   Accenture (2004) *eGovernment leadership: High performance, maximum value*. eGovernment Executive Series. New York: Accenture.

Ackhoff 1967   Ackhoff, R.L. (1967) Management Information Systems, in: *Management Science*, 14:4, December, pp. B147-B156.

Adelaku/ Enholm 1998   Adelakun, O., Enholm, K. (1998) Information Systems Quality Process in Theory and Practice: Results from a Preliminary Case Study, in: Chengular-Smith, I. and Pipino. L.L. (Eds.) *Proceedings of the 1998 Conference on Information Quality,* Massachusetts: MIT, pp.116-136.

Agosta 2000   Agosta, L. (2000) *Data Quality Methodologies and Technologies*, Giga Information Group, Planning Assumption, August 30, 2000. URL: www.gigaweb.com [14.08.2001]

Akman 2000   Akman, V. (2000) Rethinking Context as a Social Construct, in: *Journal of Pragmatics* 32(6), pp. 743-759. URL: http://www.cs.bilkent.edu.tr/~akman/jour-papers/jprag/jopfinal.ps [09.07.01]

Albrecht 2001   Albrecht, K. (2001) Information Quality, in: *Executive Excellence*, Vol. 18 Issue 8, p.11.

Alesandrini 1992   Alesandrini, K. (1992) *Survive Information Overload, The 7 best ways to manage your workload by seeing the big picture*, Homewood: Business One Irwin.

Alexande/ Tate 1999   Alexander, J. E.; Tate, M. A. (1999) *Web wisdom: how to evaluate and create information quality on the web*, Mahwah, NJ: Erlbaum.

Allen 1994   Allen, N. (1994) *How to Use Gartner Group's Probabilities*, Gartner Research Note, September 8, 1994, URL: www.gartnerweb.com [10.08.01]

Alvesson 2000   Alvesson, M. (2000) Social Identity and the Problem of Loyalty in Knowledge-intensive Companies, in: Journal of Management Studies, December, 37:8, pp. 1101-1123.

Ambrozia/ *Ambroziak 1999*	Ambroziak, B.M., Ambroziak, J.R. (1999) *Infinite Perspectives. Two Thousand Years of Three-Dimensional Mapmaking*, New York: Princeton Architectural Press.
Anderson 1983	Anderson, A. (1983) *Graphing financial information: How accountants can use graphs to communicate*. New York: National Association of Accountants.
Andersen/Smith *1999*	IEW Scenario: *Virtualizing the Office*, Gartner, Strategic Analysis Report, October 27th 1999. URL: www.gartnerweb.com [13.08.2001].
Arbnor/Bjerke ***1997***	Arbnor, I., Bjerke, B. (1997) *Methodology for Creating Business Knowledge*, Thousand Oaks: Sage.
Argyris 1983	Argyris, C. (1983) Action science and intervention, in: *Journal of Applied Behavioural Science*, 19, pp. 115-140.
Argyris & Schön *1989*	Argyris, C., Schön, D.A. (1989) Participative action research and action science compared: a commentary, in: *American Behavioural Scientist*, 32, pp. 612-623.
Aristotle 1976	Aristotle (1976) *The Nicomachean Ethics*, London: Penguin Books.
Arnold 1995	Arnold, S.E. (1995) Information Manufacturing: A Historical View of Quality Engineering, in: Basch, R. (Ed.) *Electronic Information Delivery. Ensuring Quality and Value*, Aldershot: Gower, pp. 13-30.
Astley/Zammuto *1992*	Astley, W.G.; Zammuto, R.F. (1992) Organization Science, Managers, and Language Games, in: *Organization Science*, 3: 4, pp. 443-460.
Augustin/ *Reminger 1990*	Augustin, S.; Reminger, B. (1990) Trotz Datenflut jede Menge Informationsdefizit! - Ist das erfolgreiche JIT-Konzept auch in der Info-Welt realisierbar?, in: Bäck, H. (Ed.) *Der informierte Manager*, Köln: TÜV Rheinland, pp. 73-82.
Bair 1998	Bair, J. (1998) *Dimensions of KM Technology Selection*, Gartner Inc. Research Note, 13th of October, source: www.gartnerweb.com, download date: 9.3.99.
Baker/Fraser *1995*	Baker, R., Fraser, R.C. (1995) Development of review criteria: linking guidelines and assessment of quality, in: *British Medical Journal*, 311, pp. 370-373.
Ballou/Pazer 1987	Ballou, D. P.; Pazer, H. L. (1987) Designing Information Systems to Optimize the Accuracy-Timeliness Tradeoff, in: *Information Systems Research*, 6(1), pp.509-521.
Ballou/Wang/ *Pazer/Tayi 1998*	Ballou, D. P.; Wang, R., Pazer, H., Tayi, G. K. (1998) Modeling information manufacturing systems to determine information product quality, in: *Management Science*, Apr98, Vol. 44 Issue 4, pp. 462- 484.
Baburoglu & *Ravn 1992*	Baburoglu, O.N./Ravn, I. (1992) Normative Action Research, in: *Organization Studies*, 13: 1, p. 19-34.

Barnes & Vidgen 2003	Barnes, S. and Vidgen, R.T. (2003) Assessing the Quality of a Cross-National e-Government Web Site: a Case Study of the Forum on Strategic Management Knowledge Exchange, in: *Proceedings of the 36th Hawaii International Conference on System Sciences (HICSS'03)*, Hawaii: IEEE.
Barry & Schamber 1998	Barry, C.L., Schamber, L. (1998) Users' Criteria for Relevance Evaluation: A Cross-Situational Comparison, in: *Information Processing & Management*, Vol. 34, No. 2/3, pp. 219-236.
Bateson 1972	Bateson, G. (1972) *Steps to an Ecology of Mind.* London: Ballentine.
Baur 2001	Baur, R. (2001) *Kontextualisierung von Information und Wissen in wissensintensiven Prozessen.* Unpublished Master Thesis, St. Gallen: University of St. Gallen.
Becker et al. 2004	Becker, J., Algermissen, L., and Niehaves, B. (2004) Processes in e-Government Focus: A Procedure Model for Process Oriented Reorganisation in Public Administrations on the Local Level. *Proceedings of the Second International Conference on Electronic Government.* Prague, Czech Republic. Lecture Notes of Computer Science: 147-150.
Belcher et al. 2000	Belcher, M., Place, E., Conole, G. (2000) Quality assurance in subject gateways : creating high quality portals on the Internet, in : *Library Consortium Management : An International Journal*, Vol. 2 No. 3/4, pp. 81-96.
Belleza 1983	Belleza, F.S. (1983) Mnemonic-device instruction with adults, in: Pressley, M., Levin, J.R. (Eds.) *Cognitive Strategy Research: Psychological Foundations.* New York: Springer
Berelson & Steiner 1964	Berelson, B., Steiner, G. (1964) *Human Behavior: An Inventory of Scientific Findings*, New York: Harcourt Brace Jovanovich.
Berger & Luckmann 1966	Berger, P.L., Luckmann, T. (1966) *The Social Construction of Reality*, New York: Doubleday.
Berti 1998	Berti, L. (1998) From Data Source Quality to Information Quality: The Relative Dimensions, in: Chengalur-Smith, I.; Pipino, L. L. (1998) *Proceedings of the 1998 Conference on Information Quality*, Cambridge, MA: Massachusetts Institute of Technology.
Bertin 1973	Bertin, J. (1973) Sémiologie Graphique, Paris: Mouton.
Bradley/Braude 1995	Bradley, Braude, M. (1995) *The "Magic Quadrant" Process*, Gartner Research Note, February 22 1995, URL: www.gartnerweb.com [10.08.01]
Brien 1991	Brien, J. O. (1991) *Introduction to Information Systems in Business Management*, Sixth Edition. Boston: Irwin.
Brocks 2000	Brocks, M. (2000) *Wissensarbeit im Consultingkontext: Die Rolle der Informationsqualität*, unpublished Master Thesis, St. Gallen: Universität St. Gallen, 2000.

Burkert & Eppler 1999	Burkert, H., Eppler, M. (1999) Wissensmanagement im Recht: Möglichkeiten und Grenzen einer wissensorientierten Rechtsbetrachtung, in: *Multimedia und Recht*, Nr. 10, 1999, pp. 627-630.
Buzan/Buzan 1997	Buzan, T., Buzan, B. (1997) *Das Mind-Map Buch*, Landsberg: mvg.
Cantoni et al. 2003	Cantoni, L., Di Blas, N. and Bolchini, D. (2003) *Comunicazione, qualità, usabilità.* Milan: Apogeo.
Carlisle/Dean 1999	Carlisle, Y., Dean, A. (1999) Design As Knowledge Integration Capability, in: *Creativity and Innovation Management*, Volume 8, Number 2 (June), pp. 112-121.
Carter & Belanger 2004	Carter, L. and Belanger, F. (2004) Citizen Adoption of Electronic Government Initiatives, in *Proceedings of the 37th Hawaii International Conference on System Sciences (HICSS'04)*, Hawaii: IEEE.
Chae et al. 2000	Chae, M., Kim, H., Choi, Y., Kim, J. and Ryu, H. (2000) Premier pas of mobile Internet business: A Survey research on Mobile Internet business, in: *Proceedings of KMIS/OA'2000*, pp. 218-222.
Clausen 1996	Clausen, H. (1996) Web information quality as seen from the libraries, in: *New Library World*, Vol. 97, Number 1130, pp. 4-8.
Clikeman 1999	Clikeman, P.M. (1999) Improving Information Quality, in: *Internal Auditor*, June 1999, Vol. 56 Issue 3, pp. 32-34.
Collins 1997	Collins, D. (1997) Knowledge work or working knowledge? Ambiguity and confusion in the analysis of the "knowledge age", in: *Employee Relations*, Vol. 19, No. 1, pp. 38-50.
Cornell/Brenner 1993	Cornell, P., Brenner, P. (1993) Field Research on Knowledge Work Process – In Situ Learning, in: *Proceedings of the IFMA 1993 Conference*, September 1993. URL: www.steelchase.com/knowledgebase/insitu.htm [12.07.2001].
D'Arcy 1999	D'Arcy, J. (1999) Bridging the Knowledge Gap, in: *Security Management*, Vol. 43 Issue 7, pp. 31-34.
Davenport 1993	Davenport, T. H. (1993) *Process innovation - reengineering work through information technology*, Boston: Harvard Business School Press.
Davenport 1997	Davenport, T. (1997) *Information Ecology: Mastering the Information and Knowledge Environment*, Oxford: Oxford University Press.
Davenport et al. 1996	Davenport, T.H., Jarvenpaa, S.L., Beers, M.C. (1996) Improving Knowledge Work Processes, in: *Sloan Management Review*, Volume 37, No. 4 (Summer), pp. 53-65
Davenport / Prusak 1998	Davenport, T. and Prusak, L. (1998) *Working Knowledge: How Organizations Manage What They Know*, Cambridge: Harvard Business School Press.
Davis/Naumann 1997	Davis, G.B., Naumann, J. (1997) *Personal Productivity with Information Technology*, New York: McGraw Hill.

Dawes et al. 2003   Dawes, S.S., Pardo, T.A., and Cresswell, A.M. (2003). Designing Government Information Access Programs: A Holistic Approach, *in: Proceedings of the 36th Hawaii International Conference on System Sciences (HICSS'03)*, Hawaii: IEEE.

Decina et al. (1999)   Decina, M., Cantoni, L., Lepori, B., Mazza, R., Januzzi, P., (1999) The SwissCast information push service: A multidisciplinary research, a multifaceted experience, in: *ACM SIGIR'99 Workshop on Customised Information Delivery*, URL: www.ted.cmis.csiro.au/ sigir99/decina

Del Percio 2000   Del Percio, V. (2000) *Valutare la qualità di siti web: proposta di uno schema per una metrica*, Memoria di Licenza, Lugano: Università della Svizzera Italiana.

Deming 1986   Deming, E.W. (1986) *Out of the Crisis,* Cambridge, MA: MIT Center for Advanced Engineering Study.

Despress/Hiltrop 1995   Despress, C., Hiltrop, J.M. (1995) Human resource management in the knowledge age: current practice and perspectives on the future, in: *Employee Relations*, Vol. 17, No 1, pp. 22-32.

Doelker 1997   Doelker, C. (1997) Ein Bild ist mehr als ein Bild, Stuttgart: Klett Cotta.

Donath 1998   Donath, B. (1998) 'Show me the money': How marketers measure "value.", in: *ISBM Insights*, Vol. 8 No.2, Institute for the Study of Business Markets, Smeal College of Business Administration, Penn State.

Driver/Streufert 1969   Driver, M.J. and Streufert, S. (1969) Integrative Complexity: An Approach to Individuals and Groups as Information Processing Systems, in: *Administrative Science Quarterly*, June 1969, pp. 272-285

Drucker 1991   Drucker, P. F. (1991) The new productivity challenge, in: *Harvard Business Review*, Nov-Dec, pp. 66-79.

Drucker 1994   Drucker, P.F. (1994) The Age of Social Transformation, in: *The Atlantic Monthly*, Vol. 274, No. 5 (November), pp. 53-80.

Drucker 1999   Drucker, P.F. (1991) Management. An Abridged and Revised Version of Management: Tasks, Responsibilities, Practices. Oxford: Oxford University Press.

Drucker 1999   Drucker, P. F. (1999) Knowledge-Worker Productivity: The Biggest Challenge, in: *California Management Review*, Winter Issue.

Eisenhardt 1989   Eisenhardt, K.M. (1989) Building Theories from Case Study Research, in: *Academy of Management Review*, Vol. 14, No. 4 (October), pp. 532-550.

Eisenhardt Sull 2001   Eisenhardt, K.M. and Sull, D.N. (2001) Strategy as Simple Rules, in: *Harvard Business Review*, January 2001, pp. 107-116.

Eisenhardt et al. 1988	Eisenhardt, P., Kurth, D., Stiehl, H. (1989) *Du steigst nie zweimal in denselben Fluss. Die Grenzen der wissenschaftlichen Erkenntnis.* Reinbeck: Rowohlt.
Elden & Chisholm 1993	Elden, M., and Chisholm, R. F. (1993) Emerging varieties of action research: introduction to the special issue, in: *Human Relations*, 46(2), pp.121-142.
English 1999	English, L. (1999) *Improving Data Warehouse and Business Information Quality.* Wiley & Sons: New York.
Eppler 1997	Eppler, M. (1997) Information oder Konfusion – Neue Kriterien für die betriebliche Kommunikation, in: *io management*, Nr. 5, pp. 38-41.
Eppler 1998	Eppler, M. (1998) *Informative Action: An Analysis of Management and the Information Overload*, unpublished Ph.D. thesis, Geneva: University of Geneva.
Eppler 1999	Eppler, M. (1999) Qualitätsstandards – Ein Instrument zur Sicherung der Informationsqualität in Multimedia-Produktionen, in: Merx, O. (Ed.) *Qualitätssicherung in Multimedia-Projekten*, Berlin: Springer Verlag, pp. 129-148.
Eppler 1999b	Eppler, M. (1999) *Knowledge Management Terminology*, Arbeitsbericht des Kompetenzzentrums EKM der Universität St. Gallen, Bericht Nr.: HSG/MCM/CC EKM/24 vom September 1999, St. Gallen.
Eppler 1999c	Eppler, M. (1999) *Conceptual Management Tools: A Guide to Essential Models for Knowledge Workers*, St. Gallen: NetAcademy Press.
Eppler et al. 1999	Eppler, M., Röpnack A., Seifried P. (1999) Improving Knowledge Intensive Processes through an Enterprise Knowledge Medium, in Prasad, J. (Ed.) Proceedings of the 1999 ACM SIGCPR Conference *Managing Organizational Knowledge for Strategic Advantage: The Key Role of Information Technology and Personnel*, pp. 222-230.
Eppler/ Muenzenmayer 1999	Eppler, M., Muenzenmayer, P. (1999) Information Quality on Corporate Intranets: Conceptualization and Measurement. In: *Proceedings of the 1999 Conference on Information Quality*, Massachusetts: MIT.
Eppler/Sukowski 2000	Eppler, M., Sukowski, O. (2000) Managing Team Knowledge: Core Processes, Tools and Enabling Factors, in: *European Management Journal*, June 2000, pp. 334-341.
Eppler 2001	Eppler, M. (2001) Increasing Information Quality through Knowledge Management Systems, in: *Proceedings of the 2001 International Conference on Information Systems and Engineering*, Las Vegas: IEEE Print, 2001.
Eppler & Probst 2001	Eppler, M., Probst, G. (2001) Informationsqualität statt Information-Overload, in: *Manager Bilanz*, Ausgabe III, p. 38-41.

Eppler et al. 2001   Eppler, M., Snoy, R., Mathis, R. (1999) *Qualität im Internet: eine empirische Studie zu den Gütekriterien, Erfolgsfaktoren und Defiziten von Websites aus Sicht der Benutzer*, Hergiswil: IHA·GfK.

Eppler 2003   Eppler, M. (2003) Managing Information Quality: Everyone has a role to play. *Cutter IT Journal*, 16 (1):13-17.

Eppler et al. 2003   Eppler, M., Algesheimer, R., and Dimpfel, M. (2003) Quality Criteria of Content-Driven Websites and their Influence on Customer Satisfaction and Loyalty: An Empirical Test of an Information Quality Framework, in: *Proceedings of the 8th MIT Information Quality Conference*. Boston: MIT, 108-120.

Eppler et al. 2005   Eppler, M.J., Gasser, U., and Helfert, M. 2005. Information Quality: Organizational, Technological, and Legal Perspectives. *Studies in Communication Sciences*. 2(4): 1-16.

Evans/Lindsay 1999   Evans, J.R., Lindsay, W.M. (1999) *The Management and Control of Quality*, 4th Edition, Cincinnati: South-Western College Publishing.

Ewing 1974   Ewing, D.W. (1974) *Writing For Results in Business, Government, and the Professions*, Geneva: Management Editions, 1974.

FASB 1980   Financial Accounting Standards Board (1980) *Statement of Financial Accounting Concepts No. 2: Qualitative Characteristics of Accounting Information*, FASB, May, 1980.

Flasch 2000   Flasch, K. (2000) *Das philosophische Denken im Mittelalter: von Augustin bis Machiavelli*, 2nd Edition, Ditzingen: Reclam.

Fleming/ Phifer 1998   Fleming, M., Phifer, G. (1998) *Personalizing Content on an Intranet Portal*, 5th of October 1998, Gartner Inc. Research Note.

Fleming 1999   Fleming, M. (1999) *Measuring the Value of Knowledge Content*, 21st of January 1999, Gartner Inc. Research Note.

Frownfelter-Lohrke/Fulkerson 2001   Frownfelter-Lohrke, C., Fulkerson, C.L. (2001) The Incidence and Quality of Graphics in Annual Reports: An International Comparison, in: *The Journal of Business Communication*, Vol. 38, No. 3, July 2001, pp. 337-358.

Fuld 1998   Fuld, L.M. (1998) The Danger of Data Slam, in: *CIO Enterprise Magazine*, 15th of September, on-line, URL: http://www.cio.com/ archive/enterprise/ 091598_ic.html [2.08.01]

Galloway 1994   Galloway, D. (1994) *Mapping Work Processes*, Milwaukee: ASQC Quality Press.

Garvin 1988   Garvin, David A. (1988) *Managing Quality*, New York: The Free Press.

Gasser 2000   Gasser, U. (2000) Zu den Möglichkeiten einer rechtlichen Erfassung von Medien- und Informationsqualität, in: *Zeitschrift für Schweizerisches Recht*, Band 119, I. Halbband, Heft 4, pp. 379-412.

Gerkes 1997   Gerkes, M. (1997) *Information Quality Paradox of the Web*, online manuscript, URL: http://izumw.izum.si/~max/paper.htm [18.7.01.].

Glazer 1993	Glazer, R., (1993) Measuring the value of information: the information-intensive organization in: *IBM Systems Journal*, 32(1), pp. 99-110.
Goodman et al. 1994	Goodman, S.N., Berlin, J., Fletcher, S.W., Fletcher, R.H. (1994) Manuscript Quality before and after Peer Review and Editing at 'Annals of Internal Medicine', in: *Annals of Internal Medicine*, 121, pp. 11-21.
Goldstein 1999	Goldstein, J. (1999) Ockhams Beitrag zur modernen Rationalität, in: *Zeitschrift für philosophische Forschung*, Band 53, I, pp. 112-130.
Götz/Hilt 1999	Götz, K., Hilt, A. (1999) Wissensmanagement in der kaufmännischen Berufsausbildung, in: Götz, K. (Ed.) *Wissensmanagement*, München: Rainer Hampp Verlag, pp. 215-267.
Grant/Clau, D. 2005	Grant, G. and Clau, D. 2005. Developing a Generic Framework for E-Government. *Journal of Global Information Management*, 13(1): 1-30.
Grice 1975	Grice, H. P. (1975). Logic and conversation. In P. Cole (ed.) *Syntax and Semantics. Vol. 3.* New York: Academic Press, pp. 41-58.
Günther/Voisard 1997	Günther, O., Voisard, A. (1997) *Metadata in Geographic and Environmental Data Management*, New York: McGraw Hill.
Gurney 1999	Gurney, C.M. (1999) Lowering the Drawbridge: A Case Study of Analogy and Metaphor in the Social Construction of Home-Ownership, in: *Urban Studies*, Vol. 36 Issue 10, pp. 1706-1722.
Habermas 1983	Habermas, J. (1983) *Theory of Communicative Action Vol. 1: Reason and the Rationalization of Society,* Beacon Press: Boston.
Hammer 1996	Hammer, M. (1996) *Beyond Reengineering*, Harper Business, New York: 1996
Hanselmann 2001	Hanselmann, J. (2000) *Wissenstransfer zwischen Produktentwicklungsprozessen.* Heimsheim: Jost Jetter Verlag.
Harkins 1999	Harkins, P. (1999) *Powerful Conversations: How High Impact Leaders Communicate,* New York: McGraw-Hill.
Harris/Flemming 1998	Harris, K.; Fleming, M. (1998) *KM and Content Quality: What Can You Trust?*, 29.12.98, Gartner Inc. Research Note.
Held/Russ-Mohl 2000	Held, B., Russ-Mohl, S. (Ed.) *Qualität durch Kommunikation sichern*, Frankfurt a.M.: FAZ-Institut.
Honey/Mumford 1982	Honey, P., Mumford, A. (1982) *Manual of Learning Styles*, London: P. Honey.
Horn 1989	Horn, R. E. (1989) *Mapping Hypertext - Analysis, Linkage, and Display of Knowledge for the Next Generation of On-Line Text and Graphics*, Waltham: The Lexington Institute.

Hu et al. 1997	Hu, J., Huang, K.-T., Kuse, K., Su, G.-W., Wang, K.-Y. (1997) Customer Information Quality and Knowledge Management – A Case Study Using Knowledge Cockpit, in: Strong, D.M., Kahn, B. (Eds.) *Proceedings of the 1997 Conference on Information Quality*, Cambridge, MA: Massachusetts Institute of Technology.
Huang et al. 1999	Huang, K.-T.; Lee, Y.W.; Wang, R.Y. (1999) *Quality Information and Knowledge*. New Jersey: Prentice Hall.
Huesing 2000	Huesing, T. (2000) *Motorola's Approach to Knowledge Management*, Presentation given at the Geneva Knowledge Forum, 24th of March.
Huff 1990	Huff, A. (Ed.) (1990) *Mapping Strategic Thought*, New York: Wiley.
Iselin 1988	Iselin, E.R. (1988) The Effects of Information Load and Information Diversity on Decision Quality in a Structured Decision Task, in: *Accounting, Organization and Society*, Vol. 13, No. 2, pp. 147-164.
Jessup/Valacich 1999	Jessup, L.M., Valachich, J.S. (1999) *Information Systems Foundations*, Indianapolis: Que Education / Macmillan Publishing.
Joshi 2001	Joshi, K.D. (2001) A Framework to Study Knowledge Management Behaviors During Decision-making, in: Sprague, R.H. (Ed.) *Proceedings of the 34th Annual Hawaii International Conference on Systems Sciences* (HICSS), Los Alamitos: IEEE Press.
Kahn/Strong 1998	Kahn, B. K.; Strong, D. M. (1998) Product and Service Performance Model for Information Quality: An Update, 1998, in: Chengalur-Smith, I.; Pipino, L. L. (1998) *Proceedings of the 1998 Conference on Information Quality*, Cambridge, MA: Massachusetts Institute of Technology.
Kaplan/Norton 1992	Kaplan, R., Norton, D., (1992) The balanced scorecard – measures that drive performance, in: *Harvard Business Review*, Jan. – Feb., pp. 71-79.
Khalil et al. 1999	Khalil, O.E.M., Strong, D.M., Kahn, B.K., Pipino, L.L. (1999) Teaching Information Quality in Information Systems Undergraduate Education, in: Informing Science, Vol. 2 No. 3, pp. 53-59.
Kinnel 1997	Kinnel, M. (1997) Benchmarking for information service excellence: The pharmaceutical industry, in: *Total Quality Management*, Vol. 8, No. 1, pp. 3-13.
Knorr-Cetina 1981	Knorr-Cetina, K. (1981) *The Manufacture of Knowledge. An Essay on the Constructivist and Contextual Nature of Science*, Oxford: Pergamon Press.
Königer/ Reithmayer 1998	Königer, P.; Reithmayer, W. (1998) *Management unstrukturierter Informationen*, Frankfurt: 1998.
Lakoff 1987	Lakoff, G. (1987) *Women, Fire, and Dangerous Things. What Categories Reveal about the Mind*, Chicago: University of Chicago Press.

Langley 1999	Langley, A. (1999) Strategies for Theorizing from Process Data, in: *Academy of Management Review*, Vol. 24, No. 4, pp. 691-710.
Laudon/Laudon 2000	Laudon, K.C., Laudon, J.P. (2000) *Management Information Systems: Organization and Technology in the Networked Enterprise*, Sixth Edition, Upper Saddle River: Prentice Hall.
Laudon/Starbuck 1996	Laudon, K. C., Starbuck, W.H. (1996) Organizational Information and Knowledge, in: Warner, M. (Ed.) *International Encyclopaedia of Business and Management*, London: Routledge / Thompson Business Press, Vol. 4, pp. 3923-3933.
Lesca/Lesca 1995	Lesca, H.; Lesca, E. (1995) *Gestion de l'information, qualité de l'information et performances de l'entreprise*, Paris: Litec.
Lichtenberg 1987	Lichtenberg, G.Chr. (1987) *Aphorismen*, Stuttgart: Reclam. [Written 1755-1806]
Lim et al. 1999	Lim, K.K., Ahmed, P.K., Zairi, M. (1999) Managing for quality through knowledge management, in: *Total Quality Management*, Vol. 10, Nos. 4&5, pp. 615-621.
Lionel/ Herxheimer 1970	Lionel, N.D.W., Herxheimer, A. (1970) Assessing Reports of Therapeutic Trials, in: *British Medical Journal*, 3, pp. 637-640.
Marcus 1998	Marcus, A. (1998) Metaphor Design in User Interfaces, in: *The Journal of Computer Documentation*, May 1998, Vol. 22, No 2, pp. 43-55.
Marshall/ Rossman 1989	Marshall, C., Rossman, G. B. (1989) *Designing Qualitative Research*. Newbury Park: Sage.
Matson 1996	Matson, E. (1996) The Seven Sins of Deadly Meetings, in: *Fast Company*, issue 2, p. 123.
May 1995	May, M. (1995) Diagrammatisches Denken: Zur Deutung logischer Diagramme als Vorstellungsschemata bei Lakoff und Peirce, in: *Zeitschrift für Semiotik*, Band 17, Heft 3-4, 1995, pp. 285 – 305.
McDermott 1995	McDermott, R. (1995) Designing and improving knowledge work, in: *Industrial Management*, Vol. 18 Issue 2 (March), pp. 72-78.
Megginson 1958	Megginson, L.C.(1958) The Pressure for Principles: A Challenge to Management Professors, in: *Academy of Management Journal*, Vol. 2 Issue 1, pp. 53-57.
Mengis 2001	Mengis, J. (2001) *The Importance of Dialogue within the Innovation and Knowledge Creation Process. How Conversational Tools Enable Dialogue*, Unpublished Master Thesis, Lugano: Università della Svizzera Italiana Facoltà di Scienze della comunicazione.
Mengshoel & Delab 1993	Mengshoel, J., Delab, S. (1993) Knowledge Validation: Principles and Practice, in: *IEEE Expert: Intelligent Systems and their Application*, June, pp. 62-68.

Merrill 1987	Merrill, M. D. (1987) The New Component Design Theory: Instructional Design for Courseware Authoring, in: *Instructional Science*, 16, pp. 19-34.
Merx 1999	Merx, O. (Ed.) (1999) *Qualitätssicherung bei Multimedia-Projekten*. Heidelberg: Springer.
Meyer 1996	Meyer, J.-A. (1996) *Visualisierung im Management*, Wiesbaden: Deutscher Universitäts-Verlag.
Miller 1996	Miller, H. (1996) The multiple dimensions of information quality, in: *Information Systems Management*, Vol. 13, Issue 2, Spring 1996, pp.79-82.
Minto 1995	Minto, B. (1995) *The Pyramid Principle, Logic in Writing and Thinking*, London: Pitman Publishing.
Mintzberg 1975	Mintzberg, H. (1975) The Manager's Job: Folklore and Facts, in: *Harvard Business Review*, July-August, pp. 49-61.
Moody/Shanks 1998	Moody, D., Shanks, G. (1998) What Makes a Good Data Model? Evaluating the Quality of Data Models, in: *Australian Computer Journal*, 08/98.
Moore/Wiener 2001	Moore, C. & Wiener, S. (2001) *Best Practices in Web Content Management*, Giga Information Group, Planning Assumption, August 6th 2001. URL: www.gigaweb.com [13.08.2001].
Morris et al. 1996	Morris, S.; Meed, J.; Svensen, N. (1996) *The Intelligent Manager*, London: Pitman Publishing.
Mok 1996	Mok, C. (1996) *Designing Business*, Indianapolis: Adobe Press/ Macmillan.
Muenzenmayer 1999	Muenzenmayer, P. (1999). *Informationsqualität im Intranet*. Unpublished Master Thesis, St. Gallen: University of St. Gallen.
Mumford 1995	Mumford, A. (1995) Putting learning styles to work: an integrated approach, in: *Industrial and Commercial Training*, Vol. 27 Number 8, pp. 28-35.
Naumann & Rolker 1999	Naumann, F., Rolker, C. (1999) Do Metadata Models meet IQ Requirements?, in: Lee, Y. W. and Tayi, G.K. (1999) *Proceedings of the 1999 Conference on Information Quality*, Massachusetts: MIT, pp. 99-114.
Nienhüser 1989	Nienhüser, W. (1989) *Die praktische Nutzung theoretischer Erkenntnisse in der Betriebswirtschaftslehre*, Stuttgart: Poeschel.
Nielsen 1993	Nielsen, J. (1993) *Usability Engineering*. Boston, MA: Academic Press.
Nielsen 2000	Nielsen, J. (2000) *Designing Web Usability: The Practice of Simplicity*. Indianapolis, IN: New Riders Publishing.

388   References

Nohr/Roos 2001   Nohr, H.; Roos, A.W. (2001) Informationsqualität als Instrument des Informationsmanagements, in: *doculine online* (9.6.01): http: www.doculine.de

Northcraft/Neale 1990   Northcraft, G.B., Neale, M.A. (1990) *Organizational Behavior, A Management Challenge*, Chicago: Dryden.

Nurmi, 1998   Nurmi, R. (1998) Knowledge-intensive Firms, in: *Business Horizons*, May/June, Vo. 41 Issue 3, p. 26-37.

Oden 1978   Oden, T.C. (1978) *Parables of Kierkegaard*, Princeton: Princeton University Press.

O'Conner/ McDermott 1997   Joseph O'Connor, J. and McDermott, I. (1997) *The Art of Systems Thinking, Essential Skills for Creativity and Problem Solving*, London: Thorsons.

O'Reilly 1980   O'Reilly, C.A. (1980) Individuals and Information Overload in Organizations: Is More Necessarily Better?, in: *Academy of Management Journal*, Vol. 23, No. 4, pp. 684- 696.

Oxman et al. 1984   Oxman, A.D., Guyatt, G.H., Cook, D.J., Jaeschke, R., Heedle, N., Keller, J. (1984) An Index of Scientific Quality for Health Reports in Lay Press, in : *Journal of Clinical Epidemiology*, 46, pp. 987-1001.

Penco 1999   Penco, C. (1999) Objective and Cognitive Context, in: Bouquet, P., Serafini, L., Brézillon, P., Benerecetti, M., Castellani, F. (Eds.): *Modeling and Using Context*. Berlin: Springer, pp. 270-283.

Peterson 1995   Michael P. Peterson, M. P. (1995) *Interactive and Animated Cartography*, New Jersey: Prentice Hall.

Pettigrew 1987   Pettigrew, A.M. (1987) Context and Action in the Transformation of the Firm, in: *Journal of Management Studies*, vol. 24, no. 6, pp. 649-670.

Pfeffer/Sutton 2000   Pfeffer, J., Sutton, R.I. (2000) *The Knowing-Doing Gap: How Smart Companies Turn Knowledge into Action*, Boston: Harvard Business School Press.

Pfeffer/Sutton 1999   Pfeffer, J., Sutton, R.I. (1999) Knowing "What" to Do is Not Enough. Turning Knowledge into Action, in: *California Management Review*, Vol. 42, No. 1 (Fall), pp. 83-108.

Pfiffner/ Stadelmann 1995   Pfiffner, M., Stadelmann, P. D. (1995) *Arbeit und Management in der Wissensgesellschaft - Konzeptualisierung, Problemanalyse und Lösungsansätze für das Management von Wissensarbeit*, PhD Thesis, St. Gallen: University of St. Gallen.

Polanyi 1974   Polanyi, M. (1974) *Personal Knowledge, Towards a Post-Critical Philosophy*, Chicago: The University of Chicago Press, (First Edition: 1958).

Popper 1994   Popper, K.R. (1994) Knowledge and the Body-Mind Problem. In defence of interaction, edited by Notturno, M.A., London: Routledge.

Porter 1991	Porter, M.E. (1991) Towards A Dynamic Theory of Strategy, in: *Strategic Management Journal*, Vol. 12, pp. 954-117.
Poundstone 1988	Poundstone, W. (1988) *Labyrinths of Reason*. New York: Doubleday.
Powell 2001	Powell, T.C. (2001) Competitive Advantage: Logical and Philosophical Considerations, in: Strategic Management Journal, Vol. 22, No. 9, September 2001, pp. 875-888.
Prahalad/ Krishnan 1999	Prahalad, C.K., Krishnan, M.S. (1999) The New Meaning of Quality in the Information Age, in. Harvard Business Review, September-October, pp. 109-118.
Probst & Raub 1995	Probst, G., Raub, S. (1995) Action Research: Ein Konzept angewandter Managementforschung, in: *Die Unternehmung*, 49: 1, pp. 3-19.
Probst & Gomez 1989	Probst, G., Gomez, P. (1989) *Vernetztes Denken: ganzheitliches Führen in der Praxis*, Wiesbaden: Gabler.
Probst et al. 2000	Probst, G., Deussen, A., Eppler, M., Raub, S. (2000) *Kompetenz-Management: Wie Individuen und Organisationen Kompetenz entwickeln*, Wiesbaden: Gabler.
Rasmus 2001	Rasmus, D.W. (2001) *Transferring Knowledge with Technology*, Giga Information Group, Planning Assumption, August 9th 2001. URL: www.gigaweb.com [13.08.2001).
Redman 1996	Redman, T. C. (1996) *Data quality for the information age*, Boston, MA: Artech House.
Renn/Webler 1994	Renn, O., Webler, T. (1994) Konfliktbewältigung durch Kooperation in der Umweltpolitik – Theoretische Grundlagen und Handlungsvorschläge, in oikos (Ed.): *Kooperationen für die Umwelt*, Chur: Rüegger, pp. 11-52.
Reuters 1998	Reuters (1998) Out of the Abyss: Surviving the Information Age. London: Reuters.
Rittberger 1999	Rittberger, M. (1999) Certification of Information Services, in: Lee, Y. W.; Tayi, G. K. (1999) *Proceedings of the 1999 Conference on Information Quality*, Cambridge, MA: Massachusetts Institute of Technology, pp. 17-37.
Rhodes 1994	Rhodes, J. (1994) Conceptual Toolmaking, Expert Systems of the Mind, Oxford: Blackwell Publishers (1st Edition: 1991).
Rogers 1995	Rogers, V.M. (1995). *Diffusion of Innovations*. Fourth Edition. New York, NY: The Free Press.
Ross/Murdick 1977	Ross, J. E., Murdick, R.G. (1977) What are the Principles of "Principles of Management", in: *Academy of Management Review*, Vol. 2 Issue 1, pp. 143-147.
Russ-Mohl 1994	Russ-Mohl, S. (1994) *Der I-Faktor*, Osnabrück: Fromm.

Sandy 1991	Sandy, W. (1991) Avoid the Breakdowns Between Planning and Implementation, in: *The Journal of Business Strategy*, September/October 1991, pp. 30-33.
Saracevic 1999	Saracevic, T. (1999) Information Science, in: *Journal of the American Society for Information Science*, 50(12), pp. 1051-1063.
Schamber et al. 1990	Schamber, L., Eisenberg, M.B., Nilan, M.S. (1990) A Reexamination of Relevance: Toward A Dynamic, Situational Definition, in: *Information Processing & Management*, Vol. 26, No. 6, pp. 755-557.
Schanz 1988	Schanz, G. (1988) *Methodologie für Betriebswirte*, Stuttgart: Poeschel.
Schick et al. 1990	Schick, A.G., Gordon, L.A. and Haka, S. (1990) Information Overload: A Temporal Approach, in: *Accounting, Organization and Society*, Vol. 15, No. 3, pp. 199-220.
Schmid/ Stanoveksa-Slabeva 1999	Schmid, B., Stanoevska-Slabeva, K. (1999) Knowledge Media: An innovative Concept and Technology for Knowledge Management in the Information Age, in: *Proceedings of the 32rd Annual Hawaii International Conference on Systems Sciences* (HICSS), Hawaii: University of Hawaii.
Schneider 1987	Schneider, S. C. (1987) Information overload: Causes and consequences, in: *Human Systems Management* (7), pp.143-153.
Schooley 2001	Schooley, C. (2001) *Quality of Content Is Most Critical When Assessing E-Learning Content Vendors*, August 23 2001, Giga IdeaByte, URL: www.gigaweb.com [06.09.2001].
Schopenhauer 1988	Schopenhauer, A. (1988) *Aphorismen zur Lebensweisheit*, Stuttgart: Reclam. [First published in 1851]
Seifried / Eppler 2000	Seifried, P., Eppler, M. (2000) *Evaluation führender Knowledge Management Suites: Wissensplattformen im Vergleich*, St. Gallen: NetAcademy Press.
Sekaran 1992	Sekaran, U. (1992) *Research Methods for Business*, 2nd Ed., London: Wiley & Sons.
Sengle 1987	Sengle, F. (1987) Einführung, in: Lichtenberg, G.Chr. (1987) *Aphorismen*, Stuttgart: Reclam, pp. 1-8.
Simon 1971	Simon, H.A. (1971) Designing organizations for an information-rich world, in: Greenberger, M. (Ed.) *Computers, Communications, and the Public Interest*, Baltimore: The John Hopkins Press, pp. 37-72.
Simon 1981	Simon, H.A. (1981) *The Sciences of the Artificial*, Second edition, Cambridge: The MIT Press (first edition: 1969).
Simpson/Prusak 1995	Simpson, C.W., Prusak, L. (1995) Troubles with information overload - Moving from quantity to quality in information provision, in: *International Journal of Information Management*, Vol: 15 Issue 6 (December), pp. 413-425.

Shenk 1997	Shenk, D. (1997) *Data Smog, Surviving the Information Glut*, London: Abacus.
Snowden 2001	Snowden, D. (2001) Story telling as a strategic communication tool: How the use of simple but not simplistic stories can enhance communication, in: *Strategic Communication Management*, Apr/May 2001, Vol. 5 Issue 3, pp. 28-32.
Sperber/Wilson 1995	Sperber, D., Wilson, D. (1995) *Relevance. Communication and Cognition*, Oxford: Blackwell.
Spradley 1978	Spradley, J.P. (1978) *The Ethnographic Interview*, New York: Holt, Rinehart and Winston.
Sther 1994	Sther, N. (1994) *The Knowledge Society*, Sage: Cambridge.
Stanoveksa-Slabeva/Schmid 2001	Stanoevska-Slabeva, K., Schmid, B. (2000) A Typology of Online Communities and Community Supporting Platforms, in: Sprague, R.H. (Ed.) *Proceedings of the 34th Annual Hawaii International Conference on Systems Sciences* (HICSS), Los Alamitos: IEEE.
Starbuck 1992	Starbuck, W. H. (1992) Learning by Knowledge-Intensive Firms, in: *Journal of Management Studies*, 29(6), pp. 713-740.
Strassmann, 1985	Strassmann, P.A. (1985) *Information Payoff: The Transformation of Work in the Electronic Age*, New York: The Free Press.
Strassmann 2000	Strassmann, P.A. (2000) *Governance of Information Management : Principles and Concepts*, The Information Economics Press.
Strong et al. 1997	Strong, D. M., Lee, Y. W., Wang, R. Y. (1997) 10 Potholes in the Road to Information Quality, in: *Computer IEEE*, 30(8), pp. 38-46.
Strong et al. 1997b	Strong, D. M., Lee, Y.W., Wang, R.Y. (1997), Data Quality in Context, in: *Communications of the ACM*, 40 (5), pp. 103-110.
Schultze 2000	Schultze, U. (2000) A Confessional Account of an Ethnography about Knowledge Work, in : *MIS Quarterly*, March, Vol. 24, Issue 1, pp. 3-39
Talisayon 2001	Talisayon, S. D. (2001) *Dialogue: So essential, yet so elusive*, online column, October 8th, URL: www.itmatters.com.ph/column/talisayon_10082001.html [15.1.01]
Taylor 1986	Taylor, R.S. (1986) *Vale-Added Processes in Information Systems*, Norwood: Ablex.
Teflian 1999	Teflian, M. (1999) *Information Liquidity*, Cambridge: Perot Systems.
Thorpe 1999	Thorpe, G. (1999) On-line focus groups: Mainstream in the millennium?, in: *Quirk's Marketing Research Review*, December 1999, URL: www.quirks.com [4.8.2001]

Tornatky & Klein 1986   Tornatzky, L. and Klein, K. 1986. Innovation characteristics and innovation adoption-implementation: A meta-analysis of findings. *IEEE Transactions on Engineering Management*, 29(1), February: 28-45.

Ulrich 1984   Ulrich, H. (1984) *Management*, Bern/Stuttgart: Haupt.

Van Dyke et al. 1997   Van Dyke, T.P., Kappelman, L.A., and Prybutok, V.P. (1997) Measuring Information Systems Service Quality : Concerns on the use of the SERVQUAL questionnaire, in: *MIS Quarterly*, No. 21 (June), pp. 195-208.

Von Krogh et al. 1994   von Krogh, G., Roos, J., and Slocum, K. (1994) An Essay on Corporate Epistemology, in: *Strategic Management Journal*, Vol. 15, pp. 53-71.

Von Krogh & Roos 1995   von Krogh, G., and Roos, J. (1995) Conversation Management, in: *European Management Journal*, Vol. 13, No. 4, pp. 390-394.

Von Krogh et al. 2000   Von Krogh, G., Ichijo, K. and Nonaka, I. (2000) *Enabling Knowledge Creation. How to Unlock the Mystery of Tacit Knowledge and Release the Power of Innovation*, New York: Oxford University Press.

Wahren 1996   Wahren, H.-K. (1996) *Das lernende Unternehmen, Theorie und Praxis des organisationalen Lernens,* Berlin: de Gruyter.

Wang et al. 1998   Wang, R. Lee; Y.W., Pipino, Strong, D. (1998) Manage Your Information as a Product, in: *Sloan Management Review*, 39 (4), pp. 95-105

Wang/Strong 1996   Wang, R. Y.; Strong, D. M. (1996) Beyond Accuracy: What Data Quality Means to Data Consumers, in: *Journal of Management Information Systems*, Vol. 12, No. 4, Spring 1996, pp. 5 – 33.

Waterman 1996   Waterman, B. (1996) Does Total Quality Management Apply to Knowledge Work? Absolutely!, in: *Journal for Quality & Participation*, Vol. 19, Issue 6 (October/November), pp. 6-12.

Ware/Degoey 1998   Ware, J., Degoey, P. (1998) *Knowledge Work and Information Technology*, Working Paper #98-WP-1028, February 1998, Fisher Center for Management and Information Technology, Walter A. Haas School of Business, Berkeley: University of California.

Weeks 2001   Weeks, H. (2001) Taking the Stress out of Stressful Conversations, in: *Harvard Business Review*, July-August, pp. 112-119.

Weick 1979   Weick, K.E. (1979) *The Social Psychology of Organizing*, Reading: Addison-Wesley Publishing Company, 2nd Edition.

Weick 1996   Weick, K.E. (1996) Cosmos vs. Chaos. Sense and Nonsense in Electronic Contexts, in: Pugh, D. S. (Ed.): *Organization Theory. Selected Readings*, New York: Penguin, pp. 213-226.

West 2004	West, D.M. 2004. E-Government and the Transformation of Service Delivery and Citizen Attitudes. *Public Administration Review*, Jan/Feb: 15-27.
Whitaker 1996	Whitaker, R. (1996) Managing Context in Enterprise Knowledge Processes, in: European Management Journal, Vol. 14, No. 4 (August), pp. 399-406.
Windrum/ Tomlinson 1999	Windrum, P., Tomlinson, M. (1999) Knowledge-intensive Services and International Competitiveness: A Four Country Comparison, in: *Technology Analysis & Strategic Management*, Vol. 11., No. 3, pp. 391-408.
Winograd/Flores 1986	Winograd, T., Fernando Flores, F. (1986) *Understanding Computers and Cognition*, Norwood: Ablex Pubishing Corporation.
Wolf 1999	Wolf, P. (1999) *Konzept eines TQM-basierten Regelkreismodells für ein „Information Quality Management" (IQM)*, Dortmund: Verlag Praxiswissen.
Wong & Dalmadge 2004	Wong, R.M., Dalmadge, C. (2004) Media Choice for complex knowledge-intensive Processes, in: Proceedings of the 37th Hawaii International Conference on System Sciences (HICSS).
Wortman/Max 1970	Wortman, M., Max, S. (1970) Shifts in Conceptual Approaches Which Underlie Principles of Management, in: *Academy of Management Journal*, Vol. 13 Issue 4, pp. 439-449.
Wurman 1996	Wurman, R.S. (1996) *Information Architects*, Zurich: Graphis.
Wurman 2001	Wurman, R.S. (2001) *Information Anxiety2*, Indiana: Que / Macmillan Publishing.
Xu et al. 2001	Xu, H., Koronis, A., Brown, N. (2001) *A Model for Data Quality in Accounting Information Systems*, online conference presentation, URL: www.sb.ccsu.edu/dataquality/Submitted/XU-sci2001-diq2001.ppt [20.12.01]
Yin 1994	Yin, R. K. (1994) *Case Study Research – Design and Methods*, Beverly Hills, CA: Sage Publications.
Zbaracki 1998	Zbaracki, M. (1998) The Rhetoric and Reality of Total Quality Management, in: *Administrative Science Quarterly*, 43, pp. 602-636.
Zidel 1998	Zidel, M. (1998) Retention hooks for keeping your knowledge workers, in: *Manage*, August, Vol. 50, Issue 1, p.21-22.
Zinsser 1990	Zinsser, W. (1990) *On Writing Well: An Informal Guide to Writing Nonfiction*, Fourth Edition, New York: Harper Perennial.
Zulauf 2000	Zulauf, R. (2000) *Informationsqualität: Ein Beitrag zur journalistischen Qualitätsdebatte aus Sicht des Informationsrechts*, Dissertation, Zürich: Schulthess.

Index